LUTHERANS IN AMERICA

LUTHERANS IN AMERICA

A New History

MARK GRANQUIST

To Beth, my colleague in Ministry,

[signature]

Fortress Press
Minneapolis

LUTHERANS IN AMERICA
A New History

Cover image: © Thinkstock: USA Map/9comeback/iStock/Thinkstock; Watercolor Texture/13UG13th /iStock/Thinkstock.
Cover design: Alisha Lofgren

Library of Congress Cataloging-in-Publication Data
Print ISBN: 978-1-4514-7228-8
eBook ISBN: 978-1-4514-9429-7

The paper used in this publication meets the minimum requirements of American National Standard for Information Sciences — Permanence of Paper for Printed Library Materials, ANSI Z329.48-1984.

Manufactured in the U.S.A.

CONTENTS

LIST OF IMAGES

Maps

Graphs

Tables

Images

CREDITS

Earlier versions of Excurses 1-2, 4-6, and 8-12 originally appeared in the "Faithful and Reforming" columns of the *Metro Lutheran* newspaper, all written by Mark Granquist. Thanks to the *Metro Lutheran* for their generous permission to use this material.

For permission to reprint the maps in the book, we thank Oxford University Press.

For permission to reprint the images in the book, we thank the generosity of the following persons and institutions.

1. John Peterson, Lutheran Archives Center, Philadelphia, Pennsylvania.
2. Lutheran Archives Center, Philadelphia, Pennsylvania.
3. Lutheran Archives Center, Philadelphia, Pennsylvania.
4. Abel Ross Wentz Library, Lutheran Theological Seminary, Gettysburg, Pennsylvania.
5. Abel Ross Wentz Library, Lutheran Theological Seminary, Gettysburg, Pennsylvania.
6. Lutheran Archives Center, Philadelphia, Pennsylvania.
7. Wilberforce University, Wilberforce, Ohio.
8. Concordia Historical Institute, St. Louis, Missouri.
9. Lutheran Archives Center, Philadelphia, Pennsylvania.
10. Luther College Archive, Decorah, Iowa.
11. Archives of the Evangelical Lutheran Church in America, Elk Grove Village, Illinois.

12. Archives of the Evangelical Lutheran Church in America, Elk Grove Village, Illinois.
13. Archives of the Evangelical Lutheran Church in America, Elk Grove Village, Illinois.
14. Archives of the Evangelical Lutheran Church in America, Elk Grove Village, Illinois.
15. Archives of the Evangelical Lutheran Church in America, Elk Grove Village, Illinois.
16. ELCA Region Three Archives, Luther Seminary, St. Paul, Minnesota.
17. Archives of the Evangelical Lutheran Church in America, Elk Grove Village, Illinois.
18. Archives of the Evangelical Lutheran Church in America, Elk Grove Village, Illinois.
19. Archives of the Evangelical Lutheran Church in America, Elk Grove Village, Illinois.
20. Archives of the Evangelical Lutheran Church in America, Elk Grove Village, Illinois.
21. St. Olaf College Archives, Northfield, Minnesota.
22. Archives of the Evangelical Lutheran Church in America, Elk Grove Village, Illinois.
23. Archives of the Evangelical Lutheran Church in America, Elk Grove Village, Illinois.
24. Archives of the Evangelical Lutheran Church in America, Elk Grove Village, Illinois.
25. Archives of the Evangelical Lutheran Church in America, Elk Grove Village, Illinois.
26. Archives of the Evangelical Lutheran Church in America, Elk Grove Village, Illinois.
27. Archives of the Evangelical Lutheran Church in America, Elk Grove Village, Illinois.

INTRODUCTION

T his is a book that has had a long gestational period. I have been working in the religious-history field for over twenty-five years, and the standard history of American Lutheranism, *The Lutherans in North America*, edited by E. Clifford Nelson, was already fifteen years old when I began my own study on the topic. In the past few years, as I have been teaching this history to students at Luther Seminary, it has become clear that although the older histories were (and still are) invaluable, the story of American Lutheranism has shifted in significant ways during the past forty years. Besides updating the narrative to include the most recent past, new questions and new research have shifted how we look at the subject at hand, and these new elements need to be incorporated into the historical narrative. Beyond this, the context for Lutherans, as well as for the whole of religion in the United States (which will be the geographic limit of this book), has shifted dramatically during the last few decades of the twentieth century. As is proper, we now view this almost four hundred-year historical record with new eyes and from new positions, so it is time for a new attempt to tell the story.

The "new" can never obliterate past attempts to tell this history, however; all the "new" history can do is to modify and add to the historical record. This history would have been absolutely impossible without the work of generations of American Lutheran historians who recorded the history that they saw and discovered, from Israel Acrelius's *History of New Sweden* (1759) to the flood of historical writings that have been produced in the years immediately preceding this volume. I am aware that I stand on the shoulders of giants, women and men whose painstaking efforts have made this work possible. My current teachers, colleagues, friends, and fellow historians continue to help all of us see our common tradition in new and deeper ways, while those who have preceded us continue still to enlighten and inspire our work. The writing of such a history is, in the final measure, a collaboration of immense proportions, and I am keenly aware of the assistance that I have received, even from those whom I have never met.

So what makes this present work new? Obviously, the last two chapters of this book cover new territory that have not been seen in previous histories, and in this sense it is new. But beyond these obvious additions, this work attempts to look at the history of Lutherans in America with new questions and through new lenses. It also attempts to think about this history, especially the history of the twentieth century, through a new interpretative framework, which is only natural, given the time that has elapsed since the last great wave of American Lutheran histories in the 1960s and 1970s. First, I will talk about the new questions and perspectives, then the shift in interpretation.

Much of what is lasting and continuous about the history of Lutherans in America are the institutions that they have built: the denominational structures, schools, hospitals, social service agencies, and the like. Because of their prominence in this history, it is natural that these institutions might take a leading role in any historical narrative. Yet this would be to miss some very important elements of the story. This is a history of Lutheran *people* in America; certainly, the institutions that they formed are an important part of their story, but they are not the main focus. This history tries to strike a balance at this point, giving enough of the history of institutional formation, mergers, and continuation to provide an understanding of this element, without making it the primary aspect of the story. This history also attempts to tell the individual and social history of Lutherans in America, their own struggles to live lives of faith and to adapt to a new and different religious culture. This is a much more difficult undertaking, for two reasons. First, given the millions of individual Lutherans who comprise this history, it is difficult to determine which stories are truly representative. And, second, the materials we have to tell these stories are also often skewed toward those who were both literate and in positions of power. This history tries to balance these narratives wherever possible, with special effort to highlight not just the stories of Lutheran leaders and clergy, but to attempt a narrative that includes the experiences of laypeople, women, and non-European Americans as well. This is difficult, because the sources we have on these people, who comprise the majority of American Lutherans, are not nearly as complete as might be wished. Yet, to keep this expanded vision of Lutherans in America in mind is perhaps at least one step toward a fuller and more complete history.

Now, the question of interpretation. If there was a "golden age" of writing the history of Lutherans in America, it was the 1960s and 1970s. This was the period of time when many of the standard histories of the various American Lutheran denominations were written, as well as the last complete major American Lutheran history, *The Lutherans in North America*, produced by a team of writers headed by E. Clifford Nelson. This burst of historical research and writing is still extremely valuable, and, in all honesty, this present history is deeply indebted to the labors of these fine historians. Yet, it is important to understand the circumstances behind this wave of historical writing, which gives some clue as to the motivations behind it. The 1960s and 1970s were a time of profound institutional merger and rearrangement in American Lutheranism, and many wished for the formation of an institutionally united American Lutheranism. This was also a time of great growth and optimism, and some historians saw a single American Lutheran denomination as almost inevitable, a perspective that is reflected in a number of these histories. But there was another motivation at work here, especially in the histories written about the individual Lutheran denominational traditions that were being subsumed into these new, united Lutheran denominations. Though there was a sense of tremendous hope about the future, there was also a palpable sense of great loss as the familiar Lutheran traditions merged into single entities. Many of these denominational histories were written both to celebrate these individual Lutheran denominational traditions, and to assuage the deep sense of loss that their partisans were feeling at their ending. Much of this history said to these partisans, in effect, "Yes, we had a great tradition, but it was the destiny of this tradition to come together with other American Lutherans and form a new, united American Lutheranism." These histories celebrated the Lutheran arrival as a united force on the American religious scene; this was their destiny, and their future. Mergers were good—and inevitable.

This present history has been written forty years later, and much has happened among Lutherans in America during the meantime. Although there was another merger in 1988, forming the Evangelical Lutheran Church in America (ELCA), the vision of a single, united American Lutheran entity has receded with every passing year, as the two major denominations, the ELCA and the Lutheran Church–Missouri Synod (LCMS), seem to be moving ever further apart from each other. And American Lutheranism has undergone three very public and painful schisms since 1970, which have further clouded the optimistic vision of inevitable unity, if not killed it entirely. Further, recent developments, including a reexamination of past histories, have produced a more nuanced reading of unity movements and mergers, a reading that also takes into account the difficulties and losses that institutional realignment has meant. Mergers were, as it now seems, neither inevitable nor completely good, and could actually be seen in another view as costly distractions and painful detours from the real work of American Lutheranism. This present history will not jump from one end of this spectrum to another, but will at least attempt to consider both sides of the major institutional realignments that have dominated American Lutheranism in the twentieth century.

A further challenge might be the often-heard assertion that the writing of denominational history itself is a rather poor substitute for "real" American religious history. This view generally sees these kinds of denominational histories as inferior substitutes for "true" historical scholarship, prone to self-absorption and self-congratulation as they are. To be sure, there are enough denominational histories (even among American Lutherans) that reinforce this critical viewpoint, but the existence of some mediocre historical writing does not negate the attempt. Instead, it suggests that the real push should be to write *better* denominational histories, rather than to abandon the field altogether. Further, I would assert that in fact *all* American religious history is actually denominational history, in some very important ways. Given American religious pluralism and institutional diffusion, one cannot truly write on any aspect of American religious history without locating one's subject within a specific institutional and denominational context; to fail to do this is to write a monodimensional history. Lutherans definitely have been underrepresented in the writing of American religious histories, and it is my hope that this volume will begin to redress this imbalance.

One other note, hinted at above: this book is very consciously a history of Lutherans within the territorial confines of the United States of America. This limit means that the work pays little attention to Lutherans in other parts of North America, especially to Canada and to the scattered Lutheran groups in the Caribbean, particularly after the colonial period. This limit is deliberate, but not because the history of these other areas is unimportant. Rather, it is because their history is both important and distinct; in other words, these grouping of Lutherans outside the United States have formed their communities within distinctive religious and social milieus that are different from those of the United States. Good histories of Lutheranism in Canada and the Caribbean (of which there are several; see the bibliography) root their stories in the distinctive cultures of their areas, and should not attempt to be told as an adjunct or an afterthought to the history of Lutherans in the United States. Thus, unless otherwise noted, my use of the word *America* and its variants throughout this book will denote, and serve as shorthand for, the United States.

This volume is laid out in a basic chronological fashion, moving the history from beginning to end, although there are times when it will be necessary to jump either backward or forward to help make sense of something in the text. The chapters themselves, especially after the first three, will cover roughly twenty-five to forty years of history at a time. Between the chapters are brief excurses, which lift interesting nuggets of historical materials out of its preceding chapter, to examine further. At times these excurses will duplicate materials mentioned elsewhere, but hopefully these slight duplications will not bother the reader. The first chapter—on Lutheranism in Europe, 1500–1900—is an attempt to explain the European background for the American narrative; it is separate, so as not to digress for an explanation for a European trend in the middle of a discussion of something concerning American Lutheranism. Finally, in order to improve the readability of the text, the number of endnotes have been limited, and in their place is an extended bibliographic essay at the end of the volume.

As mentioned above, this present history could not have been written without the work of numerous historians who have written their histories before me. Certainly, I have pointed out areas where my own historical vision differs from theirs, but this is not to say that my own historical inadequacies are any less than theirs; all I can hope is that readers of this narrative and future historians will understand and be patient with me. This is an attempt to write the history of Lutherans in America from my context in the second decade of the twenty-first century, and I hope that, if nothing else, I have furthered in some way the understanding of the history of Lutherans in America. It is my hope also that current and future scholars will push this story and our understanding of it even further.

The writing of such a book is a large undertaking, and one that requires tremendous support, which I have been fortunate enough to have received. Many thanks to Will Bergkamp and his team at Fortress Press; Will suggested a project of this shape, and has been of invaluable assistance in the composition and writing of this book. A number of colleagues in the field of American Lutheran history have read drafts or portions of the book and given valuable advice, including David Settje, Maria Erling, Walter Sundberg, Mary Jane Haemig, David Preus, Martin Marty, Patrick Keifert, and many others. Special thanks must be given to Jim Albers of Valparaiso University, who read through the draft and provided copious suggestions and revisions. Thanks as well to my students at Luther Seminary, some of whom read this manuscript in preliminary form for their classes and gave their honest insights into its effectiveness; this book is intended for them and for other students yet to come. So many others assisted with this work, and the book has been greatly strengthened by their suggestions; if the book has its limitations (and certainly it does) it is due to me alone. Special thanks should be given to Victoria Smith for the preparation of the index. Finally, I must give my deepest appreciation to my family—my wife, Kathy, and adult children, Beth and Rob—for their patience and support. Without their love this book could never have been written.

Chapter 1

THE EUROPEAN BACKGROUND TO AMERICAN LUTHERANISM

B efore beginning the history of Lutherans in America, it is important to understand the origins and progress of Lutheranism in Europe. When Lutherans began to come to the New World early in the seventeenth century, the Lutheran movement was already one hundred years old, and it continued to grow and develop in important ways, especially during the next two hundred years. Lutheran immigration from Europe to America continued in large numbers up until the beginning of the First World War in 1914, and subsequent immigrants continued to bring with them the issues and developments of European Lutheranism. Even in the twentieth century, developments within European Lutheranism continued to reverberate in important ways among American Lutherans, even though they were increasingly independent of each other. Although their paths eventually diverged in many ways, Lutherans on both sides of the Atlantic nevertheless were tied together and influenced by each other, and thus it is important to understand the European Lutheran "backstory" to American Lutheranism.

Beginnings of the Protestant Reformation

Protestants need to be careful when describing the western European Christian church of the late Middle Ages (1300–1500), as it is easy to fall into polemics and stereotypes. Many sixteenth-century Protestants described the medieval church against which they struggled in very dark terms indeed, and subsequent Protestant writers have tended to describe the period in terms of a battle between the "good guys" and the "bad guys," with the Protestants "recovering" the truth of Christianity that the medieval church had nearly lost. Roman Catholics have done the same thing, except switching the assigned roles. But a more nuanced understanding of this time period suggests that the medieval Western church was better off than might be imagined, and that there were important continuities between elements of the medieval church and the Protestant movements of the sixteenth century.

After the collapse of Roman authority in western Europe at the end of the fifth century, Christianity in western Europe struggled with two huge tasks: first, to Christianize the Celtic, Germanic, and Slavic tribes of western and northern Europe; and, second, to maintain and rebuild some semblance of Christian civilization among these tribes. Western Europe was a cultural and religious backwater, with the Byzantine Christian Empire in Eastern Europe and the Muslim empires in Asia and North Africa as the leading powers. But after the year 1200 or so, the parallel declines of the Byzantines and the Muslims led to the slow expansion of the "Latin" western Europeans. Despite disasters such as the great plagues of the fourteenth century, and almost constant infighting among the "Christian" leaders of western Europe, the center of Christian life slowly moved westward, especially when the Muslims conquered the Byzantine Empire, completed by 1453.

Western Latin Christianity flourished during the period from 1100 to 1300, the age of the great Gothic cathedrals and the Scholastic theologians, such as Anselm and Aquinas. Although the Western church was rocked by scandals in the later Middle Ages—especially by struggles between church and state, the Avignon Papacy (1309–1377), and the Great Schism (1377–1415), when there were two or even three different popes—western Europe grew in power and wealth. The Western church imagined its world in terms of "Christendom," a unitary Christian civilization in the West in which church and state cooperated together closely—always more of a dream than a reality, but an important conceptual ideal, nonetheless.

The Latin Church, headed by the bishop of Rome (the pope) grew rich and powerful within Western society. The church came to dominate many aspects of life, economic and political as well as theological, and this power in turn drew many individuals into the church who sought power and advancement. It also led to corruption within the church itself, when power and wealth overcame the mission of the church. The church became the means to an end for many ambitious people at the expense of the people it should have been serving. But this was also an age of deep piety, when there was growing concern for religious adherence and a seriousness about things religious. Piety and power were contesting with one another in the late medieval period, and when piety lost out to power, as it inevitably does, the concern for piety sought avenues for expression outside of the church, in popular devotion and movements that the church often viewed with deep suspicion, tried to manage or co-opt, and sometimes labeled as heresy.

During this time, many western Europeans decried the corruptions within the church, and many ideas were suggested to reform or purify it. Reformers were very active, trying to clean up the religious "system" by means of reform church councils such as the Council of Constance (1414–18), by the intervention of the state, and through internal means. One common call was for the election of a "good" reforming pope or the calling of a "good" reforming council to purify the church. If this could be done, many believed, the Western church could be rid of its corruptions and return to a state of relative purity. But the church system itself was not inclined toward reform and managed to subvert or ignore most attempts to change it; there were too many people within the system who still benefited from the status quo to see it changed.

Martin Luther and the Beginnings of the Reformation

Martin Luther was born in Eisleben, Germany on November 10, 1483, to Hans Luther, a peasant and self-made mine owner, and his wife, Margarethe. Martin grew up in the rich piety of late medieval Saxony, largely taught to him by his mother and through his schooling with the Brethren of the Common Life. After some form of religious crisis in his youth, he abandoned the University of Erfurt and a legal career to join the eremite Augustinian monastic order, which was especially pious and restrictive. Luther later recalled that he was a zealous monk who sought to relieve his religious crises through strict observance and disciplinary practices, contrary to later Roman Catholic charges that he was a failed monk. Both talented and restless, his order sent him to the new University at Wittenberg, where he studied Bible and theology, and where he became a professor after earning his doctor's degree. As a teacher he began to give annual serial lectures on books of the Bible, especially Psalms, Romans, and Galatians. Scholars disagree on the timing and the pace, but sometime during the 1510s Luther had a theological and religious transformation based on a new insight into God's grace and justification of the sinful person, which he determined was apart from any human works. This radical new theology was diametrically opposed to the cooperation between works and grace, a cornerstone of medieval theology.

As a priest, he was seriously interested in the reform of the church; he was especially disturbed by practices surrounding indulgences, which claimed to wipe out sins through good works and even through monetary payments. On October 31, 1517, he posted a series of ninety-five propositions in Latin critical of indulgences, which he wished to defend in academic theological debate. However Luther initially intended them, the Ninety-Five Theses were rapidly translated into other languages and achieved a widespread notoriety around Europe. Luther obviously touched a nerve among both reformers and defenders of the status quo, and he quickly became a lightning rod who attracted both intense praise and intense condemnation.

Luther wanted to debate abuses within the church; the church wanted him to shut up and retract his criticisms, and applied immense pressure to get him to do both. Over the next four years (1517–1521), Luther was attacked constantly by theologians and church leaders, and in defending himself he was pushed further in a more radical direction. By the year 1520, Luther had issued three seminal works that demonstrated how far he had come in the previous three years: "The Babylonian Captivity of the Church," "The Letter to the Christian Nobility of Germany," and "The Freedom of a Christian." His Ninety-Five Theses sought limited reform within the institutional boundaries of the church, but by 1520 Luther came to believe that the problem was the very system itself, which no amount of reform could fix. Luther was excommunicated by Pope Leo X in 1520, and hauled before the Holy Roman Emperor at the Diet of Worms in 1521, where he was condemned by the civil authorities as well.

Luther's stinging attacks on the papacy itself, the symbol and linchpin of the medieval religious system, suggested that something far beyond simple reforms or a new system was necessary. His new "evangelical discovery" was nothing less than a complete paradigm shift, a new way of conceptualizing Christian theology. This transformation was characterized in the phrase "justification by grace through faith, apart from works of the law," an understanding that the salvific grace of God comes to the human person as a divine gift, which the recipient can do nothing to earn or merit. Certainly, the medieval church did believe in justification as a part of the Christian life, but combined it with other elements. Luther made his understanding of justification the core of his new evangelical theology; all other theological or religious elements were viewed through the "lens" of justification. In his 1537 Smalcald Articles, Luther stated, "On this article [justification] stands all that we teach and practice against the Pope, the devil, and the world," and insisted that nothing in this article could be "conceded or given up."

Luther could very well have ended up like the fifteenth-century reformer Jan Hus, who was burned at the stake in 1415. Luther, however, was both very popular and protected by a powerful German ruler, Frederick, Elector of Saxony. After the Diet of Worms, Luther was whisked away into a form of protective custody for eleven months, during which time he translated the New Testament into German. But in Wittenberg, radical elements hijacked the new reform movement and, in order to regain control and moderate the pace of change, Luther returned to the city in early 1522. Radical religious and political elements led to the rise of Anabaptist and Spiritualist movements, as well as a revolt of the peasants in 1525, all of which Luther strongly opposed.

After 1522, Luther began to direct personally the reform of the territorial churches in northern and central Germany, either through his own efforts or through the legions of students who studied with him in Wittenberg. As a reformer, Luther was a conservative radical—radical in the sense of cutting through the layers of theology and church structure to focus on the centrality of the Christian gospel as he understood it. But grasping the central gospel affirmation of the justification of the sinner by God's grace alone, through faith, Luther was a quite willing and eager conservative, seeking to maintain much of the medieval religious heritage as long as it did not contradict the gospel. Luther reformed and maintained the medieval mass and much of the worship and music of the church, now translated into German, and put in the hands of the lay worshipers. Luther was also concerned with order; he did not want the people simply taking power into their own hands, but sought to legitimize the reform of the church by putting it in the hands of the lay political leaders in Germany, and in this way to retain the traditional complementary relation of church and state.

Luther continued his reformation of the churches in the German states through the 1520s and 1530s, issuing a flood of theological treatises, catechisms, worship materials and hymns, devotional materials, and sermons. He directed a network of reformers centered in Germany, but also stretching into Scandinavia and eastern Europe. This reformation drew the ire of church and political officials, especially the Holy Roman Emperor, Charles V, who began to move militarily against the rebellious Protestants, as they came to be known; Luther preferred the term *Evangelicals*. From the late 1520s through his death in 1546, Luther and his newly reformed churches were threatened by the military power of the emperor and the Catholic rulers in central Europe. The Protestants united to defend themselves and the balance of power swung back and forth, but the reform was never completely extinguished. Luther remained the center of this new movement until his death, interceding between quarreling theologians and among feuding rulers on whom the nascent Evangelical churches depended.

Theologically, Luther continued to write voluminously, engaging not only his Roman Catholic opponents, but also other Protestant reformers, such as Ulrich Zwingli from Zürich, whose symbolic interpretation of the presence of Christ in the Lord's Supper Luther strongly opposed. Luther also opposed the Anabaptists and Spiritualists, along with condemnations of the Jews, who angered Luther by refusing to accept the new Evangelical teachings. Sometimes, to the despair of his friends and colleagues, Luther could remain stubborn and intransigent on points of theology when he felt important elements of the gospel were at stake. An example was Luther's disagreement with Zwingli over the presence of Christ in the Lord's Supper. This dispute came at a difficult point in the late 1520s, when Protestant unity against the Roman Catholic armies was sorely needed, but Luther was unable to reach agreement with Zwingli, and the Protestants remained divided. Luther's theological output was huge, and is usually described as "occasional," in that he never wrote a complete, systematic theology but, rather, theological works to address specific theological issues or controversies. This being said, however, it must be clear that Luther himself worked and wrote within the framework of a coherent and consistent theology. His Small Catechism and Large Catechism (both from 1529) are masterpieces of this integrated theology, and have been of enduring importance to the formation and continuation of Lutheran theology across the centuries.

The Initial Formation of Lutheranism

In the sixteenth-century Lutheran territories of central and northern Europe, a new Lutheran church pattern evolved. In the core areas of Germany and Scandinavia, where they were supported by the local states and rulers, the Lutheran churches were organized territorially, with all the congregations in any particular state gathered into one church organization, closely allied to the secular power. Just because they themselves had separated from the Church at Rome did not imply that these territorial churches believed in pluralism or religious toleration; rather, they held to an establishment model of Christendom, only now on a regional level rather than on a more universal scale. Most Lutheran territories did not allow for the presence of other religious groups, Catholic or Protestant, believing that it was vital for both church and society that religious uniformity be maintained. While this situation was fairly stable in Scandinavia, the situation in Germany was much more complex. In 1555, the Peace of Augsburg brought religious warfare to a temporary halt within the Holy Roman Empire and legalized the new Lutheran churches for the first time. It also enshrined the principle of *cuius regio, eius religio* ("whoever rules determines the religion"), which meant that every dynastic change in the German territories was a potential opportunity for confessional mischief. Indeed, a number of territories shifted from Protestant to Catholic, or the reverse, and the later presence of Reformed Protestantism complicated the issue even further. War and the conquest of territory simply added to the mix. Soon there were pockets of religious minorities within the German states due to dynastic changes.

In eastern and southern Europe, there were also groups of Lutherans living in otherwise Catholic territories, and later, in Eastern Orthodox or Reformed territories. There were Lutherans in the areas of Bohemia, Slovakia, and Hungary, as well as in pockets around Salzburg, Austria, and Slovenia and Croatia. Later, with Lutheran migrations to the east, there were Lutheran settlements in Transylvania, Ukraine, and Russia. For these communities of Lutherans any idea of a territorial church was impossible, so they had to develop a communal or congregational manner of organization, in which the local gathering of Lutheran leaders decided issues, often referring back to the theological faculties of German Lutheran universities or to established Lutheran church authorities. This model would become important for Lutherans settling in colonial America.

Lacking the magisterial function of medieval bishops and the institution of the papacy, Lutherans instead looked to the theological faculties of their universities to provide guidance and judgment. These were the places where pastors were trained and evaluated for ministry, and they became places of leadership (and strife!) within the new Lutheran communion. Regular visitations of the local parishes and pastors provided guidance and evaluation of Lutheran theology and practice on the local level. In the German territories, local rulers appointed superintendents to oversee the Lutheran churches, along with groupings of senior clergy often known as consistories. In the Scandinavian state churches, which had turned over directly from medieval Catholicism, the new state-church structure maintained many of the medieval institutions, even the office of bishop and the local diocesan structures. Scandinavian Lutherans were clear, however, that they maintained reformed or "evangelical" bishops. The apostolic lineage of the bishops was broken in Denmark and Norway, and though it was incidentally maintained in Sweden, Swedish Lutherans did not hold or emphasize the medieval idea of the apostolic succession of bishops, or the "historic episcopate."

On the local parish level, especially in the rural areas, change came very slowly. Certainly, the pastors were now married and the forms of worship were changed to conform to the new Evangelical understandings, but many of the old medieval traditions persisted, in some places (such as rural Norway) for centuries. Luther and his companions used sermons and new educational tools such as the Small Catechism and catechetical hymns to teach their understanding of the Christian gospel, but this took time. Pastors, too, had to be schooled in the new Evangelical teaching and provided with pastoral manuals to assist them in their ministry. In Protestant areas of Europe literacy rose, as it was considered important for laypeople to read Bibles and catechisms.

The Development of the Lutheran Confessional Documents

Another important element of European Lutheranism in the sixteenth century and beyond was the development of a set of theological writings that came to have confessional authority for the various churches, specifically the Augsburg Confession (1530) and the various works in the *Book of Concord* (1580). Besides defining Lutheran theology and attempting to settle intra-Lutheran theological debates, these confessional documents became the standard by which Lutheranism was judged. A group was Lutheran insofar as it acknowledged the authority of these documents; in some minority situations, such as in southern and eastern Europe, Lutheran churches were referred to as the Church of the Augsburg Confession rather than by the term *Lutheran*. Even though Lutherans have long debated the theological content and meaning of these documents, and have also disputed the exact nature of confessional subscription, these documents have provided them with a common ground over which they can argue. Unlike Reformed Protestants, Lutherans have also decided that these sixteenth-century documents are sufficient, and occasional attempts to modify or supplant them have been rejected.

The Augsburg Confession of 1530 (Latin, *Confessio Augustana*) is the most widely accepted Lutheran confessional document. It was written by Luther's younger colleague Philipp Melanchthon in 1530 to present a definition of the Lutheran theological position to the emperor and Imperial Diet at Augsburg. Unlike his older and more polemical colleague, Melanchthon was a conciliatory figure, and his carefully crafted document attempted to firmly establish the Lutheran evangelical position, while insisting upon its continuity with the faith once confessed by the Roman Church. The document itself quickly became the standard for defining Lutheranism. Ten years later, in 1540, during a difficult period for German Lutheranism, Melanchthon attempted to revise the Augsburg Confession in order to meet Catholic objections and appeal to reformers in Switzerland and southwest Germany. Not only was this attempt unsuccessful, it also drew widespread condemnation from other Lutherans. Even today, many Lutheran groups signal their allegiance to the "Unaltered" Augsburg Confession, suggesting that attempts to modify it are unwelcomed.

During the decades after Luther's death in 1546, German Lutheranism went through trying times internally and externally. From the outside, Lutheran territories were attacked by Catholic forces and faced major inroads made by Reformed Protestantism, especially in western Germany. Internally, Lutherans fought over a series of theological issues revolving around the nature of faith, grace, and the human person; without the authority of Luther himself to adjudicate these disputes, these conflicts threatened to tear the Lutheran movement apart. Followers of Melanchthon (Philippists) fought with the so-called Old Lutherans (Gnesio-Lutherans) over the theological direction of the movement. Even though the Peace of Augsburg in 1555 gave the Lutherans some much-needed political breathing room, these disputes were still dangerous to the new movement. In the 1560s and 1570s, a group of mediating Lutheran theologians, including Martin Chemnitz and Jakob Andreae, began to negotiate these disputes and to draw together a common confession that most of the disputants could accept, a document called the Formula of Concord (1577; in Latin, *Concordia*). Besides gathering the disputing Lutherans together, this document also strongly attacked the Roman Catholics and other Protestants, especially the Reformed; its tone is much more combative than the Augsburg Confession, in part reflecting the brutal religious situation of the later sixteenth century. The Formula of Concord was gathered together with other writings, including the Large and Small Catechisms, Luther's Smalcald Articles (1537), the treatise on "The Power and Primacy of the Pope" (1537), and the Augsburg Confession, into the *Book of Concord*, all of which were publicly attested to by the leading Lutheran powers in Germany. Although some other Lutherans, especially in Denmark and Norway, have not given the Formula of Concord as much weight as the Augsburg Confession, in general the *Book of Concord* is the defining set of Lutheran confessional documents and has not been supplanted by any later writings or statements.

Perennial Issues within Lutheranism

Luther and the first generation of Lutheran leaders left their descendants a rich theological legacy; sometimes it seems almost too rich, because the range of options and positions within Lutheranism has at time led to internal conflicts and disputes. This is surely the case with the situation in the mid-sixteenth century that led up to the Formula of Concord in 1577, and even the adoption of the *Book of Concord* in 1580 did not bring these dynamics to a conclusion. Luther developed a dynamic theology that relied heavily on dialectical elements held in tension with each other, such as the nature of the human person as fully saint and sinner at the same time (*simul justus et peccator*), the relation between law and gospel, the hidden and revealed God, and the finite's capability to bear the infinite. These dialectical elements have been hard for Lutherans to continue to hold in tension and to explain to subsequent generations, and reductionism was a constant danger. As well, there are implications of the Lutheran theological positions that have needed to be fleshed out, especially as Lutherans have encountered new historical situations and new intellectual movements to which these insights needed to be applied. Finally, since the early Lutherans did not consider any particular church structure or liturgical orders to be absolutely normative, allowing and evidencing a great deal of latitude on these elements, Lutherans have also argued often about the nature of the church and worship.

From Luther onward, the chief Lutheran theological cornerstone has been the centrality of justification: that the human person is justified, or made right with God, by God's grace alone, through divinely granted faith. This is the chief article of faith, by which all other elements of the faith stand or fall. Luther intended this to oppose any element of human works as being involved in the process; one can do nothing to cooperate with God's grace or to merit salvation in any way. To Luther's opponents, both Catholics and other Protestants, this appeared deeply problematic, as it seems to absolve the believer from any sort of moral or ethical imperatives, and may even lead to antinominanism (opposition to the law). Lutherans have continually struggled to express the nature of grace and faith in such a way that avoids turning faith into a human work, on the one hand, or that leads to an utter determinism, on the other hand. Especially difficult for Lutherans has been the doctrine of sanctification, or the holiness of the believer. Luther made a number of remarks on the need for believers to live out personal holiness and regeneration, but later Lutherans have struggled to find a means to express the need for holiness within the confines of the doctrine of justification. Lutherans have always been clear, however, that sanctification is gift of God through the work of the Holy Spirit. Other Protestants, especially the Calvinist or Reformed Protestants, have made sanctification a much more prominent part of their theological patterns. When Lutherans immigrated to the United States, where the religious culture was dominated by Reformed Protestantism, this became a point of contention between the Lutherans and other Christians.

Lutherans have also been remarkably flexible on questions of church structure and worship practices, within some boundaries, of course. Historically, Lutherans have evidenced a wide degree of different church structures, enabled by a rather pragmatic stance on the matter. Luther famously and enigmatically remarked that even an seven-year-old child knew what the church was, but since theological faculties are not usually constituted by seven-year-olds, they have not always been able to agree. Lutheran church organizational patterns run the gamut from centralized episcopal systems, such as in the state churches in Scandinavia, through synodical forms prevalent among American Lutherans, to Lutheran congregationalism, but this has not kept some Lutherans from arguing that particular forms of church polity or organization are normative. The situation is similar with regard to worship and liturgical practices, although there are some traditional theological positions that are generally considered normative, such as a Lutheran understanding of Christ's real presence in the sacrament of Holy Communion, something that has produced confusion among non-Lutherans and Lutherans alike. The Augsburg Confession clearly stated that "it is not necessary [*satis est*] for the true unity of the Christian church that ceremonies, instituted by human beings, should be observed uniformly in all places" (Augsburg Confession, article VII). But this has not restrained some Lutherans from criticizing other Lutherans on the sole basis of their liturgical rites and their perceived "un-Lutheranness."

Finally, Lutherans have struggled continually to define their relations to the larger social and political worlds around them, and what the appropriate boundaries of these relations should be. In its first centuries, Lutheranism was protected by state and military power in Germany and Scandinavia, and many of the Lutheran territorial churches developed a close relationship with the political powers that protected and funded them. This situation led to a number of instances where the Lutheran churches became, in effect, the religious wing of secular power, which made it difficult to truly differentiate the two, even in subsequent situations where it became clear that the state did not always have the best interests of the church in mind. Elsewhere, other Lutheran churches were established as minorities within states that were either essentially pluralistic, such as the Netherlands, or in Roman Catholic areas, where Lutheranism was harassed and at times persecuted, such as southern Germany and eastern Europe. These "minority" forms of Lutheranism developed independently of the state, and became important models for American Lutherans establishing themselves within the voluntary religious situation in the United States. But the level of religious and theological engagement with, and critique of, society and government has always been an issue for Lutherans, and remains so to the present.

Patterns and Relations with Other Christians

As we have seen, the dominant Lutheran pattern, especially in Germany and Scandinavia, was the territorial church, closely related to the local government. Many of these territorial churches developed their own distinct form of Lutheran organization, practice, and piety, so that the "feel" of Lutheranism differed from one territory to the next, a situation that increased as time went along. This situation was most dramatic in Germany, where the medieval jumble of hundreds of different territories continued to exist until the late eighteenth century, when the French emperor Napoleon forcibly reorganized the German territories. Indeed, though there was a limited linguistic and cultural sense of "German-ness" within central Europe, most Lutherans in these areas thought of themselves first as Saxons or Friesians or Hanoverians or Prussians, and only second as Germans. Hence, when these "Germans" immigrated to the United States, though others considered them German Lutherans, they often grouped in local congregations that reflected their European localities. Scandinavians also demonstrated many of the same regional variations as did the Germans, with immigrants clumping in regionally specific congregations dependent on the local area of origin. These elements faded over time, but still remained important elements of American Lutheranism until the end of mass immigration after World War I.

But there were even more complications, especially within Germany. With the religious and political upheavals and changes from the sixteenth to the eighteenth century, the religious patterns were also often disrupted. A Lutheran territory might find itself coming under the rule of Reformed or Roman Catholic rulers, or combined with another territory of differing religious background. Then what would become of the territorial church? In some places, especially in western Germany where the German Reformed church was strong, the local territorial church might consist of separate groupings of Lutheran and Reformed congregations, both under the rule of the local state. In some areas of Germany, Lutherans and Reformed Protestants developed long traditions of living and working together, habits that were continued in the United States, especially in the colonial-era "union" churches. Some American Lutherans felt very close to these other German Protestants, Reformed and Moravians alike. In other places, governmental pressure to combine Lutheran and Reformed led to greater confessional resistance, such as when the new Reformed rulers of Brandenburg-Prussia attempted to unite the largely Lutheran population with existing Reformed churches, the so-called Prussian Union of 1817. This forced attempt at union resulted in a confessional Lutheran backlash against the Reformed, one that especially colored the development of the Lutheran Church–Missouri Synod in the nineteenth-century United States. These different patterns and experiences meant that Lutheran and Reformed relations in Europe were varied and complicated, and these variations and complications would be transferred to the United States. Lutheran relations with Roman Catholicism remained rather uniformly negative throughout this period in Europe, and historically this antipathy remained a fairly constant pattern in the United States as well.

The Age of Lutheran Orthodoxy, 1580–1675

European Lutheranism entered a new phase after the codification and adoption of the *Book of Concord* in 1580, a period often referred to as the age of Lutheran Orthodoxy. This period, especially in Germany, was dominated by attempts further to define and defend Lutheran theology by means of academic, university-based theology, by intellectual conflict with other Christians, and by open military conflict between Lutheran and Roman Catholic territories. The old charge that this was an age of "sterile" orthodoxy has largely been disproven; this period was important for the survival and development of German Lutheranism, and for the development of a rich Lutheran devotional and worship tradition. But the endemic warfare of this time also led to a steep decline in the societies of central Germany, one that took decades to remedy.

In the late sixteenth and early seventeenth centuries, European Lutheranism was on the defensive in many ways. The "growing edge" of Protestantism in Europe during this time had passed from Lutheranism to the Reformed Protestanism, and a number of the ruling families of German territories had switched to the Reformed camp. More ominously, the reforms of the papal church achieved under the Council of Trent (1545–1563) established a militant and resurgent Roman Catholicism that sought to regain "lost" territories and populations from the Protestants. This Roman Catholic "Counter-Reformation" saw aggressive attempts to win back Protestants, either by persuasive or coercive means. New Roman Catholic orders, such as the Jesuits, sought to carry the Counter-Reformation to all corners of Europe, and through missionaries to the Americas, Africa, and Asia. The Counter-Reformation was most successful in such eastern European countries as Poland and Lithuania, but also made significant inroads in Germany as well.

Although the military situation in Europe remained relatively quiet after the Peace of Augsburg in 1555, a type of confessional "cold war" generally smoldered beneath the surface. This conflict "went hot" after 1618, with the Thirty Years' War in Germany (1618–1648). This brutal and deeply destructive conflict began with Roman Catholic armies pressing northward into Lutheran territories, and almost completely overrunning them. At a critical point, with Protestant fortunes in Germany held in the balance, Swedish Lutheran king Gustavus Adolphus entered the field with his armies, and pushed the Catholic forces back into southern Germany. But with Gustavus Adolphus's death on the battlefield in Lützen in 1632, the conflict degenerated into a bloody and destructive stalemate, in which both sides lost control of rampaging armies and German territories were devastated. Finally, the conflict was ended with the Peace of Westphalia in 1648, with a general return to the prewar religious situation, but some areas of Germany lost between one-third and two-thirds of their populations. The states gained even more control over the churches, which became departments of the states.

Theologically, the development of Lutheranism continued after the adoption of the *Book of Concord*, going in directions that were equally polemic and academic. Facing challenges from both the Reformed and the resurgent Roman Catholics, Lutherans had to defend themselves intellectually and to define themselves as over and against their opponents. Theological disputation was a "contact sport" in this time period, and Lutherans had to develop their skills and their positions in order to keep up. During his life, Martin Luther often spoke dismissively of the medieval Scholastic traditions, especially the Aristotelian philosophy that undergirded much of it. But the intellectual *lingua franca* ("common language") of seventeenth-century Europe was Aristotelianism, and Lutheran theologians after Luther quickly adopted Aristotelian philosophy as their means to express Lutheran theology, even if Luther himself had hated Aristotle. There was a trend to conceptualize and intellectualize theology; true faith was expressed in terms of "correct doctrine." Getting doctrine straight was almost equal to having faith, so the proclamation of the gospel in sermons was often a primarily intellectual exercise.

This tendency can be overstated, however. Later critics often lambasted this period of "Protestant Scholasticism" as a period of "dead" orthodoxy, and suggested that the subjective element of faith and piety was nowhere to be found. Certainly, some of these stereotypes did have some basis in reality, but this is to overlook the deep Lutheran piety of this troubled period, as expressed in the hymns of Phillip Nicolai, Paul Gerhardt, and Johann Crüger, and the Lutheran spiritual classic, Johann Arndt's *True Christianity*, written in 1606. But because of the Thirty Years' War and its devastations, the moral life of Lutheran Germany declined precipitously, and church life slipped badly as well. However, the focus on the development of "correct doctrine" also has had its supporters among later Lutherans, especially in the United States, who have looked to seventeenth-century scholastic Lutheranism as a golden age of Lutheran clarity, and who have sought to repristinate the theology of this period. It is often the case that later Lutherans have either loved or hated the Lutheranism of the seventeenth century.

Some of the problems within seventeenth-century Lutheranism can also be traced to church leaders and the clergy within the European state churches. The close relationship and support between church and state led some church leaders to see themselves essentially as state officials, whose primary allegiance it sometimes seemed was to the state. Some Lutheran pastors were educated in the rarified atmosphere of the German universities and Protestant Scholasticism, and embodied these characteristics in their clerical careers. Other pastors were poorly educated and had difficulty in articulating both the gospel and Lutheran distinctives. Again, this criticism can be overstated, but there were many church leaders who seemed to be incapable of providing spiritual and theological leadership to their congregations. Granted, this was a very difficult period of time, but many of these troubling trends continued even after the relative calm and slow rebuilding that were occasioned after the Peace of Westphalia in 1648. One hundred and fifty years after its inauguration in 1517, it seemed to some that the power of the Lutheran Reformation had run out of steam.

Pietism and Awakenings

Or perhaps it had not run out steam. In the late seventeenth century, there was a wave of renewal and awakening movements in Europe, a cluster of movements that have been described overall as "Religions of the Heart" for their emphasis on the subjective and personal elements of the Christian faith. This cluster would include such Christian groups as the Janssenists within Roman Catholicism, some of the Puritans and later the Methodists in England, the Moravians in Germany, and, among the continental Protestants, the movement known as Pietism.

Pietism has been dismissed and caricatured by some later Lutherans as a deviation from "true" Lutheranism because of its stress on personal conversion and sanctification, but in many ways Lutheran Pietism is simply a restatement of theological and religious themes that can be traced from Luther through many of the later Lutheran theologians. Lutheran Pietism forced Lutheran churches and church leaders to return to an emphasis on the development of personal faith within the believer, something that had diminished within Lutheranism during the turbulent years of the seventeenth century. It would be wrong to overstress the changes brought by Pietism, however, as much of what they urged was in harmony with Luther and with the earlier traditions of Lutheran religious practices and faith.

The "father" of German Lutheran Pietism was a Lutheran pastor in Frankfort, Philipp Jakob Spener (1635–1705). When a new edition of Arndt's *True Christianity* was published in 1675, Spener added to the work an introduction strongly critical of the state-church Lutheranism of his day. This introduction was eventually republished independently under the title *Pia Desideria* ("Pious Wishes") and became a sensation. In this work, Spener decries the "spiritual desolation" of his age, conditions that he attributes to the spiritual decay of the church and especially of the pastors. Spener graphically describes the moral laxity of the churches of his day, and the inability or disinclination of the pastors to do anything about it. As a pastor himself, Spener knew the difficulty of trying to attack these problems, so he suggested the development of "conventicles," small groups of lay Christians who would meet together for Bible study and mutual encouragement in true and living faith. These believers would be guided through the *ordo salutis* ("order of salvation"), a directed path by which the believer would move, step by step, to a deeper and genuine Christian faith.

Spener's criticisms of the church and his proposals for renewal were highly controversial. Many Lutherans, lay and clergy, welcomed his renewing vision and sought to implement them in their local congregations. But many others, especially church leaders, were highly critical of Spener and the Pietist movement. They thought that his emphasis on active faith and sanctification was essentially a form of "works righteousness," which many attributed to the influence of Reformed Protestantism. Pietism played down the importance of "correct doctrine" as a key to the church, and instead urged a "living faith," leading the Lutheran Orthodox theologians to attack the Pietists as being doctrinally suspect and indeterminate. Church leaders found the concept of the conventicle to be a "dangerous innovation" in which laypeople without proper theological training and guidance from their pastors would be led into heresy and error. Others worried that the creation of conventicles within local congregations would lead to the creation of groups of "super Christians" who would consider themselves better than the rest of the congregation, and even better than the pastor, if he were not one of the spiritually developed. To be sure, there were instances where all of these criticisms of Pietism proved accurate, but in many other cases the Pietist pastors and conventicles proved to be forces for deep renewal within the Lutheran churches. In some cases, criticism of the Pietists came merely out of jealousy, embarrassment, and fear among pastors and church leaders of lay religious activity. Women, too, were active in Pietist circles, and this participation also resulted in additional criticism.

The reception of Pietism within European Lutheranism varied from one state church to another. In some of the territorial churches, and among the church superintendents in Germany and bishops in Scandinavia, the Pietist initiatives were welcomed and Pietist pastors were encouraged. In other places, church leaders maintained a harsh opposition to Pietism in whatever form, and Pietist activities had to go underground or keep a very low profile in order to survive. Pietism itself took on institutional forms, especially through the formation of the University of Halle by August Hermann Francke (1663–1727). Besides the university itself, Halle also included a cluster of related educational and social ministry institutions at which the Pietist pastors and missionaries were trained, and from where a worldwide network of Pietist ministries and activities was directed.

In many ways similar to Lutheran Pietism were the Moravians. This group has its roots in the pre-Reformation followers of Jan Hus in Bohemia and Moravia, some of whom in 1722 found refuge from Roman Catholic persecution at Herrn-hut, the estate of Ludwig von Zinzendorf, in Saxony. Zinzendorf, who had been influenced by Spener and Francke, developed an awakened community of believers who spread out from Herrnhut all over Europe and beyond, preaching Christian renewal and ministering to both Christians and non-Christians. They were some of the first Protestant missionaries, and by their example and challenge pushed the Lutheran Pietists themselves into global missionary activity. Both Moravians and Lutheran Pietists alike had a strong ecumenical bent, believing that the rigid doctrinal and denominational boundaries that church officials had erected were artificial and damaging. They themselves were open to relations with any "true Christian," and often worked in conjunction with one another. In the colonial United States, Pietist Lutheran leaders such as Henry Melchior Muhlen-berg sometimes worked together with the Moravians, but often came into sharp conflict with them as well.

Most of the Lutheran Pietist leaders could well be considered "churchly" Pietists, in that they wished to work within the established Lutheran churches of their time, and did not consider separation from them. Many of the Lutheran leaders in the United States in the eighteenth and nineteenth century were exactly this, moderate churchly Pietists, and their commitments were deeply stamped on American Lutheranism. But there were separatist elements within European Pietism during this time as well, groups that considered it necessary to leave the state-church congregations to form their own independent congregations. These separatist or radical Pietists believed that those who were spiritually converted Christians could no longer stay within the spiritually mixed state-church congregations, especially those with "unconverted" pastors, and that "spiritual" Christians had to form pure and separate congregations of their own. Such radical Pietist groups arose in Germany in the eighteenth century, such as the Dunkers and the Brethren, and many of these groups immigrated to Pennsylvania, complicating matters for the colonial American Lutherans. A similar dynamic would arise in Scandinavia and among Scandinavian American Lutherans in the nineteenth century.

The Enlightenment of the Eighteenth Century and Rationalism

The eighteenth century saw a radical transformation of the intellectual climate of Europe, a grouping of ideas and assumptions that came to be known as the Enlightenment, from the German term *Aufklärung*. The intellectuals who developed the set of Enlightenment principles essentially presided over a radical transformation of epistemology, or the theories of knowledge and authority. These intellectuals dismissed the traditional forms of knowledge and authority, which had been static conceptions of divine revelation, and the traditions of Western culture that surrounded them. These new thinkers, rather, privileged human reason as central to knowledge, especially the knowledge that came into the human senses through their examination of the natural world. Humans, through the development of their faculty of reason, could come to know the essence of the created world that the God of creation had placed in nature. Such an intellectual movement also necessitated a complete transformation of the ideas of the human person (anthropology): human persons had to be essentially good, or at least perfectible, and able to train their minds through reason to make moral progress for themselves and for human society. Humans were the center of creation and the human mind the highest order of creation. The Enlightenment had an air of optimism to it, that human civilization was progressing and would continue to progress if led by "reasonable" and enlightened leaders.

In defining religion, the Enlightenment thinkers took a range of positions, from "reasoned" and enlightened forms of Christianity to outright Deism. Many moderate Enlightenment thinkers believed that traditional religions, such as Christianity itself, could be molded through the elements of Enlightenment rationality, to "purify" them of their irrational, medieval accretions. One example of this approach can be seen in the works of the English philosopher John Locke, who wrote a book entitled *The Reasonableness of Christianity*, giving an essentially rationalistic explanation of traditional Christianity. Other, more radical figures, such as Voltaire in France and Thomas Paine in America, sought to completely replace traditional, "revealed," and irrational religions with a rational, universal Deism. Deists believed in a rational Creator God who created the world, embedded in it the rational laws of nature, and then set the world to run on its own, without divine interventions or interferences. Human beings, through their rational faculties, could discover the laws and will of the Creator God in nature, and act rationally and ethically on the basis of this knowledge. There was usually some element of some sort of final judgment, in which the divine would sort out human beings on the basis of their moral actions, or lack thereof.

Obviously, the Enlightenment was a huge challenge to traditional religions such as Christianity, which had been based on the ideas of special revelation and God's continual and often miraculous intervention in the created order. Enlightenment ideas sought to undercut most of the assumptions and ideas on which Christianity itself had been based for centuries, and often ridiculed its practices and theologies. The Enlightenment's direct impact on Christianity was rather minimal in the eighteenth century, however, as these thinkers were a rather rarified group of intellectuals who often conversed primarily with each other. Indeed, many Enlightenment thinkers, such as the American "Founding Fathers" (Franklin, Washington, Jefferson, and others) believed that the maintenance of traditional Christianity was vital to public morality and virtue, as the morality derived from universal reason was only available to the "enlightened" and reasonable elite. But they saw particular forms of religion as at root only important for their moral characteristics, which they saw as derived only from universal morality available through the natural creation and not from special revelation. To them, Jesus was above all the teacher of this universal morality, and they downplayed any idea that he was especially divine or had miraculous powers.

The direct impact of the Enlightenment on the churches came through the universities where the pastors were educated and trained. The philosophical and religious assumptions of the Enlightenment began to affect the educational processes, and in turn had an impact on how some pastors preached and conducted their churches, a development within Western Christianity that is sometimes referred to as religious rationalism. There were important rationalist theologians within the German church, such as Baron Christian von Wolff, Johann Semler, and Johann Mosheim, who sought to develop Lutheranism on a "reasonable" basis. Rationalistic clergy saw their primary responsibility as inculcating universal morality within their parishioners and raising the moral and educational level of their communities. Among some of these rationalistic clergy, traditional Lutheran law-and-gospel sermons were replaced with addresses about such things as the merits of vaccinations, or discourses on the proper methods of farming or similar subjects. Rationalistic clergy continued to teach the Bible and the catechisms, but now as essentially moralistic texts shorn of miraculous, superstitious, or unreasonable elements. Of course, many other pastors maintained an emphasis on traditional religion, and the congregations, being essentially conservative institutions, were slow to change. There were, however, definite signs of Enlightenment influence within the churches, especially in the cities, by the end of the eighteenth century.

Christian theological writing began to change as well, especially on the university and academic levels. One of the clearest examples of his shift can be seen in the German theologian Friedrich Schleiermacher (1768–1834), in whom the transition from Pietist spirituality to Romanticism can be clearly seen. Schleiermacher was deeply concerned that the essential insights of Christianity were being lost among the educated classes of his day, and in 1799 wrote a work entitled *On Religion: Speeches to Its Cultured Despisers*, in which he attempted to convince them of the value of Christianity. But to do so, Schleiermacher had to argue on essentially rationalistic grounds; since he could not claim special, revealed, and divine authority for Christianity, his argument was reduced to suggesting that Christianity as he styled it was the highest and most refined form of the universal religion and morality, which was available to all rational beings. This strategy, which is the basis of most modern forms of liberal Christianity, was hardly successful in winning over the "cultured despisers" of traditional or orthodox Christianity, but began to create an increasingly wide gap between Christian traditionalists and the new Christian liberals, such as in the new Unitarian movement. The intellectual world of western Europe began to move away from traditional Christianity, and Christians themselves became increasingly divided among themselves as to how to address this growing challenge.

Other developments in the eighteenth century affected traditional European Lutheranism. Memories of the devastations of confessional warfare of the previous century, combined with the "awakening" movements' drift away from theological disputation and the Enlightenment stress on universal rather than particular forms of religion, all led to the development of Christian ecumenism, in which particular differences between Christian groups were downplayed and commonalities were stressed. The idea of confessional strife between Christian groups, whether theological disputation or outright persecution or warfare, was dismissed as "primitive." The growing and centralizing power of the new European states, such as Prussia in Germany, combined a degree of Enlightenment religious toleration with a rigid state control of all elements of life, including religion. In some places, like the Austro-Hungarian Empire in central Europe, this made life somewhat easier for the minority Lutheran populations, which had suffered under persecution by the Roman Catholic authorities.

The Enlightenment was not, however, enamored of democracy, which it viewed with horror as the rule of the unenlightened and uneducated masses. Even in the new United States, the direct power of the people was limited by franchise and by forms of government that blunted the direct effects of popular sovereignty. But with the French Revolution of 1789, and the increasingly radical nature of that reform, movements toward popular democracy in Europe accelerated. The military conquests of the French emperor Napoleon, though eventually reversed, permanently altered the political and social landscapes of Europe, especially in France and Germany. Because Lutheranism was a state church, changes on the political level could not help but affect the churches. Although the ruling elites attempted to regain their autocratic control over church and state after the final defeat of Napoleon in 1815, the "cat was out of the bag" and popular forces of democracy continued to push for greater freedoms.

European Lutheranism in the Nineteenth Century

Tied to the European states and threatened by rationalism and the Enlightenment, most European Lutheran churches were at a fairly low state of vitality by the end of the eighteenth century. In the next century, they would be both challenged and reinvigorated by movements from below, such as lay awakening movements in Scandinavia and Germany, and by the resurgence of confessional Lutheranism, which often came through individual pastors and theologians. The rise of the mission movements during this century saw the expansion of Lutheranism into the Americas and Australia through European Lutheran emigrants, and through missionaries to native populations in Africa and Asia. Although some church leaders were hostile or skeptical to these directions, others found room to cooperate with these popular movements, which led to a stronger Lutheranism during the century. This was important, because the century also saw the rise of strong secularist movements hostile to religion, such as the new science of Darwin and others, the socialist and communist movements, and other intellectual challenges, such as Freudian psychology.

The awakening movements in Scandinavia and Germany during the nineteenth century drew on the heritage of Lutheran Pietism, but also were influenced by elements of popular democracy and other mass movements of the time. The revivals of the nineteenth century saw a strong emphasis on lay preaching and lay Bible study, along with a critique of the state churches that contained a strong suggestion of class resentment. There was also an element of incipient nationalism in some of these movements, especially in Norway and Finland. The Moravian movement in the late eighteenth century formed a bridge between the older Pietism and the new awakenings of the nineteenth century, but as that period moved along, its influence was supplanted by Lutheran connections with the strong and vigorous Anglo-American religious revivals that were making themselves felt around the world.

The Scandinavian awakenings began with sporadic revivals early in the century, and crescendoed through the middle of the century, especially from the 1840s to the 1870s. The revival movement later divided between those who wanted to remain within state-church Lutheranism and those who developed independent movements—Covenant, Methodist, Baptist, and eventually Pentecostal. These awakenings had a profound effect on Scandinavian American Lutheranism as well; most of the leaders of these American Lutheran denominations were deeply affected by them. The pioneer of this awakening was the Norwegian lay preacher and revivalist Hans Nielsen Hauge (1771–1824), who combined a deeply spiritual revivalism with a populist and nationalistic movement. Hauge ran afoul of the church and secular authorities, and was imprisoned for long stretches of time, but his activities (especially his preaching) had a deep impact on a significant portion of Norwegian Lutheranism. His message urged repentance of sin, conversion, and living a holy and sanctified life. Hauge urged his followers to remain within the state church, but they also gathered in local *Bedehus* ("prayer houses") for revivalistic preaching.

The next generation of revivals blanketed Scandinavia at mid-century. In Norway, Hauge's mantel fell on a theological professor, Gisle Johnson (1822–1894), who directed a major revival movement in the 1850s and 1860s. The revivalist movement in Sweden was led by another layperson, Carl Olof Rosenius (1816–1868), who was initially "converted" by George Scott, an English Methodist preacher working in Stockholm. Although a popular and effective preacher, Rosenius's main impact came through his devotional writings and by publishing a popular magazine called *Pietisten*, which was influential throughout Scandinavia. He also founded the National Evangelical Foundation in Sweden to direct the work of revivals, and which also encouraged popular and deeply effective hymnwriters and composers, such as Carolina Sandell Berg (1832–1903) and Oscar Ahnfeldt (1813–1882). In Denmark, the populist vision and hymns of N. F. S. Grundtvig (1783–1872) had a deep and abiding influence on Danish Lutheranism, though distinctive elements of his theology, such as the theological primacy of the Apostles Creed, did not have a permanent influence. The Pietist leader Vilhelm Beck (1829–1901) led the revival movement in Denmark, but was equally influential through the establishment of the "Inner Mission" movement, which spread across Europe, combining revival preaching with social reform. In Finland, important revivalists like Lars Levi Laestadius (1800–1861), Paavo Ruotsalienen (1777–1852), and Frederick Hedberg (1811–1893) led popular movements inside and outside the state church.

The nineteenth-century Pietist awakenings in Scandinavia were deeply concerned with both personal and societal transformation. Their strict personal morality has often been ridiculed by outside critics who allege that the Pietists "robbed the joy out of life," a charge that is actually quite baseless. Scandinavia was deeply affected during this time by the rampant abuse of alcohol, and the temperance movement, pioneered by Pietist leaders, had a huge positive influence on Scandinavian life and society. Through the Inner Mission movement, the revival leaders developed widespread social-service programs long before the state took notice of these needs. This emphasis also transferred to Lutheran immigrants to the United States, for whom these social-service and educational institutions became the hallmark of their denominations.

Later in the nineteenth century, the awakening movement in Scandinavia also developed a separatist wing, with the formation of the Mission Covenant in Sweden under P. P. Waldenström, and in the Methodist and Baptist movements in Scandi-navia and Germany. Toward the end of the century, leaders such as Frederick Fran-son and Lewi Pethrus, influenced by Anglo-American Protestantism, brought the Free Church and Pentecostal movements into the world of European Lutheranism. These later developments were deeply trans-Atlantic movements, with strong and repeated influences between Europe and America.

Confessional Movements in Nineteenth-Century Europe

Another important element of nineteenth-century European Lutheranism was the revival of confessional Lutheranism. This movement, essentially conservative in the best senses of the word, sought to regain the distinctive and particular elements of Lutheran confessional identity that had been downplayed by the Pietists and scorned by the rational Enlightenment. The leaders of this movement, some influ-enced by the Romantic movement, sought to rebuild traditional Lutheran theology and practice, which in some areas were threatened by movements toward a general pan-Protestantism, especially in Germany. One of the first leaders in this was the German theologian Claus Harms (1778–1855), who for the three-hundredth anni-versary of the Reformation in 1817 issued his own contemporary set of ninety-five theses, attacking rationalism and the loss of Lutheran theological distinctives. His call for a return to the Lutheran confessions reverberated throughout Lutheran ter-ritories, and made him an influential teacher and writer.

The nineteenth-century movement toward German unification was led by the rulers of Prussia, whose continual expansion of their state systematically absorbed the territories of northern and central Germany, sometimes by force. For a number of rea-sons, the Reformed Prussian ruling family sought a union of Reformed and Lutheran churches in their newly acquired territories. In 1821, the Prussian Union, under King Frederick William III attempted to impose a single liturgy on the Protestant churches within his territory, provoking vigorous opposition from a number of the Lutheran territorial churches and their leaders. Confessional Lutheran pastors such as Martin Stephan in Saxony and Friedrich Brunn in Nassau protested the enforced "union-ism," and some even formed independent "free" Lutheran bodies in Germany. Other church leaders, such as E. W. Hengstenberg in Berlin wrote and organized against what they saw as the loss of Lutheran identity. Inspired by this movement, some Lutherans left Germany for America, including C. F. W. Walther of the Missouri Synod and Johannes Grabau of the Buffalo Synod. They carried this confessional revival with them, while other American Lutheran leaders were simultaneously mov-ing in a more definite confessional direction in the middle of the nineteenth century.

The confessional revival also influenced some of the German university faculties, especially at the University of Erlangen in Bavaria. The "Erlangen school" was an important element in the revival of confessional Lutheran identity, both in Germany and among Lutherans in Scandinavia and the United States. Theologians such as J.K.C. von Hoffmann, Gottlieb Harless, and others sought to strengthen a Lutheran confessional identity over and against the Reformed, the Roman Catholics, and rationalist and secularist forces. Influenced by the confessional revival and the Erlangen school, German pastor and theologian Wilhelm Löhe organized a famous mission school at Neuendettelsau, which sent confessional Lutheran pastors out into the world especially to work with German immigrants. These pastors were very important in the origins and shaping of the Iowa and Missouri synods in the United States. Löhe was also important in the Inner Mission movement, especially in his attempt to establish the deaconess movement both in Europe and America.

The Mission Movement

Although the European Roman Catholics led the first wave of European missions in the sixteenth and seventeenth centuries, European Protestants began to participate in this worldwide movement during the eighteenth century, with the Moravians leading the way. Copying the Moravians, and under the influence of Pietism, European Lutherans began to send their own missionaries abroad. The first mission fields were among areas of the North, such as to the Sami in Scandinavia and the Inuit people in Greenland. Missionaries followed European Lutheran immigrants to North America, the Caribbean, and other areas, and America would remain the object of European missions throughout the nineteenth century. European mission activity often went hand in hand with colonial activity but, despite initial attempts by the Danish and Swedish monarchies to develop colonies, these efforts did not last. Since Germany was so weak and divided internally, the Germans did not enter the colonial "race" until after German unification in 1870. In 1706, the Danish king sent the Lutheran missionary Bartholomaeus Ziegenbalg (1682–1719) to India, where he developed a successful mission at Tranquebar.

European Lutheran mission activities were greatly enhanced in the nineteenth century, not initially through the efforts of Lutheran territorial or state churches, but through independent mission societies and mission schools. These institutions were developed under the influence of Pietism and the awakening movements, and by contact with the example of voluntary mission societies in the Anglo-American world. The initial Lutheran mission society was organized in Basel in 1780, followed by Berlin (1824), the Rhenish Mission (1828), Leipzig (1834), and a flood of other societies to follow. Mission societies were initially formed in Norway beginning in 1842, in Denmark in 1821, in Sweden in 1835, and in Finland in 1859. Some of these mission organizations were cooperative ventures with other Protestants, while some were exclusively Lutheran. Many of these mission groups were independent of their local Lutheran churches, but others worked in close cooperation with them. A number of Lutheran state churches, such as the Church of Sweden, eventually developed their own official missions. Along with the mission societies came the mission training schools, such as Neuendettelsau, Brekum, Hermannsburg, and St. Chrischona in Germany, and Fjellstad, Ahlsborg, and Stavanger in Scandinavia, which were created to train pastors and other workers for the mission fields; quite a number of Lutheran pastors and leaders in America can be traced to these schools.

Although Lutherans were somewhat slow to join the greater nineteenth-century mission movement, they participated in it with great success, forming Lutheran missions in many areas of Asia and Africa, but especially in India and China, and in southern and eastern Africa. Although their mission churches in America had their own struggles with building an indigenous Lutheranism in the United States, these also caught the mission "fever" and began to cooperate with the European Lutheran mission societies, eventually forming their own independent missions.

Liberalism and Secularism

Although European Lutheranism showed great movements of renewal, awakening, and mission through the nineteenth century, it was against the background of growing liberalism and secularism, which was deeply affecting the entire continent. The European Lutheran state churches remained strong during this period of time, but worrying trends, especially first among the educated classes, and then among the middle classes, of a movement away from Christian practice and belief could not be masked. Certainly, in the Enlightenment the elites (Schleiermacher's "cultured despisers of Christianity") were disaffected, but in the great democratic movements of the nineteenth century others joined the parade. The rise of the "new" science embodied by Darwin seemed to suggest that religion was no longer necessary, and that science and technology could not only explain the universe, they also had the potential to "save" it, in ways that seemed better than the answers provided by religion. Later elements, such as the psychology of Sigmund Freud, not only denigrated religious belief as an unhealthy neurosis, but suggested "salvific" forms of therapy. Other antireligious movements arose, especially socialism and communism, appealing both to the educated and working classes. While some elements of socialism were open to working with organized religion and created forms of Christian socialism toward the end of the century, more militant forms of socialism and the communist movement of Marx and Engel strongly opposed religion, seeing it as a bourgeois plot to keep the working classes enslaved. Toward the end of the nineteenth century, and into the twentieth, many western European countries saw a rise in movements for labor reform and democracy, and these movements often came to see the state churches, both Protestant and Roman Catholic, as the enemies of progress in their country; when these new elements took political power, they often strongly curbed the power and influence of the churches.

European Christians were divided as to how to respond. Many in the churches attempted to ignore the new movements and to continue on with their work. The Inner Mission and other groups attempted to work with the disaffected workers in the new industrial cities, with limited results. Some traditionalists "came out swinging" with critiques of the new movements and updated restatements of traditional Christian theology. But there was also the rise of a new movement of liberal Christian theology that sought to take the critiques of secularism seriously and to reshape Christian theology and practice to meet the new situation. German Lutheran theologians Adolf von Harnack (1851–1930) and Albrecht Ritschl (1822–1889) were two such liberal Protestant thinkers, and their work creatively responded to this new situation, even if, in the end, they were no more successful in countering it than Schleiermacher had been before them. But the rise of liberal Protestant theology did seriously divide the churches, just when they needed to meet the new world with a strong united front.

Conclusion

This overview of European Lutheranism from its beginnings with Martin Luther to the end of the nineteenth century has been primarily to show the European movements and developments that influenced the growth of American Lutheranism. Certainly, this development was, in the seventeenth and eighteenth centuries, essentially a one-way street, with things flowing from Europe to America. In the nineteenth century, however, there was more of a creative interchange between the two worlds, although the European side still definitely predominated. With the end of mass European immigration to America around the First World War, and the maturation of uniquely American forms of Lutheranism, there was less of an interchange between the two, and when there was interchange, it was more on an equal footing. Indeed, because of the effects of war and secularism in Europe, American Lutheranism has at times during the twentieth century taken the lead. So it is to the history of the development of those uniquely American forms of Lutheranism that we now turn.

Excursus 1

RASMUS JENSEN AND DANISH EXPLORATION

He thought he was going to India. He wasn't even supposed to be in North America, but he ended up dying there, and never did make it to Asia. But one thing makes us remember the name of Rasmus Jensen, that he was the very first Lutheran pastor in North America.

In the seventeenth century, all the European nations were establishing trading posts in Asia, and King Christian IV of Denmark wanted to do so as well. So, in 1619, the king sent out two expeditions to India. One traveled the usual route around the southern tip of Africa and established a Danish colony in India. The other, under the command of an adventurer and explorer, Jens Munk, went the other way, trying to force its way through the legendary Northwest Passage. It was believed back then that you could sail between Greenland and Canada, across the Arctic and into the Pacific, in a shortcut to the riches of India, China, and Japan.

Among his crew, Munk was assigned a young Lutheran pastor named Rasmus Jensen. Jensen had studied at the University of Copenhagen and was appointed by the king to be a "Ship Pastor to the East Indies," in charge of the spiritual life and condition of the expedition itself, and to the Danish colony in India once he had arrived. He was promised a salary of one hundred dollars a year.

The Munk expedition through the Northwest Passage was neither the first nor the last of such attempts, but it did share one thing in common with many others: it ended in tragedy. Munk's ships sailed into the Canadian Arctic regions in the summer of 1619, entering Hudson Bay in August. But despite their constant attempts to do so, they could not find a suitable water route to the riches of Asia. In late September, with the Arctic winter quickly upon them, Munk made the fateful decision to spend the winter in Hudson Bay, hoping to find the fabled route west in the next spring. They moored their ships near the present town of Churchill, Manitoba.

Initially, the winter was not too bad. The holidays of the Christian year were regularly celebrated, including St. Martin's Day on November 10, in honor of the fourth-century saint and his namesake, Martin Luther. At Christmas, Pastor Jensen celebrated the customary religious services in the traditional liturgy of the Church of Denmark. Captain Munk recorded the following entry: "The Holy Christmas Day was celebrated in customary Christian fashion. We had a sermon and Communion; and our offerings to the minister after the sermon were according to our means."[1] Since they did not have money, they gave Pastor Jenson white fox skins.

Those fox skins came just in time, as the winter suddenly turned frigid with the New Year. The expedition was short on food and supplies, and their health began to decline rapidly. Before Christmas, Pastor Jensen had already presided over the funerals of two crew members, a boatswain and the ship's surgeon. For the funeral of the surgeon, they had to wait two days for the cold to let up, and even then Pastor Jensen had to abbreviate the service, as the cold was so bitter.

After Christmas, Pastor Jensen became so weak from poor food and illness that he, like the rest of the crew, could barely survive. By January 23, Pastor Jensen was confined to his bed, and the log records, ". . . the minister sat up in his berth and preached to the crew, which was his last sermon in this world." Munk later recorded on February 20, 1620, ". . . toward evening the Rev. Rasmus Jensen died after having been sick for some time."[2] Thus ended the career of the first Lutheran pastor in North America. Munk and only two other men survived that brutal winter, and made their way back to Denmark.

Believing that he been called to India, Pastor Jensen found himself instead stranded in the harsh winter of the Canadian Arctic. He ministered faithfully to the crew for as long as he was able, leading worship and celebrating the sacraments, and even preaching from his sickbed, until he could no longer do so. He was buried in an unmarked grave on a foreign shore far from home, the first of many brave Lutheran pastors to serve in this New World.

Notes

1. Captain Jens Munk, "Navigato Septentrionalis" (1624), quoted in Carl R. Cronmiller, *A History of the Lutheran Church in Canada*, vol. 1 (N.p.: Evangelical Lutheran Synod of Canada, 1961), 16.

2. Ibid, p. 16.

Chapter 2

Beginnings, 1619–1720

The Transition to Colonial America

Lutheran beginnings in America were generally a byproduct of seventeenth-century exploration and economic adventure by European individuals and government-sanctioned groups. As Europeans looked to the west, they saw opportunity and adventure in the "unsettled" lands of North America, and they sought to make their fortunes there. Although initially they focused mainly on trading and fishing expeditions, it soon became clear that permanent European settlements in America were needed to sustain and further prosecute the economic ventures that had already begun. These initial colonial trading centers slowly evolved into full-fledged settlements; though they were still colonies dependent on trade with European countries, they gained in permanency and economic vitality as the century progressed.

As a part of the European exploration and settlement of America, colonists brought with them the religious traditions, practices, and attitudes of western European Christendom. Although the settlement of America was not primarily driven by religious considerations—and indeed, at times immigrants to America rejoiced in being freed from the religious considerations of their former continent—in the main these were people whose lives were deeply influenced by a millennium of Christian traditions in Europe, and so they transplanted these strongly held traditions into their new American settlements. But it was not a simple matter of transferring religious traditions from one continent to another, as the new situations of colonial America profoundly affected and reshaped how Christianity would be organized and practiced in the New World. Lutherans brought with them the beliefs and practices of various Lutheran regions of northern and western Europe, but had to integrate these different Lutheran traditions into a new land predominantly shaped by Reformed and Anglican Protestantism, by voluntarily formed religious communities, and by an increasingly pluralistic religious environment. The religious realities of the New World both challenged and transformed Lutheran tradition and practice, eventually forming an authentically American Lutheranism.

With French Roman Catholic settlements to the north in Canada, and Spanish Roman Catholic settlements to the south in Florida and the Caribbean, European Protestants concentrated their colonization on the eastern coast of North America, stretching from the Maritime provinces in Canada to the southern colony of Georgia. Unlike the Catholic settlements, however, the Protestant colonies were settled by distinct groups of people from various European countries, primarily England, but also by companies from Holland, Sweden, and Denmark. Initially, these groups were commercial ventures, economic "companies" such as the Dutch West India Company, but closely sponsored by their various Protestant states. Eventually, these commercial settlements would be absorbed into the larger imperial adventures of the English state, sometimes by force. But these various colonial ventures were distinct enough to ensure that the English colonies along the Atlantic would differ from one another in significant ways, including different religious profiles.

Beginning with the Virginia Company in 1607, royally chartered colonies were established from Virginia to Georgia. Being closely linked to the government in England, these colonies all had an established, state-supported Anglican Church, at least on paper. Outside of Virginia, these establishments were generally nominal. Because of the weakness of the colonial governments, and the fact that there were no resident bishops in the colonies, the actual funding and management of these Anglican parishes was largely dependent on the local large landowners such as George Washington. In the colonies of New England to the north, the Puritan settlers (Plymouth Plantation in 1620 and the Massachusetts Bay Company in 1630) opted for a different kind of established church, a congregational church that was organized along Calvinist lines, as a model to show old England what a realized Puritan commonwealth could be. But royal or Puritan, the establishments in these colonies made no room for religious dissent or differences, and heterodox individuals and groups were not welcomed. In the Dutch colony of New Amsterdam (New York and New Jersey), and the Swedish colony of New Sweden (along the Delaware

River), the Dutch Reformed and Swedish Lutheran churches, respectively, were singularly established, although both colonies were short-lived.

Despite the general failure in forming viable state-supported established churches in the English colonies, the vision of religious establishment died hard. Religious uniformity in society was seen as a desirable and necessary thing, and, given the religious conflict and warfare in England and on the European continent during the seventeenth century, it is plain to see why this attitude persisted. Religious diversity within a state was widely seen as leading to social destruction, and there were many examples to back up this viewpoint. In only two of the English colonies—Baptist Rhode Island and Quaker Pennsylvania—was there any sort of official religious toleration. For these two religious groups, any form of state-enforced religious conformity was seen as detrimental to "true religion," and they wished for religious organization free from the meddling of the state. Given this attitude, it is clear why religious minorities from Europe were attracted to these colonies, and especially to Pennsylvania (it also did not hurt that Pennsylvania had some of the richest farmland along the Atlantic coast).

Yet, even the seventeenth-century preference for religious establishments could not make religious uniformity practical in the American colonies. Most of the religious establishments (outside of New England and Virginia) were weak or nonexistent, or, like the Dutch and Swedish versions, went out of existence rather quickly. The overarching need in colonial America was for labor (free, indentured, or enslaved), leading employers not to be overly concerned about their workers' religious commitments. As well, the American colonies were rather minimally organized, and there was not nearly enough coercive power to keep religious societies uniform or to expel religious minorities. Puritans in Massachusetts tried to keep out the Quakers, and royal sheriffs in Virginia attempted to expel Baptist and Presbyterian preachers, but with little success. Practical realities resulted in *de facto* pluralism in many American colonies, which, when combined with the later eighteenth-century Enlightenment views about religious toleration, led to the First Amendment declarations of religious liberty in the U.S. Constitution.

The actual practice and organization of local religious life was often quite removed from the distant ideals of establishment. In most cases, if individuals or groups wanted to establish religious congregations in their area, the initiative was solely up to them. They needed to organize a congregation, erect a building, call and pay a pastor, and operate it on their own—essentially, the standard idea of American religious voluntarism. There were very few European pastors in the seventeenth-century American colonies, and they often had to serve multiple congregations in harsh conditions, with very little support. Even by the beginning of the American

Revolution in 1776, organized religion was still very weak, with fewer than 20 percent of colonists reckoned as church members. This was partially due to the lack of congregations and pastors, but it also perhaps owed something to those who wished to be free of organized religion altogether and found in the American situation the ability to realize this goal.

Religious minorities such as the Lutherans did not have religious establishment or state support as an option. For these colonists, the only religious organizations that they could form would be voluntary, and they would often have to struggle with Dutch or English authorities to be allowed to practice their religious traditions at all. Poverty and isolation meant that forming and sustaining congregations was difficult, and that precious resources and great patience were necessary. Usually, scattered Lutherans initially gathered in homes for lay-led religious services, singing hymns and reading the Bible, along with the reading aloud of printed sermons, usually from Luther or from devotional books. Occasionally, a Lutheran pastor visited them, traveling great distances to provide confession and absolution, Holy Communion, and other ministerial acts, such as baptisms and weddings.

If a particular group grew large enough, they might form a congregation, erect a church building, and attempt to find a resident pastor. This generally entailed a lengthy process of writing to Lutheran officials in Europe and waiting (often for years) for a pastor to be sent to them. Even when European Lutheran pastors were sent to the American colonies, they were usually unprepared for their new ministry situation, and many could not adjust to the physical demands of colonial life. Even more, many pastors were unable to deal with the new realities of voluntary religious life and the fact that laypeople now had a new sense of power and ownership for their hard-wrought congregations. Conflicts between pastors and congregations were frequent, and pastors often complained about a lack of support from their flock.

The basic outline of religion in America formed during the colonial period, and because of the twin aspects of voluntary religion and religious pluralism (both pragmatic and idealistic), a religious culture much different from that of Europe developed. From these two elements emerged a basic pattern of religious life that was based roughly on Free-Church models of European dissenters, as opposed to the various state churches. In this pattern, the local congregation was the core of identity, with individuals voluntarily associating themselves with it as they chose. Of course, this was mitigated by local social dynamics and patterns of familial and ethnic bonds. European Lutherans immigrated and settled together, and their use of languages other than English often caused them to seek ethnic religious organizations, but these bonds worked only so long before eroding under the freedom of American religion. The lack of an established state church, which, for better or worse, provided in Europe a stable context for the practice of religion, meant that the religious dynamic in colonial America would be much more fluid and confusing.

As it worked out in reality, Lutherans had to make major adjustments, not so much in their theology but in their practice of religion and in the forms of organization that they developed to support that practice. The basic pattern of voluntary Free-Church congregationalism, with its stress on membership, meant a dramatic shift in how individual Lutherans related to each other, to their congregations, and to their pastors. The transition to a membership model was difficult because of its stress on personal initiative; one was not instantly defined by a given religious identity (provided by birth and citizenship), but had to decide in an active way what one's religious identity would be (or not be!). Ethnic and family ties were still quite influential in these decisions, but over time the power of these bonds could be eroded and new identities formed or assumed. Some of those who remained Lutheran probably did so out of habit or inertia, but many others did remain Lutheran out of a renewed, voluntary decision that this identity meant something to them. But what Lutheranism itself might mean in this new country was also in the process of development, as the movement itself encountered and appropriated the new American religious culture.

For the Lutheran clergy who came to colonial America, the transition to this new religious environment was even more disruptive. They were no longer supported by an established religious system, underwritten by the state, but had to rely on their own initiative and on the voluntary participation of their congregational members to sustain Lutheranism in the New World. While a number of European Lutheran pastors in colonial America were able to make this transition, many others simply could not do so, and the supply of European Lutheran pastors willing to come to America was limited. Some of the best of these transplanted pastors were those who, like Henry Melchior Muhlenberg, were trained originally for the mission field and approached the colonial America situation with that mentality. Lutheranism in America was essentially a missionary enterprise, and would remain so until the twentieth century.

The shortage of trained European clergy meant that other means had to be developed to supply pastoral leaders for the developing American Lutheran congregations. Any number of clerical adventurers and imposters were active among colonial Lutheran congregations; failed European pastors or those who posed as pastors often created difficulties and conflicts within these congregations, and without any real church structure it was difficult to evaluate, let alone to discipline or remove, them. Given the limited supply of European clergy and their uneven quality, American Lutherans were forced to develop and ordain their own pastors. Promising candidates for the ministry studied under the tutelage of an established Lutheran pastor, "reading" theology and assisting that pastor in providing pastoral services to the grouping of multiple congregations that most pastors served. Besides raising up new pastors, this system also encouraged the development of cooperative and coordinating efforts among colonial pastors, leading to the formation first of informal and then of formal structural arrangements, and eventually synodical organizations.

Slowly but surely, over the course of the colonial period (1607–1775), Lutherans made the contextual transition to becoming a truly American religious group. In their encounter with the new world of American religion, they created the basic conceptual and organizational transitions that would allow them to flourish and grow in America, decisions that continued to shape and affect the course of American Lutheranism down to the present. It is to these decisions and developments that we will turn our attention in what follows.

The Beginnings of Lutheranism in America

One of the immediate backgrounds to European exploration and settlement of the Americas was the sixteenth-century interreligious conflict between European Roman Catholics and Protestants. National competition for trade and territory was often overlaid with confessional competition among countries. Although the confessional labels of "Protestant" and "Catholic" were often convenient and simplistic labels for deeper levels of contention, there was often a religious element to the settlement of North America. There are sporadic references in the early sixteenth-century Spanish sources to *Luteranos* who settled in the Americas, and specifically to a colony established in Florida in 1564, which was actually a group of French Reformed Huguenots, a colony that the Spanish destroyed. The Spanish often did not distinguish between different forms of Protestantism, and *Luteranos* was a common label for any Protestant. Although there was an early sixteenth-century German attempt to form a trading colony in Venezuela, this did not last. At that time, Germany was not developing into a modern nation-state, and the devastations of the Thirty Years' War (1618–1648) diverted its nascent colonial and economic ambitions, which tended to be focused more on eastern Europe and the Baltic than on the Americas. There were small colonies of German traders established locally, such as in Guyana and Suriname, where Lutheran congregations were eventually formed in the eighteenth century.

The first recorded Lutheran presence in the Americas came in a strange place and from an unexpected quarter. In the early seventeenth century, King Christian IV of Denmark encouraged economic exploration and colonization, and in 1619 sent out two ships to explore the northeastern corner of North America, searching for the illusive Northwest Passage through the Arctic ice to the riches of Asia. Commanded by Danish captain Jens Munk, the expedition was trapped in Hudson Bay near Churchill that winter, and most of the members of expedition died. The Lutheran chaplain to the expedition, Pastor Rasmus Jensen, held the first recorded Lutheran worship services in the Americas during the winter of 1619, but he died in Canada before the remnants of the expedition could straggle back to Denmark. Later in that same century, in 1663, the Danes established a colony on the Virgin Islands in the Caribbean, thus becoming a permanent Lutheran presence on those islands. Although the initial ministry was to the European settlers only, eventually the Lutheran mission was extended to enslaved Africans on the island, creating a creole Lutheranism in the Virgin Islands. When the islands were sold to the United States in 1917, these congregations became a part of American Lutheran synods.

Although generally labeled officially by the nations that sponsored these first expeditions and colonies, Danes, Swedes, Dutch, and English, in fact many of the individuals who comprised these efforts came from a variety of nations. The early Danish efforts included many Dutch and Norwegians, while the Dutch colonies had sizable numbers of Germans and Scandinavians in their number. The Swedish colony on the Delaware River was guided by Dutchman Peter Minuit, and consisted of many ethnic Finns who had previously taken up residence in Sweden. In such a way, many individual Lutherans came to colonial America, not as part of intentional, organized settlements, but as part of larger and more varied economic colonies. It took some time for these individual Lutherans to find each other and to begin to create worshiping communities.

Lutherans in New Netherlands: New York and New Jersey

Newly independent from Spain, in the early seventeenth century the Dutch Republic began an aggressive program of trade, exploration, and colonization, including substantial settlements along the Hudson River in North America. Permanently settled beginning in the 1620s, the Dutch colony of New Netherlands quickly grew to a prosperous string of settled villages along the Hudson River, from Manhattan to Albany, out along Long Island, and down into New Jersey and the Delaware River valley. Governed by the Dutch West India Company, this colony was organized along the model of the Dutch homeland, including a state-supported, established Dutch Reformed church, complete with Reformed pastors from Holland. Well positioned to take advantage of trade with the Native Americans, the colony flourished, enough so to draw the attention of the English colonies to its north and south, which resulted in the English capture of New Amsterdam in 1664, out of which the English created the colonies of New York and New Jersey.

As with other early settlements in colonial America, the Dutch colony was a mixed bag of peoples: primarily Dutch, of course, but also numbers of Germans and Scandinavians, many of whom had first settled in Holland for trading and economic opportunities. Out of these disparate individuals, along with some ethnic Dutch, Lutherans created a thriving string of congregations in Holland in the late sixteenth century, especially in Antwerp and Amsterdam. Since these Lutheran congregations developed within the context of the Dutch Reformed state church, they received no state support and limited recognition and freedoms. These Dutch Lutheran congregations were some of the first "free" Lutheran congregations, free in the sense that they were independent, voluntary congregations supported and governed without the efforts of the Dutch Republic. The example of these free Dutch Lutheran congregations served as a model for later Lutherans in colonial America, coming through the struggles of Dutch Lutherans in New Amsterdam to form their own independent Lutheran congregations within that colony.

Although it is unclear when the first Lutherans settled in New Netherlands, it is clear that they were present at least by the 1640s (if not much earlier), and by 1649 they had organized a congregation and sent a request to the Lutheran consistory in Amsterdam for a Lutheran pastor. The founding date of this Dutch Lutheran congregation in New Amsterdam makes it the oldest continually surviving Lutheran congregation in America, now First Lutheran Church, Albany, New York. The Lutheran consistory in Amsterdam entered into a long process of negotiations with the Dutch West India Company to allow for the sending of a pastor, efforts that were generally unsuccessful.

Seventeenth-century religious conflict did not always just involve Protestant–Roman Catholic tensions, but also long-simmering tensions between Lutheran and Reformed Protestants, especially in western Germany and Holland. The Dutch Reformed pastors in New Netherlands resented competition from the Lutherans (or anyone else) and strongly opposed the Dutch Lutheran efforts to obtain a Lutheran pastor for their colony. In 1654, the Dutch West India Company denied the Lutheran request and attempted to suppress non-Reformed groups in the colony. In 1657, the Amsterdam Lutherans sent their American congregation a German Lutheran pastor, John Ernest Gutwasser, but Dutch colonial authorities forbade him from exercising any pastoral role whatsoever. New York Lutherans thus informed the Amsterdam Lutheran consistory, in the face of colonial prohibitions: "On the 20th of October, we sent the Reverend Goetwasser quietly away to a farmer and if he should be further persecuted by the Director Governor and Council we shall send him outside the jurisdiction, being 6 or 8 mile away, under the jurisdiction of the English, to stay there until your honors send us a complete license from the fatherland to practice our religion unmolested."[1] Local Lutheran attempts to shield Gutwasser from the authorities eventually failed, and in 1659 he was arrested and deported back to Europe.

When the English captured the New Netherlands colony, in 1664, prospects brightened for local Lutherans. Although the English immediately moved to establish the Anglican Church in New York and New Jersey, they declared respect for the rights of the Dutch Reformed, and by extension the other religious groups in the area, to free expression of their religious traditions. The Lutherans immediately applied to Amsterdam for another pastor, though it was not until 1669 that they received Pastor Jacob Fabritius, a refugee from Hungary. Although he began his work with a flourish, the New York Lutherans found him rather odd, and when he decided to move down into the Delaware River valley, no one seemed to be too upset. The third Lutheran pastor from Holland, Bernard Arnzius, arrived in 1671 and served the New York Lutherans until his death in 1691.

The early Lutherans in New Netherlands were a varied lot; besides the native Dutch Lutherans, their numbers also included German and Scandinavians Lutherans who were involved in the colonial trade. Since the Lutheran congregations were under the care of the Lutheran consistory in Amsterdam, Dutch was the leading language of the New York congregations, though there was an effort in some places to alternate with worship in German, given the growing numbers of Germans in the colony. Of course, this later led to conflict between the two groups, Dutch and German Lutherans. Pastors were expected to be fluent in Dutch and German, and, as leaders of the Lutheran community, to have at least a working knowledge of English as well. The original two Lutheran congregations were functionally one parish, one branch in Manhattan, and the other in Albany. Pastor Arnzius divided his time between the two towns, spending the winters in Albany and the rest of the year in New York City. The congregation on Manhattan built its first church building opposite Wall Street, on the property now occupied by Trinity Episcopal Church.

As the colonies grew, first under Dutch rule, and then under English control, the colonists spread out into the territories of New York and New Jersey. Small groupings of Lutherans were established along the Hudson River valley at Loonenberg (Athens), Kingston, and Newburgh, New York, and in Jersey City, Bayonne, Hackensack, and Saddle River, New Jersey. Several of these preaching points eventually became fully independent congregations.

Although the numbers of Dutch Lutherans were relatively small, and the use of the Dutch language in Lutheran worship was soon eclipsed by German, these first Dutch Lutherans contributed some important features to American Lutheranism. The most important item came through their Free-Church organizational models, which came into their congregations through the Lutheran consistory in Amsterdam. In Holland, the Dutch Lutherans were independent congregations outside of the state-church system, and so had to adopt models for how to organize and run their congregations on their own. Based on Calvin's consistorial court in Geneva, the local Lutheran congregations in and around Amsterdam formed their own consistory, a board of local pastors established to regulate the affairs of local Lutheranism and, as has been seen, the affairs of the Lutherans in New Amsterdam as well. The congregational constitutions of the local congregations in New Amsterdam provided important models in structuring and regulating communal life, and these early constitutions were influential in shaping later Lutheran immigrant congregations. When Henry Melchior Muhlenberg, the eighteenth-century American Lutheran leader, came into contact with the Dutch Lutheran congregations in New Jersey, these models were important in his institutional formation of German Lutheranism in Pennsylvania.

Swedish Lutherans in New Sweden, on the Delaware River

Along with Denmark and Holland, Sweden was a rising Protestant political power in the early seventeenth century. Gustavus Adolphus, the ambitious Swedish king, was eager to involve Sweden in the business of exploration, trade, and colonization, and began efforts, with Dutch help, to organize a Swedish trading company. Even with the king's untimely death at the battle of Lützen in 1632, his chancellor, Axel Oxenstierna, moved the plans forward. In 1638, a Swedish expedition landed in the Delaware River valley near Wilmington, Delaware, where they built a fortified settlement called Fort Christina. Subsequent expeditions brought several hundred Swedish settlers to the new colony, many of whom were actually Finns who had settled first in Sweden, and who were induced to populate the new Swedish colony. When the Dutch shareholders withdrew from the project, the Swedes formed their own organization, the New Sweden Company, and sent John Printz as royal governor to the colony, where he arrived in 1642. The colony grew, and settlements of Swedes were formed in the areas of Delaware, southern New Jersey, and southeastern Pennsylvania. This territory was also claimed by both the English and the Dutch, and the Swedish officials granted religious toleration to the local Dutch settlers (more than the Dutch Lutherans received in New Netherlands).

The first Swedish Lutheran pastor to hold regular services in North America arrived in 1639, and was referred to in the records as "Reorus Torkillus," or Torkillus the Preacher. In 1640, soon after his arrival, a little log church was built at Fort Christina, which was the first Lutheran church building in North America, and where Torkillus held regular services until his death in 1643. He was replaced by Pastor Israel Fluviander, who arrived with Governor Printz in 1643, and remained in the colony until 1647, when he returned to Sweden. These initial two Swedish Lutheran pastors typified the general pattern of clergy in New Sweden, which was of generally short-term pastorates that ended either with the death of the incumbent or his return to Sweden, although there were notable exceptions to this general rule.

The Swedish settlements expanded up the Delaware River valley, from Fort Christina (Wilmington, Delaware) to the settlements of Wiaco and New Gothenburg (Philadelphia and Tinicum, Pennsylvania), and across the river into the areas of southern New Jersey. Churches were built at many of these settlements, most notably at Philadelphia, and there were usually one or two Lutheran pastors who served the scattered congregations. Each congregation had its own lay leadership, and during the periods of time when the pastor was absent or there was a pastoral vacancy (which could go on for years), the lay leaders endeavored to hold regular worship services and keep the struggling congregations together.

When Governor Printz arrived, he brought with him a second Lutheran pastor, Johan Campanius, who served in New Sweden until 1648. Although Campanius only served the colony for six years, he threw himself into his work with intensity and intelligence, and brought about the further establishment of the Lutheran congregations along the Delaware. He was also interested in relations with the local Native American tribes, a Delaware branch of the Algonquin family who referred to themselves as the Leni Lenape. The Swedish government instructed the New Sweden settlers to live in peace with the local Native Americans, and Campanius set out to learn their language; he developed a word list and reduced their language to written form. The Lenape often came to hear Campanius talk (they referred to him as "Big Mouth"), and he tried to converse with them about the basic tenets of the Christian faith. As he was a Lutheran pastor, Campanius decided that the best way to reach out to the Lenape was to translate Luther's Small Catechism into their language. Although he probably started this work while in New Sweden, he continued to work on it after his return to Sweden. The Algonquin catechism was eventually published in Sweden in 1696, and copies were sent to the Swedish settlements in North America, although there is no evidence that they were ever used with the native populations.

Like many of the other Lutheran pastors in early colonial America, Campanius found life and working conditions in the New World to be harsh and debilitating. In a 1647 letter to the Swedish archbishop, Campanius asked to be released from his charge on the Delaware and given a parish in Sweden where he could adequately support his family. Complaining about his personal frailty and poor health, he continued: "And now I am the only clergyman in the land, and . . . am obliged, however, without any regard to the weather, be it bad or fine, to go between the places from one to another to visit them with the Word and the Sacrament, something I am quite willing to do, but my strength is becoming more feeble for every day . . ."[2] Campanius had reason to complain of the workload. Colonial law required three services (morning, afternoon, and evening) on Sundays for the town churches, although only one service for the country churches. The High Mass on Sunday morning generally went about four hours, and the sermon itself usually forty-five minutes to an hour. This is not to mention the full schedule of Holy Days of the Church of Sweden, with sermons on Wednesdays and Fridays, and morning and evening prayer with psalms and hymns on the other days. No wonder he complained about being exhausted.

The little Swedish colony on the Delaware was small and underresourced in many ways, and could not stand up economically and militarily to the Dutch to the north and the English to the south. In 1655, the Dutch took over the Swedish colony, allowing the Swedes their own religious freedom, but only one Lutheran pastor to remain in the area. This pastor, Lars Lock (a Finn), arrived in the Delaware valley in 1647 and, contrary to the usual pattern, continued to serve the Swedish congregations for forty years, until his death in 1688. When the English took over the Dutch colony in 1664, the Swedish settlements came under English rule; they continued to tolerate the Lutherans, but moved aggressively to establish Anglican congregations in the area.

Lock continued to serve the Delaware congregations single-handedly until 1671, when Jacob Fabritius moved down to the Delaware valley from his congregations in New York. Lock continued to serve the congregation in Wilmington and New Castle, Delaware, while Fabritius began to supply the congregations in Philadelphia and on Tinicum Island, Pennsylvania. The move to Pennsylvania did not seem to improve either Fabritius's mood or his character, as he was hauled into court in 1675 for leading a "rebellion" against the colonial officials, who wanted to draft Swedish labor for the construction of river dikes. His wife, Annetje, had him in court numerous times; in one case she described her husband as ". . . a drunken and constant profaner of God's name, a deviant Lutheran preacher . . . her married but unfaithful husband, who has driven her out of her own house and chamber . . ."[3] The local Swedish congregations also complained that he could only preach in Dutch or German, and that he was very slow to learn to preach in Swedish. But, despite his possible failings, Fabritius continued to preach and preside in the upper Delaware congregations, as there were no other possible candidates to replace him.

Apparently, things along the Delaware must have improved a bit, for Fabritius seems to have settled down; his congregations came to appreciate his services, and his wife ceased taking him to court on a regular basis. The Philadelphia congregation continued to retain his services and even began to support him financially. Unfortunately, in their later years, both Lock and Fabritius suffered from health problems that limited their ministry to the Swedish congregations. Lock went lame and had great difficulty in getting around to his congregations, and died in 1688. Fabritius went totally blind in 1683, and for the last nine years of his ministry had to be led from congregation to congregation to carry out his work. He had to cease his ministry in 1691, and died five years later.

Even considering their limitations, both Lock and Fabritius seemed to have carried out their ministry faithfully. But with Lock's death in 1688, the death of Arnzius in New York in 1691, and Fabritius's retirement that same year, no Lutheran pastors remained in colonial America. The leaders of the Swedish congregations on the Delaware did what they could to find new pastors, appealing first in 1691 to the Amsterdam Consistory, and then in 1693 to the Royal Government in Sweden, for pastors and other resources to support them. They sought two regular Swedish preachers, one for the upper Delaware congregations, and one for those on the lower Delaware. Their requests were answered in 1697, when two pastors were sent from Sweden, Andreas Rudman (who settled in Philadelphia) and Erick Bjork (who settled in the Wilmington area). Although Rudman only served his congregations for five years, he had a significant impact on these Swedish churches, having the Philadelphia church rebuilt, having additional outlying churches built, and reestablishing the church order and religious patterns in this area. Similarly, Bjork had a new church building erected at Wilmington and helped to reestablish the vitality of the Swedish congregations in Delaware and New Jersey. When Rudman left Philadelphia in 1702, Dutch Lutherans in New York convinced him to minister to them for a while. During this time, he became acquainted with a young German theological candidate, Justus Falckner, and eventually had Falckner ordained for these New York congregations.

Rudman was replaced in Philadelphia by Pastor Andreas Sandel, who served these congregations from 1702 until 1719, when he returned to Sweden. Sandel continued the energetic pattern established by his predecessor and seems to have been greatly appreciated by his congregations. Sandel endeavored to defend the Swedish settlers and the rights that had been granted them by the Dutch and English governments in turn, rights that were often neglected by the colonial administrations. Sandel also sought to defend them against the religious pluralism of the American colonies. In his letter of 1710 to the Swedish bishop, Jesper Svedberg, Sandel observes: "But in spiritual matters there is in this country great differences and discord, so that if any place in the world is full of heretics and wrong teachings, it is surely one. . . . [God's power] has markedly proven among our Swedes in this country . . . [because] they keep steadily to the Lutheran teaching . . ."[4] Sandel observed that while the Lutheran court preacher in London sent supplies and pastors to the German immigrants to Pennsylvania, he and the other Swedish preachers were not so well supplied by the Church of Sweden, and they had to struggle to maintain their congregations.

Rudman, Sandel, and Bjork were three of at least twenty-five Swedish preachers to serve the Delaware congregations during the eighteenth century. For the most part, they served faithfully and well, but there were never really enough of them, and at times there were lengthy pastoral vacancies that often undid the hard work that the resident pastors had endeavored to accomplish. Most of these preachers did not expect actually to stay in colonial America permanently, but saw this as mission service, from which they intended eventually to return to Sweden. The Swedish pastors and congregations never identified and trained pastors from among the local colonial populations, and so they were at the mercy of the Swedish officials for their pastors.

Religious officials in Sweden urged their colonial pastors and congregations to have especially good relations with one other religious group, namely the priests and congregations of the Church of England in colonial America. To these Swedish leaders, the Anglican Church seemed a "real" church, with bishops and priests and liturgy (in contrast to the many American "sects"), and they urged cooperation with the "English." In his documents, Sandel reflected such attitudes, rejoicing that the colonial Swedish congregations and pastors had good relations and cooperation with the local Anglican pastors. Given the scarcity of ordained pastors in colonial America, the Swedish Lutherans and Anglicans often supplied each other's congregations when vacant, and the Swedish Lutherans began a long tradition of close work with the Anglicans. They often cooperated with each other in Pennsylvania, for example, against the Quaker elites who established and initially ran the colony. These ties expanded through the eighteenth century, especially as the younger generations of Swedes became increasingly proficient in English, even preferring it for worship over Swedish.

Danish Lutheranism in the Virgin Islands

Danish interests in exploration and trade in the New World continued even after the ill-fated Munk expedition of 1619–1620, during which most of the expedition members (including Pastor Rasmus Jensen) died. In the 1660s, the Danish West

India Company secured the island of St. Thomas for a Danish colony, and, in 1666, an expedition arrived on that island with a Danish governor and a Danish Lutheran pastor, Kjeld Slagelse. Pastor Slagelse quickly established a Lutheran congregation in the town of Charlotte Amalie, which, following the New Netherlands congregation, is the second oldest surviving Lutheran congregation in the western hemisphere. The Danish population of the island was, however, always a smaller part of the total, and there were significant populations of Dutch, Germans, and English, as well as Africans (free and enslaved). Danish-language ministry continued under royal patronage, but the dominant language was a Dutch Creole, which eventually became the language of the Lutheran congregations. Although the Lutherans were slow to evangelize among the African populations, the pioneering efforts of Moravian missionaries in the area (beginning in 1717) eventually prodded the Lutherans to extend their own efforts. The Lutheran evangelization among the African population went slowly at first, as converts were initially required to learn Danish (which few understood). Eventually, by the end of the eighteenth century, Lutheran evangelization was shifted to the Creole language, resulting in a significant African Lutheran population in the Virgin Islands. This tradition was carried to the United States later on by migrants from the Virgin Islands to the New York City area.

Early German Immigration to Colonial America

German immigration to colonial America was organized differently from the examples we have already seen. Unlike the English, Dutch, Swedish, and Danish settlers in colonial America, there was no centralized German government to direct exploration, trade, and settlement in the New World. In the seventeenth century, the area of central Europe known today as Germany was divided into hundreds of different states of varying sizes; the unified German nation did not come into political reality until 1870. Moreover, the territory of the German states had been devastated by religious warfare during the Thirty Years' War (1618–1648), which caused widespread economic hardship and depopulation. There were large parts of Germany that lost between one-third and two-thirds of their population during this time due to warfare, starvation, and disease. The problems in Germany did not cease with the Treaty of Westphalia in 1648, which ended this destructive war, and the western Germany territories along the Rhine saw continued warfare and harsh conditions throughout the century. Germany was also religiously divided among the Lutherans, Reformed, and Roman Catholics, and there were continuous efforts to impose religious change and conformity within the German states, especially on minority religious populations.

Besides the three main religious groups in Germany (Lutheran, Reformed, and Roman Catholic), there were many other small religious groups, most of whom were dissenters from the larger state churches. Some of these groups had their origins in the sixteenth century: Anabaptists (Mennonites, Hutterites, and Amish) held that the only true Christian churches were those voluntarily composed of "true" adult converts, while the Spiritualists (Schwenkfelders and others) rejected the authority of any external norms or organizations, believing religion was a matter of the individual heart. Other groups had their roots in the seventeenth-century Pietist awakenings, such as the Moravians, under the leadership of Count Zinzendorf, and more radical pietist groups, like the Dunkers, moved strongly in the direction of the Anabaptists. Because of its chaotic condition, Germany was home to dozens of radical groups led by charismatic leaders; there were mystical and communal groups that practiced all sorts of alternative religious community, ranging from celibacy to free love. Most of these groups were harshly persecuted for diverging from the norms of the state churches, and either wandered constantly in exile or sheltered uneasily under the temporary protection of local landowners (like Count Zinzendorf).

The combination of weak governments, economic devastation, and the effects of religious competition and fragmentation meant that while there were many individuals and groups that might have wished to immigrate to colonial America, there were few external resources to assist these immigrants in their journey. Some of the persecuted religious groups, such as religious minorities and radical groups (mainly Protestants), received outside assistance from friendly Protestant nations, such as the English and Dutch, but most were forced back on their own resources. Smaller religious sects pooled their resources to cross the ocean and reestablish their particular communities in the New World, especially in the religious freedom of Pennsylvania, which drew dozens of these groups. But most ordinary Germans, Lutherans among them, had to emigrate on their own. For those who lacked the money to immigrate, there was the practice of indenture, or redemptionism, which was a form of voluntary and temporary slavery. In return for the cost of the Atlantic passage, German immigrants would go into a period (usually seven years) of voluntary bondage, laboring for the landowners who sponsored them. Conditions for such indentured servants were often very harsh and punitive, but it shows the poverty and desperation among them that as many as half the Germans who came to colonial America did so initially as indentured servants.

Many of the first Germans to come to colonial America were persecuted religious groups, either the smaller religious sects, or mainline Protestant refugees from religious conflict, such as the Palatines in New York or the Salzbergers in Georgia. Later on, the composition shifted toward immigrants coming for economic opportunity, whether indentured of free. These latter immigrants were generally Protestant, either Lutheran or Reformed, and many of the German communities in colonial America were mixed groups of these two populations, who lived and worked side by side, and sometimes even pooled their religious resources. Although they shared a common German ethnic heritage, their communities often suffered from religious competition and conflict, and were challenged by free-thinking Germans who attacked all forms of organized religion.

Early German Settlements

Although there were German Lutherans in the settlements in New Amsterdam, the first recognizable German settlement in colonial America was a group of Germans (mainly sectarians) who settled in the Germantown section of Philadelphia in 1683. An eclectic group of Germans, the Rosicrucian Brotherhood (a secret society with mystical tendencies), arrived in 1694. This community did not last, but two individuals connected with it, theological students Daniel and Justus Falckner, became early Lutheran pastors in colonial America. Daniel arrived first, in 1694, serving as a land agent for the colony. He also served as a Lutheran pastor, organizing a Lutheran congregation in New Hanover, Pennsylvania, in 1703. From 1708 until his death he served congregations first in New Jersey and then in New York. Justus arrived in 1700, and was soon identified as a possible Lutheran pastor for the New York Lutheran congregation. But, although he was a Lutheran theological student and candidate, Justus Falckner was not yet ordained. This was resolved through the auspices of the Swedish Lutheran pastors in the Delaware region, Andreas Rudman and Erick Bjork. Rudman had been granted the authority to perform ordinations by his superior, the archbishop of the Church of Sweden, and eventually overcame Falckner's hesitations about the legitimacy of such a move. The ordination was held in Philadelphia on November 24, 1703, the first authorized Lutheran ordination in North America.

Justus Falckner took charge of the Lutheran congregations along the Hudson River in New York and New Jersey. These congregations had deteriorated since the death of Arnzius in 1691, but the energetic Falckner's hard work pulled them back together. For twenty years, Falckner traveled throughout the region from Albany to Long Island, faithfully ministering to the scattered Lutherans in both the Dutch and German languages; he also trained and appointed lay leaders to conduct services in the congregations during his lengthy absences. His task was an exhausting job, and the exertions of his work led to his death in 1723, at the age of fifty-one. Besides the circumstances of his ordination, Falckner is also notable for his publication, in 1708, of a Lutheran catechism in Dutch, the first Lutheran book published in colonial America.

Falckner's own ministerial journal is a stoical record of pastoral functions completed and travels undertaken, one that only hints at the tremendous burden that he bore from the scattered, disorganized, poor, and often fractious congregations. He traveled constantly by boat in the summer and by sled in winter, on horseback or even on foot. He made a circuit between the two poles of New York City and Albany, visiting constantly among the congregations in New Jersey and along the Hudson River. A biographer writes of his ministry:

> The rigors and privations of pioneer life aged all of the clergy prematurely. Constant travel over non-existent roads on horseback in poor weather, lack of proper housing and insufficient salary, too little encouragement from abroad, and dealing with impoverished and uneducated parishioners, who were not always either generous or co-operative, made their lives a constant challenge.[5]

Certainly, his ministry bore fruit at times, and a number of the congregations he served eventually flourished, but the cost to pastor and parishioners alike was heavy.

Falckner's rebuilding of the Lutheran congregations along the Hudson came just in time, as the area was soon to see an influx of German Lutheran refugees from areas of western Germany along the Rhine, especially from a territory known as the Palatinate. Traditionally Protestant, this region had suffered greatly from Protestant–Roman Catholic warfare in the late seventeenth and early eighteenth centuries, and from religious oppression that forced thousands of Protestants to flee the country from 1707 to 1710. Tens of thousands of these Palatines(as they were known) fled to Protestant England for protection. The burden of caring for these religious refugees was great, and the English government devised various schemes for resettling them, one of which involved the establishment of a colony of Palatines along the Hudson River south of Albany. From 1708 to 1710, the English government sent groups of Palatine refugees to New York, eventually comprising over 2,500 people. A smaller group of Palatine refugees was resettled in North Carolina, but this settlement did not last long.

The Palatine immigration was accompanied by two pastors, one German Reformed, and the other a Lutheran pastor named Joshua Kocherthal, who established additional Lutheran congregations along the Hudson and served them until his death in 1719. The colony was originally granted land by the English government in return for the production of raw materials for the British navy, but this proved to be an impractical arrangement and was eventually abandoned. Thrust into the wilderness of the American frontier, the colony suffered from British governmental neglect, the greed of local officials, and the difficulties of establishing communities in unsettled lands. Soon the members of the initial colony, and those German immigrants who followed after them, began to disperse, seeking better conditions elsewhere in New York, New Jersey, and Pennsylvania. The early Lutheran congregations in Schoharie, New York (1714), and Tuplehocken, Pennsylvania (1723), among others, owe their foundations to this migration of the Palatine Lutherans.

German Lutherans were also at this time beginning to move southward into Maryland and Virginia, either by way of Pennsylvania, or by the direct settlement of immigrants and indentured servants in these areas. The first organized settlement of Germans in Virginia came in 1717, with a group that was contracted to manage an ironworks; when their seven-year term was concluded, they founded a community in Madison County and formed a congregation. Other families and groups moved down through the back country of Maryland and Virginia, seeking good farmland, and in their scattered communities began to gather for religious services, sometimes served by visiting Lutheran pastors. One early Lutheran pastor in these areas was Anthony Jacob Henkel, a Lutheran pastor exiled from Europe in 1717. He regularly served Lutheran congregations in Pennsylvania, and traveled to minister to scattered groups of Lutherans in Maryland and Virginia until his death in 1728. He was the patriarch of a large family of Lutheran pastors and leaders among eighteenth- and nineteenth-century American Lutherans.

By 1720, there were the beginnings of organized Lutheran congregations ranging from Albany, New York, down through the Shenandoah Valley of Virginia, and the faint beginnings of Lutheran settlements in the South. Some congregations, such as the Dutch and Swedish congregations, had been in existence for decades, while many of the German congregations were just coming into being. But there were only a few Lutheran pastors in the whole of the American colonies, far too few to serve the widely scattered congregations. Regularly, the smaller congregations might go for months or years without pastoral services, and even most established congregations would have lengthy pastoral vacancies. As the mass immigration of Germans to colonial America was just getting started, there was a desperate need for new Lutheran congregations and for Lutheran pastors to serve them.

The Nature of Early American Lutheranism

Given the generally small and haphazard nature of their early settlements in early colonial America, the early Lutherans struggled to maintain themselves and their congregations. They were also a varied group, representing a wide spectrum of

European Lutheranism, beyond that of the Dutch, German, and Swedish Lutherans. In the Dutch colony of New Netherlands there were many German and Scandinavians (mainly Norwegians) who were Lutherans, and in New Sweden there were Finnish Lutherans as well as Swedes. During the seventeenth century, there was significant military pressure on eastern Europe from the Ottoman Turkish Empire, and numbers of eastern European Lutherans (Germans and Hungarians) fled into exile in the West; Pastor Jacob Fabricius, who arrived in 1671, was a Lutheran refugee from Hungary. In 1704, Pastor Justus Falckner reported to August Francke, the Pietist leader at Halle in Germany, of the varied composition of his congregations: "God gave me grace that I learned Dutch in a short time . . . my auditors are mostly Dutch in speech, but in extraction are mostly High-Germans. Also Swedes, Danes, Norwegians, Poles, Lithuanians, Transylvanians, and other nationalities."[6] Several early Lutheran pastors reported that while they preached regularly in German, Dutch, and Swedish, they found it vital to have a good working knowledge of English for daily activities, for coexisting with their religious colleagues, and increasingly (as was the case in New Sweden) for teaching and catechizing the younger generations. The Swedish pastor Johannes Dylander, who served the Swedish congregation in Philadelphia from 1737 to 1741, translated Luther's Small Catechism into English, and it was printed in Stockholm in 1749. Even the use of the German language itself was complicated, because there was no standard German at the time, only significant dialects and regional variations of German that were difficult for others to understand.

Along with the regional and linguistic differences among early colonial Lutherans, there were significant differences within their communities about Lutheran worship, theology, organization, and the practice of ministry. There was nothing approaching a common heritage of worship patterns. Many territories within Germany had their own distinct Lutheran worship book, liturgy, and patterns of worship life. Gathering such varied Lutherans together, the early pastors had to develop or adapt their own worship materials for their congregations out of the variety of worship books that the people had available. In letters back to religious authorities in Europe, Lutherans often expressed the plea to send hymnals and catechisms to America, as such things were in desperately short supply. Theologically, some European Lutheran churches (mainly in Germany) recognized the entire *Book of Concord* as authoritative, while in other areas only the Augsburg Confession had normative status. Lutherans were also divided along Orthodox and Pietist lines, and these differences also occasioned intra-Lutheran conflicts.

Dealing with the religious pluralism of the American colonies was often quite a challenge, for though most colonists were Protestant, they were divided into a wide variety of different types, and these differences could easily descend into conflict. Lutherans struggled with the Dutch Reformed and English Anglican attempts to form their own establishments in the middle colonies, and sought to maintain their rights within these systems. In Pennsylvania, the Germans and Swedes had varying relations with the Quaker leadership of the colony, who were frequently critical of more formally organized religious groups, such as the Lutherans. Throughout the middle colonies, the Scots-Irish Presbyterians were a growing force, and the Baptists and Methodists were not far behind them. The Germans themselves were split among Lutheran, Reformed, Moravian, Anabaptist, and sectarian groups, which often resulted in local conflict.

On the other hand, Lutherans could often work cooperatively with other Protestants around them. Because of frequent clerical interims, local Lutheran congregations relied on the pastoral efforts of other, non-Lutheran pastors, and Lutheran pastors often supplied other pulpits, especially among the congregations in the Delaware valley. Mixed German communities of Lutherans and Reformed often lacked the resources to maintain separate church buildings and schools, and sometimes formed "union" congregations, in which separate Lutheran and Reformed congregations would share a common building and sometimes even a common pastor for discernable periods of time.

The Internal Life of Lutheran Congregations

These nascent Lutheran congregations struggled to form, support, and maintain themselves on their own resources in the American colonies, without state support and often without adequate clerical leadership. European assistance was sporadic and very slow in coming; it might take years to receive any pastoral assistance at all, and when these pastors did come, they were often ill suited to the New World conditions. For the most part thrown back on their own devices, lay congregational leaders tried to keep a semblance of religious life alive without consistent pastoral leadership by conducting prayer services and the singing of hymns, often with the reading of sermons by Luther and other theological leaders. The difficulties of this pattern can be heard in the 1693 letter of the Delaware Swedes back to royal officials, seeking new Lutheran pastors; they wished for: ". . . two Swedish ministers that are well-learned in the Holy Scriptures, and may be able to defend us against all false opposers . . . and also one that might defend the true Lutheran faith which we do confess."[7] As has been seen, this letter eventually resulted in the dispatch of Pastors Rudman and Bjork in 1697, and these two young energetic leaders soon set things on a better footing, though the exertion required took a heavy toll on their health.

Sometimes the arrival of a new pastor from Europe proved to be a great disappointment, if this pastor proved to be unsuited or unprepared for the task. Imagine the case of the Dutch Lutherans in New York: for years they had struggled against the persecution of the Dutch Reformed, and they finally received Pastor Jacob Fabritius in 1669 to lead their congregations. Now under English rule, they had the opportunity to grow and expand, but Fabritius proved to be a poor choice. In a letter of 1670, the congregational leaders complained to the Lutheran consistory in Amsterdam that Fabritius: ". . . does not behave himself or live as a pastor should. He is very fond of wine and brandy and knows how to curse and swear too. . . . He pays little attention to people, so that our opponents or neighbors have nothing else to talk about but the Lutheran pastor."[8] Of course, pastors had their share of complaints against their own parishioners. It is common to read of pastors who complained that the congregations were slow to provide their salaries, parsonages, and other forms of compensation, and that the members of the congregation willfully disobeyed them, ignored their teachings and counsels, and generally lived wanton, careless lives.

These litanies of mutual complaint were not uncommon, but the opposite held true as well, where congregations and pastors were well suited to each other and developed a sense of mutual respect and trust. Although Fabritius was not well received in New York, in 1671 he moved down to serve the Swedes on the Delaware for twenty years, a relationship that seemed, after a rocky beginning, to go better (though it is not clear that he ever did learn much Swedish).

Conclusion

By 1720, Lutherans had been in North America for about a century. They had founded a number of congregations, especially in the middle colonies of British North America, as well as on the Danish Virgin Islands. The Lutherans had begun the difficult job of adjusting their religious traditions and congregations to the New World, where religious pluralism and voluntary religious organizations were becoming the norm. Although European Lutherans did offer some support to these congregations, this assistance was fragmentary and not always well suited to the needs of their new situation. Although the results of Lutheran labors in colonial America were far from impressive, they did form a base of congregations from which to grow and develop. This was fortunate, for in the coming decades after 1720 tens of thousands of German immigrants would come to North America, and their arrival would push the existing Lutheran resources to their limit.

Notes

1. "Letter of the Lutherans in New Netherland to the Amsterdam Consistory," October 21, 1657, in Arnold J. H. van Laer, trans., *The Lutheran Church in New York, 1649–1772* (New York: New York Public Library, 1946), 32.

2. "Letter, Johan Campanius to the Archbishop," January 30, 1647, in Peter Craig and Kim-Eric Williams, eds., *Colonial Records of the Swedish Churches in Pennsylvania,* vol. 1, 1646–1696 (Philadelphia: Swedish Colonial Society, 2006), 7.

3. "A court held in City Hall, New Orange," February 24, 1674, in ibid., 130–31.

4. "Letter, Andreas Sandel to Jesper Svedberg," July 21, 1710, in Peter Craig and Kim-Eric Williams, eds., *Colonial Records of the Swedish Churches in Pennsylvania*, vol. 3, 1702–1719 (Philadelphia: Swedish Colonial Society, 2007), 144–45.

5. Kim-Eric Williams, *The Journey of Justus Falckner* (Delhi, NY: ALPB Books, 2003), 80.

6. "Missives to Francke," trans. Julius F. Sachse, in *Proceedings of the Pennsylvania German Society*, 18 (Lancaster, PA: New Era Printing Co., 1909), 15.

7. "Congregation's letter to Johan Thelin," May 31, 1693, in Craig and Williams, eds., *Colonial Records*, 1:183.

8. "Letter from the Elders of the Lutheran church at New York . . ." June 30, 1670, in van Laer, trans., *Lutheran Church in New York*, 76.

Excursus 2

LUTHERANS IN THE CARIBBEAN

It is somewhat ironic that, for a northern European religious tradition, a number of the first Lutheran settlements in the Americas were attempted in the Caribbean. There have been Lutherans in some parts of this region for almost four hundred years, and there are currently substantial numbers of Lutherans in the Virgin Islands, Puerto Rico, Guyana, and Suriname, with other scattered congregations in Antigua, Bermuda, the Bahamas, Cuba, and Haiti. One of the current sixty-five synods of the Evangelical Lutheran Church in America, the Caribbean Synod, is wholly in this area, consisting of congregations in the Virgin Island and Puerto Rico. As of 2010, there were more than 27,000 Lutherans around the Caribbean basin.

Historically, Lutheranism came to the Caribbean as the religion of white European and, later, American settlers. But in time some of these churches opened their doors to local inhabitants, Hispanics, African Americans, and Native Americans, and some of these congregations have become truly indigenous and multicultural ministries. More recently, North Americans moved and settled in some parts of the Caribbean, beginning other congregations for expatriates and vacationers. There are quite a variety of different Caribbean congregations; some are independent church bodies, while others are related to American Lutheran denominations, such as the Evangelical Lutheran Church in America (ELCA), the Lutheran Church–Missouri Synod (LCMS), and the Wisconsin Evangelical Lutheran Synod (WELS).

Although there are scattered historical reports of "Lutherans" (*Luteranos*) in the Spanish and Portuguese territories in Latin America, especially Florida, Venezuela, and Brazil, these reports more than likely were references to scattered Protestant sympathizers, rather than to organized groups. The *Luterano* settlement in Florida actually consisted of Calvinist Huguenots rather than Lutherans, and was destroyed by Catholic forces in 1564. A German trading colony was founded in Venezuela in the early sixteenth century, which could conceivably have contained Lutherans, but this venture quickly collapsed. The oldest surviving Lutheran congregation in the Caribbean, the Frederik congregation in Charlotte Amalie, was founded in the Virgin Islands in 1666 by the Danish settlers on the island of St. Croix; they later founded other congregations on islands of St. Croix, St. John, and St. Thomas in the eighteenth century. Although these congregations were originally intended for Danes, by the 1750s they were doing mission work with the enslaved Africans on the islands. When the Danes sold these islands to the United States in 1917, these congregations affiliated with an American Lutheran denominations. There are also several congregations of Virgin Island Lutherans on the mainland of the United States, most notably in New York City.

Similarly, Dutch Lutherans founded congregations in the area of Guyana and Suriname in the eighteenth century, as the Europeans planted colonies there. These Dutch Lutherans formed their own congregations, with some resistance from the Dutch Calvinist authorities, and received occasional Lutheran pastors sent by the Lutheran consistory in Amsterdam. These congregations initially only consisted of white settlers and their descendants, until the middle of the nineteenth century when they began to reach out to other populations. Guyana is especially racially diverse, and the Lutheran congregations there include African Americans, Native Americans, East Indians, and some Chinese. Though served by pastors from Europe and America for quite some time, these Lutheran churches eventually became autonomous. These two churches now contain approximately 17,000 members.

Although it has a long history of European colonization, Lutherans did not become established on Puerto Rico until it became a part of the United States in 1898. In that year, a young theological student moved to Puerto Rico and eventually started a Lutheran congregation there. He was eventually followed by a number of different pastors and missionaries from the United States, who began to preach in Spanish to the local population. Eventually, by 2005, there were twenty-eight congregations in Puerto Rico, with some five thousand members, as a part of the Caribbean Synod of the ELCA.

There are Lutheran congregations in some of the other islands of the Caribbean. There was a small Lutheran presence in Cuba up to the revolution of 1961, and some scattered congregations may still exist. There is a WELS congregation in Antigua, founded in the 1970s. There is one ELCA congregation in Bermuda, and two Lutheran congregations in the Bahamas, an LCMS congregation in Nassau, and an ELCA congregation in Freeport. There is also a Lutheran presence in Haiti, connected with the Church of the Lutheran Confession in Alsace and Lorraine (France).

Though many of these Caribbean Lutheran congregations were begun by European or Americans, either as settlers or missionaries, most of their members are now predominantly local people—Virgin Islanders, Guyanese and Surinamese, Puerto Ricans, and others. They may be Hispanic, Native American, African American, or other local populations, worshiping in Spanish, English, French, or other local languages. These congregations, though small, enrich the palate of world Lutheranism.

Chapter 3

EARLY COLONIAL DEVELOPMENTS, 1720–1748

B y the year 1720, a number of Lutheran congregations had been established from New York to Virginia and in the Virgin Islands, but it could hardly be said that they were thriving. Among the congregations along the Hudson River and northern New Jersey, Justus Falckner continued to serve, but the demand of this ministry contributed to his early death in 1723. The Dutch Lutherans there were the oldest group, but they were being rapidly supplanted by the Germans from the Palatinate and elsewhere. The pastor who accompanied the Palatine colonists, Joshua Kocherthal, served the scattered German congregations until his death in 1719, when their care fell to Falckner. There were several Swedish congregations and preaching points along the Delaware River, from Philadelphia, Pennsylvania, to Wilmington, Delaware, but very few Swedish pastors to serve them. Pastor Andreas Sandel left the Philadelphia-area congregations to return to Sweden in 1718, and was succeeded in that position by Pastor Jonas Lidman. Among the Germans in Pennsylvania and New Jersey, Pastors Daniel Falckner and Anthony Henkel continued to provide ministerial care as new congregations of immigrant Germans were being founded, but often without any consistent pastoral leadership. Groups and families of Germans migrated southward into Maryland and Virginia, and formed settlements. A party of Palatine Germans, both Lutherans and Reformed, had been sent to North Carolina, but the settlement fared poorly, and there was no real attempt to form a Lutheran congregation there. Scattered groups of German Lutherans had moved into South Carolina, either directly from Europe or from North Carolina, but had not as yet developed any organized congregations. In the Virgin Islands, the Danish authorities established Lutheran congregations on the islands and sent a series of Danish pastors to serve them, but their ministry was generally limited to the Danish population, a minority among the Europeans on the islands (to say nothing of the African population).

It is impossible to estimate with much precision the number of Lutherans in America in 1720. There were perhaps several thousand Lutherans in the Swedish settlements along the Delaware River, and an equal number of German Palatines in areas along the Hudson River. The older Dutch Lutheran congregations in New York and New Jersey had never been particularly numerous, and it would be equally difficult to determine the numbers of German Lutherans stretched from New Jersey to Virginia, with the majority in Pennsylvania. Certainly, there were no more than eight thousand Lutherans in colonial America in 1720, and possibly fewer.

This fairly dismal appraisal of the situation is more dire than perhaps it was in actuality. There had been a number of important developments in colonial American Lutheranism in its first seventy years that laid the foundation for future Lutheran growth. First, there were already several dozen organized Lutheran congregations in the New World, many of them struggling, but from which further growth could be launched. Second, Lutherans in America had already begun to reenvision themselves and their congregations along the lines of American voluntary religion and religious pluralism. Third, American Lutherans maintained important connections with leading centers of European Lutheranism, in Amsterdam and Hamburg, in Sweden and Denmark, and with the new Lutheran court preacher at the royal court in England. These ties would be crucial in the further growth of American Lutheranism. Finally, 1720 marked the beginning of a period of vigorous growth in the immigration of Germans to colonial America; it is estimated that by the onset of the Revolutionary War in 1775, there were 60,000 to 80,000 Germans in colonial America, and a substantial portion of these would be Lutheran.

Berkenmeyer and Lutheranism in New York

After the death of Justus Falckner in 1723, the New York and New Jersey Lutheran congregations were left without pastoral leadership. These ten congregations then appealed to the Lutheran consistory in Amsterdam for a new pastor. They identified a young German theological student in Hamburg, William C. Berkenmeyer, who agreed to serve and who arrived in New York in 1725. He brought with him a library of religious books for the congregations and a sum of money for church building, contributed by European Lutherans, both of which were put to immediate use. A new church building in New York City was erected and dedicated four years after his arrival. Berkenmeyer, an energetic young pastor, quickly went about his scattered congregations to try to reorganize then. One common issue that he faced immediately was the presence of a self-appointed, "vagabond" preacher named Johann van Dieren, who had already insinuated himself into the Palatine congregation at Schohaire, New York, and was causing divisions within other congregations. Berkenmeyer moved quickly to counter van Diernen, persuading the Lutheran congregations to submit to his own leadership and to agree not to employ any pastors other than those properly ordained and sent from reputable Lutheran authorities in Europe.

The initial years of his ministry in New York demonstrate Berkenmeyer's own theological position. Strongly influenced by his theological education in Hamburg, Berkenmeyer was a Lutheran of the Orthodox school; he held a fairly "high" view of the nature of ministerial authority and of formal liturgical practice within his congregations. He was somewhat troubled by his own, slightly irregular situation in New York—irregular in the sense that he and the congregations were not technically under the control of a recognized ecclesiastical judicatory, the ties to the Lutheran consistory in Amsterdam being rather ill-defined. When an initial proposal to put himself and his congregations under the oversight of the Swedish provost (head pastor) in Philadelphia (and by extension under the archbishop of Sweden) proved unsuccessful, Berkenmeyer went forward on his own and began to assume the role of personal oversight of the congregations along the Hudson River.

Needing assistance to serve these scattered congregations, Berkenmeyer appealed to European authorities for more pastors to serve the area. In response, they sent out several pastors to assist him, including Michael Christian Knoll, in 1732, and Johan August Wolf, in 1734. Berkenmeyer organized the growing numbers of congregations (twenty-three in total by 1750) into five separate parishes, over which he attempted to maintain oversight. Berkenmeyer served the congregations around Albany, New York, while Knoll served those around New York City, and Wolf served those in the Raritan River valley of New Jersey. Although the congregations all were technically under the control of the Lutheran consistory in Amsterdam, distance and a lack of effective controls meant that the congregations were largely autonomous, a situation that frequently led to difficulties.

Major conflict soon erupted between Pastor Wolf and his congregations in New Jersey. Although in his new parish for only a single year, Wolf had already alienated a substantial part of these congregations, who charged him with "gross incompetence" and wanted to remove him as pastor. Wolf countered that the congregations had refused to compensate him adequately and, furthermore, they had no power to dismiss him without his consent. Pastor Knoll in New York City, no stranger to conflict with his own congregation, nevertheless wrote sympathetically to the Raritan congregation: "Meanwhile, since Pastor Wolf respects neither his office nor religion, I will no longer urge him to conduct the services, nor [the parish] to build and turn over the parsonage to him, thus giving him more possessions to hold on to."[1] In his position as the senior minister in the area, Berkenmeyer found himself drawn into the conflict and attempted to resolve it. On August 20, 1735, Berkenmeyer gathered Knoll and Wolf, together with the representatives of their congregations, to form what he called a "Classical Assembly." Drawn from the Dutch Reformed "Classis," or ecclesiastical gathering, this was the first attempt at providing a Lutheran synodical structure in North America.

For this Classical Assembly, Berkenmeyer drew up a list of propositions ("points for consideration") intended to order the life of the pastors and congregations together; it was heavily weighted on the rights of the pastors and on the duties of the congregations. In summary, the propositions claimed that congregations had no rights to censure or dismiss their pastor; they could only appeal to the proper authorities (in this case, the Lutheran Ministerium at Hamburg, Germany). The seventh and final proposition called on the Raritan congregations to take Wolf back and to try to work out the situation. Under pressure, the Raritan congregations initially acceded to these propositions, but they resented the forced "solution," and when Wolf continued his objectionable ways, the situation collapsed again.

The Classical Assembly of 1735 might have grown into a permanent church structure, the first American Lutheran synodical body, but it never met again, and nothing permanent came of the meeting. Mostly, this was Berkenmeyer's fault. He held such a high view of clerical authority that he was unable to accede to the congregation's reasonable demand for the removal of an obviously unfit pastor. His solution of appeal to European church officials was clumsy and unworkable. This incident shows that Berkenmeyer had little real insight into the new situation of Lutheranism within the American religious context and lacked flexibility to deal with it. Although Berkenmeyer would continue to serve his New York congregations faithfully until his death in 1751, he had alienated the New Jersey congregations, who increasingly looked toward the Lutherans in Pennsylvania for support. Knoll had years of difficulty in New York City, where the congregation was torn between Dutch- and German-speaking factions and subsequently split into two separate congregations.

The Swedish Congregations on the Delaware

The seventeenth-century pattern of the colonial Swedish congregations was sustained into the eighteenth century. Regular Swedish pastors were sent from Europe to the Delaware congregations, usually for short periods of time, after which they either returned to Sweden or died in office. Many congregations went for extended periods of time with no regular pastoral presence at all; the pastoral office at Swedesboro, New Jersey, was vacant for twenty-one years over a forty-six-year period between 1703 and 1749. The Swedish population of the area probably numbered about two thousand people, but the long pastoral vacancies, intermarriage with outside populations, and language disputes meant that these Swedish congregations were fortunate simply to maintain their numbers, especially without new Swedish immigration since the 1650s and little likelihood of it in the future.

When Pastor Andreas Sandel left the Philadelphia congregation in 1718, he was replaced fairly quickly by Pastor Jonas Lidman, who arrived in America in 1719. Contemporary records depict Lidman as a dedicated, if not too imaginative, pastor, one who served his congregations well but only maintained them. In response to questions from Sweden about the mission to the Native Americans, Lidman responded that they had been driven so far west that he rarely encountered them, and added that alcohol abuse had taken a major toll on them. Like many other colonial Lutheran pastors, Lidman continually complained to European authorities that he barely received enough resources from his congregations to support his family. In his case, however, Lidman found that supplying the local Anglican congregations was lucrative enough to make up the difference. He wrote to a colleague in Sweden in 1727: "We help the English (Anglican) Church as much as we can with sermons and other appropriate things, yet not so much that our own congregations thereby suffer. . . . we cannot find any special difference between them and the English Church, except that which flows from misunderstanding."[2] However, some in his congregations disagreed with him, interpreting his service to the Anglicans as a neglect of his own Swedish Lutheran congregations.

This incident illustrates trends within the Swedish congregations, both toward the use of the English language among them and a relationship with the Anglicans that grew increasingly close. Without new Swedish immigration, and with younger generations preferring English to Swedish, the language transition within the congregations became an issue, as it often does within immigrant congregations. By the 1740s, English-language services were introduced in the Lutheran congregations, and in some places English services were preferred over Swedish. The clergy sent from Sweden were hardly likely to be proficient in the English language, however; a few learned it well, but most were in residence for a limited period of time and learned very little English. This complicated the language tensions even further and weakened the congregations themselves.

After the departure of Lidman in 1730, neighboring Swedish pastor Johan Eneberg ministered to the Philadelphia congregation along with his own for two years. In 1733, the Philadelphia congregation received a new pastor from Sweden, Gabriel Falk. In less than one year he demonstrated that an unworthy pastor could do serious damage within a congregation. Falk was convinced that a vestryman of the Philadelphia congregation was having an incestuous affair and repeatedly made the charge public. Unfortunately, no one else believed Falk, and due to his continued assertion of the claim, the vestryman took Falk to court. When Falk could not prove his claim, he was fined five hundred pounds and the congregation threw him out. The congregation then went almost five years without a pastor, a situation that was compounded by the death of Bishop Jesper Svedberg in Sweden in 1735. Svedberg had been the champion and ecclesiastical supervisor of the colonial Swedish congregations, and his death caused a power vacuum, until finally ecclesiastical supervision of the Delaware congregations was transferred to the Swedish Archbishop in Uppsala.

The next Swedish pastor, Johannes Dylander, arrived in 1737, and proved to be all the pastor that his predecessors were not. Dylander showed how energy and imagination, along with pastoral skills, could revive a parish. He threw himself into rebuilding the Philadelphia congregation materially and spiritually, and succeeded very well. Besides tending to his own parish, he also preached to local German Lutheran and Anglican congregations, by contemporary reckonings up to sixteen sermons a week. He led the Philadelphia congregation in the building of a parsonage and the installation of a new pipe organ. Unfortunately, he died suddenly in 1741, after only four years in the parish. In a brief period of time, Dylander had proven to be such an impressive figure that people still talked about him even long after his death. As a contemporary Swedish traveler to America wrote, a few years after Dylander's death, "He was incredibly beloved by all, high or low, rich or poor, by Englishmen, Swedes, Germans, and by members of all denominations. The reasons for this were not only his divine teaching and exemplary life, but also his social affability . . ."[3]

Following Dylander's death, the Philadelphia church was vacant for two years, until the arrival of Pastor Gabriel Näsman in 1744. Unfortunately, Näsman was hardly the pastor (or the human being) that Dylander was, and managed to seriously damage the parish that Dylander had so painstakingly rebuilt. Näsman so alienated the church members that the once-thriving congregation soon plummeted and average Sunday worship attendance fell into the single digits. Desperate, the congregation appealed to the Swedish authorities in 1748 to remove Näsman, who lingered where he was not wanted, not returning to Sweden until 1752. Such were the troubles of the colonial Lutheran congregations at times!

Further south, along the Delaware River, was a cluster of Swedish congregations around Wilmington, Delaware, including some in southern New Jersey. Erick Bjork served many of these congregations until his return to Sweden in 1714. Two Swedish pastors replaced him: Andrew Hesselius, who served at Wilmington until 1723, and Abraham Lidenius, who first served at Raccoon and Pennsneck, New Jersey, and then replaced Hesselius at Wilmington, before returning to Sweden in 1731. Pastor John Enberg took over at Wilmington in 1732, and was succeeded by Peter Tranberg, who served there until his death in 1748. Throughout this period of time, there were usually two or three Swedish pastors at a time in colonial America, though there were often gaps in their service at various congregations. While Swedish immigration was attenuated, German immigration increased.

The Growth of the German Lutheran Congregations

German immigrants began to pour into Pennsylvania, and into the surrounding colonies of New Jersey, Maryland, and Virginia in the eighteenth century. A large proportion of them were Lutherans, although some others were Reformed, Moravians, Mennonite, and Amish, or members of the smaller sects. A large number of them, estimated to be one-third to one-half, had indentured themselves into seven or more years of service to pay for their passage. Many of these Germans were farmers, seeking to own good farmland and to avoid the wars, plagues, and famines of eighteenth-century Germany. They migrated to the rich agricultural areas of the middle colonies, especially southeastern Pennsylvania. Unlike the Palatine Germans, who came over in large groups guided by pastors, this new wave of immigrants came singly or in small groups, but congregated into ethnic German settlements only once they got to America.

Some of the earliest Germans settled in the 1680s just northwest of Philadelphia, in a section that came to be known as Germantown. Early pastors such as Daniel Falckner and Anthony Henkel served early congregations there, as well as in New Hanover (originally called Falckner's Swamp). Serving New Hanover until 1728, Flackner also made wide-ranging tours of German settlements in Pennsylvania, Maryland, and Virginia. A group of Palatine Lutherans, dissatisfied with conditions in New York, relocated to Tulpehocken, Pennsylvania, in 1723, and established an early congregation there. Another German Lutheran pastor, John Christian Schulze from Württemberg, arrived in Pennsylvania in 1732, and began to serve the congregations in Germantown, New Hanover, and Trappe (New Providence), uniting them into a single parish, which he served briefly. Schulze decided to go to England and Germany to solicit funds for the Pennsylvania Lutheran congregations, but never actually returned to Pennsylvania himself.

In 1728, a German Lutheran pastor, John Caspar Stoever Sr., arrived in Philadelphia, with his son and namesake, John Caspar Stoever Jr., a young theological student. The elder Stoever served Hebron Church, Madison County, Virginia, but left America in 1734 to solicit funds in Europe for American Lutherans, and died at sea in 1738 during his return to America. The younger Stoever was eventually ordained by Schultze in 1733, who appointed him to serve the three-congregation parish that he had formed. The younger Stoever remained in Philadelphia for only two years, leaving the united parish in 1735 to begin a long itinerant career, serving various Pennsylvania congregations until his death in 1779. After the younger Stoever departed, the three congregations were served at times by an unordained theological student and by the Swedish pastor Johannes Dylander, but they were vacant for long periods of time.

This lack of regular pastoral leadership for the German congregations around Philadelphia proved to be an opening for clerical opportunists, several of which came to plague the Lutheran work. The congregations petitioned the Lutheran consistory in the German state of Hesse Darmstadt for a pastor, and though it resulted in no positive response, it did prompt a disgraced German Lutheran pastor named Valentine Kraft to immigrate to Pennsylvania. Kraft insinuated himself into the vacant congregations, claiming to be not only their pastor, but also the superintendent of all the Lutheran churches in Pennsylvania. Pastoral claimants served other congregations, including a dentist named Schmidt at New Hanover. Although these congregations were desperate for pastoral leadership, once these vagabond preachers got established in congregational positions, they were difficult to remove. Another issue was competition from other German religious groups, especially the Moravians, who at times tried to insert their own pastors into vacant Lutheran congregations.

As the best farmland in southeastern Pennsylvania was quickly settled, the immigrant Germans moved further west and south, especially into the upland areas of Maryland and Virginia, following the north-south routes along the Cumberland and Shenandoah valleys through the Alleghany Mountains. Some of these pioneer farmers pushed even further south, down into North Carolina. A number of ethnically German rural communities were formed as a result, and often these Germans would come together to form the nucleus of a future congregation. Lutheran pastors, like John Caspar Stoever Jr., would make yearly preaching trips down from Pennsylvania through the frontier areas. Other Germans came through the port of

Baltimore, and up the rivers of tidewater Virginia, and added to these German communities. As in Pennsylvania, some of these first communities eventually formed union churches, with Lutheran and Reformed congregations sharing buildings and sometimes even preachers, such was the lack of clergy.

In the back country of Maryland and Virginia, many congregations were first established between 1720 and 1750. One of the first German congregations in Maryland was organized near Frederick around 1733, and they built a church two years later. This settlement was regularly visited, first by Stoever and later by Henry Melchior Muhlenberg. When the town of Baltimore was settled after 1730, a group of German Lutherans gathered there and were supplied by Lutheran pastors from Philadelphia. A congregation of Germans in Hebron, Virginia, was formed in 1717, and soon attracted other migrating Germans coming down from Pennsylvania. John Caspar Stoever Jr. served this congregation in the 1730s, which built its first church building in 1740. Other congregations in western Virginia followed in the 1750s.

An initial settlement of Palatine Germans in North Carolina was founded in 1710, but the colony struggled and was soon mostly destroyed by Native American attacks. Later settlements of Germans coming down through Virginia and into North Carolina formed other congregations, but these were almost all lay-led, because German pastors from the middle colonies were so far away. Many of these early German colonies established congregations, but these were mixtures of Lutherans, Reformed, and Moravians, and often had little confessional distinctiveness. The situation in South Carolina was different, in that Germans started to arrive there directly from Europe through the port of Charleston. A group of German-speaking Swiss came to South Carolina in the 1730s and settled in Orangeburg. They brought with them Pastor John Geissenbanner and organized a congregation in 1735. Germans who had congregated in the port of Charleston formed their own congregation in 1742.

The Salzburg Lutherans in Georgia

The story of the Salzburg Lutherans in Georgia is one of those dramatic narratives of religious conflict and exile that happened in eighteenth-century Europe. The Protestant Reformation took hold during the sixteenth century in parts of western Austria around the city of Salzburg. The territory around Salzburg was an ecclesiastical state, meaning that the Roman Catholic archbishop of Salzburg was not only the spiritual leader of the area, he was also the secular ruler. The local German Lutheran Protestants continued to maintain their own religious congregations in the area for two hundred years, often in the face of stiff resistance and persecution at the hands of the Roman Catholic authorities. These Lutherans resisted the Counter-Reformation attempts to re-Catholicize their communities and maintained their traditional communal rights to self-determination in religious matters. But on October 31, 1731 (Reformation Day!), Archbishop von Firmian issued the Salzburg Lutherans an ultimatum: convert to Roman Catholicism or renounce your communities and your property, and be forced into exile. Despite a wave of condemnations from around Europe, this decree was enforced. Over 30,000 Salzburg Lutherans left their homes in the middle of winter and headed northward into Protestant territories, where they were hailed as heroes of the faith. If the archbishop's strategy was to force the Lutherans to become Roman Catholic, it backfired dramatically. Much as with the Palatine refugees a generation before, Protestant groups and territories around Europe endeavored to resettle these religious refugees. The plight of the Salzburg refugees came to the attention of the Englishman James Oglethorpe and his colleagues, who in 1732 were chartering a new English colony in Georgia. Through the efforts of a German pastor in Augsburg, Samuel Urlsperger, and with the support of the English Society for the Promotion of Christian Knowledge (SPCK), a party of the Salzburg refugees were sent to Georgia in 1734, where they were given land about twenty-five miles inland from the present city of Savannah. They were led by two Lutheran pastors, Johann Martin Boltzius and Israel Christian Gronau, selected and supported by the leader of the German Lutheran Pietist University of Halle, August Hermann Francke. The party of Salzburg refugees settled on a parcel of land granted them by the colonial officials. They called the settlement Ebenezer.

Establishing a new community in the southern wilderness was difficult, especially since the land itself was not the best for agriculture. The community struggled to gain a foothold, and was successful due to their hard work and persistence, traits that early visitors to the community commented upon (including a young John Wesley, who visited them in 1737). Initially, the community was organized in a communal manner, under the leadership of the Lutheran pastors, but eventually this proved to be impractical and was abandoned for more traditional arrangements. Eventually, members of the community moved outward in search of better land, but Ebenezer remained the social and religious center of the community for quite some time. The Salzburg colony grew to a population of about 1,200 by 1741.

Upon its arrival in Ebenezer, the colony formed a Lutheran congregation and built a church building; eventually, they formed four congregations (Jerusalem, Bethany, Zion, and Goshen), as well as a school and an orphanage. The latter was an important part of the community, as on the harsh frontier adults often died suddenly, leaving orphaned children for whom the community had to care. The two pastors were leaders of the community in many ways, attempting to give spiritual guidance in an unformed wilderness, where vice and temptation were common and moral structures were weak. They also settled disputes, directed community endeavors (including an attempt to raise silkworms), and acted as physicians, an important part of the job of eighteenth-century pastors.

In the American colonies, the Salzburgers encountered many new people, not only the "English" colonists, but also Native Americans and, eventually, enslaved Africans. The Salzburgers generally lived in relative peace with the Native Americans and traded with them. The Halle officials in Germany urged them to conduct a mission with the Native Americans, but they deemed that this was not practical. Boltzius supplied regular reports to his European superiors, and commented in 1736: "With regard to the heathens in the land we can at present do nothing better than that we earnestly pray for them, give them a good example, and also demonstrate genuine love. . . . Should one of us . . . learn the Indian language, the regular duties of office at Ebenezer certainly would have to be reduced . . ."[4] Early on, the community also encountered enslaved Africans, who had been imported into the colony as labor. Initially, under the leadership of Boltzius, African slavery was rejected as improper for the Lutheran community, although later it would be adopted by their descendants as a perceived economic necessity.

Although Gronau died in 1744, Boltzius continued to serve the Salzburg settlement as pastor for many years until his death in 1765. The Halle officials quickly sent a replacement, Hermann Henry Lemke, and other subsequent pastors who served the Ebenezer colony (not without difficulties) until the beginning of the Revolutionary War in 1775. The Lutheran officials at Halle were very concerned with the success of this colony, and were quite responsive to requests for aid and leadership from the Georgia Lutherans.

Henry Melchior Muhlenberg

Although the basic geographical outlines of colonial Lutheranism were generally in place by 1740, it cannot be said that Lutheranism was thriving, nor were its prospects bright. Several dozen congregations (some no more than preaching points) were scattered from Albany, New York, to Savannah, Georgia, with about a dozen pastors to serve them. But conditions among the Lutherans were poor; the congregations struggled to maintain themselves and to retain adequate pastoral services, while the pastors themselves were a mixed lot. These Lutherans were still largely looking to European church officials for guidance and support, and as of yet only one pastor, Justus Falckner, had been ordained in the New World. As the example of the Delaware Swedes was beginning to show, the acculturation of the Lutheran immigrants and their transition to the English language meant trouble, since up to that point no Lutherans had ever worshiped or written theology in English, and they had no models of how to do this. After ninety years, there were Lutheran laypeople, pastors, and congregations in America, but there was no organized American Lutheranism. For Lutherans to grow and flourish in the New World, they would have to develop their own distinctly American form of Lutheranism and begin to wean themselves away from European models and support. The man who, more than anyone else, was to begin this vital transition arrived in Pennsylvania in 1742.

Henry Melchior Muhlenberg was born in Hanover, Germany, in 1711, the seventh child in a family of nine. His parents were middle class, but they struggled to provide an education for Henry, whose school career was delayed several times. He graduated from the University of Göttingen in 1738, and served as a teacher at the orphanage at Halle and as a pastor in Germany between 1739 and 1741. He was attracted to the form of Lutheran Pietism at Halle, where he came under the influence of its leader, Gotthilf August Francke, son of Halle's founder, August Hermann Francke. Muhlenberg initially wanted to become a missionary, first to the Jewish people, and then to India, and applied to Halle for such a position.

Things took a different turn for him, however. The three united congregations in Pennsylvania had been seeking a new pastor since the departure of Stoever in 1735, and one of their appeals had been directed to the Lutheran court preacher in London, Frederick Ziegenhagen. In turn, he contacted Francke in Halle, who gave Muhlenberg the call to the Pennsylvania congregations in 1741. Traveling by way of London and Charleston, South Carolina, Muhlenberg arrived in Pennsylvania on November 25, 1742, certainly the missionary he wished to be, but to an entirely different country. Although he officially remained nothing more than the pastor of the three Pennsylvania congregations until his death forty-five years later, in reality he became the recognized leader of most colonial Lutherans and the architect of their transition to becoming a truly American religious tradition.

The circumstances that greeted him on his arrival in Philadelphia in 1742 hardly promised a bright future. The three congregations, Philadelphia, Trappe (New Providence), and New Hanover, had no church buildings and meager resources; they had been without a regular pastor since 1735, and their condition had deteriorated. Worse, other pastors had designs on the leadership of the three congregations and ignored Muhlenberg's claim, even though he had an official call to the congregations from the European church officials. Valentine Kraft had taken control of the Trappe congregation and a faction of the congregation at Philadelphia, while Schmidt held sway in New Hanover. Many in Philadelphia who did not support Kraft were drawn away by the Moravian followers of Count Ludwig von

Zinzendorf. In a series of sermons over the next few months at the three congregations, and in skirmishes with Kraft and Schmidt, Muhlenberg decisively won the day and took control.

The next battle was with Zinzendorf and the Moravians. Zinzendorf was a talented and dedicated Christian leader in Europe who had assumed the leadership of the Moravian community, a group of pietistically inclined Protestants with fifteenth-century roots. Zinzendorf himself held a broad ecumenical vision of uniting the various Protestant groups, and his Moravians are justifiably known as some of the earliest pioneers in Christian mission work. In 1741, Zinzendorf arrived in America and, in a series of meetings from January to June 1742, sought to unite all the various German Protestant groups in America in one united body. This effort failed in its larger ambitions, but did form the nucleus of the Moravian Church in colonial America. Zinzendorf then turned to the vacant Lutheran congregations and sought to gain control of them by placing Moravian pastors in their pulpits.

Muhlenberg clashed sharply with Zinzendorf in a meeting on December 30, 1742, where the younger Lutheran pastor challenged Zinzendorf's authority over the Lutheran congregations. Muhlenberg prevailed on a number of fronts and, early in 1743, Zinzendorf returned to Europe; the idea of a united German religious body in colonial America had failed to achieve existence. Though himself a Pietist and spiritually akin to Zinzendorf, Muhlenberg had a "churchly" Lutheran Pietism that was anchored by the authority of the Lutheran Augsburg Confession, and by Lutheran conceptions of a regular call and a defined church order, elements that separated him from the Moravians.

After defeating Kraft and Schmidt and fending off the Moravian challenge, all in his first six weeks in Philadelphia, Muhlenberg began the long task of rebuilding the three united congregations. Conditions were not promising; the German population was poor, there were still division and factions within the congregations from the previous struggles, and external challenges from other German groups and from the "English" churches remained. Muhlenberg eliminated the traditions of paying for baptisms and of an offering for the pastor at communion, all in an attempt to discourage self-appointed itinerant preachers from profiting at the hands of the congregations. He began efforts to solicit funds and gather materials for the construction of new church buildings, preached and taught school regularly, and tried to heal the divisions within the congregations. And, while doing all this, in 1745 he managed to become married to Anna Maria Weiser, the daughter of a leader within the Pennsylvania German community, Conrad Weiser.

Because of both his abilities and his recognized position as a legitimately called Lutheran pastor in America, Muhlenberg was soon drawn into the affairs of the surrounding local Lutheran congregations in Pennsylvania. In a number of these congregations, there were issues with self-appointed itinerants like Kraft and others, as well as the Moravians. At Tuplehocken, the congregation had actually split into three different factions and had nearly disintegrated in four years of conflict, until 1747, when Muhlenberg and Conrad Weiser succeeded in partially reuniting the congregation. At Lancaster, the Lutheran congregation was served by a Swedish pastor, Lawrence Nyberg, who had strong sympathies with the Moravians and a deep antipathy toward Muhlenberg. Claiming that his call was from the archbishop in Uppsala and that Muhlenberg had no authority over him, Nyberg resisted the congregation's wish for an Orthodox Lutheran pastor. The case ultimately ended up in the courts, which in 1746 eventually ruled in favor of Muhlenberg and the Lutherans. Nyberg, Kraft, and others continued to agitate against Muhlenberg and the Lutheran congregations for the next several years, but by 1748 some semblance of order had returned to the Pennsylvania Lutheran congregations.

As both his reputation and authority spread, Muhlenberg was drawn further afield. The next case was the long-running struggle between Pastor Wolf and the Lutheran congregations in the Raritan River valley of New Jersey. William Berkenmeyer attempted to resolve this issue in 1735, but his solution so favored Wolf that the attempt collapsed. For years, the congregation attempted to oust Wolf through the Lutheran consistory at Hamburg, but this was slow and cumbersome and achieved nothing. In 1743, the New Jersey congregations contacted Muhlenberg, who resisted their overtures until 1745, when he agreed to serve on a civil arbitration panel. Berkenmeyer saw Muhlenberg's involvement as a usurpation of his own authority, and when Muhlenberg eventually managed to broker a solution that resulted in Wolf's departure, relations between the two worsened. As an Orthodox Lutheran, Berkenmeyer was deeply suspicious of Muhlenberg and Halle because of their Pietism. The situation got even worse in 1747, when Halle sent John Christopher Hartwick to be the pastor of the Central Hudson congregations in New York. Hartwick initially stopped in Philadelphia to visit with Muhlenberg, which upset Berkenmeyer, who spent the next four years trying to oust Hartwick from his congregations. Muhlenberg simply responded to the request of the Raritan congregations, but gradually his influence spread into the congregations in New Jersey and New York as well, and overrode that of Berkenmeyer.

Although his personal authority expanded and he was able to stabilize the situation in many of the Pennsylvania and New Jersey congregations, Muhlenberg's position was irregular. He had no call except to the three united congregations, and critics could certainly claim rightly that though he was acting as a type of superintendent over the American congregations, he had no ecclesiastical authority to do so.

He also had a great need for clergy assistance, which he hoped to get through Halle, since he had no right to ordain pastors on his own personal authority. On the other hand, no real progress could be made among the American Lutheran congregations as long as all the real decisions had to be referred to European Lutheran authorities. Then, in 1745, Halle sent three men to Pennsylvania—Pastor Brunnholtz and two unordained catechists, John Nicholas Kurtz and John Helfrich Schaum—to assist Muhlenberg with the Pennsylvania congregations. Halle did not understand the American situation; Kurtz and Schaum were not needed as teaching catechists, but as fully ordained pastors with the authority to lead congregations. Muhlenberg had little precedent and no explicit authority to ordain them. Needed was a new, official framework for legitimately making church decisions, such as ordinations, in colonial America.

The first attempt to do so had been Berkenmeyer's Classical Assembly of 1735, but it was limited to the Raritan situation and never met again. In 1744, two Lutheran laymen—a Swede, Peter Kock, and a German, Henry Sleydorn—proposed that an official relationship be established between the Swedish and German congregations, including regular meetings of the pastors and lay leaders of the congregations. An initial meeting was held, which included Muhlenberg and the Swedish pastors Tranberg, Näsman, and Nyberg (Muhlenberg's opponent), but they could not agree on an organizational plan and the meeting degenerated into name calling. As a later Swedish pastor recorded the incident in 1759, "In regard to the other projects, nothing was done. Mr. Mühlenberg called Nyberg 'Moravian,' and Nyberg called him 'Hallensian.' Mr. Naesman received the name of 'Orthodox' and 'Scholastic.' And thus the meeting ended without coming to any conclusion."[5] While the Swedes did have ecclesiastical authority from the archbishop of Sweden, this did not turn out to be the basis of a further consolidation of the Lutheran congregations in colonial America.

Muhlenberg installed Kurtz and Schaum in congregations, but because of their nonordained status, their assistance was limited. Conrad Weiser, Muhlenberg's father-in-law, urged him to ordain the two, but Muhlenberg did not feel he had the proper authority to do so. Finally, in early 1748, a third ordained pastor, John Frederick Handschuh, arrived in Pennsylvania from Halle. With three regularly ordained pastors from Halle (Muhlenberg, Brunnholtz, and Handschuh), Muhlenberg finally felt he had the support to consider ordinations. In early August, Pastors Muhlenberg, Brunnholtz, and Hartwick met in Pennsylvania to examine and to consider ordaining John Nicholas Kurtz, who passed the examination handily. Muhlenberg then assembled the four recognized pastors and delegates from ten of the German Lutheran congregations, who met August 24–26, 1748, to form the first permanent Lutheran synodical structure in America, an organization that came to be known as the Ministerium of Pennsylvania. Muhlenberg addressed the gathering: "We are assembled for the purpose of establishing better order among the congregations, and if this is the will of God, we will meet annually. This is only an experiment. We ministers who are present have not come of our own accord, but have been regularly called to the work. We must render an account before God and our own consciences."[6] Also present was the Swedish provost, and lay representative Peter Kock, but they did not formally join the arrangement.

The assembly considered three items of business, the ordination of Kurtz, the dedication of a new church building for the Philadelphia congregation, and the approval of a common liturgy that had been prepared the previous spring. These items were approved, with some modifications to the liturgy. But there were also some matters for which they failed to take action. Four men who were acting as Lutheran pastors, including John Caspar Stoever and Tobias Wagner, were specifically not included in the ministerial gathering. Muhlenberg explained the reasons they were not included: "We can have no fellowship with them because 1, they decry us as Pietists, without reason; 2, they have not been sent hither, have neither an internal nor an external call; 3, are not willing to observe the same Church Order that we do . . . 4, six year's experience has taught Mr Mühlenberg that they care for nothing but their bread; 5, they are under no Consistorium . . ."[7] The assembly also considered a complaint from Tobias Wagner against Muhlenberg concerning Wagner's expulsion from the Tulpehocken congregation, which was dismissed, and discussed the question of Moravian defectors. Finally, the assembly agreed to meet yearly, alternating between Philadelphia and Lancaster, Pennsylvania. No formal rules or constitution were written for the Ministerium, which seemingly operated on custom and consensus for the next thirty years, under Muhlenberg's own firm guidance.

So what was really accomplished here? By this point in 1748, Muhlenberg had been in America for almost six years, and had been active in promoting the cause of Lutheranism in the colonies. Facing challenges from many sides, he was fairly successful in stabilizing the Lutheran situation. Muhlenberg first won control of his own three congregations and set the self-appointed Lutheran preachers in Pennsylvania on the defensive. He blunted the designs of Zinzendorf in creating a nonconfessional union of German-speaking churches in Pennsylvania, keeping the Lutheran congregations from Moravian control. He stepped in to resolve the long-running dispute in the Raritan congregations in New Jersey, a situation made worse by Berkenmeyer's heavy-handed ecclesiasticism. Although Muhlenberg had not been able to reach agreement with the Swedish pastors and congregations, he was able to pull together the German congregations and began to supply them with pastors as well as provide them with a framework by which they could become a regular, self-governing Lutheran church in America.

Already, Muhlenberg had demonstrated a moderate, pragmatic, and flexible version of Lutheranism, one that was enlivened by the renewing power of the Pietist movement, but one also firmly rooted in the Lutheran confessions and the formal patterns of Lutheran liturgy and ecclesiastical governance. He recognized that Lutheranism in the American context would be different from Europe, but did not jettison European Lutheran precedents lightly. Of his approach, a biographer has written:

> The heritage he left to American Lutheranism was a blending of both pietistic and orthodox elements. With the pietists, Muhlenberg believed that individuals must undergo a conversion experience. . . . This, however, he tempered through orthodox thought, for the conversion experience had to be rational, not sensible . . . grace must issue through the means entrusted to the church, and good works must not negate the need for a sacramental life. He was a revivalist, but a liturgical revivalist.[8]

More than his leadership, or the structures that he formed, this basic approach, which one might call a "churchly Pietism," was his greatest contribution to Lutheranism in America.

Besides the ordination of Kurtz, the most important concrete development of the first meeting of the Ministerium in 1748 was the adoption of a common liturgy for the German Lutheran congregations in Pennsylvania. The need for a common order of service was evident to many, especially as in opposition to not only the "freer" worship of the Moravians and the German sectarians, but also to many of the "English" churches. But there was no common Lutheran liturgy, either in colonial America or back in Germany. Each German territorial church had its own liturgy, and pastors and people brought their own books and traditions with them, causing no end of confusion and controversy in the congregations. In spring 1748, Muhlenberg, Brunnholtz, and Handschuh met to draw up a common liturgy for the German congregations. Of this process, Muhlenberg wrote in his journal: "We consulted together in Providence with regard to a suitable liturgy. . . . the Swedish liturgy did not appear either suitable or necessary. . . . Nor could we select a liturgy with regard to every individual's accustomed use since almost every town and village has its own."[9] They selected as a model the German Lutheran liturgy used at the Savoy Lutheran congregation in London and had this common liturgy adopted at the first meeting of the Ministerium, with some alterations. Although never printed, each pastor and congregation had their own handwritten copy for use. This model of a common pattern of moderate liturgical worship was to become not only a norm, but a precedent, for future Lutheran worship in America.

Religious Life among the Colonial Lutherans

On the whole, the European Lutherans who immigrated to colonial America during the eighteenth century were generally both poor and ambitious. Poor, not in the sense of being destitute, but, rather, lacking good farmland, as well as experiencing disease, death, war, persecution, or overcrowding (and sometimes all of the above!). They would be hard pressed to maintain even modest livelihoods in Europe, let alone get ahead or provide for their children. The ambitious among these, and among their children, decided that the promise of free land in colonial America was incentive enough to overcome the loss of familiar location and culture, to endure months of often brutal sailing across the ocean, to brave the wilderness of America, and even, for some (the indentured), to survive seven years of virtual slavery. Most were driven by economic forces and were not necessarily fleeing from the culture and religion of their European homelands, much of which they sought to replicate in colonial America. But, in many ways, American culture and community were far different from what they had left. These immigrants would soon become acculturated to the New World, and some would even seize on the new ways of America to transform their communities and their churches.

For these new Lutheran settlers in colonial America, the church was often a central part of their personal and communal identity, and it was so important that it moved many of them to sacrifice out of what little they had to establish and support it. The church provided a symbol of an ordered society in the midst of a world that had little order or stability, and it was the place whereby the rituals of life (baptism, confirmation, marriage, and burial) could be conducted. In a world where one easily felt threatened and disconnected, the church provided familiar and important communal rituals that bound the congregation together as a community, as well as to God, who was present through the worship, even in this often disordered land. Certainly, not all the European Lutheran immigrants felt equally strongly about the need for the church and its ministry; some were probably glad to be freed from enforced religious duties. But the primacy that many of these immigrants gave to establishing Lutheran congregations in colonial America suggests that they found the congregations to be vital parts of their community.

The congregations were also, ironically enough, a source of major conflict within the immigrant communities; religion was important enough to them that they would fight over it, if necessary. The Germans settled in religiously mixed communities where Lutherans, Reformed, and Moravians (not to mention the sectarian groups) were all present. The new freedom of American voluntary religion, and a vacuum of settled religious authority, meant that either out of necessity or opportunity laypeople had a much greater voice in the affairs of their congregations than they had in Europe. Congregations longed to have pastoral leadership and often wrote passionate letters to European authorities to be supplied with pastors, but they also quarreled frequently with the pastors once they arrived. To be honest, the pastors gave as good as they got. Unlike Europe, there were neither ecclesiastical nor secular authorities willing or able to settle these disputes, so Lutheran pastors and lay leaders had to create new means by which to govern themselves and settle their disputes.

An important symbol of their religious life was the construction and maintenance of a church building, important for its definition of a sacred place where the important elements of religion could be maintained. Although initially religious services might be held in a private home, or even in a barn, such a state of affairs was not practical, nor was it considered "holy" enough for more than temporary expediency. Berkenmeyer's initial report to Amsterdam in 1725 noted the poor state of a neglected church building: "The church building, we fear, will not only be demolished by the first heavy storm, but looks more like a grain barn than a house of God; it only has two windows. . . . As the church is not paved, but merely floored with loose boards . . . one cannot pass through it without stumbling."[10] But materials for building, and the money to buy them, were difficult to obtain, and congregations often struggled with the task of completing their churches. When circumstances allowed, they preferred to build churches out of stone or brick, for, as Muhlenberg observed, wooden churches did not last long in the American climate. Examples of early church buildings that still survive, such as Muhlenberg's Trappe church, or the Swedish Gloria Dei congregation in Philadelphia, were constructed out of more permanent materials.

Maintaining the church building was also difficult, especially during periods without strong lay or pastoral leadership. Control over the church building was also a major problem. The presence of many union congregations, with both Lutheran and Reformed congregations sharing the same building, frequently led to disputes. As often happened, other congregations endured divisions and splits, causing protracted conflicts over the ownership of the building that usually ended up in secular courts.

The pastors and congregations attempted to maintain a regular worship life for the congregations, but this was difficult due to the shortage of ordained clergy. Since pastors often served multiple congregations, even if the congregation was fortunate enough to have a pastor, they did not see him every week, and sometimes, when the pastor was out on an extended mission trip, they might not see him for months. When the pastor was not available, the congregation held weekly services anyway, with the singing of hymns and psalms, the reading of Bible passages, and the reading of a sermon from a book of sermons, led by one of the lay elders of the congregation. When Pastor Näsman served the Swedish congregation at Philadelphia (1744), he proposed that:

> Sermons on the Catechism should be held at Matins from Pentecost to Advent . . . that the people should be assembled several times a year for the recital of the Catechism, that they should, in good time and without delay, present their children for baptism and confirmation, that the Lord's Supper should be held in proper esteem, and celebrated in the church at least four or six times a year, together with the hearing of confession on the Sunday next preceding.[11]

As has been seen, there were no standard liturgical forms and a great lack of hymnals; pastors and congregations used what they might have available, or that with which they were familiar. Conflicts arose because of the differences between regional custom concerning the various elements and arrangements of the liturgy. For example, Muhlenberg did not want to use the Swedish liturgy as a basis for his 1748 common service because his congregations, mainly from southwestern Germany, regarded the Swedish custom of singing the collects as "papistical."

The central part of any service was the sermon. The Lord's Supper might not be celebrated weekly, or even at times monthly, but the pastor was expected to preach at length every Sunday. The 1748 common liturgy suggested a sermon of forty-five minutes to an hour, though not longer than that. In the larger congregations, the pastor might preach multiple times a week, on Sunday morning and evening, and several days during the week. These sermons were expected to be stirring and affective; one of Pastor Wolf's problems in the Raritan congregations was that he would not preach his sermons from memory, but merely read them aloud (reportedly, he said that was good enough for "stupid farmers"). Some pastors had to learn to preach in several different languages from among Dutch, German, Swedish, and English, and to do so on a regular basis.

Since colonial America was often an unsettled and wide-open territory, it was inevitable that freedom might breed moral laxity and disorder among the people, and old standards sometimes broke down. Pastors and congregational leaders attempted to maintain the traditional European custom of the moral discipline of congregational members, but this was difficult to accomplish. Without the traditional ecclesiastical structures of Europe (backed by secular courts), enforcement of church discipline was impossible, and those who broke the moral laws often simply ignored their censures. On the other hand, congregations often called on their pastors in another traditional role, that of druggist or physician; most pastors had a box of traditional medicines (sent from Halle or elsewhere in Europe) and attended the sick with both spiritual and physical care.

Pastors and Their Congregations

Lacking resources, the congregations often struggled to pay their pastors, generating frequent clergy complaints to their superiors in Europe. Most congregations paid their pastors in multiple ways; the promised annual salary was collected by a subscription (often involuntary) from the congregational members, but cash was often scarce. Pastors were also given payments in kind, such as firewood, hay, and other commodities, as well as a parsonage in which to live and fields in which the pastor could farm or pasture animals. Direct payments to pastors for baptisms, weddings, funerals, and other pastoral acts were common, but often became a source of conflict, especially for opportunistic itinerant clergy, which is why Muhlenberg attempted to ban such payments. Certainly, there were difficulties between some pastors and their congregations, as is usually the case, but congregations could also deeply love their pastors and value their services. Pastor Boltzius in Georgia wrote to his uncle in Europe in 1734: "(God) has given me . . . (an) entire congregation who, with a very few excepted, could be called in truth a community of saints, of which I regard myself to be completely unworthy. They love me to a degree that I must often be ashamed because of my unworthiness and let it serve me to love them all the more . . ."[12] Some things about the congregations have changed very little since the eighteenth century; the Swedish pastor Lidman noted in a parish meeting of 1727 that "it was very crowded in the back of the church, and on the contrary, the pews in the front quarter stand empty."[13]

Many (but not all) of the Lutheran pastors who came to colonial America in the eighteenth century were inclined toward Lutheran Pietism and sought to cultivate a warm Lutheran piety in the members of their congregations. Many in the congregations were not similarly inclined toward the stricter spiritual practices of Pietism and often failed to live up to the standards of their pastors, which sometimes caused conflict. In a letter of 1737, Pastor Boltzius related that, "For some, especially the older people, we find the obstacle to a thorough conversion to be that they believe themselves to be already converted."[14] In a report for May 1744, he wrote: "When and if the people in Ebenezer convert truly to the Lord and seek His kingdom as a first and only thing, they will certainly not regret their departure and arrival here. . . . Still the people among us remain mouth-Christians."[15] There was evidently a difference in religiosity between the Austrian Salzburgers, who had already evidenced a deep attachment to their Lutheran heritage, and the Halle-influenced Boltzius.

Sometimes the problem could go the other way, with too much religious enthusiasm among the laypeople, which led them in the direction of the "freer" German groups, such as the Moravians and the various radical Pietist groups. Since these groups were already in the colonial German settlements, the attraction of a "purer" form of Pietism was strong toward those who sought a community of the like-minded. In his journal for 1747, Muhlenberg wrote of an encounter he had with an old man, who had been converted in Germany:

> When he came to this country, he joined the turbulent sect of people who like to call themselves the Newborn. This sect claims a new birth, which they receive suddenly. . . . When they receive the new birth in this way, they are God and Christ himself, can no longer sin, and are infallible. They therefore use nothing out of God's Word . . . The holy sacraments are to them ridiculous . . .[16]

Such individuals could cause havoc in the Lutheran congregations, where they challenged the spiritual authority of the pastors and denied the efficacy of the means of grace. In their self-anointed power, they saw themselves as the spiritually elite and condemned the pastors as "unregenerate."

This problem must be seen in the light of the wave of spiritual awakenings that passed though the American colonies in the early 1740s, a movement that is known as the First Great Awakening. Encouraged by the preaching of Jonathan Edwards and John Wesley, and spread through the efforts of itinerant evangelists, such as George Whitefield, this movement spread throughout many of the "English" churches in the colonies. Decidedly Calvinistic in tone, the movement also worked into the German community through the efforts of Dutch Reformed pastor Theodore Freylinghuysen and the American Presbyterian leaders William and Gilbert Tennent. Many Lutherans also attended the revival preaching of Whitefield, especially in Philadelphia, and were deeply affected by both his style and his message.

The Lutheran pastors had a mixed reaction to Whitefield and his revival preaching. Some, like the Swedish pastors, did not think much of him. Writing later, a Swedish pastor suggested that the early 1740s were "an unfortunate time for a (Swedish Lutheran) clergyman," because "Mr. George Whitefield, had established in Philadelphia a congregation of people of every variety of faith, which was called

'*New Lights*' . . . With these many Swedish families united."[17] Pastor Boltzius in Georgia worked closely with John Wesley in the 1730s, during the latter's brief time in Georgia, and also with Whitefield, who was a great supporter of the Ebenezer settlement; Boltzius referred to him as "an upright man, zealous for the honor of the Savior, and our close friend in the Lord . . ."[18] Muhlenberg, too, was a friend of Whitefield and the Tennents, and appreciated the warmth of their preaching. Muhlenberg, however, held to the traditional Lutheran understanding of baptismal regeneration and, as we have seen, sought renewal and revival within the worship and sacramental system of Lutheran worship, and so could not agree with Whitefield's understanding of conversion and new life. These Lutheran pastors sometimes cooperated with the spiritual awakening around them, but usually within the context of their Lutheran congregations alone. But with Whitefield and Zinzendorf in and around Philadelphia in the early 1740s, this distinction was not always an easy one to draw.

Conclusion

By 1748, the situation among the Lutherans in colonial America had started to stabilize and even strengthen. New congregations were started, more pastors had arrived, and the beginnings of an organizational path forward had begun. Lutheran leaders started to chart a path through the wilds of American voluntary religion, one that was open enough to appreciate the varieties of Christians among whom they lived without losing a distinctive Lutheran identity. And this distinctive Lutheran identity also gradually developed into a distinctly *American* form of Lutheran identity, fit for the religious situation in which they found themselves. The core of much of this development came from the work of Henry Melchior Muhlenberg, whose vision of a "churchly" Lutheran Pietism and a self-reliant American Lutheranism would prove to be the foundation of efforts moving forward.

Notes

1. "Letter, Rev. Michael Knoll to the Lay Leaders of the Lutheran Parish at Rareton, New Jersey, April 17, 1735," in Samuel Hart and Harry Kreider, eds., *Lutheran Church in New York and New Jersey, 1722–1760* (New York: United Lutheran Synod of New York and New England, 1962), 75.

2. "Letter, Jonas Lidman to Eric Benzelius, November 28, 1727," in Peter Stebbins Craig and Kim-Eric Williams, eds., *Colonial Records of the Swedish Churches in Pennsylvania*, vol. 4, 1719–1750 (Philadelphia: Swedish Colonial Society, 2008), 49.

3. Adolph B. Benson, trans., *Peter Kalm's Travels in North America*, vol. 2 (New York: Wilson, 1937), 671.

4. "Letter, Johann Martin Boltzius and Israel Christian Gronau to Gotthilf August Francke," January 8, 1736, in Russell C. Kleckley, ed., *The Letters of Johann Martin Boltzius, Lutheran Pastor in Ebenezer, Georgia: German Pietism in Colonial America, 1733–1765*, vol. 1, (Lewiston, NY: Edwin Mellon, 2009), 158.

5. Israel Acrelius, *A History of New Sweden* (1759), trans. William Reynolds (Philadelphia: Historical Society of Pennsylvania, 1874), 248.

6. Quoted in S. E. Ochsenford, ed., *Documentary History of the General Council of the Evangelical Lutheran Church in North America* (Philadelphia: General Council Publication House, 1912), 24.

7. Richard C. Wolf, *Documents of Lutheran Unity in America* (Philadelphia: Fortress Press, 1966), 11.

8. Leonard R. Riforgiato, *Missionary of Moderation: Henry Melchior Muhlenberg and the Lutheran Church in English America* (Lewisburg, PA: Bucknell University Press, 1980), 153.

9. Henry Melchior Muhlenberg, "Journal entry for April 28, 1748," in *The Journals of Henry Melchior Muhlenberg*, trans. Theodore Tappert and John Doberstein, vol. 1 (Philadelphia: Muhlenberg, 1942), 193.

10. "Letter, Rev. W. C. Berkenmeyer to the Amsterdam Consistory," October 21/November 1, 1725, in Arnold J. H. van Laer, trans., *The Lutheran Church in New York, 1649–1772* (New York: New York Public Library, 1946), 139.

11. Acrelius, *History of New Sweden*, 243–44.

12. "Letter, Johann Martin Boltzius to Pastor Johan Müller," May 6, 1734, in *Letters of Johann Martin Boltzius*, 1:82.

13. "Records of the Parish Meeting, May 1, 1727," in *Colonial Records of the Swedish Churches in Pennsylvania*, 4:43.

14. "Letter, Johan Martin Boltzius and Israel Christian Gronau to Gotthilf August Francke," July 29, 1737, in *Letters of Johann Martin Boltzius*, 1:199.

15. George Fenwick Jones and Renate Wilson, trans., *Detailed Reports on the Salzburger Emigrants Who Settled in America*, vol. 18, 1744–1745 (Camden, ME: Picton Press, 1995), 59.

16. Muhlenberg, "Journal entry for June 10, 1747," *Journals*, 1:148.

17. Acrelius, *History of New Sweden*, 244.

18. "Letter, Johann Martin Boltzius to Gotthilf Francke," August 28, 1738, *Letters of Johann Martin Boltzius*, 1:244.

Excursus 3

Colonial Lutheran Pastoral Care

The life of a Lutheran pastor in colonial America was difficult. Without much of anything in the way of material support, pastors struggled just to survive, let alone care for their poor and scattered flocks. They had to be prepared to meet many different kinds of situations that most never envisioned in their European ministerial training. Yet, a number of them gave devoted and heroic service in the new American colonies, proclaiming the gospel and guiding their people as best they could. The following entries from the notebooks of colonial Lutheran leader Henry Melchior Muhlenberg illustrate their lives and ministries; these selections are culled from just one month, November 1763 (note: these entries are much condensed).[1]

November 1: In the forenoon I had all sorts of running in and out and troublesome interruptions. Visit from the late Pastor Steiner's widow, who had many laments to make.

November 5: Saturday. Visit from Josua Pawling, of Providence, who said I must again take over the Providence church and congregation, otherwise everything would go to ruin.

November 6: I went to church with Mr. Brycelius, baptized three children, and preached to a crowded auditorium. As soon as church was over I was taken to Germantown to bury Mr. Jacob Gänsle. About five-thirty in the evening I drove away and arrived home in the dark near eight o'clock.

November 9: I felt unwell, but I had to carry out my promise to go to Mr. [George] Whitefield. He received us very cordially. I received a courteous letter inviting me to visit Chief Judge Coleman and furnish a testimonial to the deceased wife of a certain Lutheran man. I also visited the silversmith, Mr. Carben; had a refreshing visit with the family.

November 13: Sunday. Early in the morning Mr. Jacob Graef took me to Germantown. At eleven o'clock went to church [and] I preached on the Gospel. My companion drove me back to Philadelphia, but we had to drive very fast to be able to hold the [funeral] service at the right time. After the service I baptize Gr——'s sick child. In the evening I married a couple, then went to the home of Mr. Graef where I found a fine group of awakened members of the congregation [and] had an edifying and inspirational conversation with them from seven to nine o'clock.

November 16: Learned that the church council had rejected the petitions I had submitted to them. This bewildering and miserable affair is hastening my death and is almost rendering me unfit for my office.

November 17: Today we had the first deep snow and unhealthy, wet weather. Had a visit . . . The rest of the time I meditated and wrote. Otherwise I was distressed and depressed over the intricate dispute in this poor congregation . . . my health is suffering from it.

November 21: Visit from the poor widow of a Reformed preacher. She was in great straits and besought me to be surety for her, but I was unable to do so. Today I borrowed £50 *currency* at interest in order to meet my needs. At home I had many visitors, among them a young blacksmith who some year ago had married an old widow [who now] refused to live with him. The said blacksmith asked me whether he might now marry someone else. Reply: No.

November 22: More and more murders and burnings are occurring on the frontiers, and almost daily there are robberies in and around the city. The city itself is swarming with unruly mobs. I visited a godly family which had retained much of last Sunday's sermon and gained consolation from it.

November 25: Last night I was unable to sleep because of worry and concern of soul about the coming church council meeting and the fact that old quarrels are to be brought up again. I took refuge in quiet prayer to Almighty God. [After a long meeting it was noted] The entire church council and the complainants have settled all points of controversy and made peace. Henceforth there shall be no further discussion or mention of the old controversy.

November 29: Tuesday. Early in the morning I journeyed to Germantown. At home I heard that immediately after my departure on Saturday several dissatisfied persons had come into my house and blustered against me and the church council. At 1 pm I married Daniel Sorg and Margretha Heidel. In the evening we had a heavy rainstorm. Refreshing visit from Mr. Kressler.

November 30: A visit from [Swedish pastor] Wangel, with whom I conferred on various matters and strengthened myself. In the evening I read the History of the Martyrs to my family for edification.

Note

1. Henry Melchior Muhlenberg, *The Journals of Henry Melchior Muhlenberg*, trans. Theodore Tappert and John Doberstein, vol. 1 (Philadelphia: Muhlenberg, 1942), 700–716.

Chapter 4

Establishment of Eastern Lutheranism, 1748–1781

J ust as the Lutheran immigrants were getting settled into colonial America during the middle of the eighteenth century, the whole context itself was changing and evolving. American Lutherans had to do the same. At the beginning of this period, relations between the colonists in North America and their compatriots in Great Britain were relatively good; Americans were happy, even proud, to be counted as English subjects, especially when the alternatives (French to the north and Spanish to the south) were universally viewed as unacceptable, even threatening. American colonists saw Britain as their protector from the Roman Catholic powers (and their Native American allies), and the champion of the overwhelmingly Protestant colonists. But by the end of this period, the American colonists' attitudes had completely changed. They rejected British authority through a military rebellion and established a new, independent country on the eastern seaboard of North America. It was quite a dramatic social and political change in the space of about thirty years.

Issues of money and power occasioned these dramatic changes, as so often happens. To understand the background of these developments, it is important to think first about the nature of what colonies were intended to be and how they were intended to relate to the home country, in this case, Great Britain. The American colonies were to provide direct economic benefits to Britain through trade and by providing land and opportunity for British settlers. The primary role of the colonies was trade, initially the supply of raw materials to Britain, and, secondarily, to consume finished goods sent from Britain to the colonies. This trade was designed to be exclusive, and the colonies' sole market was to be the home country. The colonies were intended to make money for Britain and not to cost too much to administer and defend. The thirteen colonies generally related directly to Britain, and intercolonial ties were much less important.

There were two problems with this relationship, however. The colonies became more expensive to administer, especially in the matters of defense. The French and Indian War (1754–1763) required a major expenditure of British funds to defend the American colonies, and the British felt that the American colonists should bear part of this cost. British attempts after 1763 to introduce taxes to shift the costs onto the American colonists were a major source of friction and a leading cause of the American Revolutionary War (1775–1781). British authorities, especially the monarchy, sought more stringent British oversight of colonial affairs, including the introduction of royal governors in colonies that did not already have them. American colonists, on the other hand, resisted both taxes and tightened British control, feeling that their traditional liberties as British subjects were being infringed; "No taxation without representation" (in Parliament) was the cry.

The other problem was economic, rooted in the exclusivity of trade between Britain and the colonies. The arrangement was a monopoly for Britain and not to the economic advantage of the colonists, who complained that prices were low for their commodities and high for finished British goods. The colonists chafed under this arrangement, believing (probably correctly) that they would do better economically if they had the rights to trade with a larger world market. In the face of such restrictions, American colonists sometimes turned to smuggling as an economic activity, which upset British authorities even further. British authorities also discouraged American colonists from moving westward into the inland regions, which would limit their economic benefit to Britain, but which Americans saw as a prime economic opportunity, land being the primary basis of wealth at the time.

These common complaints began to draw the leading citizens of the American colonies more closely together, to a degree previously unknown. Although they still viewed themselves primarily as citizens of a particular colony, such as Virginia or Massachusetts, they also began to think of themselves as Americans, having common cause with those from other colonies. They also began to think primarily in terms of what was most advantageous for themselves and for the colonies as a whole, rather than what was best for Britain. Slowly, the direction of ties turned, from the trans-Atlantic to the transcontinental. A new American identity was slowly being formed.

Muhlenberg and the Further Development of American Lutheranism

The same transformation of vision and affiliation was slowly occurring among American Lutherans, who were beginning to seek ties with each other, rather than with European religious officials. The increase in numbers of Lutheran congregations and pastors, along with the formation of the Pennsylvania Ministerium in 1748, signaled the beginning of a transformation whereby Lutherans in America came to understand themselves as an indigenous communal group, rather than as scattered outposts tied to European churches. This transformation would be gradual and uneven, and American Lutherans would still be somewhat dependent on European aid and advice, but, by the end of the American Revolution in 1781, American Lutherans would be ready for self-determination and self-support.

Henry Melchior Muhlenberg played a key role in making this transformation possible. His leadership role among American Lutherans grew yearly and was generally unchallenged, except by the self-appointed itinerant preachers whose positions Muhlenberg was attempting to eliminate. From Georgia to New York, when colonial American Lutherans needed assistance (usually interventions in church quarrels or splits), new pastors for their congregations, or guidance, Muhlenberg was often consulted. Although his official call was never more than to be the pastor of the three united Pennsylvania congregations, as the leading figure within the Pennsylvania Ministerium for forty years, he was the superintendent of Lutheran congregations in America in everything but title.

His early battles with the Moravians and the itinerant preachers continued after 1748. Although Zinzendorf's plan to unite the German-American congregations into a single organization collapsed before it could be implemented in 1742, it led to the formation of an organized Moravian church in America. Although the Moravians had some close affinities to Lutheran Pietism (Zinzendorf was at one point ordained as a Lutheran pastor), they did not hold formally to the authority of the Augsburg Confession, and Muhlenberg considered them to be schismatics. Moravian preachers were very active within the German community in Pennsylvania in the 1740s and 1750s, and were often drawn into disputes with Lutherans over control of local German congregations. Lacking permanent ordained Lutheran pastors, congregational differences frequently escalated into factionalism, sometimes with one of the factions inviting a Moravian preacher to be the leader of their part of the Lutheran congregation. Some congregations, such as those in Tuplehocken,

Reading, and Lancaster, were divided into two or even three factions, causing untold confusion and distress. The Swedish preacher Nyberg, who inclined toward the Moravians, was extremely hostile toward Muhlenberg and the Ministerium and caused great disturbances. It took many trips and much effort on Muhlenberg's part to overcome these factional disputes and retain the congregations for Lutheranism. At times the whole mess, especially questions of who owned the church buildings, was subject to lengthy litigation. The disputes between the Lutherans under Muhlenberg and the Moravians were sharp and pointed, and neither side could be said to be entirely blameless.

Muhlenberg also was drawn into conflict with Lutherans pastors who remained outside of the Ministerium (like Kraft and Stoever) and with the self-appointed itinerants. Many of these pastors were decidedly not Pietists, and their leadership appealed to those factions and congregations who chafed under the moral strictures of the Pietist preachers, Lutheran or Moravian. Kraft and Stoever initially formed a loose consistory, which Muhlenberg dismissed as a means for them to "ordain a few more lazy and drunken schoolmasters and place them as preachers in vacant places."[1]

Gradually, Muhlenberg's authority spread over the congregations outside of Pennsylvania, especially among the congregations in New York and New Jersey. At first, Muhlenberg was hesitant to become involved with these congregations because they were in Berkenmeyer's territory, but Berkenmeyer proved unable to deal with the situations, especially the prolonged dispute between Wolf and the Raritan congregations. When John Christopher Hartwick came to his congregations in New York in 1747, Berkenmeyer attacked him ceaselessly, largely because of Hartwick's perceived Pietism and his friendly contacts with Muhlenberg. Disputes within the New York congregations continued, and from 1748 to 1752 Muhlenberg was drawn into their conflicts. One by one the New York and New Jersey congregations joined the Pennsylvania Ministerium, and when they needed new pastors, the Ministerium provided them. The final chapter in this transition came in 1784, when John Christopher Kunze, Muhlenberg's son-in-law, was called to the Lutheran congregation in New York City.

Often, however, Muhlenberg's travels had less to do with conflict, and more to do with the neverending needs of the immigrant Lutherans and their fledgling congregations. He traveled constantly, visiting struggling congregations in eastern and central Pennsylvania, and down into Maryland and Virginia. He traveled so much that his own congregations grumbled about his prolonged absences, although he had assistant pastors to help with the work. Being relatively late immigrants, the Germans had to go far afield to find available land, which caused them to push deeper and deeper into the frontier. In a journal entry for 1762, Muhlenberg spoke of a "recently founded, poor congregation" in Winchester, Virginia, which had appealed to him and the Ministerium for assistance. They wanted financial aid to build a church and asked Muhlenberg to examine their schoolteacher, so he could administer the sacraments to them. Muhlenberg commented: "It is exceedingly difficult to say yes or no in these circumstances. Ordained preachers live far away and are hardly able to visit such remote groups. The people would like to cling to the religion and practices of their ancestors."[2] Although he worried that the schoolmaster was poorly educated and inadequate, he also knew that there was a good possibility that, in their need, one of the self-appointed preachers might latch on to the congregation, which would be even worse.

Constant travel took its toll. Traveling conditions in colonial America were wretched, most often on horseback over barely cleared tracks, open to all the elements of the weather. A biographer wrote: "He wore himself out by these skirmishing about the country in all seasons and weathers, making night journeys through rain and snow while his body was plagued by fever or dysentery . . . arriving at his destination so nearly speechless with weariness and catarrh that he could admonish angry elders and deacons only from a bed and in a whisper."[3] Travels further afield often required hazardous voyages by ship, such as a trip to South Carolina and Georgia in 1774–75. Once the Revolutionary War started in 1775, his traveling was greatly reduced, and his advancing age also made extended trips much less feasible. But through letters and personal representatives he managed to remain in the center of things.

When Muhlenberg married Anna Maria Weiser in 1745, he not only gained a supportive and patient wife, but married into a prominent Pennsylvania German family with many connections, both to the German and the "English" communities. His father-in-law, Conrad Weiser Jr., was at times a colonial official, military officer, justice of the peace and judge, and a leader of the German community in Pennsylvania. Coupled with his hard work and gifts of leadership, these family ties helped Muhlenberg to achieve his own position of leadership. Anna and Henry had five surviving children (four others died in infancy), and several of them became prominent Lutheran pastors or colonial leaders. Sons [John] Peter Gabriel, Frederick Augustus, and [Gotthilf] Henry Ernest was educated in Europe at Halle, and Peter and Henry became Lutheran pastors in their own right. Daughter Peggy [Margaret] married Lutheran pastor John Christopher Kunze, while daughter Sally married Continental soldier (later U.S. Congressman) Matthias Richards. The second and succeeding generations of the Muhlenberg family distinguished themselves in the Lutheran ministry, in military service, and, above all, in politics. There were Muhlenbergs prominent in Pennsylvania politics well into the twentieth century.

Lutheran Growth in New York and New Jersey

Despite organizational progress in Pennsylvania, things in New York did not move forward, and many of the congregations and pastors remained in conflict. The New York Lutherans continued to depend on the consistories at Amsterdam and London for assistance and resolution of conflicts, but these European officials were too far away and too unfamiliar with the American situation to be of much assistance. Berkenmeyer himself was too heavy-handed and too much a proponent of clerical privilege to solve these problems, and he often made matters worse by getting involved as a partisan rather than as an impartial arbiter.

The long-running conflict within the congregation at New York City was between the older Dutch Lutherans who had founded the congregation and newer German inhabitants who moved into the congregation as the city grew. Beginning in 1742, the German-speaking section of the congregation requested German-language services, which the Dutch leaders generally resisted, offering only token concessions. The debate festered for several years, and Pastor Knoll was unable to deal with the situation. The Germans became frustrated, claiming that the lack of a German service was causing families to go over to the Anglicans. Finally, in 1749, most of the Germans split from the congregation and formed their own, calling a Pastor Ries to serve them when Knoll resigned. Berkenmeyer failed to effect a settlement, leaving it to Muhlenberg, who spent several months in the New York City congregation in 1751 and again in 1752. The situation was stabilized, but never fully healed.

Another problem arose with the call of John Christopher Hartwick to the Central Hudson parish in 1746. Although sent by the Orthodox consistory at Hamburg, he was educated at Halle at the same time as Muhlenberg, and on his trip to America he visited Muhlenberg at Philadelphia. All this aroused Berkenmeyer's suspicions, and he wrote several heated pamphlets and many letters to Hamburg against Hartwick, accusing him of being a "secret Moravian." Although the Hamburg leaders did nothing against Hartwick, Berkenmeyer and his clerical allies Knoll and Sommer tried and failed in an attempt to oust Hartwick in 1750, leaving it again for Muhlenberg to visit the congregations and to bring about at least a partial solution to the situation. One by one, the New York and New Jersey congregations were slipping out of Berkenmeyer's control.

The situation of the New York congregations was problematic, to say the least. Most of the Hudson River parishes consisted of several small, struggling congregations, who quarreled with each other and their pastors. In a letter of 1754 to the Hamburg consistory, Hartwick described the obstacles that he had endured in eight years of ministry:

I have had to conduct services in poorly constructed houses which they call churches, or in barns and farm huts. I have no comfortable parsonage, but have to live in poor huts and travel from one place or the other . . . (no) Cossack . . . has ridden a horse more than I have. My health is also gone. . . . My parish is widely scattered and requires great effort to bring about small accomplishments. There are many opportunities here for temptation and a willingness to sin.[4]

Hartwick turned out to be a restless sort and served various congregations in upstate New York over the succeeding years, until his death in 1796. Because of the loyalty of a substantial part of his congregations he survived Berkenmeyer's relentless attacks on him, but seemingly he was scarred by the experience. A lifelong bachelor, Hartwick amassed a large estate through shrewd land purchases and donated the proceeds to Lutheran charitable and educational causes in his will.

There were virtually no Lutherans in New England during the colonial period, with the exception of a Lutheran colony established in Maine in 1740. An entrepreneur named Samuel Waldo founded a colony of German immigrants at a place called Waldoborough, and soon induced forty families who had emigrated from Brunswick and Saxony to come to New England. They brought with them a Lutheran pastor, Tobias Wagner, who worked among them until 1743, when he went south to the Lutheran congregation at Tulpehocken, Pennsylvania. For almost twenty years this congregation was lay-led, and grew to the point that, in 1762, they successfully called Pastor John M. Schaeffer from New York. But Calvinist New England was generally not a hospitable place for Lutheran immigrants.

Swedish Congregations on the Delaware

As has been previously seen, the pattern among the Swedish Lutheran congregations along the Delaware River was for the presence of two or three pastors at a time from the Church of Sweden, most of who stayed for five or ten years (on average), and then returned to Sweden. This arrangement had two defects, as there were often extended periods of vacancies between pastors, and some of the pastors themselves were not well suited to the American situation (or, frankly, to the ministry in general). Occasionally, strong pastors, such as Dylander in Philadelphia (1737–1741) built up the struggling congregations, but then vacancies and incompetence would simply drive them down again.

For these reasons, the 1740s and 1750s were a depressed time among these congregations. Pastor Tranberg at Wilmington served adequately in his parish, but he died of smallpox in 1748, and there was no satisfactory replacement for him immediately.

Pastor Näsman came to Philadelphia in 1743, two years after Dylander's death, but was such a disaster that the congregation immediately began to decline. The Philadelphia congregation wrote to Swedish Lutheran officials to complain about Näsman: "We pass by his dark, wrath-filled and affected, several hours' long sermons, which no one can understand . . . his audacity to spread such lies . . . because of his less than edifying behavior, (now) hardly less than 4, 6, 8, or 10 people are present on any Sunday . . ."[5] Fortunately, Swedish officials sent several replacements within a short period of time. Pastor John Sandin arrived in 1748, but died less than a year later. Pastors Erik Unander and Israel Acrelius came to America in 1749 to begin a resurgence among the congregations.

The conflicts and vacancies among the Swedish congregations gave room for other religious groups to work among the Swedes, and for Swedish members to drift off into other, non-Lutheran congregations. During the troubled 1740s, the main source of friction was, as among the German Lutherans, the activities of the Moravians. Lutheran pastors complained regularly about the inroads of the "Herrnhutters" (Moravians), who were also active in Sweden at the time. Acrelius wrote, in 1759, that the Moravians were ordaining Swedes, who "called themselves Swedish ministers when they came among the Swedish people. They all gave themselves out as Lutherans, and had no doctrine than that which was established in Sweden. And although they held to the Moravian Brotherhood . . . if they were accepted by a Swedish congregation . . . they would follow the established-church regulations."[6] One of these Swedish Moravians, who occasioned much difficulty for both the Swedish and German Lutherans, was Laurence Nyberg, who was actually called to the German congregation at Lancaster in 1744. After his ouster from Lancaster by Muhlenberg, he attempted to gain a position at the vacant Swedish parish in Raccoon and Pennsneck, New Jersey. When a letter arrived in 1748 from Swedish officials disavowing Nyberg, he set up a Moravian congregation in the same area and continued to be a threat to the Lutherans.

The small size of the Swedish community, the increasing prevalence of intermarriage, and the religious pluralism of colonial America was a major problem for the Swedish congregations. Once the language transition took hold in the eighteenth century, the basis of "Swedishness" in this community was infant baptism; one was a "Swede" if one had been baptized and recorded in a Swedish congregation. With intermarriage, especially Swedes with the "English," this became increasingly difficult to maintain, and family battles erupted; Acrelius tells of a family whose children were never baptized because the parents could not agree on which church should do it. The problem of intermarriage with the local Quakers was even more difficult, because the Quakers downplayed the external rite of baptism altogether.

Swedes had the closest affinity to the local Anglicans, whose church rites and traditions seemed to be closest to their own. The relations between the Swedish Lutherans and the local Anglicans deepened throughout the century, and pastors served both kinds of congregations interchangeably.

Israel Acrelius, who served from 1749 to 1756, was generally considered a good pastor, though, by his own admission, he could never master the English language, which limited the effectiveness of his ministry. He was also the first historian of American Lutheranism; his 1759 "History of New Sweden" is a very useful observation of the situation among American Lutherans in the eighteenth century. His able successor, Carl Magnus Wrangel, who served from 1759 to 1768, had a good ability to preach in German and English, was sympathetic to Pietism, and was a close associate of Muhlenberg. In this period of the First Great Awakening, Wrangel was a very popular revival preacher, not only among the Swedes, but generally among people in Philadelphia. He began two new congregations, one at Kingsessing and the other at Upper Merion, the members of which were not specifically Swedish, but included a preponderance of "English." Wrangel's tenure in the 1760s marked the beginning of the end for the Swedish language among the Delaware congregations, leaving open the question of Swedishness as an ethnic category apart from language. Although Wrangel was personally fluent in English, few other Swedish pastors were, causing a dilemma about the future of receiving pastors from Sweden.

Lutherans in the American South

Lutheranism in the southern colonies grew slowly, as German immigration to the region was limited and they were far from the Lutheran centers in the middle colonies. The example of the Salzburg colony in Georgia was atypical for most Lutherans in the South, as Ebenezer was intentionally settled by a group of Lutherans who brought with them their own pastors and had long-running support from European officials. Most other German Lutheran settlements were more individual and much less planned, and Lutherans had to go great distances to find each other and to obtain pastoral leadership.

In Virginia, the southward migration of Germans from Pennsylvania continued, as these migrants pushed out along the frontier looking for good farmland. The congregation at Hebron was originally served by Pastor John Caspar Stoever, then by his assistant, George Klug, and then by Pennsylvania pastor, John Schwarbach. These congregations struggled to find adequate pastors, generally because they were so far into the frontier that the distances between them made travel very difficult. Additional congregations were established at Strasburg in 1747, in Winchester in 1753, and in Woodstock in 1772. The case of the Winchester congregation has already been noted in their appeal to Muhlenberg, in 1762, for permission for their schoolteacher to provide the sacraments to them. Without such arrangements, and lacking the services even of an itinerant pastor, congregations could go years without the administration of confession and absolution or the Lord's Supper.

Lutherans in North Carolina were even slower to form congregations. Most came down through Virginia into the western part of the state, centering around Salisbury and the counties to the west. There was the beginning of organized religious life during this period of time, with three or four congregations formed, but no Lutheran pastors made the trip that far south. In 1773, some of the North Carolina congregations sent two lay leaders across the Atlantic to London, where they received monetary assistance from the king (a Hanoverian German) and promises to send pastors from the consistory of Hanover and the University at Göttingen. The first pastor, Adolph Nassmann, along with a teacher, John Arends, arrived shortly thereafter. The German population in North Carolina was a religious mixture of Lutherans, Reformed, and Moravians. Unlike the situation in Pennsylvania, Lutherans and Moravians worked closely together in North Carolina.

The situation in South Carolina was different, as the German Lutherans slowly spread inland from the port of Charleston. The original congregation at Orangeburg was founded in 1735, and Lutherans moved west from there toward Lexington. Several congregations were founded along the frontier before the Revolutionary War, but, of course, without pastors to serve them. Other Germans congregated in Charleston, and there was a congregation there in the 1740s, but progress awaited the arrival of a pastor from Germany, John George Friederichs, in 1755.

In Georgia, the Salzburg Lutheran colony grew, naturally and by immigration, so that by 1741 its population numbered about 1,200 people. The original design of the colony was almost a theocracy, with Pastors Boltzius and Lemke taking not only religious authority, but a great deal of secular authority as well. The population was organized tightly around the settlement at Ebenezer, with the churches as the primary focus. This could not, and did not, last. The population growth of the colony, as well as the relatively poor fertility of the immediate land, caused members of the community to expand and disperse. Boltzius continued to maintain a great personal authority over the colony, and he served it diligently, but that situation would not last forever.

The Georgia colony, run by a group of trustees in London, was originally organized without enslaved Africans, and the trustees attempted to maintain this prohibition. But Georgians felt themselves at an economic disadvantage to South Carolina, where slavery flourished, and, beginning in the 1740s, they began to agitate for a reversal of this position. Boltzius and the Halle officials also opposed slavery, but even a number in the Ebenezer colony began to support this change, and Boltzius became the target of abuse over his antislavery stance, both inside the community and within the wider colony. In 1750, the London trustees relented and reversed the ban on slavery, and its practice began to spread throughout the colony. At Boltzius's request, much of the secular administration of the Ebenezer community was transferred to a civil official.

With the death of Boltzius in 1765, and Lemke three years later, a single Lutheran pastor, Christian Rabenhorst, remained to serve the community. This was not adequate, and Halle officials sent another young pastor to Ebenezer, Christopher Triebner, which was the beginning of a great period of difficulty. Triebner challenged Rabenhorst for control of the community, which split into two camps, each supporting one of the pastors. The situation was bad enough that by 1774, Henry Melchior Muhlenberg, then aged sixty-three, was persuaded to travel down to South Carolina and Georgia to negotiate a reconciliation. He stayed there for three months and effected a truce of sorts, but Triebner soon found himself in moral trouble and was forced to resign. Rabenhorst only lived until the end of 1776, and his death and the traumas of the war were hard blows to the Ebenezer community.

Lutheranism on the Frontier and in Canada

The "frontier" has always had a deep hold on European settlers in North America as a place of both opportunity and freedom. At a time when land was synonymous with wealth, and its scarcity in Europe held back most people, the vision of free land was downright irresistible. Free land was also very useful to American colonial officials, who desperately needed labor in the colonies and who sought it in mass immigration. There was, however, a major tension involved in this situation: colonial officials and landowners wanted immigrant laborers to remain in the settled areas and work as hired labor, while the immigrants themselves wanted to move west and carve out their own farms. Even indentured service was only a temporary thing, and after seven years the German laborers had to be freed. This is why enslaved Africans became such a popular choice, because they were slaves forever.

Since the German immigrants did not begin coming to colonial America in large numbers until the eighteenth century, they missed out on the good farmland along the Atlantic coastal regions, and so streamed inland, especially to the middle colonies. When the British settled the Palatine refugees in New York, their design was to exploit the Germans' labor for the production of naval supplies, concentrating them along the Hudson. But the Palatines resisted such treatment, and soon drifted inland to upstate New York and down into Pennsylvania. Colonial officials also wanted to keep the settlers on the eastern side of the Allegheny Mountains and away from encroaching on Native American territories, but were often unable to corral the settlers.

Religion on the frontier was an element of familiarity and comfort in a land where much was unsettled and harsh. Frontier settlers often brought with them religious books such as the Bible, psalmbooks and hymnals, Luther's Small Catechism and books of his sermons, and devotional books, such as Johan Arndt's *True Christianity*. Although Lutheranism in Europe had long since moved in a clerical direction (and away from evangelical freedom), without pastors to guide them on the frontier, communities of Lutheran settlers maintained what they could of traditional religious life. In an important sense, they began to regain ownership over their religious traditions, an important discovery that would soon affect the direction and growth of Lutheranism in America.

Lutherans soon began to push into Canada, both along the Atlantic coast and inland. The first settlements of Lutherans in Canada came among German immigrants in Nova Scotia. Partially as a bulwark against the French population, British officials sought to plant communities of Germans there and encouraged settlements by deeding land to these communities. Germans organized a congregation in Halifax around 1750 and built a church there in 1755. Further down the coast, in Lunenberg, another German community developed, along with a Lutheran congregation, but neither area had a pastor. After a series of itinerant pretenders and abortive attempts to obtain a pastor (they, too, appealed to Muhlenberg), these Canadian Lutherans finally obtained a permanent pastor in 1772, Friedrich Schultze, who resided in Lunenberg. At the outbreak of the Revolutionary War, these communities received other German Lutherans loyal to the British king. Other loyalist Lutherans from New York created settlements in upper Canada, around Niagara and Toronto.

Women in Colonial American Lutheranism

Our knowledge of women's experience in colonial American, especially among the Lutherans, is limited by the fact that very few, if any, written materials produced by women still survive. What we do know about Lutheran women during this time comes from their mention in letters, church documents and proceedings, and even legal documents, such as court transcripts and wills. What is available, then, is an indirect reading of their experience and their influence, one that can be teased out of and inferred from available materials. Nevertheless, colonial Lutheran women can at times come to life in a very vivid form, when the implications of these materials are considered.

The Reformation, and its subsequent establishment in the Lutheran territories of Europe, was a mixed experience for women. On the negative side, the rejection of monasticism meant the loss of one independent vocational course for at least some women. On the positive side, the Reformation pushed for the education of girls and women, and considered their domestic role as mother in religious terms, especially in the raising and education of children. Clerical marriage meant a new role for some women as pastor's spouse, a position that grew to be an important leadership role in the community, especially with the rise of the multigenerational clergy dynasties. Lutheran women also fiercely guarded their traditional and legal rights, many of which were conservative holdovers from medieval times.

The colonial Lutheran women that we know best as individuals are the wives and the daughters of pastors, who were very important figures, not only in their own families, but also in their local religious communities. Lutheran pastors coming from Europe were generally not married before they arrived in America, and their marriages to local Lutheran women were an important way by which these pastors gained entrance into the local community. Henry Muhlenberg's marriage to Anna Maria Weiser (daughter of prominent citizen Conrad Weiser) is the best example of this, but also the marriage of Annetje Cornelis and Jacob Fabritius, and Gerritje Hardick and Justus Falckner, among others. Other times, these marriages involved closer ties with other Lutheran pastors: William Berkenmeyer married Beinigna Sybilla Kocherthal, daughter of his colleague Joshua Kocherthal; John Christopher Kunze married Margaretta Henrietta (Peggy) Muhlenberg, which tied him into that family; and Johan Boltzius married Gertraut Kroehr, the sister of the wife of his colleague Israel Gronau. When Gronau died in 1745, his replacement Hermann Lemke arrived in 1746 and promptly married Gronau's widow, Catherina Kroehr. These women were at the center of important social and religious networks that helped hold the colonial Lutheran communities together.

The institution of the Lutheran parsonage (German: *Pfarrhaus*) was a key to the community and modeled the Lutheran ideal of a "holy home." As one scholar described it: "By marrying locally, the management of the *Pfarrhaus* became in important parts rooted in the American experience of the *Pfarrfrau* (parson's wife) and her already existing network of family and friends. . . . it was widely accepted that the *Pfarrhaus* had model character for congregation and community at large . . ."[7] The parsonage as a model for Christian conduct and domesticity was extremely important, and the relationships and networks it represents were crucial to the success of a pastor's ministry and the growth of the congregation itself.

When a pastor transgressed these boundaries, it brought his ministry into disrepute, such as the experience of Annetje Cornelius Fabritius, who repeatedly sued her husband, Jacob, in 1674, charging him with putting her out of her own house, and calling him "a drunken and constant profaner of God's word (and) a deviant Lutheran preacher . . ."[8] Similarly damaging to the ministry of Georgia Lutheran pastor Christopher Triebner was his forced resignation because of an alleged affair with the daughter of his pastoral colleague Hermann Lemke.

Because the main source of income for most pastoral families was agricultural land given for them to farm, and because many pastors had to travel extensively, the day-to-day management of the parsonage farm fell to the pastor's wife. Thus these women were primary economic supports for the ministry of their husbands and, to an extent, of the congregation. Most parsonage families lived on the border of poverty (if not in it!), and the wise management of these few resources was vital to their survival. Johan Boltzius praised the economic management of his wife, Gertraut, in a 1749 letter when the Ebenezer community began to experiment with producing silk. Boltzius wrote: "My dear wife will take joy in gladly serving the dear Orphan House. . . . She has, as in other things, also good skill and experience in silk making . . . in spite of her fragile body and much housework, with the assistance of a young maiden . . . made in 5 weeks 130 pounds of lovely, large silk balls, which not only is a good example . . . but is also a great assistance in our housekeeping in this expensive land."[9] Given his extensive traveling, Henry Muhlenberg was sometimes gone for weeks and months on end, and the maintenance of his household often rested on Anna Maria Weiser Muhlenberg; Henry was even absent for the birth of his second son, Frederick, in January 1750. Henry recorded in his journal: "In her anguish my wife wept over the fact that her husband was so seldom at home and that he was away just at this time. She felt that the wife of a workman or farmer was better off than she, for they could at least be home most of the time."[10] Outside observers, such as Benjamin Franklin and Thomas Jefferson, frequently commented on the willingness of German American women to undertake hard, physical labor within their own domestic economy.

German Lutheran women who arrived in colonial America came with traditional social and economic rights that had been ingrained in German peasant culture for centuries, and they guarded these traditional rights closely. Among other things, women had rights to retain their own property and to receive and maintain inheritances, rights that were actually more expansive than the English common law in the American colonies. Studies of colonial Lutheran wills in the eighteenth century show the tensions involved in such a transition from one culture to another: "(In Virginia) . . . married women's rights over the domestic economy seem to have diminished in the new legal system. Rural Pennsylvania German-speaking women, too, clearly voiced concerns over their privileges and property ..."[11] But the resources that Lutheran women controlled could also be used positively to assist the family economy, as when, in 1775, Anna Maria Muhlenberg contributed 120 pounds (from an inheritance) to the purchase of a homestead for her family, or about one-quarter of the full purchase price. Since women often outlived their husband, they were able to control important elements of family resources through inheritances. It is not an overstatement to say that in the establishment of Lutheranism in colonial America, women such as Anna Maria Muhlenberg, and many much less well known women, were important in their own right to the growth of American Lutheranism.

African Americans and Native Americans

Although the primary thrust of the European Lutheran mission to colonial America was to gather in and retain immigrant Lutherans, the leaders of this mission also envisioned other possibilities, especially the conversion of Native Americans and African Americans. While only an episodic concern occasionally expressed by Lutheran leaders, there is no doubt that colonial American Lutherans frequently came into contact with both populations and had to deal with their presence in their communities, albeit as outsiders to the European norms of their congregations. Pietist leaders in Europe urged mission work with Native Americans and African Americans, although the strained resources of colonial Lutheran pastors rarely allowed them the time to consider such ventures.

Africans were involuntarily brought to colonial America beginning in the early seventeenth century, and Africans (both free and enslaved) could be found in every colony, although they were most numerous in the South. In the middle colonies (New York to Maryland) enslaved Africans were most commonly used as servants and farm laborers, and many of these areas did not officially abolish slavery until the early nineteenth century. In the South, enslaved Africans were more numerous, both on large plantations and as servants and domestic laborers. Groups of free African Americans lived in all of the American colonies.

Since Lutherans tended to be on the poorer side of the early colonial economy, most did not own large numbers of slaves. But African Americans, free and slave, were present in their communities, were served by Lutheran pastors, and were at times a part of their congregations. In 1669, newly arrived Pastor Jacob Fabritius baptized an African American man named Emmanuel and admitted him to membership in the congregation, along with his European wife and two children. In 1705, Justus Falckner listed two free African Americans, Aree and Jora van Guinea, as members of his New York congregation, and members of their extended family show up in congregation records in New York and New Jersey across the eighteenth century. In 1712, Falcker admitted an enslaved African American named Pieter Christian into membership, provided that "he will hereafter, as well as he has done before, faithfully serve his master and mistress as servant."[12] Pieter married at least twice, to white women, and had a number of (free) children. New York pastors occasionally admitted both free and enslaved African Americans into church membership; slaves were admitted as long as they understood that they ". . . did not intend to abuse their Christianity, to break the laws of the land, or to dissolve the tie of obedience . . . ,"[13] as a congregational constitution of 1735 put it. There is at least one recorded instance of African Americans as members of the Swedish church at Raccoon, New Jersey, during the time of Pastor Nicholas Collin (sometime after 1770), who noted a husband, wife, and eight children: "The man Cudjo [was] born in Africa, and as he says, the son of a chief; Venus, his wife [was] born in America. Both are about 30 years old, kind people, quite devout and, in their way, religious. She is now free, but he is the slave of an Irishman."[14] The Swedish pastors noted in their records baptizing dozens of African Americans, although very few of them were listed as members of the congregations. Henry Muhlenberg and other Pennsylvania pastors also occasionally noted the baptism of African Americans, enslaved and free, but as with the Swedish congregations, very few of them were noted as congregational members.

In the North, several Lutheran pastors themselves owned enslaved African Americans, who were included in their parsonage community. William Berkenmeyer in New York owned two slaves, whom he baptized and married, and whose children he also baptized. When some of his parishioners criticized him for being a slaveowner, he pointedly told them it was none of their business, as he had bought them with his own money. Among the Swedes on the Delaware, Pastor Samuel Hasselius at Wilmington recorded on November 4, 1724: "A negress named Peggy was bought for the parsonage with the money received for the priest land which was sold, and as the cost of her was £45, and there was but £40 from the sale of the land, pastor Hesselius added £5 of his own money."[15] This practice of buying enslaved Africans for the support of church and parsonage lands was not uncommon in the eighteenth century, especially in the South. German Lutherans in the North were generally less financially able to own slaves, and the custom was rarer among them.

In the South, the first Lutherans in Georgia were (as has been seen) opposed to slavery, and Pastor Boltzius refused to allow it in their community. But by 1750, outside pressure overwhelmed his objections, and by the time of Muhlenberg's visit in 1774–75, he records in a number of places mention of slave owning among Lutheran laypeople and pastors. Boltzius himself became a slaveowner, and his colleagues, Rabenhorst and Lemke, "must have been two of the largest slave owners in the community during the 1760s and 1770s."[16] The Georgia Lutherans attempted to mitigate the effects of slavery on the Africans (and perhaps their own consciences) by attempting to treat the enslaved Africans better than did other Europeans around them. They regularly baptized African Americans and (contrary to colonial law) taught many to read and write so as to be able to read the Bible. They also gave the enslaved Africans more free time, especially on Sunday. Though they made sporadic efforts to Christianize their slaves, it is not particularly clear that these efforts actually worked.

In the Danish Virgin Islands, the Lutheran congregations were primarily oriented toward Danish settlers, even though the Danes were a minority even among the European population of the islands. Slavery was rapidly introduced into the islands, and a large population of enslaved Africans, speaking the local Dutch Creole language, was established. Initial Danish efforts to catechize the Africans in Danish were not successful. What forced a change in this "strategy" was competition from Moravian missionaries, who started work among the Africans in 1732, using the Dutch Creole. Their success prodded the Danish authorities, who in 1770 encouraged Lutheran pastors to translate religious books into Creole and to begin an outreach to the Africans in that language. This approach worked well, and thousands of Africans were added to the Lutheran congregations during the last thirty years of the eighteenth century. This was the beginning of a truly indigenous Lutheranism in the Virgin Islands, one that is still in existence today.

Dreams of missions to the Native Americans were also common among European and American Lutheran leaders, but the record here is much less active. The singular example of seventeenth-century Swedish pastor John Campanius Holm was atypical. Holm, who served along the Delaware from 1642 to 1648, learned the local Delaware language, conversed at length with them about Christianity, and even translated Luther's Small Catechism into Algonquin. But there is no record that any significant results came, even from his concerted efforts, and no other Lutheran pastors made more than a passing attempt to reach the Native Americans. Occasionally, a Native American might be baptized (usually one who had been enslaved by a European), but even this was rare. Although some pastors mentioned a concern for Native Americans, they tended to be completely occupied by the needs of the European settlers. As well, the Native Americans kept moving (or were pushed) westward, conveniently out of the reach of Lutheran pastors. Growing tensions between the Native and European populations, especially on the frontier, and the inherent danger of Lutheran contacts with Native Americans were considered reasons enough not to attempt them. For most colonial Lutherans, Native Americans were a dangerous, "other" people, and well outside of the bounds of their community.

Constitutions and the Structuring of American Lutheran Congregations

As we have seen before, the nature of American voluntary religion and the lack of a Lutheran state church meant a new situation for Lutherans in colonial America. Much of the strife that arose in the congregations was because the power relationships between pastors and congregations were now different, although it was not a simple two-way conflict. There were often congregational factions and disputes that developed because of tensions between different groups of laypeople in congregations as well. Sometimes, newly arrived Lutherans challenged the power and control of longtime congregational lay officials, creating a situation where there were multiple factions. American Lutheran laypeople were trying to find the right balance of power and responsibilities for the beneficial operation of their congregations.

One way to accomplish this goal was through the crafting and implementation of church constitutions, which attempted to regulate and minimize disputes, and to spell out the optimal balance of power within the congregations. Two such constitutions implemented in the Philadelphia area in the 1760s show a trend toward democratization and the balance of power, and became models of how Lutherans were adjusting to the new American realities. The first was implemented by Pastor Carl Magnus Wrangel at the Swedish parish in Philadelphia, while the other was developed by Henry Muhlenberg for the German-speaking St. Michael congregation, also in Philadelphia. Both echo religious democratization stemming from the First Great Awakening, and the developing political democratization stemming from the colonial tensions with the British royal authorities.

The Swedish congregations in the eighteenth century underwent a fundamental shift in orientation, with the old affiliational model of Swedish ethnicity (broadly understood) supplanted by a more voluntary membership model. For over a hundred years Swedish congregations had survived largely because power was concentrated in established families that held power by controlling lay offices, such as trustees and deacons. These elected positions became almost hereditary and, because of minimal formal procedures, there was often no clarity about who owned the real property of the congregations. In some cases, the deeds to church lands and buildings were actually in private hands, which resulted in long-term litigation.

Pastor Wrangel and many of the lay members of the Philadelphia parish had long been resisted by the lay trustees (vestry) of the congregation. In 1765, the three congregations adopted a new constitution that attempted to rein in the old vestry's powers, giving the annual meeting of the congregation more power over them. In the intense public debate that followed, the newly elected vestry sought to explain the reasons for the new constitution: "Many thoughtful members of our Congregations, as well as our worthy Minister, had long observed, that the Management of our valuable estate, purchased for the Use of our Churches, had got entirely into the Hands of a few Men of one or two families, who, according to some former rules of filling up their Numbers, might have continued this power to themselves and to their Children, from one Generation to another."[17] The resulting power struggle spilled into the larger community, finally confirming the rights of the whole congregation to the detriment of its hereditary leaders.

The situation at St. Michael congregation in Philadelphia was different, but many of the dynamics were familiar. In 1757, Pastor John Frederick Handschuh became pastor of the congregation, but by 1760 had managed to split the congregation into two competing factions. Since the congregation had the power to call its own pastor (unlike the Swedish congregations), one faction attempted to dismiss Handschuh from his position. Here again, class and economic differences played a key role, with the traditional families that had monopolized control of the congregation pitted against poorer newcomers. One scholar described the attitude of the more recent arrivals to the congregation, who were fearful of the leaders' economic demands: "Increasingly, by the late 1740s, these members of St Michael's saw the leadership as arrogant worthies who acted irresponsibly, squandering widow's mites instead of modestly responding to the congregation's needs for a place to worship, and occasional poor relief."[18] Handschuh was backed by the church council (representative of the old leadership), but his "highhanded" ways alienated many members.

When Muhlenberg was dragged into the mess, one of his solutions was a new congregational constitution, in 1762. Trying to bring some stability to the situation, his new constitution actually took some power from the congregation, especially over its ability to remove a pastor from office. In line with the Ministerium, the new St. Michael's constitution instituted checks and balances so that the rights of the pastor might be safeguarded. Similar checks and balances were given to the congregation as a whole, especially in its power to review and veto decisions of the church council. A scholar has written about this: "Because the *Kirchen- und Schul-Ordnung* (Constitution) restricted the laity's right to have a say in matters of personnel, it compensated for this shortcoming by democratizing the process of decision-making in congregational affairs. Neither group within the vestry—pastors (who used to officiate as trustees), trustees, elders, or deacons—could resolve on anything by themselves."[19] While the new constitution stabilized matters in the congregation, it was only the beginning of a solution, as matters simmered for several additional years. It was, however, a victory for Muhlenberg and the Pennsylvania Ministerium, in that its power over an important congregation (through the person of Muhlenberg) was confirmed.

These two congregational disputes, and the means of addressing them, were symptomatic of a wider trend at mid-century, that is, the increasing push for democratization within the congregations and for formal means (in this case, constitutions) to address the rights of all groups and to balance those rights to allow the effective management of congregational affairs. These dynamics were also just a part of larger political and social struggles within the American colonies at the same time, struggles that would eventually result in the American Revolutionary War and the formation of an independent United States.

Lutherans and the Revolutionary War

Lutherans immigrating to colonial America encountered many new realities to which they had to adjust, and one of these was a new system of political organization. Coming from the continent of Europe, Lutherans had little acquaintance with the British system of representative rule, as exemplified by English parliamentary government, and other traditions of limited royal power. In the American colonies, Lutherans encountered a number of different types of political organizations, but the colonies eventually had some forms of self-rule by means of colonial assemblies in which they could participate and make their voices known. Because of their unfamiliarity with these new political systems, and because of the language barrier that initially kept them apart, Lutherans were slow to move into colonial politics, but eventually they did learn to participate politically, to safeguard their rights.

In Pennsylvania, where Germans (Lutherans and others) constituted a significant portion of the colonial population, Lutherans played a significant role in colonial political activity. Pennsylvania was originally founded as a proprietary colony, literally the possession of one man, William Penn. Through Penn, his fellow English Quakers initially controlled the colony, even though they quickly became a minority in the colony. During the eighteenth century, the colony quickly broke down into political factions, especially over the issues of defense. The Quakers and their allies among the German sectarians (Mennonites and Moravians) were pacifists, and were loath to empower a colonial militia or pay them. Frontier attacks by Native Americans and the crisis of the French and Indian War (1754–1763) brought these and other political issues to a head. Muhlenberg and the other Lutheran pastors walked a delicate line here: they were theologically wary of getting too involved (as pastors) in the area of secular politics and governance, but they also recognized the need to protect the rights of their congregants and communities through the political processes. When urged, in 1764, to become involved in the political struggle over frontier defense, Muhlenberg replied: ". . . we preachers could not permit ourselves to interfere in such critical, political affairs. Our office rather requires us to pray to God the Supreme Ruler for protection and mercy and to admonish our fellow German citizens to fear God, honor our King, and love our neighbor, etc."[20] Nevertheless, Muhlenberg allowed the circulation of petitions regarding the matter within his congregations, permitted church councils to take a position on the issue, and worked politically behind the scenes to see that Lutheran interests were safeguarded. His longstanding religious dislike of the Quakers moved him to limited political activities against them.

During the Stamp Act crisis of 1765, however, Muhlenberg advised the St. Michael's church council to have nothing to do with agitation against the act. Quoting Romans 13:1 ("Be subject to the ruling authorities . . ."), he also suggested a political motive for restraint, that the Lutherans not be seen in England as part of the agitation: "We would do better to remain quiet and let the English act as they see fit."[21] For many Lutherans, especially older ones, traditional deference to authority (especially a German monarch on the English throne) seemed the wise choice; let the "English" American colonists and the British government sort it out. This approach would be sorely tested a decade later, with the outbreak of the American Revolution.

The American Revolutionary War (1775–1781) forced Lutherans to confront the inherent complexities of being "subject to the ruling authorities" when it was unclear just who the legitimate authorities were. This was a time when it was almost impossible to remain neutral, and when refusal to commit to one side meant being suspected of being partisan for the other side. This was particularly an issue for Lutherans in the middle colonies (especially Pennsylvania and New Jersey), where the shifting tides of war and control meant that Lutherans could find their settlements passing from control by one side to the other with some regularity. Muhlenberg attempted to follow a neutral course, praying for both sides and for a speedy end to the conflict. He delayed taking an oath of loyalty to the American government as long as he could, but toward the end of the war he moved more to support of the American cause and, in 1783, wrote in his journal that "it was the will of the Supreme Ruler of heaven and earth that there should be *independence* and not otherwise." He was unsure if God actively willed independence or simply allowed it, but saw independence as a divine test as to how the new nation would handle such power.[22]

If the older generation of Lutherans were cautious about their involvement, it seems that the younger generation was not, and this can be seen in the actions of Henry Muhlenberg's sons, Peter and Frederick. Peter was a Lutheran pastor in Woodstock, Virginia, but left his position in early 1776 to become an officer in the Continental Army (rising to the rank of major-general), and enlisted a number of his parishioners to join the army with him. In response to a letter from his brother Frederick, chiding him for this action, Peter wrote, "I am a clergyman it is true, but I am a Member of Society as well as the poorest layman & my liberty is as dear to me as any Man, shall I then sit still . . . when the best Blood of the Continent is spilling? Heaven forbid it."[23] Peter served for the duration of the war, and entered politics after the war, serving in Congress, among other places. Frederick, too, eventually left the ministry to serve in Congress, and they initiated a long line of Muhlenbergs active in national and state politics.

Other Lutherans joined the Continental cause. One hundred and thirty-seven members from the Lutheran congregation in Charleston, South Carolina, formed the "German Fusiliers" regiment and fought through the course of the war, and other Lutherans joined the Continental Army. The Georgia Salzburgers raised three companies of soldiers, and a German regiment, the "Independent Horse Troop," served as George Washington's bodyguards through much of the war. Lutheran laymen served the army in other ways: Dr. Bodo Otto was the senior surgeon in charge of hospitals, and his sons served with him. Christopher Ludwig of Philadelphia was Baker General to the army. Salzburg Lutheran John Treutlen became the first governor of the state of Georgia.

There were also Lutherans who remained loyal to the British crown and expressed their loyalty publically. Pastor Christopher Triebner in Georgia was a prominent Loyalist, and fled to England with the American victory in the South. Some Lutheran pastors, such as John Ludwig Voigt of Pennsylvania and Peter Sommer of New York, continued to support the Loyalist position until the very end of the war, sometimes coming into conflict with local Continental officials as well as their parishioners. Some Loyalist Lutherans actually left the country because of the victory of the Continental Army and moved to Canada. New York pastor Bernard Michael Hausihl moved to Nova Scotia, as did a number of other Lutheran laypeople. Pastor Johan Schwertfeger at Albany, New York, was imprisoned by American officials during the war for "meddling in political affairs which did not belong to his office" (as Muhlenberg put it),[24] and eventually moved to upper Canada with a number of his parishioners. A number of German Hessian soldiers (generally Lutherans) who fought as mercenaries for the British remained in North America after the war. While some remained in the new United States, many others settled in Canada.

The Revolutionary War created tremendous hardships for American Lutherans, no matter which side they supported. War cut off the flow of immigrants, including new pastors from Europe, and generally impoverished the population. Since much of the warfare itself took place in the middle colonies, where Lutherans were most numerous, it affected many congregations. Military disruptions meant that pastors sometimes could not hold services or travel, and many of their congregations were torn between Loyalist members and those who supported the American cause. A number of Lutheran church buildings were commandeered by one army or the other, and some were badly damaged. Lutheran parsonages and homes were commandeered for the housing of soldiers. The Salzburg settlement in Georgia was destroyed by British forces during the course of the war and its people scattered. The records of Swedish pastor Nicholas Collin of New Jersey vividly illustrate the traumas of war in a battleground state that passed from British to Continental control several times. In the middle of the war, Collins wrote: "Everywhere distrust, fear, hatred, and abominable selfishness were met with. Parents and children, brothers and sisters, wife and husband, were enemies to one another. The militia and some regular troops on one side, and refugees . . . on the other were constantly roving . . . plundering and destroying everything in a barbarous manner."[25] As a Swedish citizen, Collins remained neutral, which got him into trouble several times with the local American militias. Still, he attempted to carry out his pastoral duties, including visitation of wounded soldiers and prisoners.

With the end of hostilities in 1781, the situation for Lutherans in America began to return to normal, and they endeavored to rebuild their settlements and their congregations. Some decided to leave for Canada or elsewhere, but most remained in the new United States. Adjusting to the new political reality of an independent United States, and all that this entailed, would take some time to accomplish.

Notes

1. Henry Melchior Muhlenberg, "Journal entry, December 1, 1742," in *The Journals of Henry Melchior Muhlenberg*, trans. Theodore Tappert and John Doberstein, vol. 1 (Philadelphia: Muhlenberg, 1942), 68.

2. Muhlenberg, "Journal entry for July 1, 1762," in ibid., 1:533.

3. Paul A. W. Wallace, *The Muhlenbergs of Pennsylvania* (Philadelphia: University of Pennsylvania Press, 1950), 51.

4. "Letter, Johannes C. Hartwig to Friedrich Wagner," February 19, 1754, in Simon Hart and Harry Krieder, eds., *Lutheran Church in New York and New Jersey, 1722–1760* (New York: United Synod of New York and New England, 1962), 371.

5. "Letter, Wiacaco church leaders to Consistory, November 1748," in Peter Stebbins Craig and Kim-Eric Williams, eds., *Colonial Records of the Swedish Churches in Pennsylvania*, vol. 4, 1719–1750 (Philadelphia: Swedish Colonial Society, 2008), 275.

6. Israel Acrelius, *A History of New Sweden* (1759), trans. William Reynolds (Philadelphia: Historical Society of Pennsylvania, 1874), 332–33.

7. Marianne S. Wokeck, "The *Pfarrhaus* as Model in Identifying German-American Identities," in Han-Jürgen Grabbe, ed., *Halle Pietism, Colonial North America, and the Young United States* (Stuttgart: Fran Steiner Verlag, 2008), 223.

8. "At court held in City Hall, New Orange," February 24, 1674, in Peter Stebbins Craig and Kim-Eric Williams, eds., *Colonial Records of the Swedish Churches in Pennsylvania*, vol. 1, 1646–1696 (Philadelphia: Swedish Colonial Society, 2008), 130.

9. "Letter, Johann Martin Boltzius to Gotthilf August Francke," May 12, 1749, in *The Letters of Johann Martin Boltzius, Lutheran Pastor in Ebenezer, Georgia: German Pietism in Colonial America, 1733–1765*, vol. 2 (Lewiston, NY: Edwin Mellon, 2009), 528–29.

10. Muhlenberg, "Journal entry for January, 1750," in *Journals*, 1:234.

11. A. G. Roeber, *Palatines, Liberty, and Property: German Lutherans in Colonial British America* (Baltimore: Johns Hopkins University Press, 1993), 183–84.

12. *Kercken-boeck, 31, no. 3*, quoted in Harry J. Kreider, *The Lutheran Church in Colonial New York* (New York: n.p., 1942), 55–56.

13. Ibid., 56.

14. Nicholas Collin, *Journal and Autobiography*, trans. Amandus Johnson (Philadelphia: n.p., 1936), 283.

15. Quoted in Jehu Curtis Clay, *The Annals of the Swedes on the Delaware* (1835) (Chicago: John Ericsson Memorial Committee, 1938), 15.

16. Jeff G. Johnson, *Black Lutherans: The Untold Lutheran Story* (St. Louis: Concordia, 1991), 66.

17. *Pennsylvania Gazette*, June 25, 1767, quoted in Daniel Lindmark, *Ecclesia Plantanda: Swedishness in Colonial America*, Kulturens Frontlinjer 52 (Umeå, Sweden: n.p., 2005), 205.

18. Roeber, *Palatines, Liberty, and Property*, 244.

19. Wolfgang Splitter, *Pastors People Politics: German Lutherans in Pennsylvania, 1740–1790* (Trier: Wissenschaftlicher Verlag, 1998), 83.

20. Henry Melchior Muhlenberg, "Journal Entry for March 29, 1764," in *The Journals of Henry Melchior Muhlenberg*, trans. Theodore Tappert and John Doberstein, vol. 2 (Philadelphia: Muhlenberg, 1945), 55.

21. Muhlenberg, "Journal Entry for October 5, 1765," in ibid., 2:273.

22. Henry Melchior Muhlenberg, "Journal Entry for March 25, 1783," in *The Journals of Henry Melchior Muhlenberg*, trans. Theodore Tappert and John Doberstein, vol. 3 (Philadelphia: Muhlenberg, 1958), 534.

23. "Letter from Frederick Muhlenberg to Peter Muhlenberg, March 1776," at the end of Frederick Muhlenberg's diary, Trinity Lutheran Church, Reading, Pennsylvania, quoted in Wallace, *Muhlenbergs of Pennsylvania*, 120.

24. Muhlenberg, "Journal Entry for June 9, 1777," *Journals*, 3:50–51.

25. Collins, *Journal and Autobiography*, 244.

Excursus 4

RED AND GREEN AND BLACK AND BLUE: LUTHERAN HYMNALS AND THEIR IMPACT

One interesting factor of American Lutheranism is the tendency to refer to its various hymnals by the color of their covers. Just gather any group of Lutherans and shortly they will begin talking about, and critiquing, the hymnals that they have used in their life. "Why, I remember the old _____ (insert the favorite color) hymnal—now, that was a good one. Much better than this new _____ (insert the least favorite color) hymnal that we have now!" American Lutherans get rather passionate about their hymnals, probably because hymns and singing are such a big part of their worship and devotional lives, and changing these things can really stir up controversy. Just think about the emotions raised when favorite hymns (ones known by heart) are changed or deleted from the newest version of the hymnal.

Hymns and hymnals have always been very important in the Lutheran tradition. Luther wrote or rewrote quite a number of hymns, and the first Lutheran hymnals appeared already in the first decades of the Reformation. The century after Luther was a "golden age" of hymnody, when the great Lutheran chorale hymns were written, and later reset by composers like J. S. Bach. The immigrant Lutherans who came to North America, starting in the eighteenth century, customarily brought with them a Bible, the Small Catechism, and the psalmbook or hymnal of the region of Europe from which they came. In this new country, with few Lutheran congregations or pastors, the immigrants could at least gather with their hymnals to worship God and give thanks. They used these European hymnals for many years; they became a link to the world that they had left behind and a beloved religious resource.

In the eighteenth and nineteenth centuries, things began to change for American Lutheran hymnody, in two important ways. First, there was a dramatic surge of new hymns and types of hymns coming out of the Anglo-American world: revival hymns, gospel hymns, revivals of ancient and medieval hymns, and many others—all came to enrich the Protestant hymn traditions. These kinds of hymns, often more subjective and personal, were adopted and copied by Lutheran hymnwriters, often out of the Pietist tradition. The second big development was the translation of the Lutheran hymn tradition into English; the Lutheran immigrants began to worship in English, and this stimulated the production of dozens of new American Lutheran hymnals. Of course, this shift brought controversy: Which of the traditional Lutheran hymns should be translated and retained in these new hymnals? How many of the new Anglo-American hymns should be included? There is nothing new about hymnal controversies.

With the multiplication of Lutheran denominations in the nineteenth century came ever more and even more varied American Lutheran hymnals; each new denomination seemed to need its own hymnal. This need was important, it seems, for the group identity and sense of purpose of each of these denominations; these hymnals gave them something in common from which they could worship and sing. The same phenomenon worked in reverse, too; hymnals became important means by which American Lutherans came together and merged their denominations. The way toward merger was often preceded by the development of a common hymnal; first, get the congregations of the distinct denominations to worship and sing out of a common hymnal, it was reasoned, and the road to merger would be easier. In the later decades of the nineteenth century, the three divided colonial-era Lutheran groups adopted a common hymnal, the *Common Service Book and Hymnal*, which preceded their merger in 1918. Midwestern immigrant German groups came together in 1930, assisted by the American Lutheran hymnal. In the 1950s, eight different American Lutheran groups came together to develop a common hymnal, the red *Service Book and Hymnal*. Although the merger process ended up with two different denominations instead of one (the American Lutheran Church and the Lutheran Church in America), the result was that the majority of American Lutherans were now using a common hymnal. In the 1970s, the development of the green *Lutheran Book of Worship* was envisioned as a common hymnal for all American Lutherans (this, too, was perhaps too ambitious).

The late twentieth century saw a further expansion of Lutheran hymnody, with new hymns from Latin America, Africa, and Asia being included in the newest Lutheran hymnals, including the *Evangelical Lutheran Worship* (ELCA), *Lutheran Service Book* (LCMS), and *Christian Worship* (WELS). New hymnals broaden the ways in which Lutherans worship and tie them together with Christians from around the world. These hymnals have had a primary influence on creating the distinctive culture of American Lutheranism.

Chapter 5

Lutherans in a New Nation, 1781–1820

W hen the American army under George Washington, with the assistance of the French navy, defeated the British army at Yorktown, Virginia, in October 1781, it changed not only the political structure of the North Atlantic world but also its religious structures. One of the greatest military powers of the day, Britain, had been defeated by an army formed by its own American colonists, motivated by the preservation of the very rights that the British themselves had espoused. Although "New World" colonialism itself would continue in some form for the next two hundred years, this example of colonists seeking their own independence would help inspire other revolutions. The American aim was not only for independence, but for a revolution in the very structure of governance. Drawing from the British traditions that went back at least as far as the Magna Carta of 1215, and from social and political ideas of Enlightenment, American leaders sought not just a new nation, but a new *kind* of nation, one that was different from what had been known and tried but whose precise structure had not been worked out in advance. Thomas Jefferson would call it "a fair experiment," while Lincoln at Gettysburg wondered whether "any nation so conceived . . . can long endure." Reading history backward can lead one to interpret the unfolding of events as self-evident.

Reality, however, was quite a bit messier than some of the preceding rhetoric might suggest, as the years after 1781 were filled with struggles to ensure that this American experiment would not collapse in upon itself. The war decimated many parts of the American territory and its economy. Americans were divided over independence, and those loyal to British rule often faced the choice between staying and suffering retribution or leaving, often impoverished, for other parts of the British Empire, such as Canada. The American revolutionary struggle fed on a distrust of coercive authority, and thus many wanted a weak confederation of individual states instead of a centralized government. The Continental Congress, driven deeply in debt over the costs of the war, had very limited powers of taxation and governance, not to mention that they were even then a fractious and divided group of leaders from different states, with different agendas. The governing structure for the American colonies, the Articles of Confederation (formally approved in 1781), proved to be inadequate and ineffective to meet the challenges of guiding a new nation. It was an open question if this even was a new country, or whether it was simply an alliance among thirteen sovereign states.

During the 1780s, these issues forced leaders to consider a stronger and more permanent framework for American governance. The Federalists favored more definite power for the central government, with executive power in a presidency and strengthening the legislative branch, Congress. The Anti-Federalists resisted the implementation of more centralized authority, no matter how nuanced, and the battle between the two factions raged in print and in person. A constitutional convention developed a national constitution, generally along Federalist lines, which was adopted in 1787 and ratified by the states by 1789. To placate fears of an all-powerful federal government, the convention also approved the Bill of Rights, a package of ten amendments to the proposed constitution that granted constitutionally protected rights for citizens, limiting federal power over them. These developments were an early sign that the new United States was definitely a "work in progress," and the institutions and traditions of the newly independent nation took decades more to refine.

Developments in American Religious Life

The war and American independence also had a profound impact on the religious life and organizations of the American people. Formal religion in colonial America was weak, with fewer than 20 percent of Americans listed as church members in 1776. The privations of the war damaged many congregations; church buildings were destroyed, pastors and congregational members dispersed, and economic depredations cut into their ministry. While some Christian groups suffered more than others, it was the colonial Anglican churches who suffered the most, cut off from

LUTHERAN MEMBERSHIP GROWTH IN THE 19TH CENTURY			
Year	Congregations	Baptized Members*	Pastors
1790	314	25,000	—
1860	2,575	350,000	1,366
1875	4,792	780,000	2,795
1900	11,145	2,175,000	6,811

*Estimates

the bishops in England and weakened by the loss of a substantial number of British Loyalists who left the country during and after the war. Yet, all religious groups or denominations were required to rethink their new environment and their mission and to reorganize accordingly. Independence brought obstacles, but also opportunity. It was in this context that the American denomination was born.

The U.S. Constitution codified a preexisting trend in American life toward the embrace of personal religious freedom, of religious pluralism, and voluntary religion. Starting with Virginia in 1776, many states dismantled the state-supported Anglican religious establishments and granted religious freedoms to their inhabitants. This trend was a combination of three factors: an Enlightenment ideal that religion should not be coerced; the fear that many dissenting religious groups had of government control; and the pragmatic realization that religious establishment simply would not work in the American context. The adoption of the First Amendment of the Constitution in 1789 formalized these principles, that Americans would have the freedom to express their religious beliefs as they saw fit, and that the federal government would not favor or support any particular religious group. State establishments of religion continued into the nineteenth century in the form of New England Congregationalism, but politically their days were numbered.

The eighteenth-century European Enlightenment created a new approach toward religious belief and traditional religious systems, called Deism. This understanding of religion, which had been around in some form for centuries, criticized traditional Western "revealed" religions such as Christianity and Judaism as backward and unenlightened. Given the Enlightenment stress on human reason and natural law, these new religious thinkers dispensed with anything supernatural—miracles, chiefly, but any form of divine intervention in the world outside the laws of nature, including the idea that Jesus of Nazareth was in any way the divine Son of God. Deists believed in a God who created the world and embedded in it a singular moral code that was discernable to all human beings through their rational minds. Having acted, the Creator withdrew his involvement in the world, perhaps until a final day of judgment. Differences between and within organized religious groups were seen as absurd, since there was only one God and one universal moral law.

Most American Deists were moderates from the educated elite. Deist political leaders such as Thomas Jefferson, Benjamin Franklin, and George Washington saw organized religion in the new nation as remaining useful for inculcating a common morality among the masses of uneducated or unenlightened citizens, and they supported organized religion as a key to republican society. But they opposed any form of religious coercion, and generally did not find organized religion personally meaningful to themselves. A radical exception to this moderate Deism was Thomas Paine, the firebrand writer of the American independence movement. A self-educated man of lower-class origins, Paine reflected the radical Deism along the lines of French philosophers, who believed that organized religion was a fraud perpetrated on the common man. Paine vigorously promoted his view in a book entitled *The Age of Reason* (1794–1807), which caused a sensation in America and horrified the moderate Deists.

Deism and reactions to it became a hotly contested religious issue in America through the 1790s and well into the nineteenth century. Some religious thinkers actually welcomed Deism or sought to incorporate it into a reform of their own traditional religious systems. One such movement, the Unitarians, arose within the liberal wing of New England Congregationalism, especially those who had been opposed to the subjective expressions of the First Great Awakening. This group took over control of Harvard College in 1805, and became the core of the Unitarian Association when it was formed in 1825. Similar to them were the Universalists, who held to the doctrine of universal human salvation; socially, they represented the rural New England and New York populations, rather than the Harvard-educated Unitarians around Boston. Some within traditional Christian groups downplayed supernatural religious elements for more of a mild religious rationalism. But most traditional Christian groups saw Deism in whatever form as a dangerous attack on the core elements of their faith, and fought long and hard against it.

One strategy to oppose Deism and to reenliven traditional Christianity was the appeal to the revival of religious enthusiasm and revivalism, such as that which characterized the First Great Awakening of the 1740s. This direct appeal to the religious emotions, or what they would have called the "religious affections," of the masses of American people, was part of a larger eighteenth-century movement of "Religions of the Heart," such as Pietism and Methodism. This movement sought to appeal directly to the emotions of the individual, imploring them to repent their sins, to be "converted" to a true faith, and to begin to live a regenerated moral life. In the face of Deism, traditional Christian leaders fervently prayed and preached for a renewal of Christian hearts and minds.

The first wave of this renewal movement, eventually known as the Second Great Awakening, began in the 1790s in an unlikely place, the western frontier of Kentucky. Organized religion was very thin on the frontier, so pioneer pastors used new and direct methods for preaching for revival among the scattered populations. People from a wide area gathered in central locations for "camp meetings," intense, emotional, and nonstop revival services that hammered home the need for individual salvation and renewal—to get "saved." This new approach stirred up waves of emotional conversations, and was so successful that news of the revivals spread back to the settled, eastern sections of the United States, electrifying the religious leaders there. These frontier revival techniques were refined and adopted by eastern religious leaders, who began to preach to their congregations for similar religious revivals.

One key to the success of this revival was the adoption of the theology of Arminianism. Traditional Reformed or Calvinist Christianity (dominant in colonial America) viewed the conversion or "election" of a believer as solely the limited and predestined work of God; believers came passively to an understanding of their own election. As an active alternative to this view, Arminianism taught that God offered salvation to all, but it was up to believers to actively accept or reject this offer of salvation. Because of its effectiveness in revival settings, Arminianism quickly became the dominant form of Protestantism in nineteenth-century America. With groups such as the Methodists and the Baptists leading the way, this optimistic, emotional, and moralistic form of revival Christianity soon became the norm in American religion, and formed the core of American evangelical Protestantism. Although Unitarianism won the minds of some cultured Americans, evangelical revivalism won the hearts of the masses and quickly initiated a huge expansion of organized religion in nineteenth-century America.

Lutherans in America in 1781

The Revolutionary War generally affected Lutherans in a manner similar to many of their religious neighbors, with economic and physical losses that were severe in some locations, especially in the Mid-Atlantic states. Several factors mitigated the impact of the war: few Lutherans were departing loyalists; they were not heavily dependent on European governance; and the poverty that drove many Lutheran settlers inland to the frontier kept some of their communities away from the brunt of the fighting. Still, despite 150 years of activity on the American continent, the

Lutheran presence in America was fairly modest, and there were far too few pastors to serve existing Lutheran congregations.

To envision the core area of American Lutherans in 1781, imagine a line drawn from Wilmington, Delaware, northward to Albany, New York, a distance of about 250 miles. The vast majority of Lutherans lived within this core area of Pennsylvania, New Jersey, and New York. Although Lutherans had also begun pushing into the frontier areas of western Maryland, Virginia, and North Carolina, and there were scattered communities in South Carolina and Georgia, these groups were small. One estimate of Lutheran congregations in the United States in 1790 numbers some 314 congregations, of which 191 were in Pennsylvania alone. There were about eighty congregations from Maryland south to Georgia, and about forty-four congregations in New York and New Jersey.[1] But many of these congregations were very small and hardly much more than preaching points for the limited number of Lutheran pastors available; one enumeration counts a total of 151 Lutheran pastors who served in colonial America (1638–1775).[2]

The numbers of Lutheran church members in 1790 is difficult to determine, as congregational records are fragmentary. One approach is to count ethnic Germans in the new republic. The United States census of 1790 suggests about 260,000 Germans in the country as of this date, and if one estimated that one-third to one-half of these Germans came from Lutheran state-church territories, the "pool" of possible Lutherans in the United States was about 120,000 to 140,000 people.[3] But it is clear that the number of active Lutherans in that day was much smaller; the overall percentage of church members in America in 1776 was about 17 percent of the general population, so by extrapolation, the number of Lutherans in 1790 actively connected to a congregation was in the range of 20,000 to 25,000 members. No doubt, many other people in the wider community were served by these congregations, especially for baptisms, weddings, and funerals, but there is no way to determine such a number with any accuracy.

Since most Lutherans at the time primarily spoke German, they were removed from the mainstream of America political and religious life. But they were aware of, and affected by, the contemporary concerns about Deism and experiential religion such as revivalism, which intruded into their religious world. Deism and religious rationalism were making inroads into Lutheranism in Germany as well, even at Halle, causing American Lutheran leaders to wonder aloud: Even if they could get pastors from Germany, could they be trusted, theologically? Lutherans closely followed debates over the nature of religious freedom in America, and generally supported the Constitution and the First Amendment. But there were two overriding issues that captured their immediate attention: how to get enough pastors to serve Lutheran congregations (especially on the frontier), and how to deal with the increasing demand by congregations for an English-language ministry. These two pressing issues dominated Lutheranism in America for the next forty years.

The Reorientation of American Lutheranism

Just as American civil society was wrestling with new ideas and new forms of governance, so, too, were American Lutherans dealing with a vital reorientation of their structures and their viewpoints. The expansion of American Lutheran congregations and the rise in numbers of Lutheran pastors meant that the old, informal systems of church governance were simply inadequate to meet increasingly complex needs. During much of the colonial period, American Lutherans relied on a combination of informal pastoral networks and the direction and support they received from European church officials. Even the Pennsylvania Ministerium was mostly an informal arrangement centered around the personal authority of Henry Melchior Muhlenberg. With the end of the Revolutionary War, there was a growing sense that new systems of governance were needed, ones that were tailored specifically to the new American context. Muhlenberg himself withdrew from active leadership within the Ministerium in 1781 and died in 1787; though his successors were certainly worthy pastors, they could not claim his personal authority. The age of constitution writing and forming new democratic institutions had begun, and Lutherans would join this trend.

Lutheran organization would move faster after the war, but the process had begun already before the war. When it was formed in 1748, the Pennsylvania Ministerium was mainly a gathering of Lutheran pastors who agreed among themselves about regulating and advancing Lutheran ministry in the colonies. There was little in the way of formal organization, and although lay representatives of the congregations did at times attend the annual meetings, they had little impact on the proceedings. The Ministerium did not even meet between 1754 and 1760. But by the middle of the 1770s, it was clear that a more formal organization would be needed. Reflecting on the 1772 Ministerium meeting, Muhlenberg wrote: "There was also some talk of a better plan and constitutional regulations for future synodical meetings. I used to employ rather general regulations, adapted to the circumstances. . . . However it is right and proper to prepare a constitution which is constantly improved and adapted to circumstances."[4] By 1778, they had developed a new constitution, which was formally transcribed into the records of the Ministerium in 1781.

The second chapter or section of the 1781 constitution formalized the duties of the president of the synod, increasing their scope from simply presiding at the annual meeting to creating a position that specified a set of responsibilities to be exercised during the interim. As such, it formalized the position, but in a number of cases this new enumeration went beyond the customary role, and created a permanent position, not just someone to preside over the yearly meeting. It was parallel to the movement in secular politics to create an executive power within the American government, something hotly debated at the time. The Ministerium president also became, without naming it, a superintendent for all of American Lutheranism, representing a break with the Lutheran leaders at Halle who did not support such an action. The new formal title, "The Fraternal Association of the Lutheran Ministers of North America," implicitly claimed jurisdiction over Lutherans on the entire American continent.

Lay delegates traditionally attended meetings of the ministerium, but their role in the organization was limited. If they had concerns, these would be heard initially by the assembly, but then laypeople were dismissed. During the 1780s, the issue of increased lay involvement was raised, and the minutes of the 1788 meeting state: "A motion of Pastor Voigt was read, to the effect that it was necessary also to receive laymen as members of the Ministerium."[5] The issue was referred to committee, which led eventually to another new constitution in 1792. In this revision, lay delegates were allowed to vote on certain issues and to be present for all the sessions, although their numbers were limited so as not to exceed the number of pastors present. This important action was another step toward the variety of synodical polity that would soon become common among American Lutherans. The synod would be composed of not only pastors, but also representatives of member congregations.

Recognizing the geographical spread of American Lutheranism, the Ministerium created five regional districts at its 1783 meeting, four of which were in Pennsylvania, while a fifth covered New York. The New York district congregations left the Pennsylvania Ministerium in 1786 to form their own independent body, the New York Ministerium. The impetus for this came from Pastor John Christopher Kunze, Muhlenberg's son-in-law, who had taken charge of the New York City congregation in 1784. There was no apparent disagreement between the two groups but, rather, a realization that the distance that the New York pastors had to travel to Pennsylvania was excessive. The New York Ministerium even adopted the essential elements of the 1781 Pennsylvania Ministerium constitution. Organizing the New York Ministerium went slowly, and after the first meeting it did not meet again until 1791.

In its new constitution of 1792, the Pennsylvania Ministerium adopted a new name, the "German Evangelical Lutheran Congregations in Pennsylvania and the Adjacent States," indicative of a more regional scope of the body and of the importance of the congregations. Both of these developments were significant to the group's self-understanding and demonstrated the kind of organization to which they aspired.

Geographical Expansion

It was the policy of the British colonial officials to contain American colonists to the eastern side of the Allegheny Mountains, so as to keep their economic focus on the Atlantic world and to keep from upsetting the Native American tribes. During the Revolutionary War, these tribes were generally allied with the British and made the frontier a dangerous place. But the peace settlement of 1783 that formally ended the Revolutionary War ended British restrictions. The British ceded to the Americans all their territory east of the Mississippi River and south of Canada, leaving only the Spanish in Florida and the French in New Orleans. The peace doubled the territory of the United States, and effectively removed all the restrictions on westward expansion. Jefferson's purchase of the Louisiana Territory from France in 1803 nearly doubled again the size of the United States, which now extended almost to the Pacific Ocean. American settlers streamed westward in search of new lands, creating eight new states by 1820: Kentucky (1792), Tennessee (1796), Ohio (1803), Louisiana (1812), Indiana (1816), Mississippi (1817), Illinois (1818), and Alabama (1819). This expansion went roughly east to west along four corridors: across New York state and the Great Lakes; across Pennsylvania and down the Ohio River; across Virginia and North Carolina into Kentucky and Tennessee; and across the South into Alabama, Mississippi, and Louisiana.

American Lutherans were caught up in this westward expansion and left settled areas and congregations back east to seek out new lands on the frontier. Since Lutherans were numerically strongest in the Mid-Atlantic states, they generally moved west through Pennsylvania and New York, first into western sections of these states, and then into Ohio, Indiana, Illinois, and Michigan. Lutherans in Virginia and North Carolina moved westward through the Cumberland Gap and the Wilderness Road into Kentucky and Tennessee, but their numbers were smaller. Very few southern Lutherans at this time moved into the deep South states of Alabama and Mississippi.

Already by the 1780s and 1790s, Lutherans began moving into the western sections of states such as New York, Pennsylvania, Maryland, Virginia, and North Carolina, in some cases over the mountain ranges in these states. Lutherans moved up the Mohawk Valley and into the Finger Lakes region of New York, where traveling missionaries reported on their settlements in 1819. Substantial numbers of Pennsylvania Lutherans from the eastern parts of the state moved west of the

Susquehanna River, and new congregations were formed as far west as Greenburg and Latrobe. The oldest congregation in western Pennsylvania dates to 1772, and perhaps as many as twenty congregations were formed before 1800. In light of this expansion, the Pennsylvania Ministerium resolved in 1797 to meet every third year in the "western" part of the state, although during this period "west" meant to them nothing further than York, Pennsylvania, or Hagerstown, Maryland. In Virginia, most of the fourteen congregations formed between 1781 and 1800 were located along the far western and southwestern counties of that state, and some Lutherans from Virginia formed two new congregations in Tennessee, at Blountville (1793) and Greenville (1797). Pennsylvania Ministerium minutes from 1790 note that: "A man named Mace, who for some years had been a school teacher in Pennsylvania, had through diligent study acquired a fair knowledge of theology and who at present lives in Kentucky, had asked for a license (to preach) . . ."[6] Since there were no Lutheran pastors in Kentucky, the license was granted. In North Carolina, the same pattern held true: fourteen congregations formed between 1781 and 1800, all of them in counties west of Charlotte and Winston-Salem. New congregational formation was much slower in South Carolina and Georgia.

After 1800, Lutherans flowed in increasing numbers into the West, especially into Ohio, Kentucky, and Tennessee. Between 1800 and 1820, an additional six congregations were formed in western Virginia and seven more in Tennessee. An entire party of Lutherans from the Hebron congregation in Virginia crossed over into Kentucky, along with their pastor, William Carpenter, and formed a church in Boone County in 1806. Ministerium records from 1814 narrate that Carpenter, "after much fighting," left his congregation for "other congregations in Kentucky." The same minutes relate the plea of a group of seventy-two Lutherans near Bardstown, Kentucky, ". . . anxiously petitioning for an evangelical pastor, who is able to preach in the English as well as the German language. They present their deplorable condition and promise adequate support to a worthy pastor."[7] The first two congregations in Indiana were formed in 1810, in the southern and eastern parts of the state.

The area of fastest Lutheran growth, however, was in Ohio, where a sizable number of congregations were formed after 1800. Distance and numbers allowed for the formation of a separate Ohio Special Conference of the Pennsylvania Ministerium in 1812, which by 1818 had become its own separate synod. The minutes of the initial meeting in 1818 mention seventeen pastors and 3,551 congregant members; assuming that each pastor served several congregations, and many other congregations were without pastors, one might easily assume fifty to sixty Lutheran congregations and preaching points in the state by 1820.

The westward movement of these Lutherans pushed pastoral resources, already inadequate and strained, past the breaking point. There were hardly enough Lutheran pastors for the older, stable congregations in the East, let alone for the burgeoning frontier. In many cases, established Lutheran congregations saw their membership numbers dwindle as Lutheran families pulled up stakes and left for the new lands on the western frontier. Just as eastern Lutherans were beginning to form solid Lutheran synods, the challenge was to begin this process all over again in the new states across the mountains.

Emergency situations demand emergency actions, and this necessity was forced on American Lutheran leaders. Facing the twin dilemmas of inadequate numbers of pastors and small frontier congregations that could not support a pastor, even if they could obtain one, Lutherans had to develop new religious leaders for the frontier or risk losing their western members altogether. Some men with basic theological training (often schoolteachers) were designated as catechists, charged to carry out basic religious work within small congregations. A new category of pastors was comprised of licensed candidates: men who were studying for the ordained ministry, but who were not yet ready for ordination. The Ministerium granted these ministerial candidates a license to preach and administer the sacraments in one restricted location, reviewing and relicensing them yearly. Although fully aware that this situation was less than optimal, Lutheran leaders were desperate to get pastors out into the field, though many of these candidates were barely educated before they began their duties. One such pastor who started as a licensate was John Stough, one of the founders of Lutheranism in Ohio. Stough was a wagonmaker who, in 1787, settled his family in the wilderness 160 miles west of Hagerstown, Maryland. Local people soon called on him to perform weddings and other pastoral acts, even though he was not ordained. His wife died on the frontier and, in 1793, he went back to the Ministerium meeting at Philadelphia, where he was licensed as a catechist, and then a year later as a candidate. During his long ministry, he crisscrossed the frontier constantly and developed numerous congregations in Ohio, Western Pennsylvania, Virginia, and Kentucky.

Even these measures were inadequate to meet the needs on the frontiers. The Ministerium commissioned pastors to serve as traveling missionaries, who traveled extensively across the frontier to gather together Lutherans wherever they could be located, and to bring pastoral services to these struggling frontier congregations whenever they could. This work was brutally hard, as traveling conditions and the weather were often wretched; the frontier Lutherans often lived in squalid poverty, but these missionaries pushed on regardless of difficulties. The unsettled nature of the frontier, with its lack of education and religious instruction, was a constant lament. Traveling over one thousand miles through the frontier areas of Virginia in two months of 1813, Pastor Robert Miller observed an almost total lack of organized religion of any kind among the people. The conditions he described were widespread: "The education and habits of the greatest part of the inhabitants are such as to leave but a very slight sense of either moral or religious obligation upon their minds: in consequence there is little or no attention paid to the moral or religious education of children . . ."[8] Yet, other traveling missionaries described an often desperate desire on the part of settlers for religious preaching and sacramental ministry. In his autobiography, Pastor John Stough told of his first year in Ohio:

> My heart sickens within me when I behold the wide waste in our beloved Zion. Children baptized within the pale of the church, crying for spiritual food, or instruction, and all for want of laborers. . . . And many that were truly pious were spiritually starving and wandering. . . . Men came as far as 30 miles and told me their deplorable condition, bade me come and preach the gospel in their houses.[9]

Candidates and mission pastors were required to keep detailed records of their travels and ministerial actions. Stough calculated that in his fifty years of ministry, he had ". . . traveled 100,000 miles, preached in 5 different states. I have tried to preach more than 10,000 times, confirmed in all 1516 people, baptized more than double that. Married 481 couples and attended nearly as many funerals."[10] There were several dozen of these traveling missionaries authorized during the period from 1800 to 1820 who gave devoted service to the Lutheran cause on the frontier.

The Formation of New Synods

The rapid geographic expansion of American Lutherans doomed any idea that some might have had of making the Pennsylvania Ministerium the general organization for all Lutherans in the United States. When most Lutherans lived along the East Coast and within the general radius of Philadelphia, this may have been feasible, but even then such a plan was not practical for Lutherans in the South. Already by 1781, the Pennsylvania Ministerium recognized that distance was an issue and set up five districts within its organization. In 1792, the Ministerium made further concessions to geography by allowing for the formation of "Special Conferences," district meeting of pastors and laymen from distant areas of the Ministerium, such as Virginia and Western Pennsylvania and Ohio. These conference meetings were intended for local business and mutual edification, but were limited in scope. The

Ministerium constitution of 1792 specifically limited their powers: "A special meeting is not permitted under any pretense whatever to enter upon business belonging to the Ministerium, even if the officers of the Synod were present."[11] Two such special conferences were set up, one in Virginia beginning in 1793, and another in Ohio in 1812. One limitation of this approach was that local candidates for ministry would still have to travel to the main synodical meeting for examination and approval, an often arduous journey. Eventually, these special conferences became independent synods in their own right, beginning with the formation of the Ohio Synod in 1818, and the Synod of Maryland and Virginia in 1820.

Other regions of American Lutheranism decided to attempt formation of their own separate and independent organizations. In 1786, New York Lutheran pastors formed their own separate ministerium, not necessarily as a rebuke to Pennsylvania but a recognition that travel was difficult and local issues were pressing. In its formation, the New York Ministerium went beyond Pennsylvania in granting full rights to lay delegates from the congregations, forming a "synod" in the sense that would become the standard for the future.

In the South, it made little sense to consider formal affiliation with the Pennsylvania Ministerium, and local Lutheran pastors slowly developed plans for their own organizations. The first such attempt was in South Carolina in 1787, with the formation of the *Unio Ecclesiastica*, or Union of Churches, an organization of German congregations, both Lutheran and Reformed. Consisting of fifteen congregations and seven pastors, this group met and adopted a constitution in 1788. It continued to meet for several years, but eventually this early attempt collapsed. In North Carolina, pastors had been meeting informally since the 1790s, but it was not until 1803 that the North Carolina Synod was organized, which also included pastors from South Carolina. Theological debates within the North Carolina Synod led to a separation of some pastors and congregations in 1820 and the formation of the Tennessee Synod. Although these two bodies took separate geographical names, they generally overlapped the same territory, leading to the first situation of competing Lutheran synods (a situation that would become common in the nineteenth century).

The Language Transition to English

Since there were no English-speaking immigrant Lutherans, and since all Lutheran immigrants spoke Dutch, Swedish, or German as their first language, the use of English by Lutherans evolved over decades. With English as the dominant language in America, its use by immigrants was quickly viewed as necessary and perhaps inevitable, and they probably soon developed a rough working knowledge of this language, especially in order to interact with the "English" section of society. Yet, as with many immigrant groups, Lutherans tended to use their immigrant language among themselves as long as possible, especially in their homes and congregations. Language was itself a means whereby immigrants, a minority in a strange land, could maintain their ethnic separation from the dominant culture, a sense of ethnic solidarity, and the deep sense of community in which they belonged, were understood, and could express their faith.

Yet, the process of assimilation into the dominant culture was relentless, and generations of Lutherans born in the new world rapidly transitioned to the use of English and pressed for wider usage of that language even in worship and preaching. This trend posed a huge dilemma for Lutheran leaders at the time. Should they push to maintain the European languages, for the sake of the older generations and newly arrived immigrants, or should they move to English for the sake of newer generations? There was also the question of how to develop Lutheranism in English (liturgy, hymns, catechisms, and other materials), especially when many of the older pastors were limited in their English-language skills. To many Lutherans, it was an open question as to whether it was even possible to "do" Lutheranism in English. They had few models for how to manage this transition, and they were deeply dissatisfied with the perceived inadequacies of English-language Protestantism.

The experience of the Swedish Lutherans on the Delaware, who were furthest along in this transition, gave little reason for optimism for adopting English but remaining Lutheran. Already by the early eighteenth century, Swedish Lutherans in America transitioned toward the primary use of English, individually and in their congregations. With the complete end of new Swedish immigration after the 1650s, the language transition proceeded quickly. Early in the eighteenth century, there were requests to Sweden to send Lutheran pastors with a facility in English, and by 1754 some 76 percent of members in the Swedish congregations could use English (61 percent were bilingual) and only 24 percent could not understand English.[12] Intermarriage with the local English population complicated this situation. Already by 1742, the congregation in Pennsneck, New Jersey, decided to hold services exclusively in English, and though the other congregations continued Swedish services, the use of English in worship was on the rise.

The last Swedish pastor in America, Nicholas Collin, remarked in 1791 that the Swedish language was "dead," and in their letter of separation from the consistory at Uppsala in 1786, the Swedish congregations explained: ". . . it will be entirely unnecessary for future appointments to take place from Sweden of a minister to serve these congregations . . . as the Swedish Tongue is almost entirely extinct in Pennsylvania."[13] These congregations continued the idea of a Swedish ethnicity for some time, but the language was lost. The Swedish congregations and pastors had long had a close relationship with the local Anglican pastors and congregations, and the interchange of pastors between the two was common, especially given high pastoral vacancy rates in both groups. When the Swedes began to use English, they had no Lutheran theological resources in English, and so they turned to use of the Anglican *Book of Common Prayer*. Although the Swedish Lutherans had generally good relations with their German Lutheran counterparts, they expressed little interest in joining the Pennsylvania Ministerium. With no new Swedish pastors after the 1780s, the Swedish Lutheran congregations on the Delaware began gradually to move into the Protestant Episcopal Church.

The language transition for the German Lutherans had a much different trajectory, however. The struggle over the use of German in the Lutheran congregations and the transition to the use of English were much more conflicted than what the Swedes experienced, but did result eventually in the formation of an English-language Lutheranism in the United States. The conflicts were sharp during this period, but the transition to English was inevitable, although at different rates in different places. The transition to English happened most quickly in South Carolina and New York, where English became the official language of the Ministerium in 1807. Change also happened more rapidly in the urban areas, such as Philadelphia, and more slowly in some rural areas of Pennsylvania, especially where the German population was a majority.

Henry Muhlenberg recognized early in his career that knowledge of English was valuable to his ministry, and he learned English well enough to preach and converse in it. The language transition did not go smoothly for all, and often produced a third, hybrid version of the two languages. Muhlenberg wrote in his journal in 1772: "The old Germans, who are otherwise discerning, spoil the English language and in time produce a third language, which is neither English nor German. . . . Consequently the German preachers, unless they make some acquaintance with the English language, very readily fall into the third language . . ."[14] Often, there were was a mixing of the languages; one older pastor remarked: "Yah, English fuer gescheft, aber Duetsch for Gottesdienst ['Yes, English for business, but German for worship']."[15] The need for English-language catechetical instruction among the young led to various translations of Luther's Small Catechism into English: by Swedish pastors as early as 1749; by Pastor John Christopher Kunze in New York in 1784; and in Pennsylvania by Pastor Christian Endress in 1805.

Resistance, however, came from other Lutheran leaders, worried that the transition to English would be the death of Lutheranism in America. Some felt that English was simply not a suitable language for the complexities of Lutheran theology, while others feared that the adoption of English would dilute Lutheran identity to the point where it would be indistinguishable from the "English" Protestant denominations surrounding them. Some found the English language personally distasteful. Traveling missionary Paul Henkel observed in a letter of 1812, "I must also at times preach in English, since I cannot avoid it, but it is very unpleasant to me."[16] Defenders of German were divided by two distinctly different motivations. One group wished to retain German as a confessional bulwark against religious rationalism and Deism, which they saw as mainly resulting from English-language Protestantism. Another group wished to maintain German as a means of continuing ecumenical relations with the Reformed and Moravians, a sentiment strongest among rural union congregations.

The Pennsylvania Ministerium and many of its leaders were at the forefront of the struggle to maintain German. In 1805, the Ministerium adopted a clause that German be used exclusively for its proceedings, and in 1812, it declared: "No language other than German shall be publically preached in our German churches without the consent of the Church Council and a majority of . . . the members of the congregation which owns the church."[17] This statement reflected conflicts raging within Lutheran congregations over this issue. At St. Michael congregation in Philadelphia, leading English-speaking members, including Peter Muhlenberg, sought to allow English preaching and instruction in the congregation. They were strongly opposed by Pastor J. H. C. Helmuth and, in 1806, narrowly lost a congregational vote on the issue. English partisans withdrew from the congregation to form St. John's English Lutheran Church, and litigation between the two groups continued for years.

But the march of English could not be held off indefinitely, at least if Lutheranism was to survive in America. Lutheran leaders received alarming reports from traveling missionaries on the frontier, to the effect that scattered Lutherans without pastoral leadership were being absorbed into "English" denominations such as the Baptists and Methodists. Others deserted Lutheranism for more prominent American denominations, such as the Presbyterians and Episcopalians. A high-profile defection came with the decision of William Augustus Muhlenberg to join the Episcopal priesthood in 1820; he was the son of Frederick and grandson of Henry. There is no telling how many Lutherans joined English-language denominations during this period, but contemporary anecdotal accounts suggest the numbers were substantial.

Theological Struggles and Controversies

As already noted, this time period saw two quite different theological trends, Deism and rational religion on one hand, and the Arminian-powered revivalism of the

Second Great Awakening on the other. Lutherans attempted to navigate between these two very different theological movements while trying to establish their own theological identities, both as Lutherans and as citizens of the new American republic. Some of the struggles over language had deep overtones of these theological conflicts, with the belief of some that the maintenance of German would insulate Lutherans from Deism or revivalism. But regardless of language, Lutherans had to face these issues.

The impact of Deism and religious rationalism was mostly an external threat to American Lutheranism. The closest these movements came to finding a Lutheran proponent was New York pastor and synodical leader Frederick Quitman. Born in Germany in 1760 and educated at Halle, he was initially sent as a pastor to the Dutch island of Curacao in the Caribbean. He arrived in New York to take a congregation in 1795 and quickly became established in the New York Ministerium, of which he was president from 1807 to 1825. His theology represented the religious rationalism of his teacher Johannes Semler, prevalent in Germany during that time even at Halle, which held that a combination of human reason and divine revelation was the key to true religion. At the request of the Ministerium, in 1814 Quitman produced an English-language instructional work entitled *Evangelical Catechism*. While it made little reference to Luther or the Small Catechism, it did make many references to the role of human reason and morality. In one of his answers to the question of human knowledge of God, Quitman wrote: "God has graciously enabled us by means of reason and revelation to obtain a degree of knowledge of his glorious perfections, sufficient to satisfy our present wants, and to convince us that we are nearly allied to him."[18] Although his views seemed to some, then and now, as steps down the road to Deism, they represented a fairly mild form of religious rationalism, more problematic for its lack of traditional Lutheran theological foci.

Although Lutheran leaders worried aloud about Deism and rationalism, the more pervasive threat was "religious enthusiasm" or "experiential religion," those forms of religious revivalism brewing in the camp meetings on the frontier and being introduced back into settled areas of the East during the Second Great Awakening (1790s–1810s). This direct appeal to the religious emotions of the listeners pushed listeners for an immediate conversion experience; it was an effective tool to break through the rough shell of the frontier, but some Lutherans saw it as antithetical to traditional Lutheran worship and preaching. True, Muhlenberg and the other Pietist Lutheran pastors of the eighteenth century spoke at length about the need for conversions and a "true and living faith," and welcomed the revivals of Whitefield in the 1740s. But this new revivalism was another thing altogether, as it was completely lacking traditional Lutheran understandings of preaching and the sacraments. This new revivalism was dangerous because it was so effective, and many Lutherans, especially those on the frontier without congregations and pastors, were caught up in the revivals and became Methodists or Baptists.

The Lutheran pastors who most directly experienced these revivals were the traveling missionaries, such as Stough, Miller, Henkel, and others. They were often not sure of what to make of these revivals, as the raw and immediate power of the camp meetings was hard to assess accurately. Pastor Carl Storch in North Carolina was caught up in the great revivals of 1800–1801, and reported to a colleague in Germany in 1803: "Christians of every denomination assemble themselves in the forest, numbering four, six, and sometimes ten thousand persons; they erect tents, sing, pray, and preach, day and night, for five, six, and eight days. I have been an eyewitness to scenes . . . which I cannot explain."[19] Storch reported that the pastors were divided in their opinions, some thinking it the work of God and some of the Devil; he candidly admitted that the experience caused him "no little uneasiness." Many lay Lutherans pressed their pastors for a judgment about these revivals, asking, "Must we not also experience the same thing in order to be saved?" One observer noted, "The German ministers were at first divided in their opinion on the subject."[20] Some Lutheran pastors participated in these frontier revivals, believing them to be the effective work of God in the face of lawlessness and immorality on the frontier. But other Lutheran officials were deeply worried about these revivals. Typical was the charge of the Pennsylvania Ministerium to traveling missionary Pastor Paul Henkel, in 1811, that he should "have no dealings with camp-meetings, if he should find such departures from our Evangelical ways."[21] Yet, as Lutheranism moved west, and the frontier revivals expanded back to the east, Lutherans could not avoid this religious phenomenon.

The combined problems of Deism and religious rationalism, revivalistic enthusiasm, and the language transition confounded Lutheran leaders, who tried to address them theologically. While they believed in formal theological training and commitments, they wished to avoid the rationalism that seemed to be sweeping Lutheranism in Germany. Although they were confident in the necessity of Pietism's emphasis on "true conversion" and moral conviction, they sought to avoid the excesses of Arminian revivalism. The challenge of language meant that while maintaining the German language could assure certain traditions of worship and theology, unless there was accommodation to English, many from Lutheran backgrounds would find ways to worship in English, if not in Lutheran congregations, then in others. The road to creating an English-language Lutheranism that retained theological integrity came through the translation of traditional Lutheran emphases into good English and the adaptation of traditional Lutheran forms of worship and practice into the arena of American culture.

Some historians have pointed to signs in this period which seem to indicate that Lutherans in America were moving away from a strong commitments to traditional Lutheran theology; evidence includes Quitman's *Catechism*, the 1792 Pennsylvania Ministerium constitution, which omitted references to the Lutheran confessions, or the traditions of local cooperation with German Reformed in Pennsylvania and North Carolina, and with Episcopalians in New York. Evidence of an emerging "confessional crisis" within American Lutheranism can be mitigated by other developments that show a continuation of traditional Lutheran practice and identity. In the South Carolina Union of Churches, Lutheran and Reformed, the minutes in 1788 read that "all the Evangelical Lutheran pastors were sworn on the Symbolical books," and when some pastors in Pennsylvania petitioned for a joint Lutheran and Reformed hymnal, the Ministerium, in 1815, resolved "that it were best not to have anything to do with the same," stating that the synod alone could authorize hymnals.[22] The judgment of one historian of this period is that "in general, the picture seems to indicate that the confessions were taken for granted rather than being deliberately ignored."[23]

One evidence of the attempts to maintain a Lutheran identity, at least in some form, is found in the large numbers of catechisms printed during this period, both in German and in English. There were twenty-four different catechisms printed by Lutherans from 1781 to 1820, thirteen of them in English. The influential catechism of the Pennsylvania Ministerium, first printed in 1785, was reprinted in seventy different editions up until 1857.[24] While the Lutheran character of some of these publications can be faulted (most notably the one by Quitman), on the whole most of these catechisms were based on Martin Luther's Small Catechism. Furthermore, the whole emphasis on catechetical instruction itself demonstrated a Lutheran approach to educating Christians in faith, as opposed to the types of instantaneous conversions prevalent in revivalism.

One chief proponent of this catechetical approach was Pastor Paul Henkel, a notable Lutheran frontier missionary pastor of this time. Based in New Market, Virginia, Henkel was the founding patriarch of a clerical dynasty that became prominent in nineteenth-century Lutheranism. Henkel had first-hand knowledge both of the religious and moral crises of the frontier and of the limitations of camp-meeting revivalism. In 1804, he bought a printing press and produced a wide variety of Lutheran materials, notably catechisms and hymnals in both German and English, for use in frontier congregations. Henkel was an advocate of a more formal adherence to the Lutheran confessions than were others in his area, especially in the North Carolina and Virginia synods, with whom he soon came into conflict. Under Henkel's influence, the Virginia Special Conference in 1805 printed the doctrinal articles of the Augsburg Confession in its minutes, "for the benefit of the congregations," to which Henkel himself added "an instructive introduction to the Augsburg Confession."[25] Because of his conflicts with Lutheran leaders in North Carolina over confessional issues, Henkel and his allies founded the Tennessee Synod in 1820 as a competitive confessional Lutheran synod in this region.

Education and Pastoral Formation

From the Reformation forward, Lutherans placed a strong emphasis on the education of all Christians, with literacy being an important element of appropriating the Word of God as presented in the proclamation of the Gospel. Lutherans were urged to read the Bible and other devotional works, to study the catechisms as a means of coming to a mature faith, and to participate in the elements of worship through psalmbooks and hymnals. Luther urged the development of parish schools for the education of people of all classes, and this catechetical form of education became standard through Lutheran territories. This tradition was carried across the Atlantic and became a standard in most of the Lutheran congregations, at least in those congregations with the resources to provide such an education.

The parish school was usually a part-time venture, operated around the demands of farm work and meeting primarily during the winter months. These schools combined a basic education in literacy and other useful subjects with a strong dose of moral and religious education. Although these schools were occasionally taught by local pastors, the preferred pattern was to hire a parish schoolteacher for the position. This was usually a young man with some education in Europe who had come to America to seek employment, which was often very poorly paid. That there was a decent supply of such teachers among the Lutherans in colonial America is indicated by the number of requests by congregations without pastors who sought to have their schoolteacher licensed to provide basic ministerial functions. In several cases, these teachers became licensed candidates for the ordained ministry, although some teachers skipped this whole process and claimed ordained status for themselves without any external confirmation.

Following the Revolutionary War, German Lutherans placed an increased emphasis on the parish schools, both as a means to further Christian and Lutheran identity among their members, but also as a means of defending and continuing the German language. The Pennsylvania Ministerium constantly referenced the need for German schools, and in an 1815 printed address to its congregations made a plea for their support. By the end of the Revolutionary War there were, by one count, 139 church schools with approximately five thousand students.[26] But many of these parish schools eventually closed, both because of the increasing use of English among the Lutherans, as well as the gradual implementation of free public schools. Catechetical instruction remained a staple of parish life, however.

Lutheran leaders recognized early on that the primary reliance on a supply of European-trained clergy for Lutheran congregations was a doomed strategy. Despite the fact that some of these pastors provided excellent leadership for American Lutheran congregations, there certainly were never enough university-trained pastors willing to cross the Atlantic to meet the needs. And the transition to the American religious situation was difficult for many Europeans who were used to the forms and procedures of the state churches, and for whom English-language ministry was difficult. To provide enough Lutheran pastors for the new United States, Lutheran leaders had to identify and train pastors from within their own congregations, without the system of university training that was normal in Europe. This meant, however, that the vast majority of new Lutheran pastors would not be classically trained, as they were in Europe, lacking the heavy complement of classical languages (Greek, Latin, and Hebrew) and theological disciplines.

Without universities or seminaries in America, most Lutheran pastors learned their profession as "apprentices" to established pastors. Candidates for ministry were identified, and they then would "read" theology with a senior pastor and assist him with the care of several small congregations in the area. This process of education took a number of years, especially if the candidate had little in the way of formal education, and was rather uneven in terms of quality. Once they were considered ready, the pastoral candidates would present themselves for examination to the ministerium or synod. These examinations were intensive and took several days during the annual convention. Synodical leaders attempted to maintain high standards for their candidates, especially in the area of preaching. The Pennsylvania Ministerium minutes of 1795 include reservations about the homiletical skills of that year's candidates: "That some of them might be admonished to aim more at edification and popularity than at oratorical art, for if they preach sermons like the outlines presented, their congregations are to be sincerely pitied."[27] Yet, with the intense need for pastors, especially on the frontier, synodical leaders were often forced to license catechists and candidates for ministry who had very little in the way of formal education. Pastor John Stough, the traveling missionary and a key Lutheran leader in Ohio, had so little education that his local pastor in Pennsylvania initially dissuaded him from seeking the ministry. When he moved to the frontier, he was pressed into service as a pastor with no training or credentials, and only later became a catechist and candidate for the ministry. Eventually, he became a pastor and even supervised candidates of his own for ministry.

Although this system did produce pastors for the ministry, Lutheran leaders were often concerned about the often uneven quality of their education, and sought the means to improve ministerial education and training though the establishment of schools by which to accomplish this. The first to attempt such a school was John Christopher Kunze, who had been well trained in Europe and who had taught there in a classical academy. Although he was a full-time pastor in Philadelphia, in 1773 Kunze opened a classical "Seminarium" to provide a rigorous education for young men who might wish to study for the ministry. But when the British occupied Philadelphia in 1777, they seized the congregational buildings (including the school), which brought this initial effort to an abrupt conclusion. After the British withdrew, and the Pennsylvania legislature chartered the University of Pennsylvania in 1779, Kunze taught there, but the school attracted very few potential candidates for the Lutheran ministry. After Kunze's departure for New York in 1784, his colleagues J. H. C. Helmuth and John Frederick Schmidt also taught there, with much the same results. Kunze also taught classical languages at Columbia University in New York for many years, but results there were little different from Philadelphia.

These two initial ventures seemed to indicate that the university model of providing pastors was not going to work very well in the new United States. With the new climate in the United States after the Revolutionary War, it was also doubtful whether public-private arrangements, such as at the University of Pennsylvania, would work well or even pass political scrutiny. In 1774, in reference to the plans of his son-in-law Kunze, Henry Muhlenberg sketched out a different vision for theological education, a school where "catechists could be trained and made competent and willing to teach school during the week and preach a sermon on Sundays and festival days." Further, he proposed: "It would not be necessary to torment such candidates with foreign languages . . . it would be sufficient if they possess native intelligence, a compendious knowledge and experience of the marrow and sap of theology . . . a robust constitution . . . and pre-eminently, a heart that loves the Savior of the world and His sheep and lambs."[28] This idea, of a practical mission school along the lines of those at Halle and elsewhere, became the general outline of future Lutheran ministerial preparation in the United States.

Two initial attempts to provide such education took place. The first was Franklin College in Pennsylvania, organized through the cooperative efforts of German Lutheran and Reformed pastors in 1787 and located near Lancaster. This school never achieved much success due to limited financial assets and general disinterest from its German constituencies. Subsequently, it merged with Marshall College in 1849 and became solely a Reformed institution. The second attempt was in New York, through a bequest from Pastor John Christopher Hartwick, who, upon his death in 1796, bequeathed his extensive land holdings to the New York Ministerium for the purposes of establishing a school for the preparation of pastors and of missionaries to the Native Americans. The new Hartwick Seminary wandered from place to place through its first years, and was barely in existence by 1811, when the Ministerium decided to reestablish the institution near Cooperstown, New York. This institution, the first Lutheran seminary in the United States, continued for almost 150 years, until its closure in 1941. Neither of these two institutions were very successful, however, in producing anything near the number of pastoral candidates necessary.

Worship and Hymnody

Another indication of the growing self-confidence of Lutherans in America during this period was their production of worship materials for their own use, materials that reflect their Lutheran heritage, but which were rooted in a new American context. During the last part of the eighteenth century, American Lutherans produced hymnals and liturgies in German to replace the multiplicity of European versions that the immigrants brought with them. Toward the end of that century, and into the nineteenth, they also began to produce Lutheran hymnals and liturgies in the English language, the first time that this happened. These efforts had two general purposes: first, to provide materials appropriate to the American context, and, second, to provide a uniformity of worship that was intended to draw these scattered congregations together and to strengthen their common identity.

Henry Muhlenberg had long wished to develop a German-language hymnal for the Lutheran congregations in the Pennsylvania Ministerium, but the crush of his workload did not allowed him the time to accomplish this. After withdrawing from public leadership in the Ministerium in 1781, he finally organized and directed the formation of a new hymnal, which finally appeared in 1786, the year before his death. The new hymnal, the *Erbauliche Lieder-Sammlung*, was the first official Lutheran hymnal in the United States and was widely used for many years. The model liturgy of 1748, which had circulated unprinted for almost forty years, was also revised and printed with the new hymnal. Many hoped that this new hymnal would become the standard for all American Lutherans, and, indeed, the New York Ministerium did adopt the *Erbauliche Lieder-Sammlung* in 1796, but no other groups did. There were other German-language hymnals published after this, including ones by a group in North Carolina in 1797, by Paul Henkel in Virginia in 1810, and a joint Lutheran-Reformed hymnal published in Baltimore in 1817.

The language transition, however, pushed Lutherans toward the production of Lutheran hymnals and liturgies in English. Since the Pennsylvania Ministerium was focused primarily on German materials, these first English Lutheran hymnals came from elsewhere. Three early English hymnals came from New York, including the *Hymn and Prayer-Book* by John Christopher Kunze (1795), the *Collection of Evangelical Hymns* by George Strebeck (1797), and *A Choice Selection of Evangelical Hymns* by Ralph Williston (1806). Even Paul Henkel, hardly fond of anything English, published an English-language hymnal in 1810, recognizing that there was a desperate need for such a book on the frontier. When the New York Ministerium published an English hymnal by Frederick Quitman in 1814, it received widespread use.

As in the colonial period, the centerpiece of the Lutheran worship service at this time was the sermon, for which both pastors and laypeople had high expectations. The sermon was to engage the listeners and draw them deeper into Christian faith and holy living. Especially on the frontier people would come for miles on a Sunday to hear a good Lutheran sermon. The liturgies of this period generally simplified the traditional Lutheran liturgies and the schedule of the church year. Many reasons are advanced to explain this development, including rationalism and revivalism and the needs of worship on the frontier; yet it is hard to determine one particular or dominant reason for this. As with the colonial period, the sacrament of the Lord's Supper was offered with great solemnity, but not very often, perhaps one to four times a year in the typical congregation. When communion was offered, it was preceded by private confession with the pastor before the worship service, and pastors attempted to maintain a strict communion discipline, with mixed success. But during this period (1781–1820), the mobility of both pastors and laypeople worked against the enforcement of church discipline, and these practices generally went into remission.

Conclusion

This was a period of great transition for Lutherans in the new United States. The old colonial patterns, and the leaders that had formed them, were passing away, and Lutherans had to develop new structures and methods of meeting a rapidly changing world. When most American Lutherans still lived along the Atlantic coast, informal ties to each other and to European leaders made sense. But first the Revolutionary War disrupted these patterns, and then the postwar geographic expansion pushed Lutherans toward the frontier. There was no replacement for Henry Muhlenberg, whose personal and unifying authority was recognized from Nova Scotia to Georgia, so Lutherans had to develop new forms of independent synodical organization to organize and expand the American Lutheran church. New habits of democracy and democratic organization led Lutheran leaders to recognize the voice of laypeople within the synods. And the relentless transition to the use of

English foreshadowed a day when English would become the dominant language of Lutheran worship and theology. Just how much religious and theological "freight" was riding on these changes would be debated in coming years.

Notes

1. Theodore Tappert, "The Church's Infancy, 1650–1790," in E. Clifford Nelson, ed., *The Lutherans in North America* (Philadelphia: Fortress Press, 1975), 36.

2. Frederick L. Weis, *The Colonial Churches and Colonial Clergy of the Middle and Southern Colonies, 1607–1776* (Lancaster, MA: Society of Descendants of Colonial Clergy, 1938), 18.

3. Tappert, "The Church's Infancy," 37.

4. Henry Melchior Muhlenberg, *The Journals of Henry Melchior Muhlenberg*, trans. Theodore Tappert and John Doberstein, September 29, 1772, vol. 2(Philadelphia: Muhlenberg, 1942), 515.

5. "Minutes of the Forty-First Convention, 1788," in *Documentary History of the Evangelical Lutheran Ministerium* (Philadelphia: Board of Publication of the General Council, 1898), 223.

6. "Minutes of the Forty-Third Convention, 1790," in ibid., 232.

7. "Minutes of the Sixty-Seventh Convention, 1814," in ibid., 465.

8. *The Journals of the Reverend Robert Johnstone Miller, Lutheran Missionary in Virginia, 1811 and 1813*, ed. William E. Wright, VMHR, 61:141–66, quoted in William E. Eisenberg, *The Lutheran Church in Virginia, 1717–1962* (Roanoke: Trustees of the Virginia Synod, 1962), 98.

9. *The Autobiography of John Stough*, quoted in C. V. Sheatsley, *History of the Joint Synod of Ohio* (Columbus: Lutheran Book Concern, 1919), 29.

10. Ibid., 35.

11. "Constitution of 1792," in *Documentary History*, 259.

12. Hans Norman, "The New Sweden Colony and the Continued Existence of Swedish and Finnish Ethnicity," in Carol Hoffecker, et al., eds, *New Sweden in America* (Newark, DE: University of Delaware Press, 1995), 206.

13. "Letter, Wicaco Vestry to the Archbishop, June 16, 1786," in the Archives of the Uppsala Consistory, Sweden, quoted in Daniel Lindmark, *Ecclesia Plantanda: Swedishness in Colonial America*, Kulturens Frontlinjer 52 (Umeå, Sweden: n.p., 2005), 148–49.

14. Henry Melchior Muhlenberg, *The Journals of Henry Melchior Muhlenberg*, trans. Theodore Tappert and John Doberstein, September 29, 1772, vol. 2 (Philadelphia: Muhlenberg, 1946), 515.

15. William Frederick Ulery, *History of the Southern Conference* (Greensburg, PA: Church Register, 1902), 76.

16. "Letter, Paul Henkel to Henry Muhlenberg, April 9, 1812," in Richard Bauer, ed., *The Letters of Paul Henkel* (N.p.: Lutheran Historical Conference, 2003), 10.

17. "Minutes of the Sixty-Fifth Convention, 1812," in *Documentary History*, 438.

18. Frederick Quitman, *Evangelical Catechism*. New York, 1814, p. 9, quoted in Harry Kreider, *History of the United Lutheran Synod of New York and New England*, vol. 1 (Philadelphia: Muhlenberg, 1954), 44.

19. "Letter, Rev. Carl Storch to Rev. Dr. Velthusen, February 25, 1803," in G. D. Bernheim, *History of the German Settlements and of the Lutheran Church in North and South Carolina* (Philadelphia: The Lutheran Bookstore, 1872), 351.

20. Paul Henkel, "Report to the Virginia Conference, 1806," in ibid., 353.

21. "Minutes of the Sixty-Fourth Convention, 1811," in *Documentary History*, 428.

22. "Proceedings of the Corpus Ecclesiasticum in South Carolina, Actum, January 8, 1788," in Bernheim, *History of the German Settlements*, 301; "Minutes of the Sixty-Eighth Convention, 1815," in *Documentary History*, 476.

23. H. George Anderson, "The Early National Period," in Nelson, ed., *Lutherans in North America*, 93.

24. Arthur C. Repp Sr., *Luther's Catechism Comes to America*, ATLA Monograph Series 18 (Metuchen, NJ: Scarecrow, 1982).

25. "Minutes of the Virginia Special Conference, October 6 and 7, 1805," quoted in C. W. Cassell, et al., eds., *History of the Lutheran Church in Virginia and East Tennessee* (Strasburg, VA: Shenandoah Pub. House, 1930), 86.

26. Abdel Ross Wentz, *A Basic History of Lutheranism in America*, rev. ed. (Philadelphia: Muhlenberg, 1964), 57.

27. "Minutes of the Forty-Eighth Convention, 1795," in *Documentary History*, 280.

28. Muhlenberg, "Journal entry for October 13, 1774," *Journals*, vol. 2 (Philadelphia: Muhlenberg, 1946), 586–87.

Excursus 5

"Father" Adam Keffer
and Early Canadian Lutheranism

Early North American Lutherans often formed congregations on their own initiative, well ahead of the pastors who would come to serve them. These lay Lutherans were devoted to their religious tradition, and often would go to great lengths to engage a pastor to serve them. Perhaps the most dramatic example of this is the example of several small congregations in Ontario, when Adam Keffer, a lay leader of some Lutherans near Toronto, walked twice to Pennsylvania, in 1849 and 1850, in order to find a Lutheran pastor for his congregation. This was a round-trip journey of over five hundred miles, undertaken in difficult spring weather, when "Father" Keffer was over sixty years old.

German Lutherans started coming to Canada in the eighteenth century. There were Lutheran congregations started in Nova Scotia in the 1750s, which were reinforced by "Loyalist" American Lutherans who went north during the Revolutionary War. In 1793, a group of 350 German Lutherans, who had originally settled in New York, crossed the Great Lakes and founded settlements in Ontario, outside of Toronto. They had been unable to find land in New York, and accepted a generous offer from the governor in Ontario for 64,000 acres.

This area was wilderness; the group had great trouble reaching the area, and further trouble in settling there. But they persevered, and founded a number of small Lutheran congregations. These Lutherans had brought a pastor along with them, but he remained for only a few years before returning to Germany. After this, the fledgling congregations were occasionally served by regular Lutheran pastors, but there were long periods of vacancy in between.

In early North America, there were never enough pastors to go around, and this was especially true on the frontier. In desperation, congregations often had to resort to whatever kinds of pastors they could find, and there were many imposters running around claiming to be pastors when they really were not. Carl Cronmiller, a historian of Canadian Lutheranism, wrote, "These men may be described as clerical tramps, some of who were discharged Army officers or schoolteachers, imposters who pretended to be ordained clergymen."[1] These early Canadian Lutherans suffered from abuse at the hands of several such irregular pastors, who almost destroyed these congregations. In desperation, some Lutheran congregations were lured away and joined the Anglican Church.

In 1849, some of the remaining members of Zion Lutheran Church in Maple, Ontario, sent one of their elders, Adam Keffer, the son of one of the original founders of the congregation, to the United States to find them a pastor. Keffer set out walking for Pennsylvania and, tradition has it, carried his shoes most of the way (to save them from getting worn out). Eventually, Keffer was directed to a meeting of a new Lutheran organization, the Pittsburgh Synod, which was meeting in the spring of 1849 in Klecknerville, Pennsylvania. One of the members of the synod, Rev. William Passavant, discovered Father Keffer walking barefoot in a garden at the edge of the village, and invited him to the synodical meeting. Once at the meeting, Keffer gave an impassioned appeal to the group for a pastor and for financial assistance.

The young Pittsburgh Synod (only four years old) sent one of its pastors to Ontario that summer to survey the field, but there was no immediate aid for the Canadian Lutherans beyond this. The next year, in the spring of 1850, the Pittsburgh Synod met in Pittsburgh and, to the astonishment of all, Adam Keffer showed up again, having walked over 250 miles to reach the meeting. He delivered the same impassioned pleas as the year before, and this time got results. As the synodical newspaper, *The Missionary*, records it, "The interviews of this aged patriarch with the Synod, and his agonizing entreaties for someone to come over and help them, went to the heart of everyone, and awakened an interest for the mission cause never before felt."[2]

This time, Father Keffer's prayers were answered, and a series of Lutheran pastors from the Pittsburgh Synod began long and successful ministries in Ontario. In the next decade, several dozen congregations were reactivated or formed. By 1853, these congregations in Ontario were organized into the Canada Conference of the Pittsburgh Synod, an event that marks the first Lutheran synodical organization in Canada itself, and the oldest forerunner of the current Evangelical Lutheran Church in Canada.

All this was possible because one old man would not stand by and see his congregation die for lack of a good pastor. In current language you could say that he "walked the walk," as well as "talked the talk."

Notes

1. Carl R. Cronmiller, *A History of the Lutheran Church in Canada*, vol. 1 (N.p.: Evangelical Lutheran Synod of Canada, 1961), 130.
2. *The Missionary*, June 1850, quoted in ibid., 135–36.

Chapter 6

EXPANSION AND CONFLICT, 1820–1855

B y 1820 or so, the initial outlines of American Lutheran structures were becoming evident, as the traditions of colonial Lutheranism were becoming formed into a genuine, English-speaking Lutheranism, adapted to the conditions of a newly independent United States. For the most part, Lutherans in America had cast off their ties to European authorities, adopted and adapted to the pluralism and voluntary religion of their new country, and begun to develop institutions and traditions of their own. But these kinds of adaptive moves are always transitory, as both the situations and the solutions themselves are works in progress and constantly changing. So, in the next period, from 1820 to 1855, Lutherans continued to face new situations and developed new strategies for dealing with the evolving American context.

An Evolving America

The new American republic was still evolving in the early nineteenth century. The United States was a young country, with a raw, restless energy that was evident in the events of the time. Having broken with Europe and now beginning to develop its own institutions and traditions, Americans were coming to terms with the sheer size and scope of their new territory. Adding the Louisiana Purchase in 1803 stretched the country to almost the Pacific Coast, but seemingly this was not enough, and the United States added Texas, California, and the American Southwest to its territory as a result of conflicts with Mexico. The expansion of settlements in the new territories continued and even accelerated; at one point in this period it was estimated that the line marking the frontier was moving westward at a rate of over fifteen miles a year. Starting with twenty-two states in 1820, the United States added an additional nine states to the Union by 1850, including Maine (1820), Missouri (1821), Arkansas (1836), Michigan (1837), Texas (1845), Iowa and Florida (1846), Wisconsin (1848), and California (1850). The population of the United States grew from 4 million people in 1790, to 9.6 million in 1820, and to 23 million by 1850.

The United States developed in many ways beyond geography. In politics, the institutions of government were formed and reformed along populist lines. The triumph of Jacksonian democracy in 1828 shook up the young country, allowing for common people to have more direct political influence on government. In a series of precedent-setting decisions, the American judiciary system defined itself and set forth its claims of independence from the other branches of government. Even though the Jacksonians wanted to maintain Jefferson's vision of a rural country dominated by farmers and small artisans with very limited government, the advent of the industrial revolution transformed America. Industries and cities were mutually necessary, and both grew rapidly during this time, bringing with them a parallel growth in government institutions to administer and organize this expansion.

It was in communications and transportation, however, that United States was most greatly transformed during this time. The rapidly expanding nation necessitated new means to draw its population together, to inform them, and to create markets for agricultural and industrial goods. The development of better ocean-going ships meant that hundreds of thousands of immigrants came to the United States from Europe every decade. Steamships, canals, and railroads tied the country together in ways that were unimaginable even decades earlier and created new internal and international markets. The explosion in the scope and speed of communications created new platforms for information and opinion. The development of a regular postal system was foundational, and the invention and implementation of a telegraph system meant instantaneous communication across hundreds of miles. The explosion of print media, especially newspapers and journals, provided another important means of national communication and debate.

All this growth, however, inevitably led to social and political conflict, with competing groups and areas of the country struggling with one another. The overriding conflict of the day was the growing national debate about slavery. This debate grew increasingly intense and polarized over these decades, and slavery emerged as the dominant factor in almost every political and cultural issue. White northerners slowly eliminated slavery from their states, and even began to push for its elimination throughout the entire country. In the South, slavery took on renewed economic importance, as southerners looked for new markets and new horizons by expanding slavery into the western territories, which many northerners vehemently opposed. National political life was virtually paralyzed by this debate, and important national decisions could only be made by means of carefully balanced compromises on the issues. As radicals on both sides pushed the boundaries of the argument, they hastened open conflict. Many other issues, such as state's rights versus the power of the federal government, were also subsumed into this convulsive national debate.

In the area of religion in America, the time period saw equally vigorous developments and conflicts. The numbers and percentages of Americans claiming formal membership in local religious institutions and congregations showed tremendous growth, doubling from an average of 17 percent of the population in 1776 to 35 percent in 1850. When correlated with the fact that the population of the United States grew by a factor of six over this same time (from 3.5 million in 1776 to 23 million in 1850), this means that the number of formal church members grew from about 650,000 in 1776 to 7.6 million in 1850, with a corresponding growth in the numbers of congregations and pastors. Much of this rapid growth, a process that has been called the "Churching of America,"[1] can be attributed to the success of Baptists and Methodists in creating new congregations on the frontier. These two groups became the two dominant religious groups in America by 1850.

Although the initial wave of religious enthusiasm from the Second Great Awakening had cooled by the 1820s, this movement permanently altered American religious life. The raw, spontaneous frontier revivalism of the camp meetings was institutionalized into religious forms that could be both transferred and repeated on demand. Religious leader Charles G. Finney brought revivalism to the towns and villages of New York state and created patterns of American revivalism that have lasted until the present day. Countless others followed Finney's example, and revivalism became a Protestant staple, mostly because it was so effective in bringing new members into congregations.

This wave of religious activity led to a remarkable consensus on the underlying elements of American Protestantism, sometimes called the "Evangelical Protestant Consensus." Although the myriad of Protestant groups still differed from each other in significant ways, at their root they demonstrated important commonalities. This consensus, while built on a platform of Reformed Protestantism, was modified in significant ways by Arminianism and revivalism. Reliance on instant conversion and emotional intensity created millions of new believers who were "on fire for the

Lord" and sought ways to help build the kingdom of God on earth. Evangelical Protestantism channeled this energy into the formation of hundreds of benevolent societies, in which lay Christians worked together to fund and support various moral and religious causes. Bible societies, temperance and moral reform groups, home and foreign mission societies, and countless other groups sought the extension of Christianity and of Christian morality around the world. If there was a cause, there was a group to address it. This consensus, strongly moralistic in nature, urged a strict code of personal holiness and ethics, along with the creation of public means to implement them, such as Sabbath-observance laws and restrictions on the sale of alcohol. Many Protestants felt that though they belonged to a specific "denomination," the traits that divided them from other "true" Christians were minor and should not be a barrier to cooperation.

Although this convergence was a major facet of religion, it was also balanced by a large countermovement of religious groups differing in significant ways from one or more aspects of the consensus. Unitarians, Universalists, and other forms of "liberal" religion carved out niches in the face of the elements of consensus Protestantism. There was an explosive growth of communal religions, such as the Shakers, the Oneida community, New Harmony, the Amana colony, and dozens of other, often short-lived experiments. An outbreak of apocalyptic religion, led by William Miller in the 1840s, captivated thousands, and even though the end of the world did not come in 1845 as he predicted, these apocalyptic traditions continued. The emergence of Mormonism under Joseph Smith challenged the limits of American religious freedom. Millions of Irish Roman Catholics immigrated to America in the 1840s, along with a significant number of European Jews. And large numbers of African Americans, free and enslaved, were converted in the revivals of this period and became fervent Christians. They used their new Christian identity as a means to express their dreams and aspirations, even as the dominant white society sought to stifle these dreams.

The Continuing Expansion of American Lutheranism

The geographical expansion of Lutherans after 1820 mirrored that of the general American population. Already by 1821, there were identifiable groups of Lutherans on the west bank of the Mississippi River in Missouri. Lutherans moved into the old "Northwest" territories of Michigan, Wisconsin, Illinois, and across the Mississippi to Iowa. Noticeable groups of Lutherans appeared in Mississippi, Louisiana, and, after 1830, in Texas. By 1850, there were Lutheran congregations in most of the states of the Union except Florida, Alabama, and the New England states. The early settlement of Lutherans in the "West" were from established Lutheran areas along the East Coast, but increasingly, in the 1830s and 1840s, new Lutheran immigrants came to the frontier directly from Europe; initially Germans, but later Scandinavians. These immigrants came either through New Orleans and up the Mississippi River, or through New York City, across the Erie Canal, and into the Great Lakes region.

In response to a shifting and growing population, Lutherans continued home mission work, with settled eastern Lutheran groups sending out traveling missionaries, usually in an east-to-west pattern. The North Carolina and Tennessee synods sent pastors out through Kentucky and the Ohio River valley, including the southern sections of Indiana and Illinois. The South Carolina Synod similarly sent out pastors through the deep South and into Texas. Lutheran synods in the North worked through the Great Lakes region. There was a resumption of European Lutheran pastors being sent directly to the frontier, especially through mission schools such as Neuendettelsau in Bavaria and St. Chrischona in Switzerland, among others. Some organized groups of Germans and Scandinavians immigrated together and brought their own pastors. With the end of the Napoleonic Wars in 1815, Europeans renewed ties with the United States, and mass immigration began.

Already by 1816, a Lutheran congregation was organized in southern Illinois, at Dongola, probably by Lutherans from North Carolina. The North Carolina Synod sent Pastor David Sherer to the state in 1825, and he organized a congregation at Hillboro in 1832; there were a total of twelve congregations organized in Illinois prior to 1850. As was usual in new territories, the mission pastors organized a synod there in 1846. Across the Mississippi River, in Missouri, Lutherans were visited by a traveling pastor from the Tennessee Synod, and the Pennsylvania Ministerium sent another traveling missionary, J. C. F. "Father" Heyer, to that state in 1836. In the South, scattered groups of Lutherans from the Carolinas moved into Alabama and Mississippi, but few, if any, Lutheran congregations were formed there prior to the Civil War. The South Carolina Synod did send a traveling missionary, G. H. Brown, into Mississippi in 1846, and he organized some preaching points. There were no Lutheran congregations in Florida, Alabama, and Arkansas until later.

With the resumption of direct Lutheran immigration from Europe, many congregations and synods were organized by pastors who came directly from Europe. The first Lutheran settlements in Michigan were begun in the early 1830s, and by 1833 the Basel Mission Society of Switzerland sent a missionary pastor, Frederick Schmidt, to organize congregations there. A group of Germans were sent to Frankenmuth, Michigan, in 1845, by a remarkable German church leader, Wilhelm Löhe, who had organized a missionary training school at Neuendettelsau in Bavaria. Löhe's original idea for the Frankenmuth community was to locate a colony of Germans near a settlement of Native Americans, and thus develop a dual ministry. The plan worked briefly, but soon the Native American mission collapsed, leaving only the German congregation. Löhe sent as many as eighty-one mission pastors to America from 1845 to 1872; besides the mission in Michigan, the "Löhe men" also created many of the early Lutheran congregations in Iowa, which eventually formed the Iowa Synod. The first Lutheran congregations in Wisconsin were formed in 1846 by German immigrants who had come by way of Buffalo, New York, and were part of the Buffalo Synod. About that same time, Norwegian immigrants settled in southern Wisconsin and were served by missionary Elling Eielsen.

Another significant group of German Lutherans from Saxony, under the leadership of Martin Stephan, arrived in Missouri in 1839. These Lutherans were upset by changes in their German territorial church, where government authorities sought to force Lutheran and Reformed congregations into a single entity, with a common liturgy that compromised the Lutheran understanding of "genuine" worship. This group settled outside of St. Louis, but ran into initial difficulties when Pastor Stephan proved to be unfit and had to be expelled from their community. The group was soon revived by the strong leadership of Pastor C. F. W. Walther, who organized the group into the Missouri Synod.

By the 1830s and 1840s, groups of Germans settled in Texas, and Scandinavians arrived a bit later. The early conditions were deplorable and word of their situation reached back to the East. The South Carolina Synod in 1854 sent Pastor G. F. Guebner, and the Pittsburgh Synod sent Pastor Caspar Braun, to Houston to organize congregations. But the heart of early Lutheranism in Texas was provided by six mission pastors from the missionary institute at St. Chrischona, in Switzerland, who arrived in 1851 and immediately began to form congregations and the Texas Synod.

Besides the colonial Lutheran congregation in Maine, the only other Lutheran congregation in New England was formed in Boston in 1831 by German immigrants. Another singular Lutheran congregation was formed by Germans in New Orleans in 1853.

The Organization of the General Synod

The continuing geographic expansion of Lutheranism in America meant at least two things. First, new synods would continue to be formed; and, second, the Pennsylvania Ministerium could no longer be the central organizing body for all American Lutherans. As an organization, Pennsylvania clearly dwarfed all the other synods, but the expanding distances involved made it impossible for it to function effectively for the entire country. Given the number of different synods, Lutheran leaders began to consider means for intersynodical cooperation and coordination. Effective planning and cooperation in sending out missionaries and traveling preachers could be done more effectively if pastors from one synod could be recognized by the others. Also desirable would be a procedure for the establishment of new synods. Some Lutherans also envisioned a more expansive national organization for all Lutherans, one that provided elements beyond the local synods, such as a theological seminary or common worship materials. This national organization would unite all American Lutherans into a single, unified whole. By 1820, the dream appeared possible, although turning it into reality turned out to be much more difficult than initially imagined.

About 1818, the Pennsylvania Ministerium began to inquire of the other existing synods (New York, North Carolina, and Ohio) about their interest in some formal means of cooperation. When they responded positively, a leader within the North Carolina Synod, Gottlieb Schober, circulated a "Proposed Plan" (*Plan Entwurf*) for such an organization. The plan proposed a "General Synod" that would meet every third year and would have substantial powers to regulate the ministry, publications, and the formation of new synods. During 1819 and 1820, the four synods debated the possibility of such a body, and there was enough positive interest that a formational meeting was scheduled for October 22, 1820, in Hagerstown, Maryland. Representatives from Pennsylvania, New York, North Carolina, and the very new Maryland-Virginia Synod met and formed the new General Synod, the first national organization for American Lutheranism. Unfortunately, the "devil was in the details," and the new General Synod got off to a rocky start.

Opposition to the new General Synod came from a number of quarters. Some critics, such as those from the Ohio Synod and the New York Ministerium, worried that this new organization would have too much power over the constituent regional synods. Sections of the Pennsylvania Ministerium, especially where union congregations still existed, were concerned that the new organization would limit cooperation with Reformed Protestants. The biggest obstacle concerned the exact confessional position of the new General Synod; namely, How strictly would it hold to the authority of the Lutheran confessional documents? Since the confessional issue already disturbed American Lutheranism, finding the right balance on this issue proved to be impossible.

Tensions were running high on this issue within the North Carolina Synod, which traditionally held loosely to the Lutheran confessions and worked closely with the Reformed and Moravians. Schober, its leader, was originally a Moravian. A dissenting group within the synod, led by Paul Henkel and his pastoral allies, wanted a stronger and exclusively Lutheran identity, reinforced by an explicit subscription to the Augsburg Confession. Tensions within the synod ran high and proved to be irresolvable, so, in July 1820, the Henkel group split off from the North Carolina Synod to form the Tennessee Synod. Although the new body took a different geographical name, the Tennessee Synod had congregations in North Carolina and Virginia as well, leading to the first of many situations where competing Lutheran synods occupied the same territory. The Henkels and their allies strongly opposed the new General Synod because its confessional identity appeared too weak, and subsequently mounted a sustained attack on the new organization.

In response to concerns about the General Synod, organizers altered the documents of the new organization to limit its power over the constituent synods, and made its powers more advisory than coercive. Although officially titled "The Evangelical Lutheran General Synod of the United States," it did not define a confessional measurement of Lutheranism, either for itself or for its constituent synods. To allay fears, the constitution was revised to say: ". . . no General Synod can be allowed to possess, or arrogate unto itself 'the power of *proscribing* among us *uniform ceremonies of religion* for every part of the Church;' or to introduce such alterations in matters pertaining to the faith . . . as might in any way tend to burden the consciences of the brethren in Christ."[2] However, the new General Synod did retain specific powers concerning the establishment of a theological seminary and various benevolent institutions, as well as procedures for recognizing and admitting new constituent synods. The constitution of the new General Synod was approved and send back to the local synods for ratification; at least three of these synods had to approve the new organization before its next meeting in 1821 for it to achieve existence. So the battle over the fate of the new General Synod shifted back to the local synods.

Trouble soon arose. The new Ohio and Tennessee synods had not participated and would not join the new General Synod, and neither would the New York Ministerium. The three remaining synods, Pennsylvania, North Carolina, and Maryland-Virginia met in 1821 to form the General Synod, but additional difficulties followed. Suspicion of the new General Synod had been growing in some sections of the Pennsylvania Ministerium and, in order to keep that body from splintering, it was forced to withdraw its membership in the General Synod in 1823. With only two synods left within its ranks, and with the oldest and largest synods not participating, the newly born General Synod was close to collapse. Its future was saved through the actions of an energetic young Lutheran pastor from Virginia, Samuel Simon Schmucker.

Although only twenty-four years old in 1823, Schmucker had not only been a pastor for three years, but was training pastors himself in Virginia. Educated at the University of Pennsylvania and Princeton Seminary, Schmucker had well-established family connections within American Lutheranism and had been a strongly in support of the new General Synod. In 1823, though he had just suffered the death of his young wife, Schmucker swung into action and attempted to save the General Synod. Schmucker and allies in Pennsylvania and Ohio ensured that enough delegates came to the 1823 General Synod meeting to save the organization, and in 1825, the West Pennsylvania conference of the Pennsylvania Ministerium split off to form an independent synod, which promptly joined the General Synod. Although still lacking the influential ministeriums of New York and Pennsylvania, the General Synod became a viable entity and would grow stronger in the decades to come. Eventually, the New York Ministerium joined the General Synod in 1836, and the Pennsylvania Ministerium rejoined in 1853. The General Synod would never at any point in its existence contain the whole of Lutherans in America, however, frustrating the visions of its founders. Lutheran unity had been achieved, but only in part.

The Further Organization of Synods

The multiplication of Lutheran synods continued after 1820, and in fact accelerated at a dramatic rate. Dozens of new synods were formed between 1820 and 1855; at least twenty-nine from 1840 to 1855 alone, and perhaps more about which the records no longer survive. Obviously, geographic expansion was one important factor here, as scattered Lutherans in new territories came together to form new organizations. But this was not the only reason for the proliferation of synods after 1820. Synods came into existence for a number of different reasons, including differences over confessional and theological positions, language and worship, ethnicity, membership in the General Synod, and positions regarding social issues, including the abolition of slavery. Other synods would be organized like the Tennessee Synod, as a competing synod on the same territory as an existing synod. The synodical history of some regions, most notably the state of Ohio, became extremely complicated. In the land of the free expression of religion, any handful of pastors and congregations could form a new synod, and often did.

One impetus toward founding new synods was confessional; many synods arose that were more formally tied to the authority of the sixteenth-century Lutheran confessional documents, especially the Augsburg Confession of 1530. In the West, the Henkel family was especially early and active among the proponents of such developments; the Tennessee Synod was formed out of this concern, and affirmation of the Augsburg Confession can be seen in some of the synods in Ohio elsewhere. These groups were not in sympathy with the confessional position of the General

Synod. Other newly arrived groups of German immigrants shared similar concerns, and formed their own even more strictly confessional synods. Examples include the Michigan (1840), Buffalo (1845), Missouri (1847), and Iowa (1854) synods. Differences in language and ethnicity also played an important foundational role. The Missouri and Iowa synods themselves eventually became national organizations of their own, despite the geographic restrictions implicit in their name.

Sometimes, the primary focus on a new synod would be language, often when one synod would be formed out of the territory of another, existing synod. As was seen previously, the transition to the use of English had moved quickly forward after about 1800 or so, but the resumption of German immigration in the middle of the nineteenth century complicated this movement. Some of the German immigrants did form their own ethnic-language synods, but others joined existing synods, complicating or at times even reversing the language transition. The New York Ministerium was early to adopt the English language, but because of the formation of new English synods on its territory, and because of renewed German immigration, this synod became predominantly German-speaking again. In Ohio, where German settlement was strong, English-speaking pastors formed two independent synods, both called the English Ohio Synod. Although some Scandinavian immigrant pastors joined other American Lutherans in the formation of the Synod of Northern Illinois in 1851, most Scandinavian immigrants eventually formed their own national ethnic synods.

Some new synods were formed by pastors and congregations who were frustrated by the refusal of their present synod to join the General Synod. The West Pennsylvania (1825), Pittsburgh (1845), and Central Pennsylvania (1855) synods were carved out of the Pennsylvania Ministerium, as were the Hartwick (1830) and Franckean (1837) synods from the New York Ministerium, and the English Ohio (1836), Miami (1844), and Wittenberg (1847) synods from the Ohio Synod. Linguistic issues also contributed to the formation of many of these new synods. Other new synods resulted from conflicts over worship and revivalism, or certain moral and social issues, such as temperance, Sabbath observance, and the abolition of slavery. Attention to such issues had been growing among some American Lutherans during the early nineteenth century, and certain synods, such as Hartwick, Franckean, English Ohio, and Wittenberg found these issues central to their formation and identity.

Thus, not only did the number of synods multiply during this time period, but also their shape and scope, as many synods came to stand for specific positions and characteristics beyond a simple geographical territory. These developments also meant quite a number of different and competing synods, all of whom were striving to gather in their own Lutheran populations. Perhaps from the standpoint of Lutheran unity this could be seen as problematic, but this competitive situation also meant many more pastors seeking to gather in unchurched Lutherans, and more choice for Lutherans seeking a congregation or a synod that matched their own religious views.

Seminary Education

One key reason for the organization of the General Synod was the growing perception among Lutherans of the need for an institution to educate pastors. The old system of either receiving pastors from Europe or educating them as "apprentices" with established pastors was simply not producing enough pastors for the rapidly expanding Lutheran population. The use of catechists and licensed candidates, begun in the colonial period, had been simply a stopgap measure with many drawbacks, as might be expected from a system where barely trained young men were thrown into isolated congregations. Although traveling pastors and home missionaries founded new congregations, there were not enough pastors to serve them permanently. The establishment of a school for educating pastors was the obvious solution, but the resources and coordination necessary to accomplish this was difficult to manage. Still other religious groups were founding their own seminaries at this time, and the Pennsylvania Ministerium even contemplated joint theological work with the Reformed at Franklin College.

The first Lutheran seminary in Hartwick, New York, initially opened in 1797, though it remained a small, struggling, and wandering institution for almost two decades. Its prospects stabilized about 1815 when it became permanently located in a building near Cooperstown, New York, under the direction of Pastor Ernst Hazelius. Although never large, it became the principal seminary for New York Lutherans. Of much greater significance for East-Coast Lutherans was the founding of the Lutheran Theological Seminary at Gettysburg, established by the General Synod in 1826. Even more than its parent organization, Gettysburg Seminary owed it founding and early progress to the restless energy of Samuel Simon Schmucker, its first professor and the guiding light of its progress for the first thirty-eight years of its existence. As Gettysburg grew, it quickly became the leading seminary for English-speaking Lutherans in America. Although the Pennsylvania Ministerium was not a member of the General Synod, many of its pastors were educated there. It is estimated that Schmucker educated as many as four hundred Lutheran pastors during this time period, and through them exerted an immense influence on American Lutheranism.

While useful, these seminaries could not be the complete solution, especially for areas of the country far removed from Pennsylvania and New York. In 1830, the newly formed South Carolina Synod established a theological seminary on its own territory. Southern Seminary, like Hartwick, was a wandering and struggling institution for its early existence, but was another option for theological education within the General Synod. All three of these seminaries provided instruction in English.

In the same year (1830) that Southern was formed, Lutherans in the Ohio Synod formed their own seminary, in this case a German-language institution that soon became located in Columbus, Ohio. The leaders of this synod, opposed both to English and the General Synod, resolved that this seminary should be: ". . . a German Institution . . . to educate young men for the ministry in the German Lutheran church, and to educate German Teachers of Schools, so that both the interests of our church and the education of Germans in general may be promoted, and a knowledge of the language and literature of Germany may be diffused."[3] Although it did admit "English" students, there was no mistaking the founder's desire to make maintenance of the German language a primary focus of the school. Of course, this was problematic for English-speaking Lutherans in Ohio, especially in the various English conferences and synods that were established in the state. As a result, in 1845, English-speaking Lutherans opened Wittenberg College in Springfield, Ohio, with its own theological department, which was a second Lutheran seminary in Ohio. Like most of the synods that sponsored it, Wittenberg was firmly in the orbit of the General Synod and its prevailing theological outlook.

The new immigrant German Lutherans who came to the Midwest and formed their own synods, such as Missouri, Michigan, Buffalo, and Iowa, soon followed suit by establishing German-language seminaries. The Missouri Synod grew rapidly, and soon had two seminaries. The original Saxon immigrants to Missouri founded what eventually became Concordia Seminary in Perry County, Missouri, in 1839. When the Missouri Synod itself was formed in 1847, it was moved to St. Louis and came under the direction of C. F. W. Walther. Even more than Schmucker at Gettysburg, Walther was the formative influence on both the synod and the seminary for forty years, until his death in 1887. Other immigrant German Lutheran leaders, allied with Wilhelm Löhe in Germany, formed a Lutheran seminary in Fort Wayne, Indiana, in 1846. It, too, became a part of the Missouri Synod in 1847, eventually moving from Fort Wayne to St. Louis, then to Springfield, Illinois, and eventually, during the 1970s, back to Fort Wayne. In cooperation with Löhe, who had by then broken with the Missouri Synod, the leaders of the Iowa Synod moved Wartburg Seminary to Dubuque, Iowa, in 1853. So, by that date there were a total of eight different Lutheran seminaries educating pastors for the Lutheran ministry in America.

Despite their numbers, early Lutheran seminaries were formed on shaky foundations; the schools themselves were financially poor, and their students even poorer still. The seminaries were often run by one or two professors who taught a wide array of classes, supervised the moral and theological formation of the students, and spent much time on the road to raise money to keep their schools afloat. Students came to the seminaries with wildly uneven educational background, and the professors had to do much remedial work. Some students were very young, no more than sixteen or seventeen years old; others were middle-aged. Poverty and poor living conditions were the rule; one immigrant student recorded in his diary about his days at the Columbus seminary: "I have studied diligently and have often done hard labor between school terms. Poverty has pressed me at every turn, and I have been compelled to live mostly on charity. But I have managed to get along, one day at a time."[4] Although a general course of study was prescribed, usually two to three years depending on previous education, many students were able to attend seminary classes only sporadically. Many attended for a semester and then left to earn enough money to continue. The surging need for pastors caused leaders to rush students through school quickly and send them out to congregations. What the seminaries lacked in resources, however, they made up for in piety and religious fervor. The constitution at Southern Seminary in 1833 listed specific expectations of seminary students: "Worship each morning and evening. Daily meditation and Bible reading. A Sabbath spent entirely in devotional exercises, either social or secret. Cleanliness, but not expensiveness of dress. Reasonable attention to Sacred Music if possessed of the requisite talent."[5] Candidates for the ministry were closely scrutinized in their conduct and piety, attempting to ensure godly candidates for the ordained ministry.

Academies and Colleges

As the leaders of these new Lutheran seminaries quickly learned, their candidates for the ordained ministry often came to seminary woefully unprepared academically for such a course of study. The Lutheran ideal for pastors was a heavy dose of classical languages, including Greek, Hebrew, Latin, and German, and a strong knowledge of history, philosophy, and the Bible. Few, if any, students came so prepared, and the seminary professors spent much of their time in remedial work. To improve student preparation, many seminaries established an organized system of education usually referred to as the "collegiate" or "preparatory" program, utilizing the same premises and resources as the seminary itself. Whatever they were called, they were, in all honesty, classical high schools or, according to the German model, a "gymnasium." In the Missouri Synod system, there was a seamless, six-year program of pretheological education, followed by three years of seminary.

Eventually, these preparatory schools emerged out from under the shadow of the sponsoring seminary and became free-standing institutions. Often, the school itself operated for a number of years before its legal incorporation as a separate entity. These fledgling institutions were a part of a larger movement in American education, a "golden era" of establishing religiously based academies and colleges that reached a peak before the Civil War, when an estimated seven hundred such institutions were founded in the United States. Although only about one-quarter of these schools ever achieved permanent status, this was a remarkable achievement in the establishment of higher education, one in which American Lutherans were well represented.

Early American Lutheran attempts in collegiate education, including Kunze's Seminarium in Philadelphia, Columbia College, the University of Pennsylvania, and Franklin College, operated jointly with the Reformed, were generally not successful. The first successful Lutheran college owed its existence to Samuel Simon Schmucker, who, in 1832, separately chartered the preparatory department of Gettysburg Seminary as Pennsylvania College, now Gettysburg College. This same dynamic produced Capital University out of the Lutheran seminary in Columbus, Ohio, in 1850, and Newberry College out of Southern Seminary in 1856. Wittenberg University in Springfield, Ohio, was founded as a joint college and seminary in 1845, and they continued to operate together through this time. Other early Lutheran colleges included Roanoke College in Salem, Virginia (1842), and Carthage College in Illinois (1847). The Missouri Synod's preparatory academy in St. Louis, Missouri, was moved to Fort Wayne, Indiana, in the 1860s for reasons related to the Civil War. Wartburg College in Iowa dates to the founding of the Iowa Synod seminary in 1852, while elements of Muhlenberg College in Allentown, Pennsylvania, go back to 1848. There were many more academies and schools founded by Lutherans during this time period that survived for a length of time before closing, usually for financial reasons. Although these schools were founded by Lutherans, very few of them were actually owned and controlled by the synods; rather, their Lutheran character was ensured through Lutheran representation on their boards of directors.

One interesting development during this time period was attention being given to advanced education for women, a phenomenon that developed initially during the period from 1830 to 1860, especially among Lutherans on the East Coast. Often referred to as "female seminaries," they were essentially high schools or preparatory schools for young Lutheran women. The word *seminary* here was a generic term for a place where nurturing occurred and had nothing to do with the ordained ministry. A number of synods commended to their members the Gettysburg Female Seminary, run by a Professor Haupt. Several Lutheran synods during the 1840s and 1850s, including West Pennsylvania, Maryland-Virginia, and Southwestern Virginia, passed resolutions urging the establishment of educational institutions for young women. A typical rationale for such education came from the Maryland-Virginia Synod, which stated in 1848: "The great importance of Female Education is beginning to awaken the especial attention of the church, and we believe the superior intelligence of the daughters of Christian families is identified with the prosperity of Christ's Kingdom, in consequent of the part which females are capable of taking in the movements and benevolent enterprises of the Church . . ."[6] Although several similar resolutions were passed, and committees formed to explore the education of women, the Hagerstown Female Seminary, Hagerstown, Maryland, which opened in 1853, was the only such institution formed during this time. A number of other, similar institutions formed after the Civil War.

Outreach and Missions

As had been the case for American Lutherans since the colonial period, their primary focus was to reach out and gather in as many Lutherans living in the United States as they possibly could. Lack of money and pastors, along with the rapidly expanding frontiers, had made this a difficult task, but the growth of Lutheran synods, along with their increasing pastoral resources and organization, meant that in the first half of the nineteenth-century synods began to catch up with the need. The older methods continued to be employed, with traveling pastors and home missionaries locating groups of Lutherans, and catechists and licensed candidates providing pastoral leadership to small congregations. Students and professors from the seminaries also traveled over the summer and school breaks. Following the lead of other Protestants, Lutherans created home-mission societies specifically designed for domestic outreach, which functioned as synodical auxiliaries. Early societies were organized in New York and in the Maryland-Virginia Synod in 1828, and most of the older synods soon came to have some form of home missions committee or society. Although the General Synod had been envisioned to coordinate and encourage home missions, the political minefield that this entailed stalled efforts until 1835, when an independent meeting of General Synod pastors formed the "Central Missionary Society," which operated for several years. Finally, in 1845, the "Home Missionary Society of the General Synod" was formed as an auxiliary organization and operated independently for twenty years until it became an official part of the

General Synod. Funding was always an issue, because individuals and congregations contributed to these societies only sporadically.

Conditions faced by traveling home missionaries were often difficult. Scattered groups of Lutherans on the frontier were often poor, and though many of them wanted to form congregations, they had neither the numbers nor the resources to do so. Reporting to the New York Ministerium in 1825 about his travels, Pastor John Goertner described one typical part of his journeys: "[I] went down the St. Lawrence River, and ministered to the congregation at Williamsburg. Several Lutheran congregations had once flourished there but only remnants were left, principally because their pastors went over to the Anglican Church. It was not possible to arrange for a man to go there . . ."[7] Lack of available pastors and competition from other Christian groups were constant refrains in these reports; the Methodists and the Baptists on the frontier were often cited as being the most aggressive groups working among the Lutherans.

Being only lightly settled, the frontier was often an inhospitable place for formal religious establishments, and conditions were generally difficult. In reporting on an 1836 trip for the new Central Missionary Society, veteran missionary pastor J. C. F. (Father) Heyer had a dire prediction: "During the month of April I traveled 600 miles, preached fourteen or fifteen times, baptized thirteen and administered the Lord's Supper to more than a hundred communicants . . . but unless some of our young brethren can be induced to come West and take charge of these new congregations, it cannot be expected that our cause will prosper."[8] Transportation and accommodations were often primitive, if they existed at all. At one place, Heyer was forced to stay at an inn with a "very rough" and "godless crowd." Rather than remain among such people, he stayed in the stable with horses and cattle, "where I felt more comfortable."

Lutherans and African Americans

Even as slavery was declining in the North during this period, the numbers of African Americans, enslaved and free, were rising in the South. New lands on the frontier and new agricultural methods made slavery more profitable. Lutherans in the South became accustomed to slavery, and a number of them became slave owners themselves. When waves of religious enthusiasm rolled over the country during the Second Great Awakening (1790–1810), the general evangelical fervor prompted a renewed push to Christianizing the slaves. Whether done out of a genuine concern for the slave's eternal salvation, or to justify slavery itself, the numbers of African Americans who became Christian rose dramatically after 1800.

In 1809, the North Carolina Synod passed a resolution allowing pastors to baptize enslaved African Americans, with their master's permission. By 1817, the synod had developed the "Five Point Plan" for evangelization of African Americans. In an 1818 book, synod leader Gottlieb Schober summarized this plan, and argued that the Lutheran church had a duty to evangelize African Americans, both enslaved and free; further, he said: "It is the duty of the elders of such congregations among which the Negros are living, as slaves or free, to provide a place for them in our churches; or when that cannot be done to build them a house adjoining or near the church."[9] This injunction was implemented unevenly; some congregations had a sizeable number of African American members, while others had none at all. In the early decades of the nineteenth century, the most African American baptisms were among Lutherans in North Carolina and Tennessee, but after 1830, they occurred more frequently in the South Carolina Synod. It is estimated that between 8,000 and 10,000 African Americans became a part of the Lutheran synods in the South, and just before the Civil War 20 percent of the members of the South Carolina Synod were African American.[10] St. John's Lutheran Church in Charleston, South Carolina, under the leadership of Dr. John Bachman, had a large congregation of African Americans with its own leaders and Sunday school that paralleled its white congregation.

During this time, three African American men were ordained into the Lutheran ministry for work among the Africans in the United States and in Africa. The first was Jehu Jones, a member of St. John's, Charleston, who was to be sent to Africa. After his ordination in New York in 1832, he was unable to gather the funding to make the trip. After some years in the North, Jones founded the St. Paul's Colored Lutheran Church in Philadelphia, in 1834; though it lasted only five years, it was the first African American Lutheran congregation. Jones tried again in New York in 1849, with no success. The Charleston Lutherans, especially the African Americans, did not give up on the mission to Africa and, in 1845, one of their leaders, Boston J. Drayton, was ordained by the South Carolina Synod and sent to Liberia. His mission, too, was short-lived but nevertheless remarkable.

The third, and most successful, African American leader was Daniel Alexander Payne, a school teacher from Charleston who was sent to study at Gettysburg Seminary, in 1835. Although Payne himself was a Methodist and intended to remain such, he was called by the antislavery Franckean Synod in New York and ordained in 1839. Although the Synod intended to send him as a missionary to the Caribbean, Payne had his own ideas. He joined the African Methodist Episcopal Church in 1841 and rose to the level of bishop and college president in that denomination. The careers of these three men were remarkable, given the spirit of the times, although the Lutheran synods missed an important opportunity to employ their talents in perhaps better ways and to support their ministries more fully.

Congregational Life

As was seen earlier, American religion before the Civil War was an energetic form of Protestant Christianity, marked by revivals or "experiential religion" with an intense interest in mission expansion, and a keen desire to "build God's kingdom" on earth. It was also a period of organization, when Protestant Christians of all variety banded together in voluntary societies to further the larger cause of Christ and to ameliorate the social ills of the time. This "Evangelical Protestant Consensus" spilled across denominational lines and strongly influenced English-speaking American Lutheranism as well. In the spirit of benevolent optimism and mission, Schmucker wrote in 1830: "The triumph of the Gospel will everywhere be accompanied by its legitimate train of benevolent and meliorating influences on the civil and social institutions of the world; and war itself, the prolific mother of all evil, will retire before the progress of the Prince of Peace."[11] This spirit moved Lutherans toward the ardent work in revivalism, education, and personal and social moral reform, and to the development of organizations to fulfill this vision.

By the 1830s, frontier revivalism of the Second Great Awakening had been supplanted by organized revivalism regularly conducted in congregations and towns all over the United States. Revivals were the means to shake existing Christians into new faith and to bring unbelievers into the congregations. Many Lutherans were cautiously positive about these revivals, and some, such as the new Lutheran synods (Hartwick, Franckean, English Ohio) were strong proponents of them. In 1843, the Franckean Synod rejoiced in the results: "This has been a year of revivals—such as the country has not seen since the years '31 and '32. All denominations of Christians have shared largely in the outpouring of the Spirit of God. We have enjoyed some of the most extensive revivals in some districts of this Synod."[12] Revivals lasted anywhere from three days to a week or longer, and involved continuous preaching by teams of Lutheran preachers. People gathered for revival from all over a particular area, and reports and enumerations of conversions were conspicuously displayed in Lutheran periodicals. Many Lutherans agreed that moderate revivalism was healthy, but sought to avoid the "excesses" of some other forms of revivalism. While revivals were generally seen as a welcome addition, they were considered a supplement to traditional Lutheran worship, sacramental practice, and catechesis, not a replacement. Nevertheless, more conservative and strictly confessional Lutherans, such as those in the Tennessee and Ohio synods, as well as the newer German

Midwest groups, were strongly opposed to revivalism. It is noteworthy that this age of revivalism within some sectors of Lutheranism also saw an ongoing simplification of traditional worship practices, especially the Sunday morning worship service, a development continuing from the colonial period.

A strong concern for a strict personal and social morality, especially in a resistance to the "temptations" of the world, was another religious element of this age. The 1841 South Carolina Synod constitution stipulated that congregational membership not only required participation in worship and the sacraments but also: "Abstinence . . . from profane swearing, Sabbath breaking, Intemperance, Gambling or other vices and from all Fashionable Amusements."[13] Card playing, drunkenness, fancy clothing, public theatricals, and similar activities were considered as moral failings. These moral concerns also spread beyond the congregation; Lutherans organized or joined societies to combat the use of alcohol and the profaning of the Sabbath, to reform prisons and prostitutes, to aid the "worthy poor," and to combat the evils of "rum, Romanism, and rebellion." Other organized societies supported home and foreign missions, outreach to Native Americans, African Americans, and Jews, and the publication and distribution of Bibles and other religious literature. If there was a cause, there was a society to address it. Many of these societies were denominationally specific, but Lutherans also joined other Protestants in nondenominational societies, such as the American Bible Society.

The Protestant emphasis on a Sunday school in every congregation carried into many American Lutheran synods. The Sunday-school movement started in late eighteenth-century England as an evangelistic outreach to the children of the urban poor and industrial workers, but after 1800, the schools were also viewed as a means of religious instruction within established congregations. An American Sunday School Union was formed in 1824, and its Lutheran counterpart, the Lutheran Sunday School Union, was established in the General Synod in 1829. As the traditional Lutheran parish schools of the colonial period began to be eclipsed by weekday public education, the Sunday schools offered a venue for sustained and denominationally specific religious education. Lutheran traditionalists and proponents of the German language saw them as a possible means both of religious instruction and retaining German, although some of these groups, notably the Missouri Synod, continued to urge full, parish-based parochial schools. Those more in line with the American evangelical Protestants also strongly supported Sunday schools, but for different reasons. They saw the schools as a place for inculcating personal and social morality, and the general program of revivalistic Protestantism. By the 1840s, most local Lutheran congregations sponsored some form of Sunday school, whether as a part of the Lutheran Sunday School Union, of some other group, or independently.

To connect Lutherans with one another and to spread church news and theological views, Lutheran created their own periodicals and newspapers. Progress in this field was sporadic at first; the German-language *Evangelische Magazin* (1812–1817), and English-language *Lutheran Intelligencer* (1826–1831) and *Lutheran Magazine* (1827–1831), all lasted only a few years and did not achieve a wide circulation. The first periodical to achieve lasting success and national distribution was the *Lutheran Observer*, begun in Baltimore, Maryland, in 1831. Its publisher and editor, Pastor Benjamin Kurtz, was a friend of Schmucker and a strong proponent of Gettysburg Seminary and of English-language American Lutheranism, including revivals. With Kurtz's strong and opinionated stamp all over it, the *Observer* quickly gained strong praise and strong notoriety throughout the American Lutheran world. Conservative Lutherans agitated for an English-language alternative, but this was not forthcoming until the Joint Synod of Ohio founded the *Lutheran Standard* in 1843. Many synods began to consider their "own" regular periodical as an important means to reach members and congregations and to communicate the activities and viewpoints of the synod. When C. F. W. Walther began *Der Lutheraner* in 1844, it became a means for the creation of the Missouri Synod. Within the Pittsburgh Synod, Pastor William Passavant began his own paper, *The Missionary*, in 1848. Many of these papers gained readership outside of their own synods and became forums for discussions and sometimes battles over theological and ecclesiastical issues. Two more scholarly publications for pastors complemented the more popular publications, the *Evangelical Review* (1849) of the General Synod, and *Lehre und Wehre* (1855) of the Missouri Synod. These early efforts marked the beginning of massive publication programs by Lutherans in the later nineteenth century.

Renewed Immigration and Its Effects

Mass immigration to the United States during the nineteenth century transformed the country in so many ways that it difficult to enumerate them. From 1840 to 1920, approximately thirty-three million Europeans settled in the United States, most of them coming in the period from 1865 to 1914, between the American Civil War and the First World War. But even before the Civil War, mass immigration was growing in size and influence; during the decade of the 1830s, the number of immigrants was about 145,000, but during the 1840s this rose to 600,000, and, during the 1850s, to 1.7 million. The U.S. federal census of 1850 identified 584,000 Americans either born in Germany or of German parents. Obviously, not all of these German Americans were Lutherans, but surely a substantial percentage of them came from Lutheran regions in Germany, providing at least a huge pool of potential members for American Lutheran congregations and synods.

This immigration changed the face of American Lutheranism, not least by reintroducing a large German-speaking Lutheran population in the United States before the Civil War. Among Lutherans from the colonial "Muhlenberg" tradition, the use of German was on a rapid decline by 1830, with English the new language of choice. In some synods, such as the Ministerium of New York, the influx of German immigrants and congregations literally transformed the synod. In the Joint Synod of Ohio, this immigration reversed the tide of language transition back toward German. English-speaking synods, such as the Hartwick and Franckean synods in New York, and the English Ohio and Wittenberg synods in Ohio, were formed in part as a protest against this wave of German influence. But it was in the Midwest, where antebellum German immigration was strongest, that new and large synods were formed independently by pastors who came to the United States during this immigration, groups such as the Buffalo (1845), Missouri (1847), and Iowa (1854) synods.

What marked these new Midwestern German synods was a stricter adherence to the sixteenth-century Lutheran confessional documents, including not just the Augsburg Confession but the entire *Book of Concord*, hence the use of the term *Concordia* for some of the institutions of the Missouri Synod. Many of their Lutheran leaders who emigrated from Germany were deeply upset by the rationalism and "unionism" of the German territorial churches and their lack of a strong Lutheran identity. When they came to the United States and viewed the established Lutheran synods, they were equally displeased, and considered many of them, especially the General Synod, to be barely Lutheran, if at all. One party of such immigrants settled around Buffalo, New York, starting in 1839, under the leadership of Pastor J. A. A. Grabau; they formed the Buffalo Synod in 1845. Grabau held an elevated view of the church and of the ordained ministry and urged this position on the other midwestern Lutheran groups. Grabau's own leadership, however, was soon challenged within his own small synod, which eventually split into three different, even smaller factions.

The largest of these midwestern confessional Lutheran groups, the Missouri Synod, traces its origins to a group of seven hundred Saxon Lutherans who immigrated to Missouri in 1839. They were led by a charismatic pastor, Martin Stephan, who had clashed with church and government officials in Saxony, and, as a result, sought to establish a "true" Lutheranism in the United States. When Stephan's leadership quickly became autocratic and erratic, the Saxons deposed him. The mantle of their leadership soon fell to an energetic young pastor, C. F. W. Walther, who revitalized the disillusioned pastors and lay members of the group. Through *Der*

Lutheraner, and with his knowledge of Luther, the Reformation, and of American religious freedom, he provided a vision for German Lutheranism in America, and his influence spread rapidly throughout the Midwest.

Other Germany missionary pastors also came to the Midwest from Wilhelm Löhe's missionary institute at Neuendettelsau, in Bavaria, settling in Michigan. These pastors, along with pastors Friedrich Wyneken and Wilhelm Sihler at Fort Wayne, Indiana, and several disaffected German pastors in the Ohio Synod, began discussions of a new, German-language confessional synod in the Midwest. Meeting in Chicago in 1847, the Saxon Missouri pastors, along with the Bavarian pastors from Michigan, Indiana, and Ohio, met and formed the "German Evangelical Lutheran Synod of Missouri, Ohio, and Other States," subsequently often referred to as the "Missouri Synod." The strong and definite constitutional references to the sixteenth-century Lutheran confessions left no doubt as to the primacy of these documents in the new synod. Because of the Saxons' experience with Stephan, the new synod also contained a strong democratic and congregational emphasis. The 1847 constitution stated: "Synod is in respect to the self-government of the individual congregations only an advisory body. Therefore no resolution of the former, when it imposes anything upon the individual congregation, has binding force for the latter."[14] Walther was elected as the first president, and under his leadership the Synod grew rapidly so that, by 1854, the synod had to be divided into four distinct geographical districts. Because it differed strongly with Missouri on ministry and the congregation, the Buffalo Synod did not join, and sharp theological disagreement ensued between Grabau and Walther over these issues.

Although some of Löhe's pastors initially joined in the formation of the Missouri Synod in 1847, Löhe himself remained unsure of the new organization, especially with its stance on the powers of the congregation, and on Walther's more functional doctrine of the ministry. Conversations with Walther and Friedrich Wyneken in 1851 did nothing to alter Löhe's initial assessment that Missouri's doctrine of the church was seriously deficient. One of Löhe's pastors, Georg Grossmann, arrived in Michigan in 1852 to take charge of a mission school there and promptly joined the Missouri Synod. He was soon excommunicated from Missouri, however, for refusing to accept its position on the church and the ministry. Grossmann and a number of other Löhe pastors moved their school to eastern Iowa in 1853, establishing it there as Wartburg Seminary. Having left the Missouri Synod, and dissatisfied with the Ohio or Buffalo synods, they founded the Iowa Synod in 1854, which also grew to become a national synodical body. Löhe was a strong supporter of the new Iowa Synod, and directed his missionary pastors to the new organization. Although the Iowa Synod under the theological leadership of Sigmund and Gottfried Fritschel remained firmly a confessional Lutheran body, the synod believed that some areas of organization practice and belief were "open questions," that is, topics on which Lutherans could disagree and still maintain church fellowship. Iowa even allowed some variety of theological difference within the synod itself over doctrines such as the nature of the church and ministry, and of eschatology. Walther and other Missouri leaders attacked the Iowa Synod for doctrinal "looseness," insisting that full doctrinal agreement was necessary before any church fellowship could be established. Fellowship before complete doctrinal agreement was "unionism," and not acceptable.

By 1855, the contours of conservative German Lutheran confessionalism were established in the Midwest. Missouri grew rapidly and became the largest of these synods. The Iowa Synod and the Joint Synod of Ohio would also become sizable national organizations and served as opposition to Missouri. The Buffalo Synod, and new synods in Texas (1851) and Wisconsin (1849), would remain as distinct bodies, though none of these ever reached the size of the larger synods. The three largest, Missouri, Iowa, and Ohio, engaged in often strenuous theological debate throughout the nineteenth century, and competed in the towns, cities, and countryside, seeking to gather in the large numbers of German Lutherans flooding into the United States.

The Controversy over "American Lutheranism"

As has been seen numerous times so far, one of the primary struggles for Lutherans in America was how to be both Lutheran and American, especially how one could define just which groups were truly Lutheran and which had lost this identity. Define Lutheranism too broadly, and all distinctive characteristics would be lost. Define Lutheranism too narrowly, and it could be turned into a handful of isolated sects, unable to fully participate in American public and religious life. Lutherans in America simply could not agree on the balance to strike here and just what elements should define Lutheranism in this country.

After the founding of the United States, Lutherans focused on the nature and authority of the Augsburg Confession. This document was developed by German Lutherans as a confession of faith and a document that defined what it meant to be Lutheran. The form of adherence, or "subscription," to the Augsburg Confession was itself a matter of some controversy, as was the exact nature of that document's authority. In colonial America, many Lutheran groups gradually removed formal language about the Augsburg Confession from their constitutional documents, although it is not clear exactly what they intended by such actions; they were not intentionally dropping the Lutheran identity, or so they claimed.

When, in 1826, Samuel Simon Schmucker wrote his professorial oath as the first teacher at Gettysburg Seminary, he specifically added a reference to the Augsburg Confession. After declaring his belief in the Scriptures to be the "inspired Word of God," Schmucker added: "I believe the Augsburg Confession and the Catechisms of Luther to be a summary and just exposition of the fundamental doctrines of the Word of God . . ."[15] From this and other writings, it is clear that Schmucker saw the Augsburg Confession as an important element of Lutheran identity, and in this sense was perhaps more explicitly confessional than some other American Lutherans of the time. Still, Schmucker was also wary of raising the Augsburg Confession too high as an authority; by naming it as a "summary and just exposition" of the Word of God, he was leaving some room to criticize, and even reject, certain parts of the Augsburg Confession if they seemed to him contrary to the Scriptures.

One original facet of the Augsburg Confession itself was its intention to be an overture to the Roman Catholic rulers of the Holy Roman Empire in 1530. The author of the Confession, Philipp Melanchthon, attempted to show that Lutherans were not dangerous schismatics, and expressed the Lutheran position as closely to the Roman position as he could. Schmucker and many other American Lutherans of the day were strongly anti-Roman Catholic, and believed that the Augsburg Confession contained some latent medieval Catholic elements that were contrary to Scripture, which were no longer held by American Lutherans. In 1851, Schmucker explained: "The actual doctrinal position of our church in this country at the formation of the General Synod, was that of adherence to the fundamental doctrines of the Scriptures as substantially taught in the Augsburg Confession, with acknowledged dissent on minor points."[16] So they could, and did, believe that at points the Augsburg Confession was incorrect. The main points of contention were its formulations about the real presence of Christ in the Lord's Supper, baptismal regeneration, exorcism, and the rejection of strict Sabbath observance, all of which seemed to Schmucker and others as too Roman Catholic. This position has often been labeled "American Lutheranism," which has become a sometimes confusing designation.

While Schmucker advocated for a "moderate" confessionalism within American Lutheranism, the theological tide was flowing past him toward a stricter and more formal adherence to the authority of the Lutheran confessions. Since the 1820s, the Henkel family and the Tennessee Synod had been sharp critics of the General Synod on confessional grounds. But even within the General Synod and the Ministerium of Pennsylvania there were elements moving toward a more conservative confessional position and stricter adherence to the authority of the Lutheran confessions. Important figures in this development were Lutheran pastors Charles Porterfield Krauth, son of Schmucker's colleague at Gettysburg Seminary, and

William Passavant, of the Pittsburgh Synod. The readmission of the Pennsylvania Ministerium to the General Synod in 1853 was another sign of more conservative Lutheranism in the East, which paralleled the immigration of stricter confessional Lutherans to the Midwest.

In 1855, an anonymous document was mailed to Lutheran pastors and leaders around the United States. This document, the "Definite Synodical Platform," contained an "American Edition of the Augsburg Confession," revised to remove from the Augsburg Confession language that some considered unsuitable for American Lutherans, particularly the "Roman" elements cited above. In reality, the document was the work of Schmucker, Benjamin Kurtz, and Samuel Sprecher, president of Wittenberg College. This proposal ignited a firestorm of controversy over its attempts to amend the Augsburg Confession. Although it was envisioned for synodical consideration, only three small synods in Ohio ever formally adopted the document. Kurtz strongly supported the Definite Platform in the pages of the *Lutheran Observer*, but he could not stem widespread negative reactions to the proposal. Whatever the intentions of the authors, the results of this conflict, the "American Lutheran" controversy, resulted in a sharp and general rejection of this edition of the Augsburg Confession, although it is clear that essential elements of Schmucker's general theological approach remained strong within the General Synod. Politically and strategically, the attempt to amend the Augsburg Confession was a complete failure. After a season of sharp theological conflict over the "Definite Platform," most Lutherans had had enough of the debate. In February 1856, sixty-four Lutheran leaders from both sides met to sign the "Pacific Overture," a ceasefire of sorts, intended to quiet the situation. Although the controversy died down, many of the underlying elements of the controversy and corollary issues smoldered under the surface. As American Lutherans, and Americans in general, moved toward the 1860s and civil strife, the theological conflict would definitely erupt again.

Notes

1. Rodney Fink and Roger Starke, *The Churching of America, 1776–2005: Winners and Losers in Our Religious Economy* (New Brunswick, NJ: Rutgers University Press, 2005).

2. "Article III, section 2, number 3, Constitution of the General Synod, 1820," in Richard C. Wolf, ed., *Documents of Lutheran Unity in America* (Philadelphia: Fortress Press, 1966), 27.

3. "Minutes of the Joint Synod of Ohio, 1842," pp. 36–37, quoted in Donald Huber, *Educating Lutheran Pastors in Ohio, 1830–1930* (Lewiston, NY: Edwin Mellon, 1989), 30. Although the constitution was developed in 1830, it was not published until 1842.

4. Eric Norelius, "Journal entry for July 10, 1853," in G. Everett Arden, trans., *The Journals of Eric Norelius* (Philadelphia: Fortress Press, 1967), 115.

5. "Constitution of Southern Seminary, 1833," quoted in Susan Wilds McArver and Scott Hendrix, *A Goodly Heritage: The Story of Lutheran Theological Southern Seminary, 1830–2005* (Columbia, SC: Lutheran Theological Southern Seminary, 2006), 4.

6. "Resolution of the Maryland-Virginia Synod, 1848," in Abdel Ross Wentz, *History of the Evangelical Synod of Maryland* (Harrisburg, PA: Evangelical Press, 1920), 134.

7. "Report of Pastor John Goertner, New York Ministerium Minutes, 1825," quoted in Harry J. Kreider, *History of the United Lutheran Synod of New York and New England* (Philadelphia: Muhlenberg, 1954), 61.

8. "J. C. F. Heyer, Report to the Central Missionary Society, 1836," quoted in E. Theodore Bachman, *They Called Him Father: The Life Story of John Christian Frederick Heyer* (Philadelphia: Muhlenberg, 1942), 90.

9. Gottlieb Schober, *A Comprehensive Account of the Rise and Progress . . . of the Christian Church by Dr. Martin Luther* (Baltimore: Schaeffer and Maund, 1818), 167.

10. Jeff G. Johnson, *Black Christians: The Untold Lutheran Story* (St. Louis: Concordia, 1991), 128.

11. Samuel Simon Schmucker, *A Plea for the Sunday-School System, delivered Feb. 2, 1830 . . .* (Gettysburg: H. C. Neinstedt, 1830), 32.

12. "Minutes of the Franckean Synod, 1843," 6, quoted in Kreider, *History of the United Lutheran Synod*, 114.

13. Synod of South Carolina, *Discipline, Articles of Faith and Synodical Constitution*, ch. 6, sect. 3 (Baltimore: Publication Rooms, 1841).

14. "Constitution of the German Evangelical Lutheran Synod of Missouri, Ohio, and other States, chapter IV, section 9, 1847," in Carl S. Meyer, ed., *Moving Frontiers: Readings in the History of the Lutheran Church Missouri Synod* (St. Louis: Concordia, 1964), 151.

15. Cited in Abdel Ross Wentz, *Gettysburg Lutheran Theological Seminary, vol. 1: History, 1826–1965* (Harrisburg, PA: Evangelical Press, 1965), 99.

16. Samuel Simon Schmucker, *The American Lutheran Church, Historically, Doctrinally, and Practically Delineated . . .* (Springfield: D. Harbaugh, 1851), 158.

Excursus 6

"PRAISE THE LORD": LUTHERANS AND AMERICAN REVIVALISM

When thinking about American revivalism, many images come to mind. Tent-meeting revival services on the edge of small southern towns, with sawdust, pounding gospel music, and hell-fire preaching. Perhaps a Billy Graham crusade in a big-city auditorium, with the music of George Beverly Shea, and the final altar-call invitation to the music of "Just As I Am." Or perhaps Dwight Lyman Moody or Billy Sunday . . . but my guess is that you'd never associate revivalism with American Lutherans. Guess what? Some American Lutherans did practice revivalism, and many congregations still do use elements of the evangelistic approaches honed in the fire of American revivalism. American religion was fundamentally shaped by revivalism.

Revivalism as we now know it developed after the American Revolution, during the period from 1790 to 1810 called the "Second Great Awakening." Organized religion was very weak in colonial America, and when, after the war, Americans started pouring into the frontier areas west of the Allegheny mountains, Christian churches faced an almost impossible task in "churching" this new territory. Too few in numbers to reach the settlers in any traditional ways, pioneering preachers had to develop new techniques to match the new situation. Methodist circuit riders and Baptist lay preachers went wherever they needed to reach the settlers. Other preachers decided to gather settlers from far and wide in "camp meetings," where preaching and socializing went hand in hand. Unable to reach most settlers consistently for long periods of time, preachers pioneered new ways of influencing their audiences with an emotional, immediate offer of salvation, one that hit home to thousands of people at a time.

News of these great and wonderful revivals of religion from the American frontier filtered back to settled congregations and preachers along the Eastern Seaboard, and excited spontaneous revivals there, too. A New York lawyer-turned-preacher, Charles Grandison Finney, reasoned that these spontaneous revivals could, in fact, be turned into planned revivals that could be orchestrated to reach masses of unchurched people in the new American republic. Using Finney's techniques, nineteenth-century American preachers brought millions of new converts into formal affiliations with Protestant congregations. Moody, Sunday, and Graham later took the basic elements of American revivalism and adjusted them for urban audiences and modern listeners.

With all the religious excitement going on around them, American Lutherans could not help but be swept up in revivalism. In the period before the Civil War (1800–1860), many American Lutheran pastors cooperated with other Protestant leaders to organize area-wide revivals; they also held Lutheran revival services in their congregations and among their institutions. These pastors saw the hand of God at work in the revival, bringing about a new wave of reform in American Lutheranism. One account of a four-day revival among Lutherans in South Carolina in 1831 approvingly reported that "hundreds were bathed in tears, a solemnity pervaded the whole assembly, more than one hundred individuals accepted the invitation given to those who desired to be personally conversed with on the subject of their soul's salvation."[1] Hundreds of such accounts were regularly published in some of the Lutheran newspapers of the time.

This is not to say that revivalism was universally or uncritically accepted among American Lutherans. There were some wilder elements of American revivalism, including emotional outbursts and intense pressure, which most Lutherans rejected. In 1841, one Ohio Lutheran synod passed a resolution on revivals that stated that they "recommend opposition to all disorder and ultraism (while) we earnestly encourage our Churches to promote genuine revivals by faithful preaching of the word, by prayer, and by other means in accord with the holy religion of our Redeemer." But more moderated forms of revivalism gained widespread acceptance within Lutheran congregations, though most agreed that conversions gained in such situations needed to be followed up with further Christian education.

Other Lutherans, however, totally rejected American revivalism as being un-Lutheran and un-Christian. One angry writer in 1838 chastised a Lutheran newspaper editor for his eager support of revivals, saying, "You and the other Revival Boys are advocating this Rail-Road Christianity according to which they become sinlessly perfect in an hour (so that) our people might not desert to the Methodists."[2] Newly arrived Lutheran immigrant pastors, along with other conservative Lutheran preachers, spoke out regularly against revivalism and for traditional Lutheran worship. Nothing new about the contemporary American Lutheran "worship wars"!

Revivalism remained important in American religion, and one can trace elements of it in many areas still today. For example, the revival tradition of "camp meetings" eventually evolved into the Bible camps that we know today. Gospel songs and direct preaching of the gospel for repentance and the amendment of life remain important in many congregations. If the historic revivals have become a bit of a caricature, many of their effects and techniques are still an important part of American Protestantism, even American Lutheranism.

Notes

1. *Lutheran Observer*, December 15, 1831, quoted in E. Clifford Nelson, ed., *The Lutherans in North America* (Philadelphia: Fortress Press, 1975), 136.

2. *Lutheran Observer*, March 30, 1838, quoted in Willard Allbeck, *A Century of Lutherans in Ohio* (Yellow Springs, OH: Antioch Press, 1966), 106.

LUTHERANS: 1750

CHURCHES
○ 1 Church
● 5 Churches
● 25 Churches

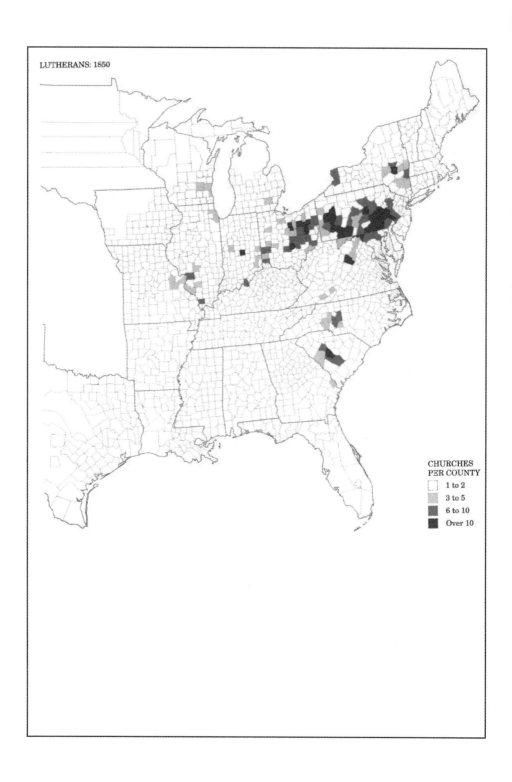

LUTHERANS: 1850

CHURCHES
PER COUNTY
1 to 2
3 to 5
6 to 10
Over 10

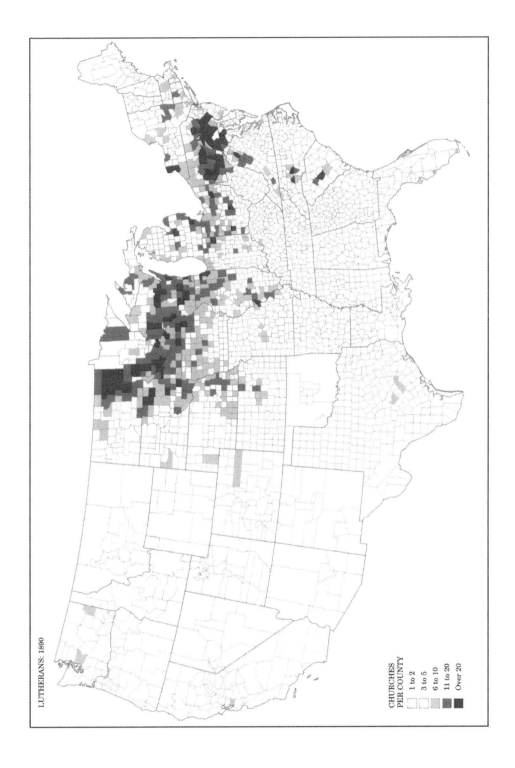

LUTHERANS: 1890

CHURCHES
PER COUNTY

1 to 2
3 to 5
6 to 10
11 to 20
Over 20

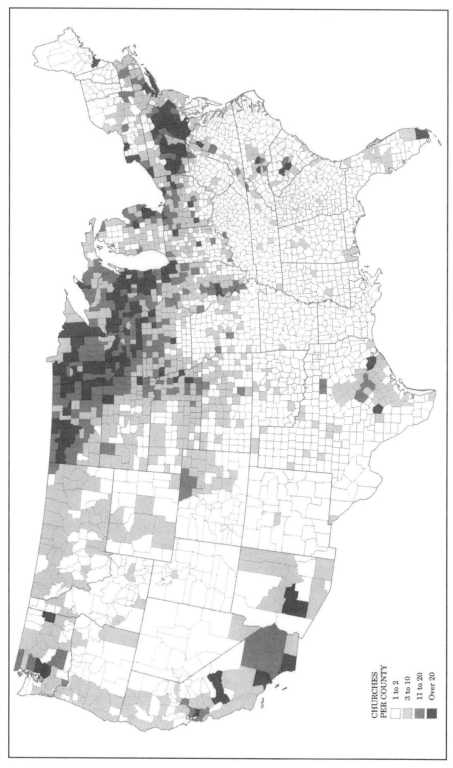

CHURCHES
PER COUNTY

1 to 2
3 to 10
11 to 20
Over 20

Lutherans, 1990

1. Augustus Lutheran Church building, Trappe, Pennsylvania, begun in 1743. One of the three congregations that originally called Henry M. Muhlenberg.

CATECHISMVS LUTHERI
Lingva
SVECICO-AMERICANA.

2. Frontispiece of the translation by Johan Campanius of Luther's *Small Catechism* into the Algonquin language, printed in Stockholm in 1696.

3. Portrait of Henry Melchior Muhlenberg, patriarch of colonial American Lutheranism.

4. Portrait of Samuel Simon Schmucker, prominent Lutheran leader in the early nineteenth century.

5. Early view of the Lutheran seminary in Gettysburg, Pennsylvania.

THE

LUTHERAN OBSERVER.

—"whatsoever things are true, whatsoever things are honest."—Phil. iv. 8.

Vol. I. BALTIMORE, AUGUST 1, 1831. No. 1.

TO OUR READERS.

The Prospectus of this publication was issued from Gettysburg, where it was intended to be conducted by Professor Schmucker and Dr. Hazelius. The Lutheran community looked with intense anxiety for its appearance under such able superintendents, but Providence has disappointed our ardent expectations. The precarious state of the health of the first gentleman has compelled him reluctantly to relinquish a field of labor in which he expected to be still more eminently useful to the church, and we all know that his distinguished qualifications would have secured for this paper an extensive circulation. In consequence of this, the whole labor of conducting the German Magazine has devolved upon Dr. Hazelius, and he did not feel at liberty to add the editorship of this journal, to his labors already sufficiently arduous. We have been requested to superintend its publication, which we have consented to do, upon the condition that all our brethren would cheerfully assist us. It is a new field of operation to us, and we need the aid of all those who feel an interest in the cause which we have espoused.

The expediency of such a periodical has not been questioned. Every other denomination of Christians has its religious Journals, and why should we be without ours? The German Magazine, though ably conducted and widely circulated, does not meet the increasing wants of the church. Our English brethren have no means of receiving information of the state of our Zion, and all agree that we should have an English paper. The Lutheran Intelligencer and Lutheran Magazine have both been discontinued, and the question now is, whether it is not possible to unite the feelings and influence of the whole church so that the permanency of one paper may be secured? May we not establish a religious semi-monthly periodical in the centre of the church, which will enlist the support of the whole denomination,—be identified with its interests, and be regarded by all as its accredited organ? We have seen that two could not be supported, —may we not then perpetuate one?

We do not think it necessary to make many professions about our system of religious doctrines and opinions. Those who are acquainted with us have had opportunities of ascertaining our opinions, and to those who do not know us, we would simply state, that we hold the great doctrines of the Reformation, and that it will be our aim to maintain them

7. Portrait of Daniel Payne, the first African American graduate of the Lutheran Seminary at Gettysburg, and later bishop in the African Methodist Episcopal Church.

8. Portrait of C.F.W. Walther, patriarch and leader of the Lutheran Church Missouri Synod.

10. Sketch of Norwegian Synod leaders arguing about slavery in 1867, drawn by Caroline (Linka) Preus, wife of one of the synodical leaders.

DEFINITE PLATFORM,

DOCTRINAL AND DISCIPLINARIAN,

FOR

EVANGELICAL LUTHERAN DISTRICT SYNODS;

CONSTRUCTED IN ACCORDANCE WITH THE
PRINCIPLES OF THE

GENERAL SYNOD.

PHILADELPHIA:

MILLER & BURLOCK.

1855.

9. Frontispiece of the Definite Platform (1855), the ill-fated proposal by Schmucker and others to amend the Augsburg Confession.

11. Typical prairie church building with congregation, Nathanael Lutheran Church, Alchester South Dakota.

12. Seventh and eighth grade class, Trinity Lutheran parochial school, Montgomery, Alabama, October, 1947.

13. Norwegian-American deaconess leader Elisabeth Fedde (front, center) and new deaconesses, Minneapolis, c. 1890.

14. Early view of the Lutheran Hospital and Deaconess Motherhouse in Pittsburgh, Pennsylvania, the first Protestant hospital in the United States.

15. Dr. William Gable serving communion at the Lutheran mission on the Rocky Boy reservation (Chippewa-Cree), Box Elder, Montana.

16. Halvor and Hannah Ronning and family in Chinese dress; Norwegian-American missionaries to China in the 1890s.

17. Lutheran pastors and native catechists in Madagascar c. 1910.

18. Lutherans ministering at a World War I training camp, NLCSSW; Rev. Julius Deckman and John W. Link at Camp Sevier, Greenville, South Carolina.

19. Helen Frost, Lutheran missionary to the Inupiaq people, in front of her tent, at the Teller Mission, Alaska, c. 1930s-1940s.

20. Lutheran World Relief feeding program for children in post-World War II Germany.

21. Temporary married student (veterans) housing, St. Olaf College, Northfield, Minnesota, 1947. Buildings were war surplus, previously used to house German POWs in Iowa.

22. Typical 1950s mission congregation, St Paul's Lutheran Church, Quincy, Washington.

23. Four acolytes bringing together quartered pieces of a large candle to symbolize the merger forming the Lutheran Church in America, Detroit, Michigan, 1962.

24. The first woman ordained as a Lutheran pastor in the United States, Elizabeth Platz, November 22, 1970.

25. The procession ("walkout") of students and faculty out of Concordia Seminary, St. Louis, Missouri, to form Christ Seminary in Exile (Seminex), February 19, 1974.

26. Rev. Nelson Trout, denominational leader and Bishop in the American Lutheran Church, 1988.

27. Denominational Ministry Strategy (DMS) protester being removed from the constituting convention of the Evangelical Lutheran Church in America, 1987.

Chapter 7

MASS IMMIGRATION, 1855–1888

A t the midpoint of the nineteenth century, the United States stood poised for both tremendous growth and devastating conflict. Geographically, the country had reached roughly the limits of its contiguous continental growth, with only Alaska and Hawaii to be added later. In 1850, there were thirty-one states, mostly east of and along the Mississippi River, with Texas and California, as well. In the next twenty-five years, seven more states would be added to the Union, including Minnesota (1858), Oregon (1859), Kansas (1861), West Virginia (1863), Nevada (1864), Nebraska (1867), and Colorado (1876), for a total of thirty-eight states by the American centennial in 1876. The rest of the western lands were rapidly populated by new settlers, many of them immigrants, and were formed into territories. Driven by demographic forces and mass immigration from Europe, the population of the United States more than doubled, from twenty-three million in 1850 to fifty million in 1880. The immigration averaged between two and three million people per decade from 1851 to 1880, and over five million from 1881 to 1890; by 1880, about 14 percent of the population of the United States was foreign-born. Although this population growth did fill the western territories, its primarily impact was a huge expansion of the cities in the East and Midwest, which grew dramatically; not only New York, Boston, and Philadelphia, but also Chicago, Detroit, Cleveland, Cincinnati, and St. Louis. With the increase in population came an equally dramatic growth in industries to employ this growing population and provide them with goods and services. During this time, the United States became a leading world manufacturer, as well as the primary food exporter to the world.

This tremendous growth came even though the United States was torn apart during the American Civil War (1861–1865), which cost at least 625,000 soldiers their lives and devastated the economy and infrastructure of the entire southern region. The conflict over African American slavery in the South, which had dominated national politics and civic life of the entire country from 1830 to 1860, resulted in the secession of eleven states from the Union in 1861 to form the Confederate States of America. This led to a destructive and bloody war between the northern and southern states. Although the Confederacy was defeated in 1865, and the enslaved African Americans were freed by the Thirteenth Amendment to the Constitution, this national tragedy continued to haunt the United States for decades afterward. Many areas of the South were excluded from the growth and industrialization that benefited the rest of the country. Although the northern and western states bounced back from the Civil War much more quickly, the war was a national trauma from which the country as a whole only slowly recovered.

The number of Lutherans in the United States grew rapidly, outstripping the rate of the general population increase. In 1860, there were an estimated 350,000 baptized Lutherans in the United States, but only fifteen years later, in 1875, that number jumped to 780,000 baptized Lutherans. Certainly, this was due in part to the immigration of Germans and Scandinavians, but there was also substantial growth in the established eastern "English" synods. The membership of the oldest synod, the Pennsylvania Ministerium, jumped from 54,000 baptized members in 1860 to 72,000 baptized members in 1875.[1] Fueled by immigration, the conservative midwestern synods grew rapidly. The Missouri Synod, founded just in 1847, expanded from an estimated 32,500 baptized members in 1860 to almost 150,000 baptized members by 1875, transforming it into a national synodical organization. Lutherans also continued and accelerated their institution-building, establishing and expanding schools, colleges, and theological seminaries, as well as social-service institutions such as hospitals, nursing homes, orphanages, and agencies to serve immigrants, seamen, and those with physical and mental disabilities. Synodical organizations were also strengthened and expanded, especially auxiliary groups for women and support for home and foreign missions.

Despite this rapid expansion and growth, this was also a time of great conflict and division among American Lutherans, as great theological and ecclesiastical controversies swept through this religious family. The eastern, "Muhlenberg" Lutherans, with their roots in the colonial period, saw the General Synod split twice, first with the departure of the southern Lutherans in 1861, and then a confessional split in 1867 that resulted in the formation of the rival General Council. Many of the confessional midwestern Lutheran groups came together in the Synodical Conference in 1872, but strong theological disputes soon wracked this section of American Lutheranism and disrupted their relations. The resulting synodical defections from the Synodical Conference meant that the large Missouri Synod came to dominate it, along with a handful of much smaller synods. The immigrant Scandinavian Lutheran synods also underwent rapid growth and internal division; at one point there were six different, rival Norwegian Lutheran synods, and there were also divisions and separate groups within the Swedish and Danish Lutheran communities. By 1875, there were three large, rival national Lutheran federations—the General Synod, the General Council, and the Synodical Conference—along with a regional federation, the General Synod South, and thirteen other independent synods, some of substantial size.

Slavery, Abolition, and the Civil War

It is hard to overemphasize the degree to which the question of slavery dominated American public life during the period from 1830 to 1860, and how it permeated all levels and organizations of American religious life. Moderates sought to find widely acceptable solutions to the issue, such as the gradual emancipation of the enslaved African Americans, compensation for their owners, and the colonization of former slaves in Africa. But in the 1830s, a new movement arose in the North, a radical push for the immediate and unconditional abolition of slavery, which elicited a similarly radical defense of slavery by southern apologists. National politics was convulsed by this issue, and even a series of carefully crafted political compromises could not settle the issue, resulting in stalemate and stagnation. In an 1858 campaign speech, Abraham Lincoln observed that "A house divided against itself cannot stand." Many observers agreed, but few saw practical and peaceful ways to unify the nation over this contentious issue.

Like most Americans at the time, Lutherans generally sought to avoid or minimize the issue because they worried about its effect on their institutions, especially the General Synod, which contained both northern and southern synods. But with the movement for immediate emancipation beginning in the 1830s, some Lutheran pastors and lay leaders attempted to have their regional synods adopt this new position. Frustrated with their unsuccessful attempts to get the Hartwick Synod to adopt a more forceful stance against slavery, a group of New York Lutherans formed the Franckean Synod in 1837. Several other regional groups, such as the

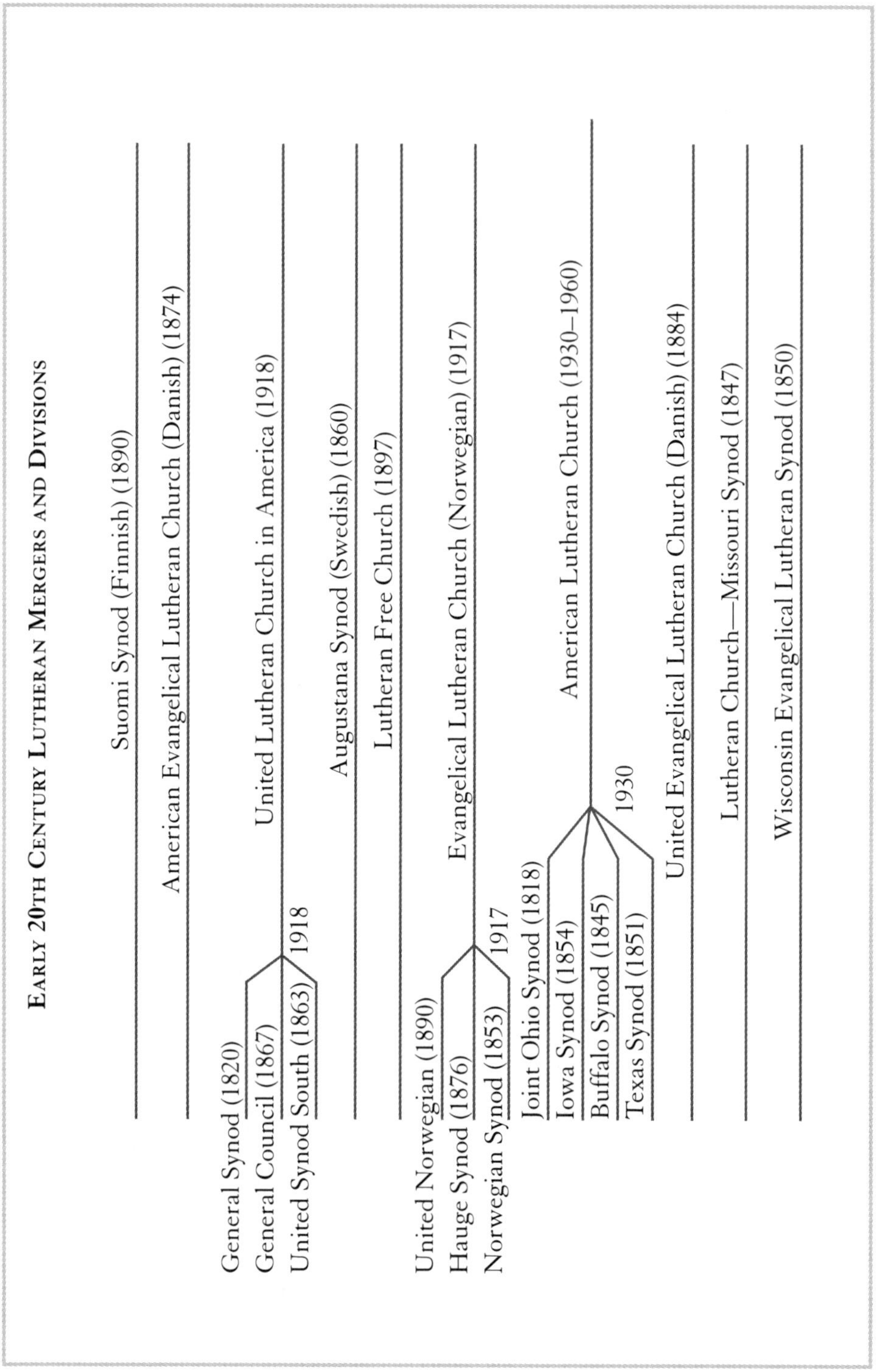

Early 20th Century Lutheran Mergers and Divisions
Suomi Synod (Finnish) (1890)
American Evangelical Lutheran Church (Danish) (1874)
General Synod (1820)
General Council (1867)
United Synod South (1863)
1918
United Lutheran Church in America (1918)
Augustana Synod (Swedish) (1860)
Lutheran Free Church (1897)
United Norwegian (1890)
Hauge Synod (1876)
Norwegian Synod (1853)
1917
Evangelical Lutheran Church (Norwegian) (1917)
Joint Ohio Synod (1818)
Iowa Synod (1854)
Buffalo Synod (1845)
Texas Synod (1851)
1930
American Lutheran Church (1930–1960)
United Evangelical Lutheran Church (Danish) (1884)
Lutheran Church—Missouri Synod (1847)
Wisconsin Evangelical Lutheran Synod (1850)

Pittsburgh Synod and the Wittenberg Synod, also adopted strong antislavery positions, referring to slavery as a "moral evil." In its 1837 constitution, the Franckean Synod stated that "the whole system of American slavery . . . was an offense to God" and that any defense of that system was sinful.[2] Although the Franckean Synod was not received into the General Synod until 1866, the Pittsburgh and Wittenberg synods were members before the Civil War.

Southern Lutherans viewed these developments within northern Lutheranism with alarm, and began to question their continued membership in the General Synod. One leader within southern Lutheranism, Dr. John Bachman, pastor of St. John's Lutheran Church in Charleston, South Carolina, produced a scholarly and theological examination of slavery in 1850. Bachman concluded that the Bible did not categorically condemn slavery as a system, though it did condemn abuses in how it was practiced. Suggesting that enslaved persons were actually better off under a system of "mild servitude," Bachman suggested that the Lutheran church ought to avoid the issue entirely because of the division and bitterness that such debate occasioned.[3] Other southern Lutherans took a more belligerent tone, however, lashing out at proponents of abolition in the North, including some Lutherans. In 1835, the South Carolina Synod adopted a resolution stating: "Resolved, unanimously, that this Synod express their strongest disapprobation of the conduct of Northern Abolitionists—and that we look upon them as enemies of our beloved country; whose mistaken zeal is calculated to injure the cause of morals and religion."[4] Increasingly, southern Lutherans looked with suspicion on their northern counterparts, with the actions of the General Synod coming under special scrutiny.

The position of Lutherans in the border states between the North and the South, such as western Virginia, Tennessee, and Missouri, was complicated. Many Lutherans in these areas were not themselves slaveowners but they lived among people who were, and the topic of the abolition of slavery was explosive. Some tried to mediate between the two opposing and polarized positions, attempting to keep the peace. Because of their tenuous position in the border states, C. F. W. Walther and the Missouri Synod attempted to stay out of this conflict and to avoid making public pronouncements of a political nature. Walther insisted the Bible did not consider slavery itself to be a sin but, rather, a moral evil in punishment for sin. Further, Walther suggested that abolitionism in opposing to slavery was anti-Christian: "Having set forth [that slavery was not, in itself, a sin] we therefore maintain that abolitionism which holds and declares slavery as an essentially sinful relationship . . . and therefore wants to abolish the former under all circumstances, is a child of unbelief . . ."[5] One Lutheran historian concluded about Walther's position, "In effect, it justified the existence of slavery,"[6] although perhaps not all its practices.

Generally, the immigrant Germans and Scandinavians who settled in the North were strongly against slavery and wanted to see it abolished. Thus when Lauritz Larsen and other leaders of the Norwegian Synod, closely allied with the Missouri Synod, adopted Walther's position on slavery, it produced a fierce controversy among the Norwegian Americans, and even back in Norway. Most Norwegian Lutheran laypeople and pastors were strongly against slavery and broke openly with Larsen over this issue. This controversy also drove many Norwegian American pastors away from a close relationship with the Missouri Synod. As many young Norwegian Americans were fighting and dying for the Union cause in the Civil War, any defense of slavery, no matter how nuanced, was anathema to this immigrant community.

When the southern states seceded from the Union in 1861, the five southern synods in the General Synod—North Carolina, South Carolina, Virginia, Southwestern Virginia, and Georgia—effectively withdrew from their northern counterparts. There was much discussion among them about forming their own cooperative body within the new Confederate States of America, but these synods did not meet to form their own organization until May 1863. Named the "General Synod of the Evangelical Lutheran Church in the Confederate States of America" or, more commonly after the war, the General Synod South, the new body attempted to support its own newspaper, colleges, and seminary through the very difficult years of the Civil War. During its formation, the new General Synod South took square aim at northern Lutherans: "As far as sympathy and harmony of action is concerned, the Northern and Southern parts of our Church have been divided. The spirit of the Northern portion is a spirit of *fanaticism*, which has been nurtured and intensified until . . . it permeates all their religious, social, and political relations."[7] Southern Lutherans struggled through the increasingly difficult war years, but continued to maintain that slavery was not itself a sin, while still attempting to urge good treatment of enslaved persons by their masters.

The northern synods remaining in the General Synod postponed their 1861 convention, hoping that the secession was temporary and that they could avoid the appearance of disunity among Lutheran synods. But as the war moved into its second year, the General Synod could wait no longer and met in May 1862. At that meeting, the northern synods termed the war "an armed rebellion against its lawfully constituted Government," and used words such as "wicked, unjustified, unnatural, inhuman, oppressive, and destructive" to describe it. Further, the proceedings resolved: "That in the suppression of this rebellion and in the maintenance of the Constitution and Union by the sword we recognize an unavoidable necessity and sacred duty . . ." Further, the resolution expressed its "most decided disapprobation" of the southern Lutheran synods and leaders for their support of "treason and insurrection."[8]

Many northern and southern Lutherans rushed to support their respective military efforts; young Lutheran men enlisted in both armies and Lutheran pastors joined army units as chaplains. The initial days of glorious patriotic fervor quickly faded as the war dragged on through increasingly bloody battles and lengthy months and years. The expectations of a quick and decisive war turned into grim determinations to see the war through, despite the costs. A Lutheran pastor, John H. W. Stuckenberg, served as a regimental chaplain to a unit that saw action at Antietam, Fredricksburg, and Gettysburg. He wrote to the *Lutheran Observer* in 1863 that battle turned the soldiers' minds toward God, and impressed itself on their very beings: "You see at once that the terrible scenes that they have witnessed, have not left them unmoved. They have shed blood and have seen it flow in streams . . . and have been at the very jaws of death, and still have escaped unhurt. . . . What they have seen and heard is indescribable . . . and they are changed beings, and can never again be what they were."[9] Southern Lutheran pastors were equally active among the army camps and units of the Confederate forces, and some observed an initial religious revival among the military men during the beginning stages of the war. But as the war dragged on and affected the southern states deeply, the tone of southern Lutherans began to turn inward and reproachful. In late 1864, the *Southern Lutheran* newspaper commented darkly, "Blasphemy, Sabbath-breaking, selfishness, avarice, hardness of heart, unbelief, and many other evils abound . . . we think we have a right claim to claim the help of the Lord, but we dishonor Him; we are not rebels against the United States, but we most assuredly are rebels against the Almighty."[10] Both sides saw the providence of God directing the ebb and flow of battle, and it was a widespread idea that success or failure in the war effort were the judgments of God. Calls for public repentance and the search for forgiveness were constant themes.

Although the human and material costs of the Civil War touched every segment of American society, both North and South, the actual destruction of battle touched some Lutherans more deeply than others. The battle of Gettysburg in July 1863 disrupted the Lutheran seminary there, which became the focal point of battle on the first day. The Confederate forces seized the seminary buildings, and one can still see a cannonball lodged in one of its building's walls. But it was in the South where Lutherans felt the direct effects and destruction of the war most vividly. All war is destructive, but in the terrible conflict that was the American Civil War, this destruction took on a form of policy. The bitter struggle to control the Shenandoah valley of western Virginia, where many Lutherans were settled, turned into a destructive rampage that destroyed buildings, farms, and fields. General William Tecumseh Sherman's "March to the Sea" across Georgia in 1864 was a purposeful campaign of destruction, and when this campaign took a turn northward into the Carolinas, southern Lutherans suffered deeply. By the end of the Civil War in April 1865, they had sustained damage to their homes, congregations, schools, and seminary. All were financially stressed. The rebuilding of southern Lutheranism took decades.

Reconstruction and African American Lutherans

The emancipation of African Americans signaled a new era for southern Lutherans, especially concerning African Americans who had been members of their congregations before the war. Now that African American Lutherans were free citizens, southern white Lutherans were unsure how to relate to them. Lacking clear directions, southern white Lutherans talked about the issue and studied it occasionally, but in the main did nothing. Schemes for educating African American pastors were proposed, but there was little will and no money for such ventures. Some local congregations maintained the old prewar patterns of including African Americans as members, but others moved to restrict their participation. St. John's Lutheran in Charleston, South Carolina, amended its constitution in 1869 to restrict congregational membership to white men, and also instituted segregated seating patterns. African American membership in the South Carolina Synod declined rapidly after 1865. To be fair, northern Lutherans at the time were equally negligent and unconcerned about outreach to African Americans, but southern Lutherans already had African Americans whom they might have retained had they made efforts to do so. The North Carolina and Tennessee synods sought to encourage the development of separate African American Lutheran congregations, and did license six African American men as Lutheran preachers, but this approach also stalled for lack of resources and lack of interest. One historian put it bluntly, "to say that black Lutherans 'disappeared' after the Civil War is not correct. They were either asked to leave Lutheran congregations or were summarily put out."[11]

White southern Lutherans struggled to rebuild their congregations and institutions through the period of Reconstruction (1865–1876). The war was financially ruinous to Lutheran institutions in the South; Newberry College and Southern Seminary in South Carolina had to be almost completely rebuilt. Roanoke College in Virginia actually flourished after the Civil War, due almost entirely to its charismatic president's fundraising efforts among northern Lutherans. The General Synod South also struggled to find its footing, which was complicated by shifting alliances in the South. The confessional Holston Synod of Tennessee entered the General Synod South in 1869, but left again in 1872. Upset by a decision to maintain Southern Seminary in South Carolina, the North Carolina Synod withdrew in 1870, only to rejoin in 1881. The Mississippi Synod joined in 1876. A cause of contention around the General Synod South was its lack of definite constitutional language formally recognizing the authority of the Augsburg Confession. There was, however, a growing trend toward confessional Lutheranism in the South after the Civil War, as traditional opponents such as the North Carolina and Tennessee synods began to reach out toward one another. Serious negotiations toward further union began in 1884, and by 1886 the Tennessee and Holston synods, along with the six synods of the General Synod South, combined into a new body, the "United Synod of the Evangelical Lutheran Church in the South," often referred to as the United Synod South. This new body contained almost all southern Lutherans with the exception of some southern congregations of the confessional Midwest synods.

Crisis in the North and the Formation of the General Council

Although the issue of the "American Edition" of the Augsburg Confession— Schmucker's "Definite Synodical Platform" of 1855—had been resolved with the widespread rejection of this document, the larger battle over the nature of Lutheran confessional authority in the Lutheran synods continued to grow through the 1850s and 1860s. Although Schmucker's plan seemed to many as an overreach that should not be adopted, he still had a large number of allies who supported his general position, if not his specific proposal. However, a significant sector of the old Muhlenberg tradition, especially in the Pennsylvania Ministerium, was moving in the direction of a stricter adherence to confessional Lutheranism based on the unaltered Augsburg Confession. These divergent streams indicated a crisis ahead for the General Synod, one that broke out into open conflict in the middle of the 1860s.

When the Pennsylvania Ministerium rejoined the General Synod in 1853, it still retained confessional reservations about that body and worried about its alleged tendencies toward centralization and usurpation of synodical power. As a condition for membership, the Pennsylvania delegates were instructed to withdraw from any meeting of the General Synod if it took actions that seemed to be contrary to confessional Lutheranism. When the Franckean Synod applied for membership in the General Synod in 1864, the confessional conflict exploded. Because of its abolitionist stance, the Franckean Synod could not have been admitted before the war, as southern synods would have viewed this negatively. In the middle of the war, and with the departure of the southern synods, the Franckean Synod could be considered. However, the Franckean Synod had only a generalized "Declaration of Faith" in its constitution and no reference at all to the authority of the Augsburg Confession. The Franckean delegates stated that, in their opinion, joining the General Synod was a *de facto* assumption of its confessional stance and, by extension, of its acceptance of the Augsburg Confession. At its 1864 meeting, representatives to the General Synod approved the admission of the Franckean Synod by a vote of ninety-seven to forty, over the heated protests of the delegates from the Pennsylvania Ministerium. Following their standing orders, the Pennsylvania delegates withdrew and reported to their synod that, in their opinion, the General Synod had violated its constitution by such an action.

The Pennsylvania Ministerium met in July 1864, and as one of its actions set up its own Lutheran seminary in Philadelphia, with Charles Porterfield Krauth, Charles Schaeffer, and William Mann as faculty, all conservative critics of Schmucker and the Gettysburg Seminary. With all sorts of public controversies over confessional issues leading up to the 1866 General Synod convention, the political intrigue was rife. The Pennsylvania Ministerium sent a group of delegates to the 1866 meeting, but they were not seated at the convention. The ruling on their credentials was that their 1864 withdrawal was a permanent action, and that to enter the 1866 convention, the Pennsylvania Ministerium would have to reapply for admission. Of course, this resulted in a complete rupture between the General Synod and the Ministerium of Pennsylvania.

At its own convention in 1866, the Pennsylvania Ministerium issued a call to all other Lutheran synods in the United States to meet and consider forming a new federation of confessional Lutherans. Later that year, at a meeting in December 1866, thirteen different synods met to discuss the possibilities of such a new organization. There was enough interest to call a constituting convention for November 1867 in Fort Wayne, Indiana, where they established a new entity, the General Council of the Evangelical Lutheran Church in America, or General Council. Although representatives from the larger midwestern German synods such as Missouri, Ohio, and Iowa attended the initial meeting in 1866, they did not join the new General Council. Missouri was especially wary of the new organization and wanted a series of free theological conferences to precede its establishment. But other synods saw no reason to delay, and so eleven synods joined the new General Council, including seven from the General Synod: the Pennsylvania and New York Ministeriums and four independent synods. Of course, these actions led to more synodical ruptures, notably within the New York Ministerium, the Pittsburgh Synod, the Illinois Synod, and others. In each of these cases, one faction stayed in the General Synod, while another faction left to join the General Council.

In the midst of division, theological suspicion and contention often spring to the fore, and such was the case with the early years of the new General Council. More conservative and confessionally Lutheran than the General Synod, the General Council still seemed insufficiently conservative and confessional for many of the midwestern German synods. Initially, the General Council adopted a document entitled "Fundamental Principles," written by Charles Porterfield Krauth, which expressed the theological position of the new federation. But midwestern groups pressed for more detailed definitions on such issues as the limits of pulpit and altar fellowship, and membership in "secret societies" such as the Freemasons and other organizations. The newly formed General Council was cautious about providing definitive answers on such contentious issues. When it did reply to the questions in 1868, the answers were not satisfactory to all. As a result, the Missouri, Ohio, and Iowa synods stayed out, and the Wisconsin and Minnesota synods withdrew. Finally, in 1872, at Akron, Ohio, the General Council formulated its rule on pulpit and altar fellowship, that is, questions about sacramental and preaching cooperation with other Lutherans and other Christians. The rule, reaffirmed at the 1875 convention in Galesburg, Illinois, and popularly called the "Galesburg Rule," stated: "Lutheran pulpits are for Lutheran ministers only. Lutheran altars are for Lutheran ministers only. The exceptions to the rule belong to the sphere of privilege, not right. The determination of these exceptions is to be made in consonance with these principles, by the conscientious judgment of pastors, as the cases arise."[12] More conservative Lutheran critics were not satisfied with such a formulation, especially with possible exceptions, which seemed to them to open the back door to these practices. With some exceptions, the General Council remained an organization of the more conservative and confessional part of the old colonial Muhlenberg tradition. By 1867, that tradition had become divided into three federative groups: the General Synod, the General Council, and the General Synod South.

Further Postwar Expansion of Lutheranism

The rapid westward expansion of the American frontier resulted in the settlement of lands beyond the Mississippi and as far as the Pacific Coast during and after the Civil War. Especially in the northern territories, many settlers were German or Scandinavian immigrants seeking cheap farmland in Kansas, Nebraska, and the Dakotas. Other immigrants went to the northwest areas of Montana, Oregon, and Washington, seeking jobs in agriculture, fishing, mining, and lumbering, especially after the best Midwest farmland was taken. The established Lutheran synods of the East and Midwest struggled to reach these pioneers and to form them into congregations. As was usually the case on the frontier, Lutherans were scattered and it was difficult for Lutheran pastors to reach them, even for visits. With the formation of seminaries, the supply of Lutheran pastors had improved, but impoverished new settlers often had a difficult time providing financially for congregations and pastors. As before, much of the ministry among these western settlers was done by traveling pastors and home missionaries, who attempted to meet the spiritual needs of the settlers and organize them into fledgling congregations. As one home missionary explained it in the 1880s, "It is extremely important that the Lutheran Church take possession of these areas from the very beginning. . . . This is to prevent the development of congregations of denominations of different faiths. It is also important to receive immediately into the Lutheran community those fellow believers who gradually move into the area."[13] Especially in the mining and lumbering camps of the West, civilization was a thin veneer, and it took many years to establish a Lutheran presence there.

German, Scandinavian, and "English" Lutheran synods all vied for the religious attention of the western settlers. Establishment of permanent congregations slowly moved west. By the 1850s, there were already Lutheran congregations in Iowa, Minnesota, and Kansas, and in Nebraska in the early 1860s. The first Lutheran congregations in the Dakotas, Colorado, and Oregon date from the 1870s, and in Montana and Washington from the 1880s. Scandinavian mission efforts to reclaim Scandinavian American Mormons led to the establishment of Lutheran congregations in Utah beginning in the 1880s. The first Lutheran congregation west of the Rocky Mountains was formed in San Francisco, California, out of the work of a traveling Missouri Synod pastor, J. M. Buehler, who arrived in that city in 1860. Some of the earliest congregations on the West Coast were actually missions formed to serve the needs of seamen who moved through ports such as San Francisco and Seattle.

The confessional conflict and the geographic expansion of Lutherans in America also meant the proliferation of synods, both in the settled areas of the Midwest and East and out on the frontiers. The division between the General Synod and General Council in 1867 led to the formation of new and rival synods in a number of locations, and the competition between the two bodies spread into the Midwest and West. A number of new synods were formed during this time, including the Minnesota Synod (1860), the Kansas Synod (1868), and the Nebraska Synod (1871), as well as western districts or conferences of other synodical bodies, such as the Western District of the Missouri Synod in 1854. As shall be seen, Scandinavian American Lutherans were seldom satisfied with just a single Lutheran option, and often broke up into rival ethnic Lutheran bodies. In 1860, there were forty-two distinct Lutheran synods in the United States, but just fifteen years later, in 1875, there were more than sixty. Although religious conflict could be locally destructive at times, all this competition and conflict between Lutheran denominations could also mean an expansion of Lutheran efforts and a Lutheran presence throughout the United States.

Scandinavian Lutherans in the United States

The mass immigration of the nineteenth century changed in composition and location as the century moved along. For Lutherans, the first wave of immigration from 1840 to 1880 was dominated by Germans, but their immigration tapered off dramatically after 1880. They were followed by a major surge in immigrants from Scandinavia, which began during the 1860s and lasted until the beginning of the First World War in 1914. About 1.2 million Swedes, a million Norwegians, and smaller numbers of Danes and Finns came to America during this time, representing a substantial loss of population to their home countries, about 25 percent of the Norwegian population and 20 percent of the Swedish. The composition of this immigration changed over time as well. The initial immigrants of the 1860s and 1870s were usually families in search of farms in the rural areas, but the later immigrants tended to be single young men and women looking for jobs in American cities. The Norwegians came to settle mainly in the upper Midwest, especially Minnesota and the Dakotas, the Swedes from Illinois to Kansas and up into Minnesota, and the Danes chiefly in Iowa and Nebraska. Later Scandinavian immigrants also founded communities in East-Coast urban centers and in the Pacific Northwest, especially Washington.

The Scandinavian immigrants came from countries where state-church Lutheranism was nearly monolithic, assuring that all these immigrants were at least nominally Lutherans. The religious situation in nineteenth-century Scandinavia was complex, however, with popular religious revival movements challenging the nature of official Lutheranism, while non-Lutheran options such as the Methodists, Baptists, Free Church, and Pentecostals were increasingly available. Very few state-church Lutheran pastors immigrated to the United States, and the Scandinavian Lutheran denominations that were established in America were generally deeply colored by these Pietist awakening movements. Even though there was a huge pool of potential Scandinavian members for these new Lutheran denominations, the obstacles to gathering them in were formidable; poverty, dispersion, and lack of pastors chief among them. Only a minority of Scandinavians actually joined the immigrant denominations; by 1920, only about 30 percent of Norwegian Americans, 20 percent of Swedish Americans, and 9 percent of Danish Americans were members of Scandinavian ethnic denominations, and this came after decades of home-missions efforts.[14]

Besides the external causes of poverty and lack of religious resources, there were many reasons that an immigrant might not formally join one of these immigrant denominations. The concepts of membership and voluntary financial contribution were alien to them, and many immigrants used the services of local congregations without joining. One estimate is that up to 50 percent of the immigrant population was within the "sphere of influence" of these ethnic congregations. Some immigrants joined "English" or American congregations, while others celebrated their new religious freedom by joining no church at all. Still other immigrants were put off by the restrictive Pietist morality of many of these congregations, while others lived where no Lutheran congregations were available.

Despite these negative factors, many Scandinavian Lutheran denominations grew to be large national organizations, and certainly the largest ethnically based groups within their immigrant communities. Besides establishing thousands of local congregations, these denominations developed schools, colleges, and seminaries, orphanages and hospitals, and many other social-service agencies, and were the primary keepers of the immigrant ethnic heritage. Scandinavian Americans joined the congregations of these denominations for many reasons: religious ones, primarily, but also for ethnic and linguistic reasons, as well as for companionship and support. Facing a harsh and sometimes unforgiving new culture, immigrants often sought out like-minded people and religious leaders for solidarity and support. But there were also significant tensions within these immigrant Lutheran traditions; they fought among themselves and divided with regularity, which was nothing unusual for other American Lutherans, either.

The Norwegian Americans were a religiously contentious and divisive lot, although, conversely, they were also the most successful in gathering their ethnic compatriots into congregations. Much of the contention within the Norwegian American Lutheran community had roots in theological and ecclesiological controversies of the nineteenth century in Norway, especially in the awakening movement that began early in the century under the leadership of lay preacher Hans Nielsen Hauge. Hauge and his followers sought a Pietist renewal of Lutheranism in Norway, but his activities such as lay preaching were strongly opposed by the state church, and Hauge was even imprisoned for seven years. Hauge's followers set up independent "Prayer Houses" in Norway, which for some became *de facto* congregations.

The earliest Norwegian immigrants to the United States settled in northern Illinois and southern Wisconsin in the 1840s and 1850s. The first Lutheran leader among them was a Haugean lay preacher named Elling Eielsen, who organized a synod in 1846, popularly called the Eielsen Synod. The synod was fiercely congregational, stressed repentance and conversion, and strongly opposed the formal liturgy and structure of the Church of Norway. Eielsen did not long have the field to himself, however, as another leader, J. W. C. Dietrichson, arrived in 1844. Dietrichson embodied everything that Eielsen detested; Dietrichson was trained at a Norwegian university, ordained by a bishop into the Church of Norway, and strongly advocated the formal liturgy and structure of that church. The two were instant competitors and ardent enemies; when the two finally met in 1845, Dietrichson challenged Eielsen's legitimacy, and Eielsen is reported to have grabbed Dietrichson by the beard and exclaimed, "Listen to me, you pope, I intend to plague you as long as I live."[15] Although Eielsen eventually moved toward the fringes, and Dietrichson returned to Norway, they defined the issues and the boundaries for Norwegian American Lutherans.

Dietrichson and others met in 1853 to form the Norwegian Evangelical Lutheran Church in America, commonly known as the Norwegian Synod. This body sought to establish the traditions of the Church of Norway in the United States, with a formal Lutheran liturgy and a learned clergy, although they never sought to establish the episcopate. Under the talented leadership of immigrant pastors such as J. A. Ottesen, A. C. Preus, and Ulrik Koran, the new synod grew quickly and gathered in the immigrants; from about 13,000 baptized members in 1860, the synod grew rapidly to over 70,000 baptized members in 1875. The leaders of the Norwegian Synod sought Lutheran allies, and after consideration found the Missouri Synod to be closest to its own confessional position. In 1859, Pastor Lauritz Larsen was sent by the Norwegian Synod to be the Norwegian professor at Concordia Seminary in St. Louis, an arrangement through which the synod hoped to train its own pastors. Unfortunately, the Missouri position on slavery did not sit well with most lay Norwegian Americans, who were strongly antislavery and supported the Republican Party. This produced an ongoing controversy between some of the Norwegian Synod leaders, who supported the Missouri Synod and its position, and the majority of the synod's pastors and laypeople, who opposed it. Because of the controversy and the Civil War, the educational arrangement with Missouri collapsed and, in 1864, Larsen instead became the head of the Norwegian Synod's new Luther College, established in Iowa in 1861.

Standing in the middle ground between the Eielsen and Norwegian synods were a number of other Norwegian American pastors. Some of them initially joined together with Swedish American pastors in 1851 to become members of the Synod of Northern Illinois, a part of the General Synod. But the Scandinavian pastors did not fit well into this new synod and were deeply troubled by the "American Lutheranism" controversies of the 1850s. In 1860, the Scandinavians withdrew from the Synod of Northern Illinois to form the Scandinavian Augustana Synod. This arrangement combined a larger number of Swedish congregations with a smaller number of Norwegian ones; though it did not lead to conflict, the minority Norwegians withdrew peacefully from the Augustana Synod in 1870. From then on, the Augustana Synod was exclusively Swedish. The departing centrist Norwegians could not form a single denomination, however, but split up into two separate groups, the Norwegian-Danish Augustana Synod, and the Conference for the Norwegian-Danish Evangelical Lutheran Church in America. There was also a split within the Eielsen Synod in 1876, which divided the Hauge's Norwegian Evangelical Lutheran Synod from the much-smaller Eielsen Synod, which soon faded into relative obscurity. So by 1876, Norwegian American Lutherans had their choice of affiliating with no fewer than five different, competing Lutheran denominations.

The religious situation in nineteenth-century Sweden was similar to that of Norway, with a Pietist awakening movement that developed early in the century, which called for reforms both of church and society in Sweden. Unlike in Norway, there was less overt hostility over this movement, and unlike Hauge, none of the Swedish awakening leaders were imprisoned. The leader of the Swedish revival movement was lay preacher C. O. Rosenius, who formed the National Evangelical Foundation in 1856 to coordinate revival activity in Sweden. Much of both Swedish and Norwegian Lutheranism in America was strongly influenced by Rosenian Pietism, which urged cooperation with Lutheran church structures while pushing for an awakened Lutheran population and a strong Pietist morality. However, there was low-level conflict and opposition to the awakening movement from many officials of the Lutheran Church of Sweden, while most of the founders of Swedish American Lutheranism came out of the revival movement. Actually, only a handful of Scandinavian American Lutheran leaders, Norwegian, Swedish, or Danish, were ordained, state-church pastors. Rather, most of those who came from Scandinavia were educated in the Pietist mission schools or in Scandinavian American seminaries and ordained in the United States.

Two of the first Swedish church leaders in the United States were state-church pastors with decided Pietist leanings, Lars Paul Esbjorn and Tuve Nilsson Hasselquist. Together with other early leaders such as Eric Norelius and Erland Carlsson, these Swedes joined with Norwegians to enter the Synod of Northern Illinois in 1851. When these Scandinavians became independent in 1860, forming the Augustana Synod, it was on the basis of their adherence to the Augsburg Confession. In 1860, the Augustana Synod also formed its own seminary, Augustana Seminary, which eventually settled in Rock Island, Illinois. The traditional core of the Augustana Synod was in the Illinois-Iowa area, although the synod had a large number of members in Minnesota and a significant presence in New York and New England. Augustana was open to alliances with other Lutherans in the United States, and in 1870 joined the General Council, although close cooperation was not always easy for a Swedish-speaking denomination in a predominantly German- and English-speaking federation.

There were also significant Swedish American religious denominations that were not Lutheran, reflecting influences that circulated from the United States and England to Sweden, and then back to North America. The Swedish Baptist movement began in the United States in 1852 with the formation of the Swedish Baptist General Conference, and Swedish Methodist congregations, dating back to the 1850s, were joined into ethnic conferences within the American Methodist denomination. Though these groups were much smaller than the Augustana Synod, they posed a strong challenge to it, especially in the 1850s and 1860s, and theological debates raged between the groups. After the death of Rosenius in 1868, a portion of the revivalist movement within the Lutheran congregations in Sweden and among Swedish Americans pushed for further separation. Through the 1860s and 1870s, these "Mission Friends" formed increasingly exclusive religious societies either within the Augustana congregations or as independent congregations. Rosenius's successor in Sweden was pastor and theologian Paul P. Waldenström, who came into conflict with official Lutheranism over the doctrine of the atonement and the nature of confessional authority. Waldenström led the Mission movement in Sweden away from formal adherence to the Lutheran confessions.

Some of the "freer" Mission Swedes in America formed their own Lutheran synods. The Swedish Evangelical Lutheran Ansgarius Synod was formed in 1873, and the Swedish Evangelical Mission Synod was formed in 1874, differing from each other in that the Ansgarius Synod affiliated with the General Synod, but the Mission Synod did not. The controversy over Waldenström and the atonement raged throughout Swedish America during the 1870s, and the Augustana Synod excommunicated a sizable number of pastors and laypeople over the issue. One of the "Free" Augustana pastors who was excommunicated, J. G. Princell, famously quipped that "synods" were nothing more than "organized sin." As the controversies developed, the Free and Mission people moved away from the Augustana Synod and from formal Lutheranism, but they could not all move toward each other, either. In 1884, the "Free" portion of the movement formed the Swedish Evangelical Free Church, and in 1885, the "Mission" people formed the Swedish Mission Covenant Church, at which time the Ansgarius and Mission synods ceased to exist. By 1885, the religious world of Swedish America was formed; the Augustana Lutherans represented about 70 percent of church members, while the Baptists, Methodist, Free, and Mission represented the remaining 30 percent. Like the Norwegians, the Swedes had five different options, but unlike the Norwegians, their four smaller groups were non-Lutheran. The Augustana Synod grew from an initial membership of about 7,200 baptized members at its founding in 1860 to 33,000 baptized members in 1875.

The number of Danish immigrants to the United States was much smaller than that of either the Swedes or Norwegians, perhaps about 350,000 prior to the First World War. They also tended to spread out further, and often associated with Norwegian Lutheran congregations, where language differences were not much of a factor. One early religious section of Danish immigrants were the Danish Mormons, who came in large numbers to Utah in the 1860s and 1870s. Later Danish Lutheran home-mission efforts tried to win these immigrants back, but with little success. Denmark had several different streams of Lutheran traditions; the two strongest during the nineteenth century were the followers of theologian and hymn writer N. F. S. Grundt-vig, and the Pietists generally centered in the Danish Inner Mission. Sometimes, the Grundtvigians are referred to as the "Happy Danes," and the Inner Mission group as the "Sad" or "Holy" Danes, referring mostly to differences over the strict Pietist life-style and rejection of "worldly" amusements by the Inner Mission people.

Grundtvig was a wonderful hymnwriter and a colorful theologian, with a strong emphasis on the nationalistic, or "folk," element of Danish Lutheranism. For him, the Danish language, culture, and nationality were inexorably linked to Christianity, and he urged expression of all these together. He valued more the "living word" of Scripture over what he saw as mechanistic understandings of biblical authority. One of his idiosyncratic theological positions involved locating an important expression of this "living word" of God in the Apostles' Creed, especially its use in the baptismal formulation. Grundtvig was very influential in the Lutheran Church of Denmark in the nineteenth century, and within Norway for a period at midcentury. Led by Vilhelm Beck and deeply influenced by the Moravians, the Inner Mission was a classic Pietist movement that urged repentance, conversion, and a regenerate lifestyle deeply opposed to the "things of the world." Both strains of Danish Lutheranism were brought to the United States by immigrants, although the masses of Danish immigrants were probably not strongly associated with either position.

The first Danish American Lutheran organization, begun in 1872, eventually became known as the Danish Evangelical Lutheran Church in America, more commonly called the Danish Church. Like the Church of Denmark, this organization included both Grundtvigians and Inner Mission people but, unlike the Church of Denmark, it could not hold them together. Independent Danish American Lutheran groups, primarily Inner Mission, were formed during the 1880s, and eventually these independent Inner Mission people, along with the Inner Mission section of the Danish Church, merged in 1896 to form the United Danish Evangelical Lutheran Church. "Happy" and "Holy," Danish Americans now had their choice, but Danish

American membership in either group was low, with only about 10 percent of all immigrants from Denmark joining a Lutheran congregation in the United States.

The Synodical Conference and the Predestination (Election) Controversy

After some flirtations with joining the new General Council in 1867, many midwestern German confessional groups decided either to leave the General Council or not to join it at all. This left many of these Lutheran groups searching for some vehicle by which to express their unity as conservative, confessional Lutherans and to cooperate on practical matters. In 1870, the Joint Synod of Ohio in 1870 initiated a call to explore the formation of such an organization, with a conference in 1871 laying the groundwork. In 1872, the Illinois, Minnesota, Missouri, Joint Ohio, Norwegian, and Wisconsin synods formed the Synodical Conference. Although close to many of the synods involved, the Iowa Synod had a history of cool relations with the Missouri Synod, and for that reason Iowa did not join. The organization was both strictly confessional and strictly advisory; its powers were constrained, although there was some initial discussions of the formation of a joint seminary. C. F. W. Walther was elected as the first president, and in its first years the Synodical Conference demonstrated considerable vitality. By 1875, the new organization represented over 325,000 baptized American Lutherans and was larger than either the General Synod or General Council.

Theological troubles soon seriously damaged relations between these midwestern confessional synods, however, which had significant negative effects on the Synodical Conference. The issue of contention was the doctrine of predestination or election: the idea that God has predetermined or chosen those who will be saved. Although Reformed or Calvinist Christians are better known for holding this doctrine, it is also essential to the Lutheran theology of grace, in which humans are saved not by their own actions but solely by the grace of God. Predestination assures that it is God's action alone that saves and not any human effort. Luther held to predestination, but did not consider it to be a central or vital doctrine of the faith, and nothing over which ordinary Christians ought to be concerned. Traditionally, in Lutheran theology, predestination has not been fully defined and is often mentioned in the negative; that is, "Calvinists believe this about predestination, but we Lutherans do not." Article IX of the Formula of Concord (1580) has a section on election, but is not precise about the doctrine.

Troubles began with a theological discussion at a meeting of the Western District of the Missouri Synod in 1877. Under Walther's leadership, this group had a long and thorough debate about the doctrine of predestination, and reports of the discussion were circulated. Several theologians in the Synodical Conference began to raise questions about Walther's formulation of the doctrine of predestination. Soon the debate spilled over onto the pages of *Lehre und Wehre*, the theological journal of the Missouri Synod. The critics, Henry Allwardt and Frederick Stellhorn of Missouri, and Friedrich Schmidt of the Norwegian Synod, suggested that Walther's position was closer to Calvinism than Lutheranism, and accused Walther of being a "Crypto-Calvinist" (secret Calvinist) on the issue. Given Walther's strong antipathy toward Reformed theology, which he perceived among the "American Lutherans," these were fighting words. So the battle was joined.

The positions involved were complicated and the stakes were high. An American Lutheran historian, Abdel Ross Wentz, summarized the dispute in these terms:

> The man who believes in Christ and his atoning merit is . . . predestined to be saved. But shall we say that God's predestination is the cause of his faith and his salvation, or shall we say that his faith is the cause of his predestination? The Missourians took the first alternative . . . [insisting] that a man cannot believe in Christ unless God causes him to do so. . . . [Missouri's opponents] took the second alternative and insisted that God elects man to salvation "in view of his faith" in the merits of Christ.[16]

Opponents suggested that Walther's position on predestination robbed human beings of their autonomy and moral responsibility, and accused him of determinism and fatalism as well as Calvinism. Walther accused his opponents of synergism, that is, human cooperation with God in salvation, as well as semi-Pelagianism. The controversy revolved around the question of whether God saved human beings "in view of their faith" or, more commonly, God's "foreknowledge" of human faith.

This controversy soon flamed into all-out theological war, and greatly complicated relations among these midwestern confessional groups. The Iowa Synod already had a history of rocky relations with Missouri, and its theologians Sigmund and Gottfried Fritschel opposed the Missouri position on predestination. The internal Missouri opponents of Walther, Allwardt and Stellhorn, left the Missouri Synod early in the controversy and joined the Joint Synod of Ohio, the group from which the main opposition to Walther and the Missouri position was to come. Key to this opposition was the Ohio Synod theologian Matthias Loy, a longtime ally of Walther who, in 1881, came out in print against Walther's position, stating: "Missouri teaches that God elected unto faith, not in view of faith. . . . If election is *unto* faith, and all consideration of man's conduct . . . is rejected as synergistic error, the sovereign will of God must determine all. . . . The Missourians have repeatedly protested that they do not teach an election without faith, although their language is not always assuring."[17] The dispute raged fiercely between the parties during and after the 1880s, and had the effect of alienating the Joint Synod of Ohio from the Missouri Synod, which culminated in Ohio's withdrawal from the Synodical Conference in 1882. The Norwegian Synod also withdrew over the same issue in 1883, which reduced the size of the Synodical Conference by one-third, leaving that body as constituted by the Missouri Synod and a grouping of several other, much-smaller synods. The Synodical Conference did not become the instrument of uniting the midwestern confessional synods, as originally attended.

Although the controversy over predestination seriously disrupted the relations between the Missouri, Ohio, and Iowa synods, it was managed without large-scale internal disruptions within each synod. The situation was very different among the Norwegians, however, especially those in the Norwegian Synod, which was internally splintered by the dispute. There had long been an undercurrent of resentment and suspicion among the Norwegians against the Missouri Synod, dating back to the slavery controversy of the 1860s. Although the leadership and about two-thirds of the pastors of the Norwegian Synod supported the Missouri position on predestination (or election, as it was called among the Norwegians), there was a substantial group who favored the second position. These positions were popularly expressed as the two "forms" of election, the first form being "election unto faith," along the Missouri lines, and the second form "election in view of foreseen faith," closer to the Ohio and Iowa position. The first form drew from Article IX of the Formula of Concord (which had an ambiguous authority among the Norwegians), while the second form came from the revered and widely used Norwegian catechism of Bishop Eric Pontoppidan, from his answer to question 548.[18]

The debate over the two forms of election raged throughout the Norwegian Synod during the 1880s; the other Norwegian American denominations, who supported the second form, generally stayed out of the controversy. This conflict filtered down into the congregations of the Norwegian Synod and caused great difficulties on the local level. For example, in the historic Norwegian congregation of East Koshkonong in Wisconsin, the controversy divided the congregation; a dissident group withdrew and established its own congregation, with its own building just several hundred yards away from the original church. It is hard to know how many other Norwegian Synod congregations were similarly affected, but the number was substantial.

Tensions ran high within the Norwegian Synod, and in 1884 they erupted into divisions within the synod itself. In response to synodical actions sought to define the position of the first form ("An Accounting"), while a minority issued their "Confession" and began to set up their own institutions, including a separate treasury to support "second-form" pastors, teachers, and seminary students, and eventually their own independent seminary associated with St. Olaf College. These dissidents became known as the "Anti-Missouri Brotherhood," and increasingly distanced themselves from the Norwegian Synod. The inevitable break between the two groups came during 1886–1887, when the Anti-Missourians formally withdrew, numbering about one-third of the synod. Much more so than with the German synods, the election controversy among the Norwegian Americans affected them on the congregational level for decades to come.

Developments among American Lutherans: Worship and Mission

Through the nineteenth century, American Lutherans continued the process of developing their own traditions, institutions, and outreach, drawing on the traditions of European Lutheranism, but increasingly adapting them to the particular conditions and challenges of America. As they gained strength and confidence, American Lutheran synods developed their own approaches to the needs of their own communities and to the world around them. Three aspects of these trends are notable during this period of time: an increasing development of American Lutheran liturgies and hymns; a growth in home missions and outreach to Native Americans; and the establishment of benevolent and social-service institutions.

Among the Lutherans of the colonial Muhlenberg traditions, their early transition to the use of English in worship and openness to American patterns such as revivalism meant that worship among them became simplified early in the nineteenth century. Many of the traditional Lutheran liturgical elements, such as the responsorial elements of the liturgy and the observance of the festivals of the church year, were simplified or eliminated. Worship was dominated by the sermon and relied on free or spontaneous responses along the lines of other American Protestants. Part of the debates over "American Lutheranism" during the 1850s focused on the nature of worship and the liturgy. The pendulum began to swing back slowly toward more formal liturgies during the latter half of the nineteenth century. The General Synod's new English liturgy in 1847 took some small steps in this direction, while the Ministerium of Pennsylvania introduced its own English liturgy in 1860, which took the process somewhat further. The General Synod, under the liturgical leadership of Beale Melanchthon Schmucker, son of the pro-revival Samuel Simon Schmucker, introduced a new, more formal liturgy, the "Washington Service" of 1869. The General Council adopted its own new hymnal, the *Church Book*, in 1868, while southern Lutherans also took steps toward liturgical renewal. These trends continued through the 1870s and 1880s, when the three groups of eastern Lutherans began to cooperate on developing a single Lutheran liturgy, which appeared as the *Common Service* of 1888. This common liturgy was not uniformly adopted, and sections of the General Synod still strongly opposed it, but this development was one sign that these three groups were gradually drawing toward closer relations.

Many of the midwestern groups depended on liturgies, psalmbooks, and hymnals brought with them from Europe and reprinted in the United States. The Joint Synod of Ohio cooperated with the Pennsylvania and New York ministeriums to develop a German liturgy in 1884 and an English one in 1894. Many German immigrant groups, especially the Missouri and Iowa synods, initially used European liturgies (in German, "*Agende*"), such as those from Saxony or by Wilhelm Löhe. Walther developed a German liturgy for the Missouri Synod in 1856, followed by a German hymnal in 1862. The various Scandinavian groups also brought with them their own national psalmbooks and liturgies, although since these represented the state-church Lutheranism of Scandinavia, the more pietistically inclined of these immigrants often modified them or used them selectively. Among the Swedish immigrants, the early leaders of the Augustana Synod generally used a Pietist revision of the Swedish Psalmbook of 1819. A collection of well-loved revival hymns, the *Hemlandssånger*, intended for devotional use, was nevertheless widely used for congregational worship. The Norwegian groups were split among themselves over the liturgy and psalmbook of the Church of Norway, with the more formal Norwegian Synod using it, while the Pietist Haugeans employed little in the way of formal liturgies. The Danish congregations evidenced similar divisions.

The nineteenth century was an expansive period of hymn writing, especially in England and America. Sometimes derided for sentimentality and subjective, individual focus, and for their use in revival settings, these Victorian Anglo-American "gospel" hymns nevertheless remained hugely popular and were exported to Europe. Revivalist leaders in Scandinavia translated these hymns and wrote similar hymns of their own, which formed an important element of Scandinavian American worship. It was not unusual for Scandinavian Americans to be singing in equal measure the hymns of American hymnwriters such as Fanny Crosby and of their own writers, like Carolina Sandell Berg.

Mission and evangelical outreach were key to the expansion of nineteenth-century American Lutheranism, and the growth that Lutheranism evidenced during this time is proof that American Lutherans did evangelism effectively. The immigrants did not automatically flood into Lutheran congregations, but had to be gathered carefully and painstakingly into the various synods by means of deliberate efforts. Throughout the nineteenth century, the growth and sophistication of these synods required a higher degree of organization in home-mission activities, with centralized home-missions committees and regularized funding. The leader in this was the General Synod, which did mainly English-language outreach, but which also formed two new German-language synods in the Midwest, the Wartburg Synod (1875) and the German Nebraska Synod (1890). Since the General Council was divided linguistically (roughly one-third each English, German, and Swedish), the evangelism was delegated to the respective linguistic synods. The Missouri Synod had an extensive German-language home-mission effort, as did the Iowa and Ohio synods; the Norwegian groups had parallel organizations.

At the major American ports of entry, there were often Lutheran immigrant houses where ethnic pastors ministered to the newly arrivals. Home missionaries regularly traveled through the Midwest, West, and Canada to organize preaching points and congregations, often following the newly built railroads. Seminarians and seminary teachers were often pressed into service for short-term assignments. Local pastors assumed responsibility for bringing word-and-sacrament ministry to settlers within range of their congregations. For example, pioneer Minnesota pastors Eric Norelius (Swedish) at Vasa Lutheran Church and B. J. Muus (Norwegian) at Holden Lutheran Church were each responsible for the establishment of a dozen or more congregations within a one-hundred-mile radius of their home congregations. English-speaking groups, especially the General Synod and the southern Lutherans, followed their members who moved west. Lutherans increasingly flocked into the new and growing American cities, but urban home missions there were slower to develop. Although each synod's concern was mainly directed at their own ethnic populations, "English," German, or Scandinavian, the fact that there were so many competing groups eager to form congregations and gather in the immigrants meant that hundreds of new congregations were formed, and hundreds of thousands of new members were enrolled.

Although the main home-mission focus of these Lutheran denominations was on their own ethnic populations, they occasionally attempted localized efforts to extend home-mission work to non-Lutherans, often other immigrant populations. There were several efforts to reach out to immigrant Jewish populations. Midwest Scandinavians formed an independent "Zion Society for Israel" in 1878, which continued its work well into the twentieth century. Other Jewish mission efforts included those of the Missouri Synod in New York City (1883), the Iowa Synod in Chicago (1893), and the Joint Ohio Synod in Pittsburgh (1896).

More widespread were Lutheran mission efforts among Native Americans, attempts encouraged by U.S. government policies, which forced Native Americans onto reservations and solicited religious groups to operate relief and educational programs there. The earliest nineteenth-century attempts were by the "Löhe missionaries" who began religious outreach to Native Americans in Michigan during the 1840s. After these efforts collapsed and Löhe's followers founded the Iowa Synod in the 1850s, the new synod continued to seek ways of doing mission work among the Native Americans. From 1859 to 1867, the Iowa Synod attempted mission work with the Crow and Cheyenne tribes in Wyoming and Montana, but due to unstable conditions, these efforts did not flourish. One Iowa Synod missionary described their difficulties, especially with the trading companies that sought to exploit the Native Americans:

> . . . we must free the Indians from the companies, or else our effectiveness will suffer. We also must have continual residence if we want to help the Indians forgo their unsteady way of living, to which they adhere so firmly. What good is all the talking about agriculture and living in houses? They must see it . . . whatever they saw in the forts . . . could have scared them a thousand times in turning their backs on agriculture.[19]

Similarly, during the late 1870s, Augustana Synod missionaries Johannes Telleen and Matthias Wahlstrom surveyed portions of the American West for possible mission opportunities, including with the Delaware tribe that the New Sweden colonists had contact two centuries earlier, but nothing came of this. When the situation was more settled, later efforts resulted in longer-established work that lasted well into the twentieth century. In 1884, several Norwegian American denominations established mission work with the Winnebago tribe in central Wisconsin, near the town of Wittenberg. In 1890, the Pietist Danes began work with the Cherokee tribe in Oaks, Oklahoma, while the Wisconsin Synod founded a mission to the Apaches in Arizona in 1893, and the Missouri Synod conducted similar efforts with the Stockbridge tribe in Wisconsin after 1899. One further effort was the mission by Pastor T. L. Brevig of the Norwegian Synod among Eskimo tribes around the remote town of Teller, Alaska, in 1894. This effort resulted in the formation of several permanent native congregations in that area. Although there was occasionally much effort and goodwill involved in these efforts, they usually suffered through inconsistent support and often yielded minimal results.

An area of importance for Lutherans in the nineteenth century was the development of institutions of mercy such as hospitals, orphanages, homes for the aged and for the physically and mentally handicapped, and sanatoriums. Since local governments supported very few of these institutions and there was little in the way of a "social safety net," religious institutions were often left to fill this need. Life was short and often difficult during this century, and average life expectancy only reached forty-seven by 1900. Cities were dangerous, crowded, and unsanitary, and frontier life was lonely, brutal, and unsafe. Life was tenuous, and even though most families endeavored to "take care of their own," this was not always possible, especially among immigrants whose extended families were often on the other side of the Atlantic. The European Pietist movement of the eighteenth century pioneered the formation of these institutions of mercy. The University of Halle was a complex of different institutions created to meet social needs, and this model was transferred to colonial America through the founding of an orphanage at the Salzburg settlement in Georgia. Such institutions were, however, not widespread in colonial America, which relied on informal networks of support to meet these social needs.

The growth and complexity of American society in the nineteenth century argued for a different approach. The great evangelical consensus in the early part of the century unleashed a wave of voluntary organizations to meet social needs, and American denominations got into the business of building and operating institutions of mercy. The Lutheran pioneer in such ministries was Pastor William A. Passavant of the Pittsburgh Synod, who tirelessly founded and promoted Lutherans hospitals and orphanages around the country, and worked with other groups, especially the Scandinavian synods, to establish their own institutions. After seeing institutions of mercy among Lutherans in Europe, Passavant returned home and founded a hospital in Pittsburgh in 1849, the oldest Protestant hospital in America. As was often the case, these early institutions were operated on large amounts of faith but little in the way of financial resources. Referring to that first hospital, Passavant later recalled:

> The first year of its existence was a time of great pecuniary difficulty. The institution was commenced in humble dependence on God. . . . Two beds, a table, a cook stove, and a few chairs composed all the furniture when the first patient was received . . . qualified nurses had to be procured at a considerable expense, and means had to be raised for support of the increasing number of sick.[20]

Staffing these institutions was a huge challenge, especially since professional medical training was in its infancy. In Europe, those in charge of religious institutions of mercy had revived an older Christian tradition, the diaconate, to provide trained medical staffing. Although there were male deacons in Europe, among Lutherans in the United States, female deaconesses were the primary examples of this movement. These deaconesses were organized into a quasi-monastic regime, tied to a central motherhouse and organized for the service of mercy. Early deaconess efforts in the

Pittsburgh hospital and among the congregations of the Iowa Synod were sporadic. It was not until the 1880s that permanent Lutheran deaconess organizations were started in America.

Many different synods started hospitals and other institutions of mercy. There were few, if any, synods that could not boast of "our" hospital, or "our" home, or "our" orphanage. Passavant organized additional hospitals in Milwaukee (1863) and Chicago (1865). Missouri Synod pastor Johan Buenger established a hospital in St. Louis in 1860. Sister Elisabeth Fedde founded Norwegian hospitals in Brooklyn (1883), Minneapolis (1888), and Chicago (1896), while the Swedish Augustana Synod founded hospitals in Saint Paul (1882), Chicago (1884), and Omaha (1890). It is estimated that during the last third of the nineteenth century, some twenty-five Lutheran hospitals were formed in the United States, along with many more orphanages, homes for the aged, and other forms of social-ministry organizations. Specialized institutions were also developed to meet particular needs, such as for the deaf and those with physical and mental handicaps. These initial efforts in the nineteenth century would continue into the twentieth, and eventually resulted in the formation of the second-largest social-service network in the United States.

Conclusion

By 1888, American Lutheranism had gone through a remarkable period of both conflict and growth. Synods were organized, divided, and re-formed, and at least three large federations of Lutheran synods coordinated their efforts. The traumas of the Civil War and Reconstruction split the country, and brought death and destruction in their wake. Millions of immigrant Lutherans poured into the United States, and synods struggled to gather them into congregations and provide pastors to lead them. Lutherans also struggled to define what it meant to be both Lutheran and American, and since they came up with divergent answers, they argued and divided and united. What impresses most about this period is the sheer energy and faith evidenced by these American Lutherans, a restless and inventive lot. These traits would only be multiplied in the decades to come.

Notes

1. This is even in spite of the fact that the Ministerium of Pennsylvania lost a fair number of congregations to newer synods during the formation of the General Council in 1867. All membership numbers in this chapter are from Robert C. Wiederaenders, ed., *Historical Guide to Lutheran Church Bodies of North America*, 2d ed. (St. Louis: Lutheran Historical Conference, 1998). Since most of these statistics before 1900 report "Communicant" members, an extra 30

percent is added to them to approximate the numbers of "Baptized" members, a category used primarily in the twentieth century.

2. *Constitution of the Franckean Synod*, 1837, Standing Resolutions, article 2 (Hartwick, NY: n.p., 1839), 53.

3. John Bachman, *The Doctrine of the Unity of the Human Race, Examined on Principles of Science* (Charleston, SC: C. Canning, 1850).

4. *Minutes of the South Carolina Synod, 1835*, 8. Quoted in Raymond M. Bost, *History of the Lutheran Church in South Carolina*. Columbia, SC: R. L. Bryan Co., 1971.

5. C. F. W. Walther, "Vorwort," *Lehre und Wehre*, 10 February 1863, p. 34.

6. August R. Sueflow and E. Clifford Nelson, "Following the Frontier," in E. Clifford Nelson, ed., *The Lutherans in North America* (Philadelphia: Fortress Press, 1975), 239.

7. *Minutes of the First Convention of the General Synod of the Evangelical Lutheran Church in the Confederate States of America . . .* 1863 (Columbia, SC: n.p., 1864), 4.

8. *Proceedings of the Twentieth Convention of the General Synod . . .* 1862 (Gettysburg: n.p., 1862), 29–32.

9. "The Effects of a Battle on a Man's Religious Views and Feelings," *Lutheran Observer*, March 6, 1863.

10. "Editorial," *Southern Lutheran*, November 10, 1864, p. 2, quoted in Paul McCullough, ed., *A History of the Lutheran Church in South Carolina* (Columbia, SC: R. L. Bryan Co., 1971), 297.

11. Jeff G. Johnson, *Black Christians: The Untold Lutheran Story* (St. Louis: Concordia, 1991), 148.

12. *Minutes of the Sixth Convention of the General Council . . . Akron, Ohio, 1875* (Pittsburgh: n.p., 1870), 46–47.

13. C. G. Eisenberg, *History of the First Dakota-District of the Evangelical Lutheran Synod of Iowa and Other States*, trans. Anton Richter (Washington, DC: University Press of America, 1982), 58–59.

14. Mark Granquist, "Swedish- and Norwegian-American Religious Traditions, 1860–1920," *Lutheran Quarterly* 8, no. 3 (Autumn 1994): 304.

15. J. A. Bergh, *Den norsk lutherske Kirkes Historie I Amerika* (Minneapolis: Augsburg, 1914), 43.

16. Abdel Ross Wentz, *A Basic History of Lutheranism in America*, rev. ed. (Philadelphia: Fortress Press, 1964), 206.

17. Matthias Loy, "Election and Justification," *Columbus Theological Magazine* 1 (1881), in Theodore G. Tappert, ed., *Lutheran Confessional Theology in America, 1840–1880* (New York: Oxford University Press, 1972), 209–210.

18. E. Clifford Nelson and Eugene L. Fevold, *The Lutheran Church among the Norwegian-Americans*, vol. 1: 1825–1890 (Minneapolis: Augsburg, 1960), 256.

19. Johann Jakob Schmidt, "Diary Entry for September 14, 1858," in Gerhard M. Schmutterer, ed., *Tomahawk and Cross: Lutheran Missionaries among the Northern Plains Tribes, 1858–1866* (Sioux Falls: Center for Western Studies, 1989), 185.

20. G. H. Gerberding, ed., *The Life and Letters of W.A. Passavant, D.D.* (Greenville, PA: The Young Lutheran Co., 1906), 186.

Excursus 7

THEA: ONE LIFE AMONG MANY

What can one person do or accomplish in such a short time that is allotted to humans on earth? Millions of people are born, live, and die; grieved by family and friends, they quickly become only a memory. Thea Rønning was one such person. She lived at the end of the nineteenth century for only thirty-two years, and now, except for the patient research of a historian, would be totally forgotten. But the story of Thea's brief life needs to be remembered, especially as an example of the thousands of other young American Lutherans who heard the call of God.

Thea Rønning was born into a pious farming family in Norway in 1865. She received a limited education and was confirmed in 1880. Greatly influenced by the Pietist revivals of her day, in 1887 Thea discovered that God had work for her, although the exact nature of her call only gradually unfolded. Together with her brother, Nils, and other young Norwegians, Thea immigrated to the United States in 1887, settling in southern Minnesota. The voyage to the new world was rough and exhausting, and the United States was a strange and disconcerting place. But Thea and Nils soon located their older brother Halvor, and found themselves a home among the Norwegian American community.

At this time, many Christians in Europe and North America were gripped by the call to take the Christian gospel to the people of Africa and Asia. Thousands of young Christians left everything behind to go to the mission fields, and not a few of them died tragically young in this calling. The call to mission work swept through the congregations, Ladies' Aid societies, mission societies, Sunday schools, academies, and colleges of Norwegian America. Young people heard God's call to go to places like Madagascar, South Africa, India, and China. Thea and Halvor discovered their call to China, made possible by the newly formed China Mission Society. In 1891, brother and sister joined a larger group headed to the mission field and, after another arduous journey, arrived in China on December 1, 1891.

Objectively, they had no business going to China. They were poor, they knew no Chinese at all, and it was a very dangerous place, with its rampant disease and starvation, not to mention the political instability and violence. But they had a deep love and confidence in their Savior, a trust in God's providence (in life and in death), and immense concern for the spiritual and physical welfare of the Chinese people.

Thea and Halvor eventually settled with other missionaries in Fancheng, an inland area of northern China. They learned Chinese and made contact with local people. Women missionaries such as Thea were very important, for the initial approach toward many Chinese families was through their women, to whom only they could gain access. Although Thea was personally used to poverty, the wretched condition of many of the Chinese women appalled her; grinding poverty and disease were combined with brutality, including female infanticide and footbinding. Thea sent letters back to her sponsoring communities; in one from 1895 she described her work:

> I have been stronger this winter than before. It is very difficult to be sick and to study this difficult language. We have 40 girls in our girls' school. . . . Now we have started to make house calls and then we really discover need. We talk to the women and children about God. It is so new they cannot fathom it, but God's Spirit has power and can open the heathen heart.[1]

Life on the mission field was not all trial, however, and in some letters she describes her joys and successes, as well as the challenges. She found her own personal joy through her marriage to another missionary, Carl Landahl, in late 1896.

This missionary work often came at quite a personal sacrifice, and too many of them paid the ultimate cost, dying on the mission field. Thea herself suffered several life-threatening illnesses, and on March 23, 1898, she died at the age of thirty-two.

Despite wars, upheavals, and persecution, Western Christian missionaries continued their work in China through the first half of the twentieth century, but after the Chinese communists came to power in 1949, they were expelled. For the next forty years very little was known about the fate of Christianity in China, and whether it would survive at all. With the opening up of China in the past thirty years, there has been a remarkable resurgence of indigenous Chinese Christianity. Estimates now range between 50 and 150 million Chinese Christians, with a substantial rate of growth. Even with all the trauma, Christianity has taken root and is growing. None of this could have happened without the efforts of Thea and thousands of others who risked all to answer God's call. Thea's was a life well lived.

Note

1. Gracia Grindahl, *Thea Rønning: Young Woman on a Mission* (Minneapolis: Lutheran University Press, 2012), 146–47.

Chapter 8

STRUCTURING AN AMERICAN LUTHERANISM, 1888–1918

I n 1900, America was a young country, strong and growing. Having put the trauma of the Civil War behind it, the country was spreading out from coast to coast, and filling out because immigration and population growth were swelling the rapidly growing cities. The United States had become the world's leading industrial power by the early twentieth century, providing jobs for the immigrants and exporting goods around the world. Growth had not always gone smoothly; the economic depression of the 1890s brought hardship and temporarily curbed both economic growth and the rate of immigration. Despite setbacks, the population of the United States grew from 63 million in 1890 to 106 million in 1920, partly due to the massive immigration from Europe. Although immigration during the 1890s dipped to 3.7 million persons, it shot up to 8.8 million in the 1900s and slowed again to 5.7 million in the 1910s, partially because of the onset of World War 1. Although this immigration brought needed workers for industry and laborers for farms and mines, its very magnitude brought serious social pressures and conflicts. During the late nineteenth century, the composition of this immigration shifted from western Europeans to southern and eastern Europeans, which brought millions of Roman Catholics, Eastern Orthodox, and Jews into an intensely Protestant nation. By 1900,

Roman Catholicism became the single largest religious family in the country, passing the Methodists and Baptists, even though there were still more Protestants than Roman Catholics overall. Nativism and calls for restrictions on immigration grew louder, resulting in some immigration restrictions, especially the exclusion of non-Christian Asian immigrants to the West Coast.

Despite its preoccupations at home, and despite its own inclinations, the United States also became involved in world affairs. A decisive victory in the 1898 war with Spain resulted in the addition of the territories of Cuba, Puerto Rico, Guam, and the Philippines, and the development of a "two-ocean" naval fleet. Hawaii was also added as a territory in 1898. The United States played an "active role" in the affairs of a number of Central American countries, especially with the formation of Panama and the construction of the Panama Canal. Although the United States actively attempted neutrality during the early years of the First World War (1914–1918), it was drawn into that conflict in 1917, and subsequently provided the essential edge in troops and materials that led to the victory of the Allies in 1918. Despite its inclination toward isolationism, the United States had become a world power.

At home, the increasingly diverse country experienced social and cultural unrest as a byproduct of its growth. Major cities filled with immigrants, often packed into fetid slums; they were also dramatically different from the established American population in religion and culture. The growth of industry and its often brutal working conditions led to the organization of labor unions and advocates for socialism (and even a few anarchists), who fought for better wages and better social conditions. Progressives pushed for curbs on the outright power of those who monopolized major industrial sectors, and the government moved, albeit slowly, to do so, as well as to ensure minimum working standards. American women sought greater rights, especially the right to vote, and during the "Great Migration," millions of African Americans moved from the deep South into the cities of the North and Midwest. The social fabric of the country was strained, but the institutions of the country learned to grow, adapt, and even at times change.

Lutherans were an important and sizable sector of this massive immigration, and the growth of the American Lutheran denominations reflect this trend. From approximately 600,000 baptized American Lutherans in 1875, their numbers jumped to 2,175,000 baptized by 1900, making American Lutheranism the third largest Protestant family in the United States, behind the Baptists and Methodists. They were the fourth largest religious family overall, with the Roman Catholics in the lead. In 1900, American Lutherans were clustered mainly along ethnic lines and formed into a dozen major denominations, with another dozen or so smaller synods. Several Lutheran mergers occurred during this time, including two rounds

LUTHERAN MEMBERSHIP GROWTH IN THE 20TH CENTURY			
Year	Congregations	Baptized Members*	Pastors
1900	11,145	2,175,000	6,811
1925	16,411	5,250,000	10,191
1950	14,795	6,248,000	14,534
1975	17,919	8,628,000	23,154
2000	19,212	8,190,000	28,755
2010	18,150	7,705,000	28,300

*Estimates

of merger to unite most Norwegian-American Lutherans, the consolidation of the Joint Synod of Wisconsin, and the reunion of the eastern Lutherans of the Muhlenberg tradition. The decades surrounding the new twentieth century saw immense growth in the institutional expressions of American Lutheranism, with an acceleration of the building of seminaries, colleges, and schools, as well as of hospitals, orphanages, and other institutions of mercy. Home-mission efforts organized new congregations and new regional synods in the Midwest and West, especially along the Pacific Coast. American Lutherans, following the religious spirit of the age, also began to participate in the then-great Christian push to send missionaries into all the world, but especially to Asia and Africa. Still somewhat removed from the mainstream of American religious life, mainly due to language differences, Lutherans were already active participants in their communities on the local, state, and regional levels, and were poised to become more involved on the national and international levels in the years to come.

The larger Western world, including the United States, was deeply affected and deeply challenged by new ideas, ideologies, and social movements at the end of the nineteenth century and the beginning of the twentieth. Nationalistic and democratic strivings were stirring the continent of Europe, with a wave of political consolidation especially in Germany and Italy. Many of these trends were echoed by parallel developments in the United States. The rise of modern science, especially the theory of evolution, shook old certainties and challenged previous perceptions of our world and of our very selves as human beings. It seemed as though scientists were discovering new wonders every month or so, to the point where, early in the twentieth century, some wondered aloud whether humanity would soon run out of new things to discover. The inner workings of the human mind and human society were being plumbed by the new fields of psychology, sociology, and anthropology, which provided new and sometimes shocking views of how our species actually developed and worked. Technology was producing wonderful new inventions, such as telephones, motion pictures, radio, automobiles, and airplanes, and improving on many existing ones. Modern medical practices and medicines were slowly beginning to positively affect the lives of many. It was a time when progress, or at least the promise of progress, was in the air. If modernity brought its own new and large set of problems, there was still a pervasive sense of optimism that the Western world had the tools and the potential to solve all issues, old and new. It seemed to many that the world had moved from a static position to one of dynamic growth and development

As it often does, religious life lagged behind the progress of the Western world, which is not always a bad thing. The nineteenth-century turn toward urbanization and industrialization challenged traditional religious views and practices, rooted in the static world of older, traditional agrarian society. Organized religion, especially in western Europe, had difficulties in developing new congregations for the masses of poor urban and industrial workers and providing basic religious services for them. The voluntary churches in the United States did better, but still struggled to keep up with dramatic population shifts. All religious groups, the traditional source of charity and relief, were hard-pressed to assist the massive needs that developed, especially during the periodic economic downturns of the new capitalism.

Religious belief, still pervasive in Western culture, was being challenged from many directions, social as well as intellectual. The rise of evolution and modern science provided alternative views of the world, ones that were mechanistic and deterministic rather than based on the providential guidance of a divine being, which challenged traditional biblical accounts. Many new intellectual developments, such as Freudian psychology, were openly hostile toward traditional religious belief; Freud believed that religious belief was simply an unhealthy or maladjusted psychological development. New social movements, especially communism and socialism, were either hostile or indifferent to traditional religious systems and sought to replace religion in the lives of the workers with their own ideologies. Marx claimed that religion was a drug used by the ruling classes to pacify and addict the workers, sedating them into accepting their sorry lot. In too many cases in the nineteenth century, Marx's analysis was more accurate than it should have been.

Although these movements had not replaced traditional religion, they became serious competitors to it and spurred a series of religious responses. Predictably, some religious responses ignored or demonized these new challengers, as Protestant conservatism and Roman Catholic traditionalism sought to blunt the force of their message. Other religious responses attempted to debate with modern realities, either to engage in a nuanced and reasoned defense of traditional religious belief or to revise and rethink religious systems so as to bring them into line with a whole-heartedly embraced modernity, which was the approach of theological liberalism. Although they were aware of many of these modern developments and recognized their challenges, American Lutherans during this period were simply too busy gathering in the masses of immigrants and building the structure of Lutheranism in the United States to engage these forces directly. Besides, there were few, if any, liberals or radicals among their ranks, so they did not undergo the kinds of internal battles over responses to modernity that wracked other sectors of American Protestantism, notably the fundamentalist-modernist controversies. American Lutherans still fought among themselves theologically, but usually over different shades of theological conservatism and degrees of confessionalism. Active Lutheran engagement with modern forces and ideologies, and internal divisions over them, would wait until later in the twentieth century.

Growth and Consolidation of American Lutheranism

The numerical growth of American Lutheranism occurred on many fronts during this period. Lutherans were traditionally rural, and located in sections of the East, South, and Midwest, but the geographic expansion of the nation's population and the rise of the large cities meant that potential Lutherans might be found almost anywhere in the country. The later immigrants, after 1885 or so, were increasingly drawn to the large cities, and they were joined there by the native-born generations of younger Lutherans from rural and small-town America seeking their fortunes. Lutherans were slow to form urban congregations, but this trend accelerated in the early twentieth century. Immigrant Scandinavians replaced Germans as the primary group of new immigrants; besides locating in traditional regions of the rural Midwest, many also settled in the eastern cities and the Pacific Northwest states.

New regional groupings—synods, districts, or conferences, depending on the denomination—were formed, especially in the West. The Swedish Augustana Synod organized a Pacific Conference in 1888, which soon divided into separate California and Columbia conferences in 1893. The California District of the Missouri Synod was organized in 1887, and the California Synod of the General Synod in 1891. The Pacific District of the Norwegian Synod was founded in 1894, along with the Oregon-Washington District of the Missouri Synod in 1899, and the Rocky Mountain Synod of the General Synod in 1891. In that same year, the General Council organized the English Synod of the Northwest, which stretched from Wisconsin to Washington. This new synod, with its English-language outreach, threatened the ethnically based synods, who perceived it as a competitor to their own congregations. In the Southwest, there were a trio of new organizations in Texas, as the Ohio Synod (1890), Iowa Synod (1896), and Missouri Synod (1906) developed their own regional bodies in that state.

The formation of the United Norwegian Lutheran Church (UNLC) in 1890 was occasioned by the fractious and divisive theological debates over election (predestination) within the Norwegian Synod during the 1880s. The majority of the leaders and congregations within the Norwegian Synod held to the "first form" of election, close to the position of C. F. W. Walther and the Missouri Synod, but there was a strong minority (about one-third) of the Norwegian Synod that opposed this position. In a series of moves during the late 1880s, this minority group pulled away from the Norwegian Synod and formed the "Anti-Missouri Brotherhood" in 1887. Organized not to become another synod but to be a movement toward union, the Anti-Missourians quickly reached out to the centrist groups among the Norwegian American community, notably the Norwegian Augustana Synod and the Conference for Norwegian-Danish Evangelical Lutheranism to form the United Norwegian Lutheran Church in 1890. This carefully negotiated union of the three denominations contained more than half of the Norwegian American Lutherans at the time (152,000 baptized members), while the Norwegian Synod (95,000) and the Hauge Synod (22,000) represented the bulk of the rest.

Rarely, however, did mergers among the Norwegian Americans go smoothly, and the new United Church quickly ran into difficulties. In this case, the question revolved around the fate of colleges and seminaries in the new church. The Anti-Missourians were closely related to St. Olaf College and had their seminary there, while the Conference supported Augsburg College and Seminary in Minneapolis. When the United Church decided to designate St. Olaf as the college of the new denomination, the supporters of Augsburg rallied to its defense. While a protracted court case over the actual ownership of Augsburg dragged on through the courts for years, supporters formed the "Friends of Augsburg" in 1893, which itself developed into a separate denomination in 1897, the Lutheran Free Church (LFC). The Lutheran Free Church and a smaller similar group, the Church of the Lutheran Brethren (founded in 1900), represented the "free" wing of Norwegian American Lutheranism, holding to congregational autonomy and the need for a converted or "awakened" membership. The difference here was that the "free" element of Norwegian American Lutheranism retained its formal adherence to Lutheranism, while among the Swedish Americans this same element dropped its formal Lutheran identity, becoming the Swedish Mission Covenant and Swedish Evangelical Free churches.

In 1892, three midwestern German synods, Wisconsin, Michigan, and Minnesota, moved into a more formal relationship with each other, with the new group called the Joint Synod of Wisconsin, Minnesota, Michigan, and Other States. This was not yet a formalized merger as such, but a closer federation of these three groups, which added a fourth in 1904, with the formation of a Nebraska Synod. The first three groups had a fairly long history, stretching back to the mid-nineteenth century, and for varying times each group had been a part of the General Council, before becoming a part of the Synodical Conference. These groups were confessional conservatives, and Wisconsin generally supported Walther during the predestination controversy, but they also attempted to maintain some independence from Missouri, while still being a part of the Synodical Conference. Eventually, in 1919, this federation of four distinct synods was melded together into a single denomination, and because about 60 percent of the congregations were in Wisconsin, the new body retained its original name, and was commonly known as the Wisconsin Synod.

New Ethnic Lutheran Groups

Early in the twentieth century, the source of the new immigrants from Europe shifted; certainly, there were still substantial numbers of Scandinavians arriving every year, but the immigration was increasingly dominated by persons from southern and eastern Europe. Although these immigrants were mainly non-Protestants, there was some Lutheran immigration from these regions as well. While Finnish, Icelandic, and Baltic Lutherans came from officially Lutheran territories, this immigration also included Lutheran minority populations in eastern Europe, especially from Slovakia, Poland, Hungary, Slovenia, Romania, and Russia. Some of these Lutherans were Slavic by background, while others, such as those from Romania and Russia, were ethnic German colonists from eastern Europe.

The largest group of these new immigrants was from Finland, with as many as 230,000 who came to the United States. Finland had long been a part of Sweden, and the state church of Finland had been Lutheran since the Reformation, even though Finland came under Russian control in 1815. Although Finns were among the settlers in the New Sweden colony, Finnish immigration to the United States did not really begin until the last decade of the nineteenth century; they settled mainly in the northern portions of Minnesota, Wisconsin, Michigan, and parts of Ohio and the Pacific Northwest. Because of the long Swedish rule of Finland, there were ethnic Swedish-speaking populations in western Finland, and these immigrants generally formed congregations associated with the Augustana Synod. The Finnish-speaking immigrants generally formed their own ethnic congregations, though there was a strong streak of socialism among Finnish immigrants, and significant tensions between the religious and nonreligious Finns, especially those active in the labor movements, socialism, or communism.

As with the Scandinavians, the nineteenth century in Finland was a time of religious and nationalistic awakenings. The state church in Finland contained the bulk of the population, but there were revivalistic movements within Finland, the largest of which were inspired by revival leaders Lars Levi Laestadius and Frederick Gabriel Hedberg. Although scattered Finnish Lutheran congregations were formed in the United States as early as 1876, it was not until 1890 that the first Finnish denomination was formed, the Finnish Evangelical Lutheran Church, popularly known as the Suomi Synod. This group, which historically was the largest denomination among Finnish Americans, was closely related to the state church of Finland, and established a school and seminary at Hancock, Michigan. It had about 14,000 baptized members in 1900. The Suomi Synod was a strong centralized polity that tightly bound the congregations to the synod itself.

A group of Finnish American Lutherans rooted in the portion of revival movement headed by Hedberg formed the Finnish Evangelical Lutheran National Church in America in 1898, in opposition to the Suomi Synod. In its beginnings, the "National" Finns represented a tradition of lay preaching from Finland, but during the 1920s came under the influence of the Missouri Synod, and eventually most of their pastors were trained in Missouri seminaries. In 1964, these National Finns merged into the Missouri Synod, ending their separate existence. Another revivalistic Finnish group were the Laestadians, or Apostolic Finns. This uniquely Finnish movement stressed emotional revivalistic preaching, the need for repentance and conversion, and individual absolution and laying-on of hands, accomplished by any awakened lay believer. The Apostolic Finns in American tended to follow specific preachers and leaders, and as a result have formed, splintered, and re-formed over the last one hundred years into over a dozen different movements and organizations. Most Apostolic Lutherans practice a strict personal and corporate morality; some groups today are closer in nature to conservative evangelical Protestantism, while others are strictly removed from the world in tight rural communities, a type of Lutheran "Amish," perhaps.

The final Scandinavian country represented was Iceland, also with a Lutheran state church. The number of Icelanders immigrating to North America was small, and they settled mainly in the upper Great Plains, especially North Dakota and the Canadian province of Manitoba. Early congregations in these areas date to the late 1870s and 1880s, and the first and only Lutheran denomination was formed as the Icelandic Evangelical Lutheran Synod of America, in 1885. Typical of the

Icelanders, they were the first Lutheran denomination in North America to allow women to vote and hold office in their organizations. Although they were not challenged by socialism, as were the Finns, there was an organized Icelandic Unitarian movement formed in North America, and there was some competition between the two groups, especially in the small, rural Icelandic farming communities. The Iceland Synod established some cooperative arrangements with the Norwegian American Lutherans, but in 1942 it became an ethnic affiliated synod of the eastern United Lutheran Church in America.

Lutheranism had roots in Slovakia dating back to the Reformation, and parts of Slovakia have remained Lutheran despite centuries of harsh repression from the Roman Catholic nations that ruled it. Slovak immigration to the United States began in the late nineteenth century and flowed to industrial and mining areas in the East and Midwest, primarily in Pennsylvania and Ohio. The Pittsburgh Synod of the General Council began work among the Slovaks and Hungarians in 1890, and the General Council formed a Slovak-Hungarian board in 1905. Scattered Slovak Lutheran congregations emerged before 1900, the first one founded in 1883, but there was no national organization until 1902, when the Slovak Evangelical Lutheran Church was formed. These Slovaks developed a close relationship with the Missouri Synod, and joined the Synodical Conference in 1908. Many of its pastors were subsequently trained in Missouri Synod seminaries. Eventually, in 1971, it merged into the Missouri Synod. As can be expected, a second group of Slovak pastors, laypeople, and congregations emerged who were wary of the Missouri Synod and refused to join the new Slovak Synod. Eventually, this group came together and in 1919 formed the Slovak Zion Synod, which became a distinct linguistic, nongeographical synod within the newly formed ULCA.

Home-mission work by larger Lutheran denominations targeted other immigrant Lutheran groups, most of whom were too small to form their own synods. The General Council established outreach to Lutherans from Hungary, Latvia, Slovenia, and Transylvania. The Missouri Synod initiated home-missions work with Lutherans from Latvia and Estonia in 1892, which grew under the leadership of Pastor Hans Rebane. The Eastern District of the Missouri Synod began Lithuanian and Polish outreach in the 1890s; by 1922, the Missouri Synod counted thirteen Estonian and Latvian congregations, along with eight Lithuanian and fifteen Polish congregations. In Texas, an early immigration of Wends (Slavs originating in eastern Germany), resulted in a number of distinctly Wendish congregations, which also joined the Missouri Synod. Finally, after 1880, there was a sizable immigration to North America of ethnic Germans from Russia, most of whom settled in the northern Great Plains. Although many of these Russian Germans were Anabaptists

(Mennonites and Hutterites), a significant portion of them who were Lutherans who formed their own distinct Russian German congregations.

Women, Laymen, and Young People

Developments in American society toward the end of the nineteenth century led to changes in relations within its various segments. Women began the long struggle for greater rights and opportunities; younger generations pushed their elders for more responsibilities and greater change; and ordinary laypeople began to press their leaders for an additional voice in the running of the country and of its institutions. Men and women organized social and fraternal organizations and joined them in record numbers. The Lutheran denominations felt the pressure from women, laymen, and young people, but change within church institutions was slow in coming. In many instances, women, laymen, and young people simply bypassed the church and formed their own parallel organizations within congregations and denominations, to meet with each other and to support the activities that they found important. While remaining loyal Lutherans, these groups made sure that their voices would be heard and their concerns addressed. After all, they were the vast majority of Lutherans in America.

The campaign for additional rights for women, especially the right to vote, began in earnest after the Civil War. Changes in society meant that many more women were formally educated, and now some had the time and inclination to work for causes outside of their domestic obligations. While most women probably did not directly identify with the more radical leaders of the women's rights movement, they nevertheless shared with them quite a number of practical concerns about issues such as women's property and marital rights and their own personal independence. Women also continued to organize to meet societal needs and support moral reforms, most notably the temperance campaign against the sale and use of alcohol.

Almost from their beginnings, most Lutheran congregations had some type of informal women's organization or society within them. Women met regularly for prayer and devotions, for sewing and charitable activities, and to support the work of the congregation. These groups often formed a substantial part of the congregation, and very often the congregation relied heavily on their support of its basic ministries. Many pastors realized that the good opinion and active support of the women in their congregation was crucial to the effectiveness of their own ministry and that to "cross" the women's group could mean a quick end to their pastorate.

Toward the end of the nineteenth century, Lutheran women began to organize themselves on the regional and national level into separate women's groups within their particular denominations, primarily for the support of home and foreign mission work. The first of these was the Women's Foreign Mission Society of the General Synod, founded in 1879. Other Lutheran denominations quickly urged the formation of similar groups; in 1879, the editor of the southern *Lutheran Visitor* complained that while many denominations had active women's groups, ". . . in the South Carolina Synod the women, with but few exceptions, are sitting idle in the church . . . because we lack organization, and our ministry itself—our Synod, is not duly interested . . ."[1] In most cases, however, the initiative for the formation of such a denominational women's society came from the women themselves, often through the efforts of well-positioned pastors' wives. Typical was the formation of the Woman's Home and Foreign Mission Society in the Augustana Synod, in 1892. The driving force behind this organization for the next fifty years was Emmy Carlsson Ewald, daughter of pioneer synodical leader Erland Carlsson and wife of Pastor Carl Ewald. Similarly, Rebecca Oline (Lena) Gjertson Dahl, wife of T. H. Dahl, president of the United Norwegian Lutheran Church, was the impetus behind the organization of the Women's Missionary Federation within that denomination. Almost every sizable Lutheran denomination had some form of regional or national women's organization by 1920.

It would be wrong to underestimate these women and the organizations they founded. Although these women generally worked within the given boundaries of the time, they knew how to push those limits and get things done. Most of these women's organizations were autonomous, and the women themselves decided their own funding priorities and, in many cases, their own mission projects. These organizations had national, regional, and local entities with their own separate treasuries, newspapers, and annual meetings, conveniently held in conjunction with the annual denominational meeting. They funded home- and foreign-mission work, domestic schools and colleges, orphanages and hospitals, and homes for girls and women. Their financial impact was enormous; in the first fifty years (1892–1942) of the Augustana Woman's Missionary Society (WMS), the group raised and distributed $2.9 million for mission work, and through the 1910s and 1920s, the WMS budget was larger than the budget of the synod itself.[2] These organizations were generally quite comfortable acting independently of the denomination when it suited their priorities.

Some American Lutheran women found another avenue for ministry through the deaconess movement, where unmarried women were enrolled in a Protestant order focused on nursing and social service. With antecedents in nineteenth-century Germany and Scandinavia, the deaconess movement was brought to America primarily to staff hospitals and social-service agencies. Early attempts, such as those by

William Passavant and within the Iowa Synod, did not have permanent results, but beginning in the 1880s permanent Lutheran deaconess movements were founded in the United States. In 1884, John Lankenau, a prominent Philadelphia Lutheran layman, funded the formation of a deaconess motherhouse in Philadelphia, marking its formal organization within the Ministerium of Pennsylvania. Other similar organizations were founded by other Lutheran denominations in America, including the General Synod, the Augustana Synod, the Synodical Conference, and the Norwegian groups. By 1899, there were 197 Lutheran deaconesses in the United States, centered around seven different motherhouses. At its peak, around 1940, the movement numbered 480 women.[3]

The deaconess movement among the Norwegian Americans owed its existence to a remarkable Norwegian deaconess, Sister Elisabeth Fedde, who arrived in Brooklyn in 1883 to work with the immigrants there. The need she saw overwhelmed her, but she gathered her resources and founded a hospital, and then a deaconess organization to staff it. She also inspired the foundation of similar Norwegian American institutions in Minnesota and Chicago, and constantly canvassed not only prosperous Norwegian Americans, but even the New York state legislature, for resources to support these organizations.

Lutheran women found other areas of service open to them, or pushed their way into them. Women within the Synodical Conference became teachers in Lutheran parochial schools, although initially in small numbers because the synods were wary of this development. In 1872, Missouri Synod educator J. W. C. Lindemann cautiously approved of women teachers in limited areas: ". . . we can never entrust our more mature male youth to 'schoolmistresses'; but also we might very well use them for the lower classes and for girls' schools far more extensively than has been done heretofore."[4] The need for teachers was urgent, and by 1923 the Missouri Synod began to allow women to attend the synodical teacher-training schools, although their enrollment was often limited to a certain percentage of the student body.

Besides simply funding missionaries, some women actually went out to the mission fields themselves, either as the wives of male missionaries, or as single young women, usually to do nursing or to work among the women of the mission field. These contacts with local women were crucial in developing the mission work, and only the women missionaries could do it. A mission writer observed in 1899: "The lady missionary gains admission either by invitation or through the children in the mission school. . . . A wide sphere of usefulness presents itself . . . since the husbands no longer oppose the work, but frequently invite the lady missionaries to come and teach their wives and daughters."[5] One of the most outstanding of these early women missionaries was Anna Sarah Kugler, who graduated from medical school in 1879 and was sent to India as a medical missionary by the General Synod in 1882. She worked tirelessly and developed a hospital at Guntur, and then an entire medical community to staff it. Dozens of young women went out to the mission fields of Africa and Asia; sixteen of the forty-one missionaries sent out before 1920 by the Augustana Synod were single women, and this does not even include the wives of the male missionaries. Life was very difficult for these women missionaries, and a number of them died of disease while serving abroad.

While Lutheran men appreciated these contributions of Lutheran women, the men were sometimes worried by their activities and by the general social movements for greater rights for women. Generally, women were not allowed to vote or hold office in Lutheran congregations, let alone in larger synodical organizations, with the lone exception of the tiny Icelandic Synod. Among some more conservative groups, the pastor himself was often the presiding officer of the congregational women's organization. When, in 1910, a congregation in Utah selected a woman to be a delegate to the annual Augustana Synod convention, it threw the whole gathering into an uproar, and rules were quickly passed to prevent such happenings in the future. In 1916, Missouri Synod seminary professor W. H. T. Dau asserted that women had limited and defined roles within the church: "Church-life and secular life are different. . . . If the secular State for reasons of its own adopts woman suffrage, the Church for reasons of its own may decline the same."[6] It would be well into the twentieth century before women could vote and hold office in most American Lutheran congregations and denominations.

In very similar ways, younger Lutherans began to organize themselves during the late nineteenth century, although their groups were more oriented toward social interaction and religious education than missions. Similar to the women's organization, but not as widespread, local societies for young men and women were being founded in Lutheran congregations around the country during the second half of the nineteenth century, with synodical and national organizations to come later. Since, at this time, most youth did not attend college or even high school, the "target audience" of these groups was generally unmarried men and women in their late teens and twenties who were working and were members of local Lutheran congregations. Some Lutheran leaders worried about such developments, fretting about the frivolous (or worse) possibilities of mixed groups of young people together, but competition from other secular and non-Lutheran religious organizations suggested that they had better develop Lutheran options of their own.

The organization of wider Lutheran youth organizations did not come until the end of the century, and then they met with some initial resistance. Missouri Synod pastor August Senne argued in 1892 for a national youth organization in the

Missouri Synod, uniting local efforts: ". . . our young Christians in different parts of the land would . . . be pushed closer together. . . . If a member of one of our societies would move to a strange city . . . then this member would have friends to whom he could turn and who would help him."[7] The urge to form wider organization overcame objections, and in the Missouri Synod the Walther League was formed in 1893, followed closely in 1895 by the Luther League, which operated primarily within the General Synod and General Council. Initially, these groups were autonomous, but increasingly during the early twentieth century they became integrated into denominational structures and eventually became the official youth-ministry outreach of the denominations themselves.

For those youth who attended Lutheran academies and colleges, there were many other student organizations in which they could participate, including literary and debating societies, ethnic groups, and social clubs. Of special interest here were the college missionary societies, patterned after the Student Volunteer Movement, which brought the cause of foreign missions to thousands of young Lutherans, encouraging some of them to become missionaries themselves.

Young Lutherans, especially those first- and second-generation immigrants, were at the forefront of encountering the new American society of the late nineteenth century. Like other American youth, young Lutherans crowded into the growing cities, searching for work and advancement. For young German and Scandinavian immigrant women in particular, a common profession was that of domestic servants, maids, and cooks in the households of middle- and upper-class Americans. These experiences brought them into direct contact with "American" society. As one scholar has noted: ". . . for young girls . . . this hiring-out experience provided an opportunity for increased self-confidence, financial independence, female networks, assimilation into American society, socialization, and technological competence."[8] Whether in the workplace, society, or schools, younger Lutherans were at the front of encountering the new modern world around them, and through them many of these innovations were gradually introduced to American Lutheranism as a whole.

Lutheran laymen also formed their own organizations within the American Lutheran denominations, often with similar goals to that of the women and youth. Although these men had relatively more power within their congregations and denominations, they often took second-place to the clergy who led these institutions. It was also the age of societies. The culture was rife with male social and fraternal organizations, such as the Elks, Moose, and Masons. In many Lutheran denominations, membership in these organizations was discouraged or forbidden due to concerns about their quasi-religious nature, so Lutheran laymen's groups were viewed as a safer religious option. These groups generally focused on stewardship awareness and raising funds to support denominational projects, scholarships, pensions, and mission efforts as well as to provide men with social opportunities.

Late in the nineteenth century, when the interdenominational Laymen's Missionary Movement began, a number of Lutheran laymen affiliated with this movement. The first Lutheran group was the General Synod's Laymen's Movement, founded in 1907. The genesis of this organization came from the efforts of a successful young Lutheran businessman, Jesse Clark. Tired of hearing about deficits in the General Synod budgets, he remarked to a colleague: ". . . I am not accustomed to being connected with a bankrupt concern, and my opinion is that if Laymen were given a chance to manage the Church finances, we might right them."[9] A similar movement was founded in the General Council in 1909, with the aim of ". . . bringing into our church management the same principles necessary to any successful business enterprise," and supporting missions and church growth.[10] Other laymen's groups were later formed within the Missouri Synod, the Augustana Synod, the Norwegian Lutheran Church in America, and other Lutheran denominations.

America's entry into World War I in 1917 generated great needs for ministry with the American troops, both in training camps at home and operations overseas. On November 13, 1917, representatives from all the major American Lutheran denominations formed the Lutheran Brotherhood of America (LBA). It charged itself with raising funds to build and staff ministry centers at major American military installations. This group of pastors and laymen worked overtime to raise funds and provide necessary resources for American servicemen. After the war, many individual Lutheran denominations formed their own men's Brotherhoods, and in 1927 the LBA reorganized itself as a federation of such organizations, the American Federation of Lutheran Brotherhoods.

At the 1917 organizing convention of the Norwegian Lutheran Church in America, the new church voted to authorize a "mutual aid" or insurance society, initially called the Lutheran Union (insurance was a controversial issue at that time). This organization soon broadened its field, inviting board members from most of the midwestern Lutheran groups. In 1920, the Lutheran Union began close cooperation with the LBA, and the insurance union took on the name Lutheran Brotherhood. When the LBA reorganized in 1927 and took a new name, the fraternal insurance agency retained the name Lutheran Brotherhood. A similar mutual aid organization, Aid Association for Lutherans, was formed in Wisconsin in 1902; these two fraternal benefits companies merged in 2001 and took the name Thrivent Financial for Lutherans in 2002.

Education and Schools

In America, the period between 1860 and 1918 saw the formation of thousands of private schools, academies, and colleges, most of which were religiously based. Of the forty-nine Lutheran colleges in existence in 2013, ten were founded before 1860, thirty were founded between the Civil War and the First World War, and only nine were founded after 1918. For every institution that survived, perhaps three or four others were founded but did not survive to the present. The nineteenth century was a time when schools could be founded relatively easily, often featuring only a single building and a handful of teachers, who often were pastors. Synods, groups of Lutherans, and sometimes even individuals established educational institutions. Every synod seemed to desire its "own" school as a part of its mission and identity, to teach its youth specific religious values and its linguistic and cultural heritage. Although some schools were established primarily to provide educated young men for the ministry, increasingly these schools broadened their approach, providing a useful secular education within a religious context. Some even educated young women and men together in the same institution.

Almost all the Lutheran schools were begun as academies, in essence a type of private high school, often with many of its students boarding at the institution. Some of these academies were founded as offshoots of theological seminaries to provide a basic education for ministerial candidates, but other academies were independently established. Among some of the German Lutheran groups, the model for such an institution was the German gymnasium, a six-year program that integrated high school and the first two years of college. All these schools offered essentially a classical education, heavily oriented toward languages (Greek, Latin, and Hebrew), with strong doses of theology, philosophy, and rhetoric. As can be imagined, many of these institutions were lightly capitalized and did not survive the economic depressions of the 1890s or 1930s.

In many of these schools, a single building (sometimes rented) served as classroom, dormitory, dining hall, library, chapel, and faculty offices and housing. Living conditions were often rather primitive, with student's life (moral and otherwise) strictly supervised by the faculty. These schools were expected to act *in loco parentis* ("in the place of parents"), and to form the students morally and religiously as well as intellectually. Students participated in numerous literary and religious societies, as well as sports and similar activities. In some areas, especially among southern Lutherans, there were special "women's seminaries," where young women were educated for their domestic responsibilities. Despite the sometimes Dickensian conditions, many students reported fond memories of their school years and deep loyalty to their teachers and institutions.

Developments in the late nineteenth century forced changes upon these schools, as the rise of free public high schools, eventually even in many rural areas, undercut the need for costly religious academies. Many of the Lutheran schools attempted, and some were successful, in adding a "collegiate department" to their institution, leading to the awarding of bachelor's degrees. In the schools that survived, the collegiate department grew and took hold while the academy portion gradually declined and was eventually eliminated. The curriculum changed over time as well. Many schools initially provided a traditional classical curriculum, but quickly broadened their offerings to include more "practical" courses of study, such as liberal arts, music, science, and business and accounting. Although Lutheran parents wanted a good religious education for their daughters and sons, there was a limited market for classical rhetoricians, and the parents also demanded practical education that would lead their children to professions and livelihoods. Women were educated for teaching and nursing; some men might be prepared to enter seminary, but others would become businessmen and professionals and lay leaders in the Lutheran congregations.

Those schools established exclusively to prepare young men for the seminary soon found themselves at a disadvantage, as there was a limited market for this kind of education, and economic pressures forced them eventually to consider a broader educational mandate, and even co-education. The Missouri Synod schools eventually had to modify the gymnasium model and many developed full collegiate programs. The synod also developed separate teacher-training institutions to staff their system of parochial schools. Some Lutheran colleges even moved into the realm of granting advanced degrees, but this trend did not last. Strangely, for a religious movement that included important roots within sixteenth-century German universities, none of the Lutheran colleges in North America developed into a full-fledged university, deciding to remain focused almost exclusively on undergraduate education.

Some of these Lutheran academies and colleges were owned directly by regional or national Lutheran judicatories, and the schools became a focal point and source of pride for them. The denominational press was full of stories about happenings at "our" schools and on developments within them. These Lutheran bodies, however, could rarely afford generous subsidies to keep the schools operating, and in the main the schools had to develop their own financial resources. Absent a well-funded endowment, which none of them had, the school's president usually undertook a yearly fund-raising tour through the congregations of his constituency, hoping to raise enough money to keep the doors open. Economic downturns and agricultural disasters had a serious and, at times, fatal impact on schools' economic viability.

These schools were designed to reinforce the religious teachings of their denominational partners, and their intellectual milieu was often quite conservative. Many of the intellectual and scientific developments of the late nineteenth century were slowly and cautiously introduced, if they were introduced at all. Some fields were avoided altogether; for example, none of the Norwegian American schools ever had departments of geology, perhaps so as not to have to address the controversial topic of evolution. Students' religious lives were actively nurtured, and many pastors and missionaries, both women and men, were inspired to this calling through their education.

Foreign Mission Work

One of the most distinguished aspects of the nineteenth- and early-twentieth century Protestant awakening in Europe and North America was the intense concern and passion for overseas missions, especially to Asia and Africa. These mission efforts over 150 years led to perhaps the greatest geographical and numerical expansion of Christianity ever. By the middle of the twentieth century, Christianity had become a truly global religion in ways matched by no other religion. Sometimes it is "fashionable" to sneer at these efforts, or to denigrate them by tying them to Western colonialism, and certainly these mission efforts at times had their faults. Yet the immense growth of indigenous Christianity in the global South (Africa, Asia, and Latin America) in the second half of the twentieth century is vivid testimony both to the power of the Christian message and the dedication of the Western missionaries who spread it to all corners of the earth.

Like their Protestant neighbors, American Lutherans were often caught by the power of this missionary vision, even if they could not always find the resources to devote to it. For Lutherans in the nineteenth century, America itself was the primary mission field, and building Lutheranism in this country was their primary task. This is not to say that home missions and foreign missions were mutually exclusive, however, and the spirit that drove the former often inspired the latter. When the Lutheran denominations themselves could not find the resources to devote to overseas missions, women, laymen, and students organized themselves to raise both funds and awareness for foreign-mission work, pushing themselves and their denominations to do more in these areas.

Initially, the most that American Lutherans could do was to funnel their resources to Lutheran mission societies in Germany and Scandinavia, who already had established mission projects in Asia and Africa. Prior to the Civil War, eastern Lutherans began several of their own overseas missions, beginning with the remarkable "Father" J. F. C. Heyer, who was sent by the mission society of the Pennsylvania

Ministerium to India in 1841, single-handedly beginning a long-running work at Rajahmundry. In 1860, the General Synod began mission efforts in the African country of Liberia, and through the rest of the century sent almost twenty missionaries to that country. The mission in India became the responsibility of the General Council, which sent numerous missionaries to India, along with the Augustana Synod, who sent their first missionary, August Carlson, to India in 1878.

Beginning in the 1890s, more American Lutheran groups began to develop their own foreign-mission projects, and by 1918 most of these denominations had at least one mission station somewhere around the world. Initial attempts were usually made in conjunction with some already-existing mission field, usually established by a European Lutheran mission agency. So, for example, the Norwegian Americans cooperated with the Norwegian Mission Society in Madagascar, the Joint Ohio Synod cooperated with the Hermannsburg mission in India, and the Augustana Synod supported the work of the Swedish Mission Society, also in India. At times, an American Lutheran denomination would negotiate the transfer or even purchase of a portion of one of these groups' "territory," to make it their own. In 1912, for example, the Joint Synod of Ohio purchased a portion of the Hermannsburg mission in India for $17,600 and brought it under their direct control.

Sometimes groups or individuals were so eager to begin their own mission work that they began it without official sanction or support from their particular denomination. In one instance, in 1898, a young Swedish American seminary student, G. Sigfried Swensson, single-handedly began a Lutheran mission in Puerto Rico and soon had convinced both the Augustana Synod and the General Council to send financial support and additional missionaries to that island. In 1890, Norwegian American pastors in the Midwest founded an intersynodical China Mission Society and started mission work in China, which was eventually taken on as an official mission of the merged Norwegian Lutheran Church in America in 1917. In 1912, a Missouri Synod pastor and teacher, Edward L. Arndt, decided that he would be a missionary to China. When the synod refused to support him, he founded his own mission society to fund the work; five years later, the synod officially took over this mission.

By the early twentieth century, American Lutherans were developing other organized mission work abroad. In Africa, the Norwegian Lutherans were active in Madagascar and South Africa, while the Lutheran Brethren began work in Cameroon in 1916, and the General Synod continued its work in Liberia. In India, in addition to the long-running General Council mission, which was also supported by the Augustana Synod, the Missouri Synod began its own mission in 1894, and the Danes supported the Santal Mission. China received multiple American Lutheran missions, from the Norwegian denominations (1890 onward), from the

Augustana Synod (1906), as well as the Missouri Synod (1906). American Lutheran mission work in Japan was begun in 1892 by the United Synod South, and in 1898 by the United Danish Evangelical Lutheran Church. The Lutheran Church in Guyana, which dated back to the eighteenth century, came under the influence of the General Synod in the late nineteenth century, and formally became one of its missions in 1915.

Lutherans also had strong interest in missions to Muslims in the Middle East, but this was a difficult undertaking. Several Persian pastors came under the influence of the Augustana Synod, which supported their mission work in Persia (Iran) from 1888 to 1912. The Missouri Synod had a ministry to Persian Americans from 1911 to 1920. The longest-running of these efforts, however, was the intersynodical Lutheran Orient Mission, which began its work among the Kurdish people in the Middle East in 1910.

African American Lutherans

African American Lutheranism in the South declined markedly after the Civil War, as African Americans either left or were invited to leave existing Lutheran congregations. In theory, white southern Lutherans envisioned that African Americans would form their own separate Lutheran congregations and that the southern synods would ordain their pastors. But there was little leadership and few resources for such a development, and the numbers of African American Lutherans declined rapidly. After the war, the North Carolina and Tennessee synods ordained a number of African American Lutheran pastors, but did little to support them. From 1883 to 1888, the Maryland Synod sponsored a program in which five African American Lutherans were educated at Howard University in Washington, D.C., and two of these men, Daniel Wiseman and Philo Phifer, became pastors and leaders in North Carolina. But the southern synods lost what little interest they had in the African American congregations, and in desperation the African American Lutheran pastors themselves organized their own synod, the Alpha Evangelical Lutheran Synod of Freedmen in America, in 1889. This struggling little synod soon lost its leader, David J. Koontz, and barely lasted for two years, though it was the first and, as it turned out, only African American Lutheran synod.

Before going out of existence, the Alpha Synod made contacts with the Synodical Conference, who had been making some sporadic efforts to do home-missions work among African Americans in the South. The early efforts of the Synodical Conference in this area, dating from 1877, were often clumsy and ineffective; African Americans were seen as "heathens" and not true Christians, and some of the first pastors to work with them were culturally insensitive to a remarkable degree. However, other Synodical Conference pastors did organize growing African American congregations in Louisiana and Arkansas, starting from the 1880s. When the Synodical Conference took over the congregations of the Alpha Synod in 1891, they began to work with these existing congregations, organizing them into the Immanuel Conference. To train future African American Lutheran pastors and teachers, the Synodical Conference opened two educational institutions in 1903, Immanuel Seminary and College in North Carolina, and Luther College in New Orleans. This work, especially in North Carolina, was effective in stemming the decline of African American Lutheranism and contributed to its modest rebirth.

On the East Coast, there were scattered African American Lutheran congregations, including Redeemer Lutheran Church in Washington, D.C., where Daniel Wiseman was the longtime pastor. The Joint Synod of Ohio sponsored a congregation and a mission-outreach program in Baltimore, Maryland, which was also successful. But most surprising were parallel efforts by the Joint Synod of Ohio and the Synodical Conference among African Americans in Alabama, which both began around 1915. The Joint Synod of Ohio opened several schools and congregations in that state, and the schools were especially successful. Work by the Synodical Conference came through the initiative of a remarkable African American educator, Rosa J. Young, who had opened a school near Selma, Alabama, in 1912. Enlisting the support of the Synodical Conference in her enterprise, this grassroots Lutheran work in Alabama began to expand at a remarkable rate, with twenty-nine congregations and twenty-seven day schools formed by 1927. In 1922, Alabama Lutheran Academy was established in Selma, Alabama, to train young African American Lutheran leaders; it eventually became the first and only historically black Lutheran college in America. African American Lutherans could accomplish remarkable things, if given adequate and continuing support for their efforts, and if white denominational leaders would allow them to lead in ways that were appropriate for their communities. Unfortunately, these two factors were not often present in many of the Lutheran mission efforts.

Further Lutheran Merger Efforts

During the second decade of the twentieth century, two important mergers united important sections of American Lutheranism. In the first, in 1917, most of the Norwegian American Lutherans joined together in the formation of the Norwegian Lutheran Church in America (NLCA). In the second, the three branches of the colonial Muhlenberg tradition reunited in 1918 to form the United Lutheran Church in

America (ULCA). These two mergers began a century that saw several more rounds of mergers, leading to the eventual unification of most American Lutherans in two major denominations, the Lutheran Church–Missouri Synod (1847) and the Evangelical Lutheran Church in America (1988). Merger discussions and negotiations were a major concern for Lutherans throughout the twentieth century.

There had been one previous merger among the Norwegian American Lutherans, in 1890, which formed the United Norwegian Lutheran Church, but sizable groups, namely the Norwegian Synod and the Hauge Synod, had remained outside this denomination. The theological issues of the nineteenth century, especially the election controversy and related topics, were still lively issues, and hard feelings and suspicions were still evident, particularly between the United Church and the Norwegian Synod. Still, during the first decade of the twentieth century, representatives of the three major denominations met regularly and began to find solutions to at least some of the issues. Riding a wave of nationalistic feelings that emanated from the independence of Norway from Sweden in 1905, widespread hopes grew among Norwegian Americans that a wider church union could be accomplished. Despite real progress, however, further union was hung up over the doctrine of election, especially its first form ("election unto faith") of the Norwegian Synod, and the second form ("election in view of foreseen faith") of the United Church and the Hauge Synod. About 1911, pressured by popular lay opinion that strongly wished further merger, these denominations resolved to restart their negotiations. Instead of the old theological leaders, however, the denominations chose new delegates to the union discussion, drawn mainly from a newer generation of parish pastors who were less bound by the disputes of the past. At Madison, Wisconsin, in 1912, this new group reached a compromise settlement (Norwegian: *Opjør*) on the question of election, suggesting that within certain boundaries both the first and second forms of the doctrine were legitimate. This compromise was widely accepted in the Hauge Synod and the United Church, but caused problems within the Norwegian Synod, where a minority of pastors strongly opposed it.

With this compromise in hand, the three Norwegian denominations carefully moved toward merger, one that attempted to balance the interests and traditions of each group. Finally, in 1917, the new Norwegian Lutheran Church in America was formed, representing over 90 percent of all Norwegian American Lutherans. Smaller groups, such as the Eielsen Synod, the Church of the Lutheran Brethren, and the Lutheran Free Church still did not participate. Some of the minority within the Norwegian Synod who had opposed the *Opjør* broke away in 1918 and formed the Norwegian Synod of the American Evangelical Lutheran Church, sometimes referred to as the "little" Norwegian Synod, and now known as the Evangelical

Lutheran Synod (ELS). This group affiliated with the Synodical Conference in 1920. The merger hinged on careful balancing of the interests of each group, and much care was taken, for example, to see that proponents of both theological positions, first and second form, were appointed equally to the seminary faculties.

The formal reunion of the three strands of the colonial Muhlenberg tradition, the General Synod, the General Council, and the United Synod South, was a gradual process that spanned over fifty years. Divided three ways in the 1860s over the Civil War and questions of confessional Lutheran identity, these groups gradually began to work more closely with each other during the last decades of the nineteenth century, cooperating on a common liturgical service and coordinating in other areas, such as home and foreign mission work. Auxiliary groups such as the respective women's and men's groups and the Luther Leagues began working together, and many laypeople, especially, began to think that there were no real reasons for continuing the divisions. Yet, significant confessional and doctrinal issues had historically divided the three groups, and these longstanding issues were difficult to overcome.

The divisions of the 1860s were usually fought over the question of authority of the Lutheran confessions, and how strictly these boundaries could be drawn. Traditionally, the General Synod had understood the Lutheran confessions to be "fundamentally correct" as explanations of doctrine and biblical truth, but held that some parts of the Augsburg Confession were "non-fundamental." The General Synod had an open attitude toward working with other Protestant groups, and was, for example, the only Lutheran denomination to join the Federal Council of Churches in 1908. The General Council held a stricter view of the authority of the Lutheran confessions, including the *Book of Concord*, and a more restrictive policy on cooperation with other Protestant groups. It also officially opposed its members joining "secret societies" such as the Masons, and limited access to Lutheran pulpits and altars, as articulated in the Galesburg Rule. In many of these issues, the United Synod South often found itself in the middle but moving more in the direction of the General Council.

Sometimes the history of this reunion is told in terms of the increasing "confessionalization" of the General Synod in the last decades of the nineteenth century. This was part of the story, but certainly not all of it, for there were important developments within the General Council and United Synod South that moved them toward the General Synod positions as well. Especially after the death of Samuel Simon Schmucker in 1873, there was, in some parts of the General Synod, a renewed appreciation both for the doctrinal utility of the Lutheran confessions and for more traditional forms of Lutheran worship, but others still held to the synod's older traditions, which were less formally confessional and liturgical. In 1893, Wittenberg College theology professor Luther Gottwald was put on church trial, in essence for being "too conservatively Lutheran" and too close to the position of the General Council. Although he was cleared of the charges, the proceedings showed that some still strongly held the old General Synod positions. It is also clear that the General Council also was moving toward the General Synod in some areas. The battles with the midwestern confessional groups, especially the Synodical Conference, had frustrated many in the General Council, who resented having their confessional Lutheran "credentials" continually questioned. This negative interaction caused some in the General Council increasingly to look more sympathetically toward the General Synod and the United Synod South.

A series of decisions by the General Synod during the first decades of the twentieth century to recognize more formally the authority of the Lutheran confessions reduced some the barriers to reunion, though progress was slow. In 1914, the three groups formed a common committee to plan for the celebration of the four-hundredth anniversary of the Protestant Reformation in 1917 and, at its last meeting, lay delegates from all three groups passed a resolution urging the three denominational presidents to arrange such a merger. From this point, things moved exceedingly quickly, and by November 1918, the new United Lutheran Church in America (ULCA) was formed, joining the General Council, General Synod, and United Synod South. The only group not to join the new denomination was the Swedish Augustana Synod. Although it had long been a part of the General Council, it was an anomaly within it: a large, national ethnic synod within a group of smaller regional synods, Augustana had often feuded with other parts of the General Council, especially over English-language home missions. Augustana declined to enter the new ULCA and went independent. As a result of synodical divisions in the nineteenth century, the ULCA had an excess of overlapping regional synods, and the process of merging these regional synods together took place during the 1920s. The new ULCA constitution also had a somewhat more centralized polity than did its three predecessors, which gave the national organization of the new denomination more authority.

Lutherans and World War I

Although American Lutherans were often preoccupied with their own pressing internal affairs, they also followed national and international development closely and had strong opinions about the course of current events. When the European powers were plunged into World War I in 1914, isolationist America attempted to avoid entanglement. American Lutherans generally agreed with this policy of neutrality, but they still had their opinions and their sympathies, which tended to be mildly pro-German and definitely anti-British. Many Lutheran authors blamed the war on British imperialism; typical was one Swedish American, who wrote in 1914: "Who had decided England's policy? The 'God Mammon,' whom the world worships and loves. There can be no other cause for England's enmity toward Germany, no other reason why for many years she has planned her neighbor's destruction."[11] Certainly the German American Lutheran denominations had sympathy for their home country, but tended to express this cautiously, usually preferring to advocate for neutrality as a means for blunting pro-Allied (English and French) sympathies. As America edged toward assisting the Allies materially, the Lutheran press protested vociferously, complaining about war profiteering.

The entry of the United States into the war in April 1917 shifted the Lutheran tone quickly and dramatically, and Lutheran leaders and Lutheran periodicals unhesitantly proclaimed their patriotism and support of their country. Young Lutheran men enlisted in the armed forces, and other Lutherans campaigned actively for the purchase of war bonds and other means of support for the troops. The nation was gripped by waves of anti-German xenophobia, which by extension was applied to all things and all people who were "foreign." This attitude hit immigrant Lutheran groups the hardest, and often did not make a distinction between Germans, Scandinavians, and others; if they used foreign languages in their worship and their schools they were suspect. Several midwestern state legislatures passed proclamations forbidding the use of foreign languages in schools and public places, and at times mobs attacked and closed Lutheran churches and schools. A few Lutheran leaders were physically attacked. The Missouri Synod, with its private German schools and reputation for aloofness from other Protestants, was particularly targeted. The editor of Missouri's English-language publication counseled in 1918: ". . . only by plainly asserting that we are with our Government and against Germany shall we overcome such doubts as are in the minds of the public concerning our 'loyalty' in the war-time sense, the only sense which now counts."[12] Although the popular storm of hysteria soon blew over, and the wartime laws were repealed or invalidated, this brief episode made a deep impression on immigrant Lutherans.

The irony of all this was that the shift from neutrality to war came in early 1917 just as American Lutherans were making large plans for the public celebration of the four-hundredth anniversary of the Protestant Reformation in October of that year. Some Lutherans had put aside their denominational squabbling, and were organizing in plans for joint, pan-Lutheran celebrations. It was a way of celebrating not only the Reformation anniversary but also the "coming of age" of American

Lutheranism, now the third largest Protestant family in the United States. Very quickly, these plans had to be scaled back and replaced by cooperative efforts to support young Lutheran men in the American armed forces. In terms of chaplaincy and troop support, the U.S. government did not want to have to deal with each Lutheran denomination individually, forcing the Lutherans to work together on such efforts.

Forced to unite, most major American Lutheran groups sent representatives to form the National Lutheran Commission for Soldiers' and Sailors' Welfare (NLC-SSW) in October 1917; the Missouri Synod did not join, already having formed its own Army and Navy Board, which quietly coordinated its efforts with the NLC-SSW where necessary. The work of the NLCSSW was conceived broadly and implemented quickly, and included the establishment of Lutheran centers at camps, military installations, and hospitals, and the commissioning of Lutheran military chaplains. Christian literature for the troops was printed in massive amounts and distributed freely. The NLCSSW also coordinated volunteer work by local clergy and by synodical women's organizations and created a permanent publicity organization, the Lutheran Bureau, in 1917.

Of course, all these efforts took money, and quite a bit of it. The efforts of the NLCSSW would have collapsed without funding, and the commission undertook a national fund drive to support its efforts. This campaign for support was a risk—a simultaneous and coordinated multisynodical fund drive, the type of which had never been attempted among American Lutherans. Imagine the surprise when the campaign nearly doubled its lofty original goal by raising $1.35 million, while the Missouri Synod raised $560,000 of its own. This meant that American Lutherans raised close to two million dollars for ministry to support the troops, in addition to their generous purchase of government war bonds.

Many, but not all, American Lutherans hoped that this wartime cooperation might be a successful first step toward a more permanent organization that could coordinate many kinds of intersynodical Lutheran activities. Major war-related activities still remained to be addressed, including support of the troops, aid to European Lutheran churches affected by the war, and the support of "orphaned" missions—German mission fields abroad that it could no longer support. But there were many other areas in which a Lutheran cooperative group could organize, including coordinating home and foreign missions, social-service and educational institutions, and chaplaincy. In September 1918, the representatives of ten Lutheran groups met to establish a permanent National Lutheran Council to address these possibilities.

Conclusion

Growth—growth in numbers, in organizations and ministries, and in public presence—is the word that describes the trajectory of American Lutheranism from 1888 to 1918. These Lutheran denominations were reaching the masses of immigrant Lutherans and providing them with pastors and congregations, with schools and hospitals, and with many other sorts of ministries. When the denominations could not or would not do it, lay Lutherans (men, women, and youth) pushed ahead of their leaders and developed institutions and movements of their own. American Lutherans were beginning to do outreach and mission around the world, and to work more closely with one another to accomplish these goals. The several major Lutheran mergers (1890, 1892, 1917, and 1918) foreshadowed even larger unity efforts that would lie ahead in the twentieth century.

Notes

1. "Editorial," *The Lutheran Visitor*, May 14, 1879, quoted in Hugh G. Anderson, *Lutheranism in the Southeastern States, 1860–1886* (The Hague: Mouton and Co., 1969), 152.

2. Maria Erling and Mark Granquist, *The Augustana Story: Shaping Lutheran Identity in North America* (Minneapolis: Fortress Press, 2008), 161–62.

3. Frederick Weiser, *Love's Response: A Story of Lutheran Deaconesses in America* (Philadelphia: Board of Publication of the United Lutheran Church in America, 1962), 70.

4. J. C. W. Lindemann, "Die Lehrthätigkeit der Frauen innerhalb der Christenheit," *Evangelische-Lutheran Schulblatt* 7 (March 1872), in Carl S. Meyer, ed., *Moving Frontiers: Readings in the History of the Lutheran Church–Missouri Synod* (St. Louis: Concordia, 1964), 374.

5. Preston A. Laury, *A History of Lutheran Missions* (Reading, PA: Pilger, 1899), 122.

6. W. H. T. Dau, "Prefatory Note," in *Woman Suffrage in the Church* (St. Louis: Concordia, 1916), 2.

7. August P. Senne, "Was Wir Wünschen," *Der Vereinsbote* 1, no. 1 (August 1892), quoted in Jon Pahl, *The Hopes and Dreams of All: The International Walther League and Lutheran Youth in American Culture, 1893–1993* (Chicago: Wheat Ridge Ministries, 1993), 18.

8. Carol K. Coburn, *Life at Four Corners: Religion, Gender, and Education in a German-Lutheran Community, 1868–1945* (Lawrence: University of Kansas Press, 1992), 121–22.

9. *Golden Anniversary Booklet, Lutheran Laymen's Movement, 1907–1957* (New York: Lutheran Laymen's Movement, 1957), 3.

10. Ernest G. Hessenbuttel and Roy H. Johnson, *Pittsburgh Synod History: Its Auxiliaries and Institutions, 1845–1962* (Warren, OH: Pittsburgh Synod of the United Lutheran Church, 1962), 286.

11. C. A. Larson, "Which Would You Choose?" *Lutheran Companion*, 22, no. 49 (December 5, 1914).

12. Theodore Graebner, "Unjustified Aspersions," *Lutheran Witness* 37 (May 28, 1918): 168–69.

COLLEGES AND CONTROVERSY

There are two things (among others) that Lutherans seem to enjoy: they are very loyal to their church colleges, and they do relish a good controversy. About 120 years ago, Norwegian Lutherans in the Midwest had the chance to enjoy a great dispute between the supporters of Augsburg College and St. Olaf College. It was such a controversy that it ended up giving birth to an entirely new Lutheran denomination, and their relative supporters dividing into two different denominations. First, a bit of background about Lutheran colleges, and then to the squabble between the supporters of Augsburg and St. Olaf.

The nineteenth century saw the birth of literally thousands of small, church-related schools, some of which survive to this day as small, liberal-arts colleges. Many of these schools originally began as academies, which were really private high schools (as public education often ended at eighth grade). A few of these academies still exist in their original form, such as Oak Grove Lutheran School in Fargo and Minnehaha Academy in Minneapolis. As public education expanded in the twentieth century, some of these academies grew into undergraduate colleges, while others eventually closed their doors for good. Lutherans founded dozens of such schools in the Midwest, and most of the Lutheran colleges that we have today grew out of such roots. It was a point of pride for Lutheran denominations that they had "their school," and Lutherans supported them with great enthusiasm, which sometimes led to controversy.

In the late nineteenth century, there were several distinct Norwegian Lutheran denominations in the United States—as many as five different ones at one time. As the century rolled to an end, great efforts were made to merge these ethnic denominations together, a difficult task made more difficult not only because of thirty years of theological dispute, but also because of the issue of schools. In the late 1880s, several denominations of Norwegian American Lutherans were engaged in a merger process that eventually led to the formation of the United Norwegian Lutheran Church (1890–1917). Mergers are difficult things to arrange, and this one was complicated by the question of "schools," in this case, Augsburg and St. Olaf. The new denomination had to decide the "school" issue, especially because it was felt that they could only support one such institution.

On the face of it, the problem seemed manageable. Augsburg was primarily an institution for training Lutheran pastors, while St. Olaf was a liberal-arts academy and college that trained students for a wide variety of careers. Simple, it would seem: St. Olaf would be the "school" of the new denomination, while Augsburg would be its seminary. But things are never as simple as they seem, as deeply felt opinions about the nature of church-related education soon came to the fore and erupted into fierce controversy.

Augsburg College was founded first, in 1869, as an institution for training Lutheran pastors for Norwegian congregations in America. Powered by the educational vision of its two primary leaders, Georg Sverdrup and Sven Oftedal, Augsburg grew into a coordinated, nine-year course of education for young men: academy to college to seminary. St. Olaf was founded in 1874 by B. J. Muus and others, first as an academy, then as a college, which was co-educational from the beginning and which sought to prepare young Norwegian Americans for a variety of positions in the world (including the ministry).

When the United Church was founded in 1890, many saw the academy and college portions of Augsburg as being superfluous, and long-term support for them was ambiguous, at best. Supporters of Augsburg saw church support for St. Olaf as a threat to their vision of a coordinated theological education, and the battle began. In good Lutheran fashion, it involved spirited letters and articles in the press, fights in church conventions, secret meetings, and even disputes in the Minnesota legislature and the state courts. As Richard Solberg summarizes the debate, "Friends of Augsburg assailed St. Olaf for its humanism and rationalism, its 'luxurious facilities,' its doctors of philosophy, its masters of art, and [its] deficits. St. Olaf supporters branded Augsburg as a 'humbug' institution offering piety as a substitute for intellectual rigor and scholarship."[1]

As it turned out, in 1893 the supporters of Augsburg formed a group of supportive congregations, the "Friends of Augsburg," which eventually became a separate denomination in 1897, the Lutheran Free Church. As a failed attempt to reconcile the Augsburg supporters, St. Olaf was cut free from the United Church in 1893 and led a precarious life until the United Church reclaimed it in 1899. Both colleges survive to this day, and their athletic teams compete in the same conference. But not very many of their supporters realize that the roots of rivalry go back to church controversies of the 1890s.

Note

1. Richard W. Solberg, *Lutheran Higher Education in North America* (Minneapolis: Augsburg, 1985), 232.

Chapter 9

BECOMING AMERICANS, 1918–1940

T he United States became involved in World War I contrary to the wishes of most of its citizens. Once the nation was involved in the war itself, Americans rallied around and supported the troops and the war efforts, but this attitude quickly faded after the war's end. Most Americans resumed their isolationist attitudes and were strongly against further "foreign interventions," despite viewing with great alarm the rise of communism in Russia and fascism in Germany and Italy. Americans simply wanted things to return to "normal" and to be able to concentrate on their own lives and business. But the world kept intruding; wars in China, Ethiopia, and Spain were simply forerunners of the great world war to come, and the revolution and upheavals in Russia extended to a "Red scare" at home. The unsettled and uneven peace of Versailles in 1918, and the impotence of the League of Nations, which the United States refused to join, meant that the world during this between-wars period remained a restless place and Americans could not help but be drawn into it. The Great Depression of 1929–1941 was felt around the world, and demonstrated that even if the United States wished to be isolated, the global economy had developed to a point that events abroad had major impacts at home, and vice versa.

Americans tried to shut out the world, as best they could. One way to do so was to scale back dramatically immigration into the United States. There had been a periodic tide of anti-immigration and nativist attitudes since the middle of the nineteenth century, especially pointed at the Irish Roman Catholics and the immigration of Asians from Japan and China to the West Coast, but by the early twentieth century these feelings ran even higher, and by the 1920s Congress had developed a series of laws that reduced immigration to a trickle. While four million immigrants were admitted to the United States during the 1920s, most of them during the first few years of that decade, only about a half-million were admitted during the 1930s. The xenophobia of the First World War continued into the 1920s, and immigrants were viewed as foreigners bringing undesirable religious traditions such as Roman Catholicism and Judaism, as well as threatening social views such as socialism, communism, and even anarchism. These attitudes weighed heavily on the immigrants already settled in the United States, most of whom sought to show themselves as "good, 100 percent Americans," even as they tried to maintain some semblance of ethnic pride.

The population of the United States continued to climb during this period of time, slowly rising from 106 million in 1920 to 123 million in 1930, and to 132 million in 1940. The rate of growth leveled off because of the restrictions on immigration and the economic effects of the Depression, but the surge of Americans moving to the urban cities did not slow at all. Americans remained a restless people, and there were great shifts of population away from the rural areas. Agriculture went through a profound downturn in the 1920s because of overproduction and natural disasters, and these factors, along with mechanization, fueled these demographic shifts.

Social and technological changes accelerated, undercutting the urge to return to the "normalcy" of the past. Modern technology was molded into consumable forms, as automobiles and appliances, modern medicines and treatments, and the development of mass entertainment culture in the forms of radio, movies, and recorded music transformed American life. Americans were connected with the larger world in ways that earlier generations could scarcely dream, and these connections engendered massive movements within society. The 1920s saw a fast-paced rate of social change, including the right of women to vote, the continued migration of African Americans to the North, the imposition of national prohibition on alcoholic beverages, and the continued expansion of the great American cities. Forms of mass communication and entertainment spread a new youth culture, with movie stars and radio crooners embodying and leading this social revolution, often to the horror of their elders. Working men and women organized into labor unions and fought with their employers for better wages and living conditions. All this was before the great economic depression of the 1930s, which brought the world to its knees, economically, and shook the social foundations of the United States to its very core.

The second and third decades of the twentieth century were a time of great changes and great challenge, and American society struggled to keep up with the rate of development.

Religiously, the United States was still a majority Protestant nation, although the great immigration brought sizable numbers of Roman Catholics, Eastern Orthodox, Jews, and Buddhists to populate portions of the country. The sheer numbers of American Roman Catholics made them a force with which to be reckoned, and American Jews took full advantage of their freedom to move into important areas of American life. American Lutherans were a somewhat difficult group to categorize in all this; as Germans and Scandinavian immigrants they were foreign "others," but since they were generally Protestants, they were viewed by the dominant American Protestants as possible allies against the encroachment of the non-Protestant "others." African Americans, though deeply Protestant, were held on the margins of society. Nativism, especially with the dramatic upsurge of the Ku Klux Klan in the 1920s, fought to oppose Jews and Roman Catholics, as well as African Americans.

American Protestants were strongly challenged by the rise of secular modernity as well, but became deeply divided over how to respond to these trends. The rise of modern science and technology, along with secular ideologies such as communism and socialism, meant that there were now competitors to religion in Western cultures, movements that threatened to replace religious belief in the lives of individuals. Modern intellectual movements analyzed and criticized the foundations and beliefs of traditional religious systems, calling their very truth into serious question. Unlike the Deist critics of the eighteenth century, who maintained a vague moral theism, these new critics imagined a life without any religion at all and evangelized this new secular "gospel" to the masses.

The divisions within American Protestantism were strategic ones, trying to devise methods by which the challenges of modernity could be blunted and religious belief could be maintained. A small but growing group of religious liberals wished to embrace the challenges of modernity and to develop new forms of Christian tradition shorn of the old superstitions of the past, which they saw as the only means of keeping Christianity relevant for modern, educated people. These religious "modernists" felt that many of the traditional forms and beliefs of Christianity were simply accretions of the ages that could be jettisoned; to get to the true "core" of the Bible, for example, one could simply cut out the superstitions and miracles of the past. Other Protestants reacted strongly against this strategy, pushing, rather, in the opposite direction. If modernity and Christianity were in conflict, then modernity was wrong, and traditional Christian beliefs, *all* of them, had to be maintained. These movements, often termed evangelical or fundamentalist, believed that all the

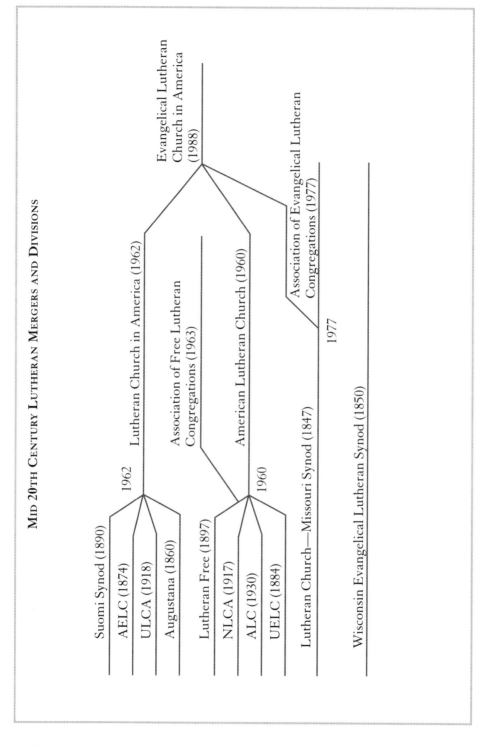

Mid 20th Century Lutheran Mergers and Divisions

Suomi Synod (1890)

AELC (1874)
ULCA (1918)   1962   Lutheran Church in America (1962)
Augustana (1860)

Association of Free Lutheran
Congregations (1963)

Lutheran Free (1897)
NLCA (1917)   1960   American Lutheran Church (1960)
ALC (1930)
UELC (1884)

Evangelical Lutheran
Church in America
(1988)

Association of Evangelical Lutheran
Congregations (1977)

Lutheran Church—Missouri Synod (1847)   1977

Wisconsin Evangelical Lutheran Synod (1850)

elements of the Bible and traditional Christian theology had to be defended; if one "brick" of the Christian edifice proved to be untrue, then the whole structure was in danger of collapse. In the 1910s and 1920s, many American Protestant denominations were wracked by the conflict and schism of the fundamentalist–modernist controversy. The bulk of moderates in these denominations tended to oppose the fundamentalists, who withdrew in sizable numbers to form their own, new denominations. American Protestantism became divided into the now familiar camps, with the older "mainline" denominations and the new evangelical-fundamentalist groups competing with each other.

The Landscape of American Lutheranism between the Wars

Even with the cessation of mass immigration in the 1920s, American Lutherans were a growing population, both in demographic growth and home-mission outreach. From a baptized membership of 3.68 million in 1920, the number of Lutherans grew to 4.7 million in 1935, averaging in the 1930s about 150,000 new members a year. In 1935, the Lutheran denominations recorded 120,000 infant baptisms and 20,000 adult baptisms among a total net gain of 180,000 members.[1] The 1935 figures give an interesting glimpse into the institutional power of American Lutheranism in that year, even with the full effects of the Depression. That year in the United States there were 20,000 Lutheran congregations, 10,300 active Lutheran pastors, and a total Lutheran benevolence of $42 million (down from $58 million in 1930). Lutherans supported four hundred social service or inner mission agencies, including eighty-seven homes for the aged, seventy-six hospitals, and sixty-four orphanages, with twenty-two theological seminaries, twenty-six colleges, and thirty-six teacher's schools and academies. They supported twenty major mission sites around the world, with 669 missionaries, 1650 schools, and twenty hospitals.

American Lutherans were divided into about ten larger denominations by this time. The United Lutheran Church in America (ULCA), at about 1.58 million members, and the Missouri Synod, at about 1.25 million, were the largest two church bodies, with another 1.7 million members divided between the eight midwestern "centrist" Lutheran denominations. This nicely illustrates the Lutheran landscape at the time, with two major American Lutheran denominations (ULCA and Missouri) constituting the borders of American Lutheranism, with a group of eight related ethnic denominations in the middle. The politics of American Lutheran affiliation and merger would play out among the shifting dynamics of these ten denominations.

American Lutheran denominations were generally gathered into one of two cooperative groups, the National Lutheran Council, begun in 1918, and the

Synodical Conference, founded in 1872. These two groups were designed to coordinate activities between the constituent synods, especially in terms of home and foreign missions, social-service and educational institutions, and other so-called external activities. The National Lutheran Council comprised the ULCA and seven of the midwestern synods, while the Synodical Conference was dominated by the Missouri Synod, and also included the smaller Wisconsin Synod and two other much smaller groups.

There were two major Lutheran mergers in 1917 and 1918, the merger of most Norwegian Americans into the Norwegian Lutheran Church in America (NLCA), and the reunion of the three branches of the colonial Muhlenberg traditions into the United Lutheran Church of America (ULCA). Between the wars, there was a great deal of talk and negotiations about possible closer relations, but only one actual merger process materialized, one in 1930 that brought together the Ohio, Iowa, Buffalo, and Texas synods to form the American Lutheran Church (1930–1960).[2] The formation of this new denomination seemed natural to most observers; all four synods were conservative, confessional midwestern German groups that had been uncomfortably situated between the General Council on the one hand, and the Missouri Synod and the Synodical Conference on the other. At various points several of these synods had actually been in either the General Council or Synodical Conference, or in both! These four synods had generally opposed Missouri in the predestination controversy, but also had their doubts about the confessional integrity of the General Council. Yet, the negotiations took a number of years, reaching a theological impasse over a common statement on the exact nature of biblical authority, which was only resolved through careful diplomacy.

Between the wars, two smaller Lutheran groups formed out of controversies within established Lutheran denominations. The first derived from the minority within the Norwegian Synod that could not accept the doctrinal compromise that resulted in the formation of the NLCA. A group of pastors and congregations met in 1918 to form a new denomination, the Evangelical Lutheran Synod (ELS) or, popularly, the "Little Norwegian Synod." Claiming to be the true heirs of the old Norwegian Synod tradition, this denomination centered at Bethany Lutheran College, Mankato, Minnesota, and had about nine thousand members in 1935. The ELS maintained close ties to the Missouri Synod and was a member of the Synodical Conference. The second group arose out of a theological controversy in the Wisconsin Synod in the 1920s, over the "Wauwatosa theology" originally espoused by Professor J. P. Koehler. Arguing against what they saw as "spiritual tyranny and dead orthodoxy" within the synod, a group of forty pastors was suspended in 1927 and formed a loose association called the Protéstant Conference.

Outside of these institutional developments, American Lutherans were beginning to gain a real sense of confidence in themselves and in their denominations as truly American religious groups. With a certain maturation, especially within the groups who had been formed in the nineteenth century, they exhibited an attitude that "we belong here." New generations of pastors and leaders, born and educated in the United States, shifted their gaze from Europe to North America. Although they still kept in contact with their European Lutheran counterparts, there was now a sense of equality with them, rather than a servile dependence. Lutherans were now educating their own pastors and running their own missions, and were confident in their abilities to do so. As the third-largest Protestant family in the United States, they felt that they had arrived and were legitimately American.

And still, they were not yet fully Americans, especially those groups that had been formed in the nineteenth century. Lutherans were still largely rural and had a tendency to "clump" together in ethnic enclaves, both in the rural areas and in the cities. They were underrepresented in American political and social life, even in those areas, such as parts of Pennsylvania and the upper Midwest, where they were the dominant group. Although American Lutherans took great notice of the larger religious and intellectual trends around them, in their discussions and theological arguments they still mainly conversed with each other about these things, often employing a distinctive Lutheran "grammar" that did not mesh well with outside religious groups. Socially, in the early twentieth century, American Lutherans were moving into the middle class and into educated and professional positions, but at a rate that lagged most other mainline American Protestants. Outsiders viewed Lutherans as generally middle class but with a mildly discernable "ethnic" veneer; many Lutherans did not seem bothered by this assessment.

Immigration and Language Transition

The rising tide of nativism and opposition to further immigration, already apparent in the late nineteenth century, resulted in the dramatic restrictions on immigration in the Reed-Johnson Immigration Act of 1924. This congressional legislation imposed tight immigration restrictions, limiting immigration to 2 percent of the total population of any specific ethnic group already in the United States. Asians had already been completely excluded, and this new act was mainly aimed at restricting immigration from southern and eastern Europe, specifically Roman Catholics and Jews. Northern European immigration had largely waned by the 1920s; the act reduced immigration from Great Britain by 19 percent, but from Italy by 90 percent.

American Lutherans were ambivalent about these immigration restrictions. Generally, they were opposed to the further immigration of Roman Catholics and Jews to the United States, and supported that aspect of the legislation, while decrying the limits placed on immigration from Germany and Scandinavia. The German immigration to the United States began a serious decline in the 1880s, which moved one Missouri Synod writer to observe in 1915: "The German immigration into this country has decreased to such an extent as to be no longer a serious factor in the building up of Lutheran congregations."[3] Scandinavian immigration was, however, in full stream right up to the First World War, and many Scandinavian Americans expected the immigration to resume once the war was over. Some Scandinavians worried that "legitimate" immigration from northern Europe was being held down simply to keep out "undesirable" immigrants from southern and eastern Europe. In 1929, one writer from the Swedish Augustana Synod protested this "conspiracy," asking how ". . . the United States will be benefited by the immigration of more Italians, Poles, and Irish . . . by limiting the quotas of Germans and Scandinavians."[4] The expectation of further Lutheran immigration led several Lutheran denominations to protest publically the new immigration laws, at least insofar as these laws applied to them.

The question of immigration was one aspect of a larger shift in American Lutheranism, the accelerating transition to the use of the English language. Although most nineteenth-century immigrants understood that they needed to learn some English to succeed economically and in the larger American society, many of them preferred to continue to use the immigrant languages in their homes and congregations. Many of the ethnic Lutheran denominations grudgingly allowed limited English-language resources for the younger generations, especially worship and educational materials and periodicals, but the main business of the synods was transacted in the immigrant language up to the 1920s. It was often a generational struggle, as older generations of laypeople and pastors generally had limited facility in English and worried about being sidelined in the very congregations they helped to build. Yet, others realized that without the transition to English, much of the younger generation would be lost to their congregations.

Although the eastern Lutherans of the ULCA had generally been using English for a century, with the exception of German elements in the General Council, most of the midwestern synods continued the dominance of foreign-language work until World War I. The primary arguments for the maintenance of the foreign languages were as follows: first was a concern that there would be enough pastors and worship services in the foreign languages to serve the needs of the older generation of Lutherans who wished them. Second was that the synods needed to maintain linguistic resources to do ministry with the waves of immigrants expected after the end of the First World War. Third, many wondered if Lutheranism could actually be done in English, at least with theological integrity. They looked at the English-speaking eastern Lutherans and laid at least part of the blame for their perceived "inadequate" Lutheranism on the influence of the English language. Already in 1891, a Missouri Synod writer suggested that the German language was a "defense" against "false teachings" and "unionistic tendencies" in congregations, while the English Lutheran congregations "are apparently placed into an entirely different position towards sectarian churches of all denominations. There is no visible barrier between them and these English churches who are following a path of error."[5] These attitudes can be summed up in the story of the old Lutheran who was asked whether God could understand English. The old man thought for a minute and then said, "Ja, God understands English, but He doesn't like it."

But the push for English was inevitable and accelerated greatly by the xenophobia of the First World War. By the turn of the twentieth century, most of the midwestern synods had a number of "English" congregations, usually intentionally formed as younger offshoots of established ethnic urban congregations and joined into some form of "English" association or conference for mutual support and encouragement. Advocates for English-language Lutheranism generally pointed out that failure to move in this direction would result in the loss of many of the younger generations of Lutherans. One Swedish Lutheran editor wrote in 1913: "No one wishes to rob the old folks of the Swedish. . . . But if we are considerate toward the old people . . . we should also be equally careful not to refuse to give our young people their spiritual support. We should be as concerned about *their* spiritual welfare."[6] Other writers complained about the numbers of prominent Lutherans who had already been lost to American Lutheranism because of limited numbers of English congregations.

The transition to the use of English was slow prior to the First World War; English was used in schools and in limited situations in most congregations, either on Sunday evenings or a couple Sundays a month, but synodical business was transacted mainly in the immigrant languages. After the war, the language transition happened very rapidly, and by the end of the 1920s it was fully complete. By 1930, most of the major Lutheran denominations were conducting their business and ministries in English; the Missouri Synod was slower to transition to English. In the Norwegian Lutheran Church in America, the number of English worship services surpassed those in Norwegian in 1924, and one observer predicted that Norwegian services would die out completely by 1942.[7] The rate of transition happened so quickly that many defenders of the immigrant languages had to form societies to protect the immigrant language and culture, which they believed were in danger of dying out completely in America. In 1921, G. A. Brandelle, the president of the Augustana Synod, saw the transition to English happening so quickly that he urged that "one or two congregations should be kept in the large cities as exclusively Swedish churches" for visitors and immigrants.[8] But the language transition was complete; most American Lutherans learned to worship God in English, whether they liked it or not. There is no record of God's opinion about this switch.

American Lutheran Engagement with the Wider World

With the formation of the National Lutheran Council (NLC) in 1918, American Lutherans had a common organization to address the needs of the world. Soon that organization was put to work dealing with needs that sprang from the war itself, especially the devastations in Europe, and the subsequent needs of European missions abroad. In 1918, the NLC voted to send five commissioners to Europe to survey the needs, and pledged to raise several million dollars for relief efforts. When the commissioners toured Europe and found that devastation was the worst among Lutheran communities in eastern Europe, from Finland and the Baltic through Poland and into Russia and the Ukraine, they immediately started channeling money to these areas through existing European Lutheran churches. American Lutheran leaders Laurtiz Larsen and John Morehead traveled extensively in eastern Europe and Russia, both to arrange for the distribution of aid and to report back to the American congregations on the enormity of the need in Europe. In fundraising drives from 1919 to 1925, American Lutherans gave 6.7 million dollars in cash and goods for European relief. Some of it went to Lutheran churches in France and Germany but more was designated for eastern Europe. This was just one part of a much-larger American response to postwar reconstruction in Europe. Americans might have been moving back toward isolationism, but they could still respond generously to needs overseas.

Another aspect of the NLC relief program was aid to "orphaned" missions in Africa and Asia. Before the war, European Lutheran churches and mission societies had established major mission stations in the global South, but the war caused havoc with them. German territories abroad, such as Tanzania, Cameroon, Namibia, and New Guinea, were taken over by the British or the French. German missionaries abroad in these countries and in British India were put into internment camps, unable to continue their missionary leadership. Without this leadership, and without European funding (embargoed due to the war), these mission stations were in danger of collapse. After the war, German mission societies did not have the funds to resume their mission work because of the postwar collapse of the German economy.

Responsibility fell to American Lutherans to pick up this mission work and to take over many of the German mission stations abroad. In India, the established ULCA and Augustana missions took over or directed much of the German Lutheran work in that country, and in 1925 the ULCA purchased the Berlin Mission Society facilities in China. In Tanzania, the Augustana Synod took over much of the work of the Leipzig Mission in that country from 1922 to 1926, and then established its own work on the Iramba plateau. The Iowa Synod cooperated with the Neuendettelsau missionaries in New Guinea and became responsible for much of that work after the war. Norwegian American groups established missions in Cameroon after the war, when that territory was transferred from Germany to France. All these new foreign-mission obligations, on top of the European relief effort, put an enormous financial burden on American Lutheran denominations, but their leaders and laypeople stepped up to the challenge. By 1935, in the middle of the Depression, American Lutherans were contributing a remarkable $1.2 million a year to the support of these missions, old and new.

These American Lutheran efforts abroad after World War I suggested to some denominational leaders that it was time to form an organization to coordinate Lutheran contacts and work around the world, similar to how the NLC was beginning to function at home. Although there had been some initial proposals in this direction as early as 1911, the first real action toward such a worldwide meeting of Lutheran churches came about through the urging of the European commissioners of the NLC in 1919 and 1920, prompting the NLC to reach out to European groups, leading to the eventual organization of the first Lutheran World Convention (LWC), held in Eisenach, Germany, in 1923. The meeting was cautiously planned as a way for Lutherans around the world to meet each other, not as the start of some further organization, which might have discouraged some Lutherans from attending. The wounds of the war were still fresh and there were some obvious tensions remaining, but representatives of five American Lutheran denominations were a part of the meeting, in which they joined nearly 150 Lutheran leaders from twenty-two different countries. The meeting established the concept of Lutheran cooperation through common confession and discussed forms of practical cooperation.

This first meeting led to the establishment of an executive committee to plan for future meetings, and NLC leader John Morehead was elected as chairman. With a successful initial meeting, four more American Lutheran denominations decided to participate at the second meeting at Copenhagen in 1929, meaning that all the major American Lutheran denominations were participating, except those in the Synodical Conference. The LWC was disrupted through the 1930s by the economic depression and by the rise of the Nazis in Germany, with the subsequent challenges to Lutherans there. A 1935 meeting was held in Paris, but this was the last meeting before World War II erupted in 1939.

The NLC and Theological Debates in the 1920s and 1930s

The National Lutheran Council, founded with a flourish at the end of World War I, was intended to continue and expand the work of the National Lutheran Commission for Soldiers and Sailors Welfare (NLCSSW). Many observers thought that it was truly out of character that these eight Lutheran denominations could join together in common work so quickly, without years of theological deliberations and confessional agreements, but perhaps the exigencies of war triggered their cooperation. Flush with enthusiasm, the eight denominations that formed the NLCSSW carried over into the NLC. Beyond the work that the NLC was doing in Europe and on the mission fields, proponents of the NLC foresaw a bright and expansive future for the new organization. They saw it coordinating Lutheran efforts in such areas as home and foreign missions, education, social service, and presenting a united American Lutheran position to the world. But the initial wartime enthusiasm quickly dwindled, and as some Lutheran leaders gave a second thought to what they had just done, they began to raise objections, which brought the NLC to an early theological crisis between 1918 and 1920.

To avoid such lengthy and often fruitless theological negotiations that usually preceded closer Lutheran cooperation or union, the founders of the NLC emphasized two points. First, they insisted that the NLC was not any kind of Lutheran union or church body, but merely a vehicle for cooperation. Second, that to avoid the traditional worries about unionism, the work of the council would be limited to cooperation in externals (*res externae*) rather than internals (*res internae*). Theoretically, externals were those forms of cooperation that could be done together without first reaching complete theological agreement. While the distinction made theoretical sense, it soon became apparent that in practice the differences between two categories were almost impossible to define. How, for example, could the member denominations coordinate home-mission work, and thus avoid duplicate efforts, without at least a tacit acknowledgment that the ministry of each of the cooperative denominations was truly orthodox Lutheranism? Later on, one of the Norwegian American proponents of the NLC, President Lars Boe of St. Olaf College, wrote to his friend, NLCA President J. A. Aasgaard: ". . . the Lord has never permitted it [the NLC] to be only an agency for cooperation in external affairs. Time and time again we re-wrote the constitution and regulations . . . to safeguard this line that we arbitrarily set up, only cooperation in externals, but the Lord . . . pushed us across the line every time."[9] Although the Missouri Synod agreed at times to limited coordination, but not cooperation, with the NLC, it refused to join the new organization and frequently criticized the other midwestern confessional denominations for their "unionism" with the ULCA through the NLC.

President Hans G. Stub of the Norwegian Lutheran Church in America soon called for an NLC "Joint Committee on Doctrine and Practice," which met in March 1919 and again in January 1920. From the papers presented to these meetings, it became very clear that there was a major theological division between the views of the ULCA and those of many of the midwestern Lutheran groups. Stub himself presented the so-called Chicago Theses (1919), which later became the basis for the so-called Minneapolis Theses (1925), which insisted that further doctrinal negotiations and agreements were necessary within the member denominations of the NLC in order to carry out cooperative ministries and to avoid unionism. Stub and a number of other midwestern leaders still harbored their doubts as to the orthodox Lutheranism of the ULCA, which, in their view, was insufficient in affirming the authority of the Lutheran confessions and the Bible and tacitly allowed its members and even pastors to belong to secret societies and lodges such as the Masons.

The ULCA representatives to these meeting, especially President Frederick Knubel and theologian Charles M. Jacobs, responded with a paper of their own, entitled "The Essentials of the Catholic Spirit in the Church" (1919), which was later rewritten and adopted by the ULCA and known as the "Washington Declaration" (1920). In their understanding of cooperation and unity with other Lutherans, they asserted that no Lutheran group has "any reason" to doubt the confessional Lutheran commitment and identity of another Lutheran group, and ". . . each of these bodies is in unity of the Lutheran Faith with every other, and that these Bodies do form one Church, according to . . . Augsburg Confession, article seven . . ."[10] Knubel and Jacobs even envisioned the possibility of limited cooperative work with other, non-Lutheran, Christian groups, as long as such work did not threaten their proclamation of the gospel.

These two documents neatly delineated the faultline running through the NLC and through American Lutheranism in the 1920s. Several American Lutheran historians have categorized the two approaches as "Ecumenical Confessionalism" and "Exclusive Confessionalism." The Ecumenical Confessionalism position sought to suggest that adoption of the Lutheran confessions was by itself sufficient, and that further theological negotiations were unnecessary; Lutherans should recognize each other as Lutherans. The Exclusive Confessional position suggested that Lutheran confessional unity could only be attained when groups were in complete theological agreement with one another, and that this agreement was necessary before cooperation could be achieved.[11] These two theological strains lived uncomfortably with each other within the NLC and characterized the parameters of Lutheran merger negotiations in the interwar years.

Theological Disputations and the Authority of Scripture

American Lutherans had long argued about theology and confessional identity, so the fact that the denominations in the NLC could not agree was not surprising. But after 1920, American Lutherans had new issues to fight over: the nature of biblical authority and terms new to the debate, namely "inerrancy" and "infallibility." The main battle for American Lutherans in the nineteenth century was the exact nature of the authority of the Lutheran confessions, especially the Augsburg Confession, and how strictly they defined Lutheran identity. While this issue did not go away, it was supplanted in the early twentieth century by a sharp fight over the exact nature of the authority of the Bible, and especially how to describe that authority. Behind this was an entire jumble of religious and cultural issues that had been rocking American Protestantism from the late nineteenth century onward, and on which American Lutherans were beginning to take positions.

In the North Atlantic world, the authority of the Bible, especially among Protestants, had long been a given, a bedrock for both religion and culture. Even when the Protestants could not agree on much of anything, they agreed that the Bible was the source and norm of their faith. Although eighteenth-century Deists asked sharp questions about the truth of the Bible, they could not shake biblical authority as a bedrock belief. Even those who were tangential to organized Christianity, such as Abraham Lincoln, often lived and worked in a world that was suffused with biblical concepts and images. But later in the nineteenth century, the solid authority of the Bible as a norm began to erode, and many scholars began to ask probing and disturbing questions about the truth and authority of the Bible. New discoveries in science and other fields suggested that the biblical description of the cosmos was inadequate; the biblical account of the creation of the world in six days, for example, could not be squared with scientific discoveries in geology and biology. Some biblical scholars themselves began to study the Bible as they would any other ancient text, measuring it against the other forms of historical and archeological evidence to determine the accuracy of the biblical text. These scholars, employing what came to be known as "higher biblical criticism," suggested that the Bible itself was a complicated human construction, spread out over centuries and multiple human authors and editors and containing much of the worldview of its time. They pointed to alleged internal inconsistencies and even errors within the texts.

Most of these higher biblical critics were religious liberals who sought to "save" the core theological message of the Bible by using their critical tools to separate out the timeless theological truths of the work itself from its temporal and historical elements, which could be wrong. Since modern science demonstrated biological evolution over millions of years, the liberals suggested that to maintain a literal six-day creation would be damaging both to the Bible and to religious faith. Although most Christians in this time did not go as far as these biblical critics, many did think (rather naïvely) that it should be possible to coordinate biblical accounts with modern science; some claimed that "Evolution is God's way of doing things." But religious conservatives were increasingly skeptical and worried, both by the claims of modern science and by those biblical critics who would critically "dissect" the Bible. Conservatives felt that even if liberals' motives were to save the Bible, their adoption of criticism would destroy its reliability and authority. Increasingly, conservative defenders of the Bible argued that it must be completely true in all respects; if it was shown to be in error in some points, then the truth of the whole Bible must be called into question.

The conservative defenders of biblical authority increasingly employed two terms to characterize the truth of the Bible, namely "inerrant" and "infallible." The term *inerrant* has roots in seventeenth-century Reformed theology, but was introduced into the late nineteenth-century debate by American Presbyterians Charles Hodge and B. B. Warfield. When the conservative position was outlined in a series of pamphlets entitled "The Fundamentals," the inerrancy of Scripture became a bedrock position. The term, and underlying concepts of biblical authority, soon became the flashpoint in the American Protestant debates over the authority of Scripture, and in the fundamentalist–modernist controversies.

Traditionally, Lutherans had not employed the English term *inerrancy* to define the authority of Scripture. The sixteenth-century Lutheran reformers held that the Bible was the "source and supreme norm" for Christian faith and life, because it was a true and authentic witness to the gospel, the living and saving reality of God's Word in Jesus Christ. Martin Luther suggested that what was important was how the biblical texts "pushed" the good news of Christ, and that the degree to which any text did this indicated its authority and importance. Later Lutheran theologians, in theological struggles with Reformed Protestants, attempted to define further the nature of biblical authority, but did not generally employ the term *inerrancy* to define the matter, although some current Lutherans will argue that the term is in harmony with their understanding.

American Lutherans traditionally held to a conservative position on the authority of Scripture, and were generally opposed to the attempts of higher biblical critics and modernists to call portions of the Bible into question factually. Since this was not an issue in the sixteenth-century Lutheran confessional documents, these issues were not a part of the confessional debates among American Lutherans during the nineteenth century, although some conservative Lutherans thought that the official position of the General Synod on the authority of Scripture was weak. Although some American Lutherans expressed positions on biblical authority that came close to the position of "inerrancy," the word itself was not used. By the early twentieth century, in the context of the fundamentalist–modernist controversy and with the transition to the use of English, American Lutherans began to search for wording that expressed in English their understanding of the nature and authority of Scripture, and some began to borrow the term *inerrant* from conservative American Protestants. It is not always clear, however, that when American Lutherans used the term *inerrant* they meant it in the classical form of Reformed Protestantism. Some American Lutherans used the term *inerrant* to describe the Lutheran position that Scripture was the "supreme source and norm," while others used it to mean that the Bible is without error in any matter whatsoever.

The term *inerrant* entered American Lutheran theological debates in the Chicago Theses of 1919, composed by the president of the Norwegian Lutheran Church in America, Hans G. Stub. The preamble to this document states, ". . . the canonical books of the Old and New Testament are the inspired and inerrant Word of God." The corresponding statement of ULCA leaders Knubel and Jacobs expresses biblical authority as: "The authority of the prophetic and apostolic Scriptures of the Old and New Testaments, as the only rule and standard by which all doctrines and teachers are to be judged."[12] At this period of time in the early 1920s, most of the midwestern Lutheran groups were generally sympathetic to the use of the terms *inerrant* and *infallible*, both because they believed it correctly expressed the nature of biblical authority and because it brought them into harmony with the Missouri Synod on the issue. When the ULCA and a few others resisted the term *inerrant* as being problematic, yet another issue developed to complicate relations between American Lutheran groups.

In the negotiations between the Iowa, Ohio, and Buffalo synods that produced the American Lutheran Church (ALC) in 1930, the groups involved ran into a snag when they discovered that although they used the term *inerrant*, they did not all mean the same thing by its use. Most notably, the Iowa Synod theologian Johan Michael Reu used the term *inerrant* to mean that the Bible could not be wrong on matters of doctrine and belief. When it was proposed that the constitution of the new American Lutheran Church (1930–1960) describe the Scriptures as "the inspired and inerrant Word of God," Reu opposed this. Although he wanted strong language about biblical authority, he resisted the formal use of the term *inerrancy* as a doctrine or as a basis for church union. Four years of theological wrangling ensued until the the constitution of the new ALC, which used the word "infalliable" but not "inerrant" for scripture. This proved an additional barrier between conservative midwestern groups, such as the ALC, and the ULCA.

In their use of the Bible, almost all American Lutherans at the time remained conservative, if not premodern. No American Lutheran biblical scholars openly promoted the use of higher biblical criticism, and all argued for a strong doctrine of biblical authority. Conservative Lutheran critics suspected that the ULCA was "soft" on biblical authority because of its resistance to inerrancy language and because of some passages in the writings of ULCA biblical scholars, but in general, American Lutherans were cautious, if not dismissive, of the liberal-modernist theological agenda.

Efforts toward Lutheran Unity

Despite the three Lutheran mergers that took place between 1917 and 1930, it was apparent to most observers that there might be more mergers to come. The vast majority of American Lutherans were now using the English language, so linguistic barriers were no longer an obstacle to union, and even the ties of ethnic heritage were fading, albeit slowly. Although through the 1920s and 1930s, for example, a minority of the NLCA maintained enough votes to block the denomination from dropping the word *Norwegian* from its official title, the push was on in most of the Lutheran denominations to become "American" denominations not just in their titles but also in their outlook and organization. The NLCA finally managed to change its name in 1946 to the "Evangelical Lutheran Church" (ELC). Once they were truly "American" denominations, it seemed natural to many to push for a single Lutheran denomination representing all Lutherans in the United States. Yet, if closer cooperative relations were difficult to achieve, further institutional merger was a goal that was even more difficult to realize.

Besides the usual problems of institutional loyalty and interest, Lutherans were also divided over the criteria for merger and who would actually be invited to the negotiating table. The basic division involved the United Lutheran Church in America (ULCA) and the Missouri Synod. These two largest Lutheran denominations were at opposite ends from each other, with other centrist midwestern groups between them being drawn one way or the other. It seemed possible during the 1920s and 1930s that the centrist groups might move in the direction of either the ULCA or Missouri, but it was more of a stretch to think that ULCA and Missouri themselves might achieve a closer relationship.

Even though they had fought with the Missouri Synod during the nineteenth century, many of the midwestern confessional denominations still held out deep hopes for closer relationships with Missouri and maintained a distrust of the ULCA. The NLCA and the ALC, especially, sought closer relations with Missouri. The Swedish-ethnic Augustana Synod, on the other hand, had been an early member of the General Council and was generally sympathetic to parts of the ULCA. Augustana also had a history of difficult relations with Missouri, so that the Swedes did not have the same kind of longing for closer ties with them as did the NLCA and ALC.

The primary questions of the day regarding unification were two: first, what organization was going to be the "path" for merger negotiations; and, second, which American Lutheran denominations would be invited to the negotiating table. Some saw the National Lutheran Council as the natural arbiter of further moves toward Lutheran unity, but the early theological struggles in that organization did not bode well for further success. Others believed that either the Missouri Synod or the Synodical Conference, dominated by Missouri, was the best path. But it seemed that getting both Missouri and the ULCA to the same table was unlikely.

To this end, in 1930, five of the centrist midwestern groups formed their own new cooperative organization, the American Lutheran Conference. The NLCA, the ALC, the Lutheran Free Church, the Augustana Synod, and the United Danish Evangelical Lutheran Church formed an organization with an aggregate membership roughly the size of Missouri or the ULCA. It was not always clear, however, to conference members or outsiders, what its primary purpose was. Would it be a vehicle for further cooperation, even though all five were already in the National Lutheran Council, or essentially a defensive alliance against the power of either the ULCA or Missouri? The early years of this conference were hindered by the Depression and World War II and by internal disagreements over strategy and direction.

Through the 1930s, in a series of formal and informal bilateral discussions, the various Lutheran denominations sought to locate themselves within the larger context of Lutheran cooperation and merger discussions. Even the most optimistic observers did not foresee any imminent mergers in the immediate future, but each American Lutheran denomination sought to define its own ground, to seek partners and allies, and to influence the course of discussions along the lines of its own position. Many groups produced their own doctrinal articles to clarify or cement their position: the "Savannah Declaration" of the ULCA (1934); the "Brief Statement" of the Missouri Synod (1932); and the Intersynodical (Chicago) Theses of the midwestern groups (1925). At their best, these documents were attempts to clarify theological positions; at their worst, they were theological "hand grenades" lobbed from the entrenched position of one group into that of another. The history of American

Lutheranism has amply shown, however, that simply issuing doctrinal position papers has rarely, if ever, achieved the goal of closer denominational relations, let alone merger.

There were several rounds of theological discussion that occurred during this time. Mention has already been made of the negotiations between the Iowa, Ohio, and Buffalo synods that produced the ALC in 1930; these talks were complicated by a long dispute about the authority of Scripture. The ALC and the Missouri Synod had ongoing conversations that seemed to have promise, but eventually came to nothing. To their credit, representatives of the ULCA and Missouri Synod sat down for a series of discussions from 1936 to 1938, though, given their previously defined positions, no one was surprised when the talks themselves quickly hit an impasse. The ULCA was also involved in talks with the ALC from 1936 to 1940, which went somewhat better and eventually achieved a common statement, the Pittsburgh Agreement. However, as is sometimes the case with these things, the agreement itself did not bring about further unity; the ALC remained distrustful of the ULCA and adopted a "wait-and-see" attitude. The ULCA negotiators acceded to the ALC on a number of key points, only to find that in giving way on important issues they had nothing to show for their sacrifice except hard feelings from the rest of the ULCA. The Pittsburgh Agreement was a bitter pill for the ULCA to swallow, and it soured the denomination on future attempts at "merger by means of theological statements."

The Depression and Its Effects

Despite external pressures and internal divisions, the 1920s were an expansive time for American Lutherans, with steady growth in members, congregations, and financial resources. Many American Lutheran denominations spent the nineteenth century playing "catch up" to the masses of immigrants that flooded into the United States, always badly behind in congregational and pastoral resources to meet the overwhelming needs. By the 1920s, the mood seemingly had shifted; immigration had slowed dramatically, allowing these denominations finally to attempt to reach out to yet-untapped pools of potential Lutherans. Many Lutheran groups made big plans in both home and foreign missions and the development of educational and social-service institutions. Expansion and growth were in the air.

And then it all came crashing down, with the stock-market crash of 1929 leading to the Great Depression. Americans were used to economic downturns; they might be severe, as with the Depression of 1893, but it seemed that these would be short-lived and that the economy would soon turn upward again. Not so with the

Great Depression of 1929–1941; every time it appeared that things might be improving, the economy took another nosedive. It was really not until the rapid expansion of defense spending in the late 1930s that the Depression came to an end. Actually, because a majority of American Lutherans were still rural at the time, the Depression began during the 1920s, when the agricultural economy collapsed due to low commodity prices and overproduction, which continued into the later stock-market collapse. This depression was more than a decade in length, and brought about a social crisis in America the likes of which had not been seen before, with rates of unemployment reaching as high as 25 percent.

Traditionally, churches had been the provider of emergency social services and the "social safety net" for their communities, but the scope, scale, and duration of this depression simply overwhelmed their resources. American Lutheran groups did what they could to provide temporary relief for their communities, but since the economic depression was so widespread, their members could not provide the financial resources to meet the needs. Because of the expansion of their missions and ministry during the 1920s, these denominations took on a greatly expanded financial obligations that they were hard-pressed to manage during the Depression. The NLCA, for example, had developed an ambitious home-mission effort during the 1920s, and was running an accumulated deficit from these operations of nearly $300,000. The deficit was covered by lines of credit from banks in Minneapolis, but when the Depression hit, the NLCA found itself in severe financial trouble, which only stringent economies eventually solved. The Missouri Synod reported in 1932 that it had a debt of $850,000, of which almost $600,000 was owed to banks. The collapse of local banks, and the loss of those funds on deposit, also affected Lutheran institutions, and almost all of the denominations cut back on spending and reduced staff.

Benevolence giving to the national denominations fell dramatically, as the Depression drained resources and local congregations struggled to keep their doors open and their ministries alive. The ULCA saw its yearly benevolence income slip from a high of $1,400,000 in 1929 to $865,000 in 1932; ULCA income did not recover until the 1940s. Congregational giving to the national church in 1939 was still 17 percent below what it had been in 1931. In the Augustana Synod, per capita giving to the denomination sank from $22.13 in 1930 to $13.82 in 1935, and similar stories could be told of all the other Lutheran groups. American Lutheran leaders continued to appeal for support from their members, and sought to reach them through organized benevolence campaigns, but money was scarce all around. In response to one appeal from the Lutheran Free Church, a member wrote in 1933 to the denominational publication, the *Lutheran Messenger*, explaining his dire conditions:

. . . the last two years my income has been so small that I have been unable to pay interest or taxes [on my farm] . . . we have enough to eat, but could easily use more clothing. . . . There are thousands of farmers in just as bad shape as I am, and many much worse. . . . there are very good reasons why not so much is coming in in donations from our farmers as might be expected. It is not miserliness in regards to God's work . . . it is plain helplessness . . .[13]

Average American household income dipped almost forty percent during the Depression, and many families were severely pinched, if they were getting by at all.

The plight of many pastors and congregations was equally dire. Many congregations saw their income drop precipitously and had to make equally drastic cuts. Many of the newly established home-mission starts and other small struggling congregations that had been on financial support from the national home-mission boards saw this support cut back or eliminated altogether. Since the largest part of most congregation's expenditures was for pastoral salaries, already comparatively low, these reductions in support affected pastors directly and dramatically. One Augustana Synod pastor wrote denominational president G. A. Brandelle in 1933, saying: "I am not getting my salary. . . . My two congregations are now in arrears on my salary to the amount of $1315.00. . . . I have not managed to lay up anything to live on and am totally dependent on my salary, myself, my wife, and three children in minor ages."[14] The Depression slowed the call process to almost a complete standstill, and even if pastors wished to move, there were few, if any, calls available to them. The situation was the worst for new seminary graduates, the vast majority of whom could not find congregations. In 1932, only twenty percent of the graduates of Augustana Seminary had calls, a situation similar to that of other Lutheran seminaries. Although a number of Lutheran seminaries had been considering the introduction of a practical "internship" year for pedagogical reasons, these programs were introduced in the 1930s in part because they kept the seminarians in school for an additional year, and provided low-cost pastoral interns to local congregations. Perhaps the worst affected were the retired pastors and their widows; pastoral pension programs were just being introduced, and few pastors had much money available for retirement. The introduction of Social Security benefits in 1935 was a great assistance to them.

Lutheran institutions struggled through the Depression, and not all of them survived. The weakest of the Lutheran educational institutions, usually academies and junior colleges, closed their doors, and the rest of them retrenched dramatically. Many faculty positions were eliminated, and salaries were cut substantially for those who remained; often, fixed salaries were eliminated, and faculty and staff were only promised a percentage share of the institution's income. As enrollments dipped dramatically, and debts from the expansions of the 1920s mounted, these institutions felt a severe contraction. A number of the colleges that were originally all-male were forced to begin accepting female students in order to survive. Missouri Synod schools that were exclusively focused on future pastors and teachers began to admit tuition-paying, non-preministerial students. Social-service agencies suffered similar declines in their revenues, even as demands on their services soared, and a number of these institutions had to retrench or close. American Lutherans had taken on a greatly expanded role in home and foreign mission, establishing new congregations and mission fields, and the worldwide scope of the Depression deeply affected these ventures.

In previous periods of economic difficulties, the nation had actually seen upswings in attendance at religious services and "revivals" of religion. But the Depression of the 1930s was different, in that it saw a religious depression as well as an economic one. It is very difficult to quantify this decline through the 1930s, but from limited data and from the observations of contemporaries, it is evident that church attendance and participation declined during the Great Depression, and if overall numbers of members did not decline, rates of growth certainly slowed.

Although the Depression and unsettled political conditions strongly affected the funding of American Lutheran mission work around the world, it did not dampen their enthusiasm for the cause itself. Neither did it lessen the general isolationism of most Americans, who sought to keep America out of "foreign entanglements." After the initial expansion in the 1920s, especially by taking over from the European mission societies that could no longer manage some of their mission stations, American Lutheran groups kept on expanding their mission presence around the world. The Norwegian Lutheran Church in America had proportionally the largest mission presence, followed by the ULCA. The Missouri Synod expanded the work it had begun in India, adding thirty-one missionaries and seven nurses between 1925 and 1930, and its mission stations expand from sixty-six in 1920 to 205 in 1940. It also expanded its work to Africa in 1936, answering a letter of invitation from the Ibo people of Nigeria to come and work among them. The Augustana Synod sent forty mission personnel abroad to China, India, and Tanzania in the 1920s and thirty-one more in the 1930s. Even some of the smaller denominations initiated their own missions; the Danish Lutheran Church in America sent its first missionary to India in 1920, and the Church of the Lutheran Brethren started work in Cameroon in that same year.

Some American Lutherans decided to move ahead of the pace of their denominations, and established mission societies independent of the various American synods. The existing work of independent mission groups, such as the China Missions

Society and Lutheran Orient Mission, were continued and new groups were formed. When he could not get the NLCA to sponsor his work in Africa, A. L. Gunderson organized the independent Sudan mission in 1923, which began work in Cameroon and the Central African Republic. A number of Lutheran students and pastors formed an independent World Mission Prayer League in Minneapolis in 1937, which started with mission work in Bolivia and central Asia. Many of these new mission personnel were inspired by their time in the recently formed group of Lutheran Bible Institutes that had been organized across the country. These were conservative, nondegree-granting Lutheran educational institutions that trained students in biblical knowledge and mission outreach; a high proportion of their graduates went out on the mission fields, whether sponsored through the denominations or through the independent societies. Many of these mission personnel were young, unmarried women, either nurses or teachers. In 1935, the total of 367 Lutheran men on the mission field were outnumbered by 402 women, of which 175 were single.

Mission work in Africa and Asia was a dangerous endeavor, and some missionaries had their tours abroad cut short by illness or political upheavals; some died while overseas. Since many American Lutheran missions of the twentieth century contained a strong contingent of nurses and doctors, the medical conditions that afflicted earlier missionaries were mitigated, but conditions could still be difficult. China, which was the "crown jewel" of Western mission efforts, was rocked by political and military upheavals, with the Chinese Nationalists fighting the Chinese Communists, as well as invasions by the Japanese in the 1930s, all leading to a general breakdown of law and order. Missionaries to China routinely had to be moved or relocated away from areas of trouble. Typical was the report of Augustana Synod missionaries in Honan in 1925: "During the first few months of the year most of our stations were visited with serious upheavals. Much looting, burning, and killing was reported. At Linru several thousand people lost their lives. By special providential care we Christians, both foreigners and Chinese, were most miraculously protected."[15] Under the auspices of the National Lutheran Council, but independent from it, American Lutheran mission executives formed the Lutheran Foreign Missions Conference of America in 1920 to coordinate efforts and share information among the various American Lutheran denominations about their foreign-mission work.

American Lutherans and the Larger American Society

In American society, the 1920s and 1930s were a time of social ferment, although each decade had a very different feel to it. The 1920s saw the development of a new, youth-oriented mass culture, with technological innovations such as automobiles, radio, and movies playing a major role. Women got the vote, alcohol prohibition was imposed, though often flouted, and Americans tried to "entertain" themselves back to normalcy after the disruptions of the war. The 1930s, on the other hand, were a more somber and even desperate time, when the deep effects of the financial collapse threatened to unwind the very social fabric of the country. The threats of communism and fascism and wars in Spain and China were harbingers of a greater military catastrophe to come. President Franklin D. Roosevelt sought to address America's malaise through his New Deal programs, but the Depression lingered stubbornly, deeply affecting an entire generation.

On the whole, American Lutherans were socially conservative and wary of many of the elements of the new culture of the twentieth century. They shared deeply in the old Protestant morality of the nineteenth century, which expressed itself in a strict personal moral code, which honored the Sabbath, read the Bible, resisted drinking alcohol and using tobacco, and avoided dancing and other "frivolous" social activities. Although this strict morality had begun to fade a bit by the early twentieth century, it was still strongly held by many, especially in the rural Lutheran enclaves. Of particular concern were the Lutheran youth, who were maturing in the midst of a changing social scene in the 1920s; parents worried that the new mass culture of the decade would draw their children away from the values of home and church. The Lutheran youth organizations sought to provide a "wholesome" alternative to the lures of the world and they grew rapidly, urged on by eager church officials. One report of a 1929 Missouri Synod Walther League convention proclaimed that instead of "worldly amusements, the young attendees ". . . were voluntarily, even enthusiastically, convened in the interests of their league and church; they had prepared for months for this strictly church assemblance. . . . Their very joyousness in church service disarmed every loose statement that the 'youth of today are the children of the devil.'"[16] Another attempt at influencing Lutheran youth was the Bible camp movement, which expanded rapidly during the 1920s. Lutheran schools and colleges sought to provide a strictly regulated living and learning environment for their students, free from the temptations of the culture around them.

For the rest of the Lutherans, pastors and church leaders tried to assist their congregants in resisting the lures of a changing culture. Prohibition was the law of the land and, generally being advocates of temperance, most Lutherans strongly supported the new law and its enforcement. Some of the more conservative German groups, especially the Missouri Synod, did not share in this enthusiasm for alcohol prohibition. With a culture that allowed moderate drinking, and with a fear of entangling church and state, they argued against the new law. The new mass-culture vehicles were suspect, especially the motion pictures, which one Lutheran editor referred to as "moral filth . . . presented as 'art,' and defended by some as a 'mirror of life.'"[17] Dancing, gambling, card playing, and "secular" entertainments were equally suspect. The new medium of radio was a much less controversial; while parts of it, especially popular "jazz" music, were regularly decried, some other programming was considered to be harmless. The medium of radio was also seen as a possible evangelistic tool, and some Lutherans embraced this use of the new technology. Beginning in the 1920s and 1930s, Missouri Synod professor Walter A. Meier pioneered a very successful program, "The Lutheran Hour," on national radio networks; his preaching reached millions of people. St. Olaf College radio station WCAL was a radio pioneer, and broadcast religious programing in multiple languages all across the Midwest.

Lutherans generally were resistant to many of the new social, scientific, and intellectual trends of the period, such as psychology and sociology, and the "isms"—socialism and communism—were seen as "godless" attacks on religion. A progressive political movement in the Midwest attracted some Lutherans, especially farmers, but the more radical wings of this movement were shunned. Despite a significant radical presence in the midwestern Finnish communities, for example, a strong ethnic antipathy existed between the "church people" and the secular social radicals. The theory of evolution was a divisive issue during the 1920s, and generally Lutherans opposed this new science, fearing it as an attack on God and on biblical truth. Norwegian American pastor Byron Nelson was an active and prolific author of works attacking evolution and urging the alternative of creationism; his books were continuously printed by the denominational publisher, Augsburg Publishing House, well into the 1950s and received generally positive reviews in the contemporary Lutheran press.

Because of the social and economic traumas of the 1930s, American Lutherans were also forced to deal with other serious matters, issues that often forced them to reconsider long-held social and political positions. In the nineteenth century, Scandinavian American Lutherans were overwhelmingly Republican in political affiliation. The German Americans were historically Democratic, but began to desert that party in large numbers after 1896. Regardless of their political sympathies, Lutherans tried to keep religion and politics separate; Lutheran denominations and periodicals generally remained apolitical. They did occasionally express opinions on political issues where these impinged on religious or denominational issues, but sought to keep these comments on the level of policy rather than politics. That said, the massive disruptions and upheavals of the Depression forced Lutherans to reconsider some of their positions. Most Lutherans were traditional capitalists and not directly linked to the labor movement, but the failures of the economic systems in the 1930s caused them to reevaluate some of these positions. Some Lutherans cautiously supported the labor movement and some of its more modest positions, especially the rights of workers in large industries. In 1938, the annual convention of the American Lutheran Church issued a statement that attacked both "atheistic communism" as well as "present day soulless capitalism, which through greed and lust for power, ruthlessly disregards the rights of the working man."[18] Cautious statements like this and others suggest that Lutherans were coming to grips with some of the large economic and political realities around them.

One controversial aspect of the 1930s was the range of New Deal programs implemented by President Roosevelt, which dramatically changed the role of the federal government in Americans' lives. Some of the less-controversial aspects of the New Deal, such as government relief efforts for the poor and unemployed, support for agricultural prices, and aspects of the Social Security program were generally acceptable to American Lutherans. Since the scope of the crisis was beyond the level that churches themselves could address, these new programs seemed to offer some hope in the midst of disaster. The Augustana Synod periodical offered a qualified endorsement of the New Deal in 1933: "Like most emergency solutions, the present project is far from ideal. Its prime movers admit their and its fallibility [but because] . . . many of the causes in it are just, it should not altogether fail."[19] But other American Lutherans were worried about the larger implications of such novel and sweeping government programs, which seemed like incipient socialism to them. Typical was Missouri Synod editor Theodore Graebner, who attacked the entire New Deal as socialistic in nature, placing the church and individual human persons under the control of the state. Many American Lutherans would have agreed with his sentiment that the Depression was equally a spiritual and moral crisis that could only be solved by repentance and a return to God.

Another aspect of the 1930s was the unsettled nature of world politics. American Lutherans were consistently opposed to communism and worried about the threat this movement in Russia posed to Lutherans in Europe. Although some were mildly sympathetic to Hitler at first, insofar as he was rebuilding Germany and creating a bulwark against communism, their initial support soon turned negative, especially in light of Nazi belligerence and war-like threats to other European nations. Above all, most American Lutherans were isolationists and, in the face of another European war, a few were moving in the direction of pacifism. Isolationist sentiments were a constant refrain during the 1920s and 1930s, as American Lutherans still had a bad taste from their experiences in World War I and did not want to be dragged into another European war. In the face of mounting evil around the world, American Lutherans expressed continuing support for institutions like the League of Nations, multiparty negotiations for disarmament, and other similar efforts. Lutheran support for President Roosevelt slid during the 1930s, in part because of widespread perceptions that his close political relations with Great Britain were in danger of pulling America into another European war.

One last influence of the interwar years left its permanent mark on American Lutheranism. This was the age of big organizations, in business, in politics, and in society. This was the age of centralization, when efficiencies of scale and "scientific" central planning seemed to offer the way to a better life for Americans, despite the controversies of the 1930s. This trend took over in American religious life as well, with the centralization and bureaucratization of many of the mainline Protestant denominations. Traditionally, most American Lutheran denominations had been rather small and decentralized bodies; they met yearly to transact business and elect committees, but there was little in the way of standing structures and permanent staffs. Typically, the president of the denomination managed day-to-day affairs in conjunction with the heads of their regional judicatories (synods, districts, or conferences). Instead of a permanent church headquarters with dedicated staff, the leaders of the denominations traveled to meet with each other at central sites, facilitated by free or reduced railroad passes. Many American Lutheran denominations did not even have a designated church headquarters, or if they did, it was a rather modest facility.

Accompanying the urge toward merger and consolidation of American Lutheran denominations was a parallel movement to consolidate denominational activities. Lutherans created permanent church headquarters with full-time staffs, so as to centralize power and create efficiencies within their denominations. Soon after the foundation of the National Lutheran Council in 1920, for example, the organization quickly established a large, permanent national headquarters in New York City. Other major Lutheran denominations soon followed suit, and even though the Depression forced them to scale back temporarily, this was a permanent and continuing trend. Lutheran laymen's groups supported this trend, especially through the establishment of permanent stewardship and fundraising organizations within the denominations, particularly so as to support the cost of these new structures. Partly this trend toward consolidation and centralization was due to the increasing size and scale of these denominations, several of which were over one million members each. But Lutherans were also "breathing the spirit of the age" and, like their mainline Protestant cousins, believed the idea that bigger was better and more effective, and that "scientific" methods of modern management could be harnessed to do the work of the gospel. The trend toward bureaucracy eventually led to a permanent structural shift in American Lutheran polity; whether this was good or not could only be seen in the future.

Notes

1. "Section 12, Parochial Statistics," in *Lutheran World Almanac and Encyclopedia, 1934–37* (New York: National Lutheran Council, 1937), 324–26.

2. Confusingly, there were two different denominations entitled the "American Lutheran Church," the one formed in 1930, and then one formed in 1960. To add to the confusion, the first ALC (1930–1960) was one of the four denominations that formed the later ALC (1960–1988). So it is necessary to use the dates with these two groups.

3. VT, "Local Church Publicity," *Lutheran Witness* 34, no. 13 (June 29, 1915): 200.

4. Carl J. Bengtson, "Editorial Comments," *Lutheran Companion* 37, no. 43 (October 26, 1929): 1349.

5. John Schaller, "Danger Ahead," *Lutheran Witness* 10, no. 8 (September 21, 1891): 57.

6. "Editorial," *Lutheran Companion*, 19, no. 28 (July 15, 1911): 1.

7. E. Clifford Nelson, *The Lutheran Church among the Norwegian-Americans*, vol. 2 (Minneapolis: Augsburg, 1960), 250–51.

8. "President's Report to the Synod," 1921, quoted in G. Everett Arden, *Augustana Heritage* (Rock Island, IL: Augustana Press, 1963), 247.

9. "Letter, Lars W. Boe to J. A. Aasgaard," October 29, 1942, quoted in Nelson, *Lutheran Church among the Norwegian-Americans*, 2:302 n.51.

10. Frederick Knubel and Charles Jacobs, "The Essentials of the Catholic Spirit in the Church," 1919, in Richard C. Wolf, ed., *Documents of Lutheran Unity in America* (Philadelphia: Fortress Press, 1964), 306.

11. The terms "Exclusive Confessionalism" and "Ecumenical Confessionalism" can be found in E. Clifford Nelson, *Lutheranism in North America, 1914–1970* (Minneapolis: Augsburg, 1972), 78–79; and Arden, *Augustana Heritage*, 270–71. The description of the two approaches is found in E. Clifford Nelson, "The New Shape of Lutheranism,' in idem, ed., *The Lutherans in North America* (Philadelphia: Fortress Press, 1975), 459.

12. Wolf, *Documents of Lutheran Unity*, 298, 309.

13. Letter from Arthur Quanbeck, "From the Mailroom," *Lutheran Messenger* (March 1, 1933), 11, quoted in Eugene Fevold, *The Lutheran Free Church: A Fellowship of American Lutheran Congregations, 1897–1963* (Minneapolis: Augsburg, 1969), 185–86.

14. Letter, E. O. Valborg to G. A. Brandelle, September 11, 1933, G. A. Brandelle Presidential Papers, Augustana Synod Collection, ELCA Archives, Elk Grove Village, IL.

15. "Minutes of the China Mission, 1926," 5, quoted in S. Hjalmar Swanson, *Foundation for Tomorrow: A Century of Progress in Augustana World Missions* (Rock Island, IL: Augustana Book Concern, 1960), 126.

16. R. D. Chappell, "To the Editor of *The News-Sentinel*," July 14, 1929, quoted in Jon Pahl, "Lutheranism in the Twenties: Youthful Perspectives," in *Interpreting Lutheran History: Essays and Reports of the Lutheran Historical Conference*, vol. 17 (St. Louis: Lutheran Historical Conference, 1996), 186–87.

17. "Editorial," *Lutheran Companion* 35, no. 13 (March 26, 1927): 291.

18. *Minutes*, Fifth Convention of the American Lutheran Church, October 14–20, 1938, p. 310, quoted in Niel M. Johnson, "Lutherans in American Economic Life," in John E. Groh and Robert H. Smith, eds., *The Lutheran Church in North American Life* (St. Louis: Clayton Pub. House, 1979), 145.

19. "National Recovery," *Lutheran Companion* 41, no. 46 (November 18, 1933): 1443.

Excursus 9

LUTHERANS AND THE LODGE

When most people think about the term *lodge*, they likely will imagine some rustic main building at a lakeside resort. So, when they hear that American Lutherans have, at times, fought long and hard about the "lodge issue," they are rightly confused. But in this case, the term *lodge* has nothing to do with summer camp, but is, rather, a synonym for social, fraternal organizations such as the Masons and many other similar groups that used to be very popular in America. So why did a large swath of American Lutherans come to the conclusion that being a lodge member was antithetical to being a good Lutheran Christian?

While groups like the Masons, Rosicrucians, and the Illuminati had a long history back to the Middle Ages (and were in their origins a religious alternative to Christianity), most of these fraternal organizations, such as the Elks, Moose, Odd-Fellows, Knights of Pythias, and dozens of others are of nineteenth-century origin. By that time, many of these groups functioned as fraternal societies for men, providing not only a social outlet, but also valuable professional contacts and even financial support for the "brothers." There were many of these groups, some of which were general in nature, while others targeted specific groups of individuals. Some early labor "brotherhoods" and college "Greek" fraternities would be an example of the latter. These groups were a widespread part of male life in nineteenth- and twentieth-century America, and many men were members of these groups.

Many of these lodges (sometimes referred to as "secret societies") were highly organized and had very detailed and ornamented rituals, complete with secret ceremonies, knowledge of which was supposed to be held only by the "brothers" themselves. Some of the groups were organized on a quasi-religious but nonsectarian basis, complete with chaplains and rituals that paralleled and mimicked traditional religious belief. There were generally no doctrinal requirements for membership, and the "brothers" could be from a variety of religious groups, including many forms of Christianity and Judaism, as well as those who were Deists and other forms of "free thinkers." American Roman Catholics, generally not accepted at the time as members in some of these groups, formed their own parallel fraternal society, the Knights of Columbus.

The major doctrinal issue that some Lutherans had with these "secret societies" was the question of "unionism," or of being in religious fellowship with others without being in doctrinal agreement with them. Many of these groups did have definite religious elements, even if many lodge members ignored or downplayed them, and their membership was often religiously mixed. As one Lutheran critic of the lodges wrote in 1899, "In most of these societies, members join in stated religious rites and exercises conducted by religious officers, chaplains, priests, etc. according to accepted rituals or books of forms."[1] Further, they did these things in mixed religious company. Whether or not you actually believed these rituals, or found them religiously persuasive, you were in essence (these critics suggested) worshiping with them.

There was a second, and more practical, set of issues. In essence, these fraternal groups were competitors to the Christian churches for the time and affiliation of men. Although many members of these secret societies were also members of their local congregations, there was often a rivalry and a tension between the lodge and the church. In their membership, churches tended to be a majority of women, and it was often a struggle to get men to commit to being active church members. Sometimes, the activities and rituals of the lodge could come into conflict with congregational life, especially funerals. The *Lutheran Book of Worship* funeral service included the following warning: "The ceremonies or tributes of social or fraternal societies have no place within the service of the Church."[2]

Since these groups were so popular, Lutherans struggled to determine the best approach to dealing with them. In some Lutheran groups, lodge membership was not a major concern, and laymen and even many pastors were members of them. Other Lutheran denominations maintained a concern about these organizations, but believed that a pastoral and persuasive approach to the issue was necessary; they would try to convince their members that lodge membership was not proper for good Lutheran Christians, and try to "wean" them away from the lodges. Still other Lutherans took a firm approach to the issue, suggesting that lodge membership was never allowable, and threatening disciplinary action against lodge members in their congregations. It even became an intra-Lutheran issue, with some Lutherans suggesting that other Lutherans were "soft" on the lodge issue.

In the twenty-first century, this issue has faded in importance. One reason for this is because the membership in these secret societies has plummeted. Still, it is a concern for some Lutherans, especially the question of divided loyalties and participation in quasi-religious organizations.

Notes

1. August L. Graebner, "Secret Societies," in *The Lutheran Cyclopedia* (New York: Charles Scribner's Sons, 1899), 438.
2. "Burial of the Dead," in *Lutheran Book of Worship* (Minneapolis/Philadelphia: Augsburg/Board of Publication, Lutheran Church in America, 1978), 206.

Chapter 10

Lutherans in War and Peace, 1940–1965

T he quarter-century between 1940 and 1965 saw an incredible transformation of the United States, from being an economically devastated and isolationist country during the 1930s, to becoming the world's economic and military superpower, actively engaged around the globe by the early 1960s. Shocked into action by the debacle at Pearl Harbor in December 1941, the United States marshaled its formidable resources, including its vast human capital, to defeat both Germany and Japan in the Second World War. After this war, Americans turned their energies toward defeating their wartime allies, the communist Russians and Chinese, and began the long "Cold War" against communism. This Cold War, tinged by the apocalyptic specter of nuclear warfare, was a game of global strategy that sometimes turned hot, such as in wars in Korea and Vietnam. Americans had become convinced that being separated by oceans from Europe and Asia was no longer a defensive strategy, and that in an age of global warfare with long-range bombers and intercontinental ballistic missiles, the United States had to maintain a strong position in the world in order to defend itself.

At home, the United States experienced a prolonged economic expansion unlike any in its history, and millions of Americans benefited from a dramatic rise in their standards of living. Having been denied anything approaching "normal" for almost two decades, with first the Depression and then the Second World War, a generation of Americans, the "greatest generation," sought to secure their own personal piece of this prosperity, buying a car and a house in the suburbs, and starting families. The resultant "Baby Boom" (1946–1964) resulted in seventy-eight million births during the period, as the population of the United States expanded from 132 million in 1940 to 194 million in 1965. Prosperity led to an age of optimism, when it seemed that America should be able to succeed at doing whatever it wanted, if the country put its resources to work. Advances in science and technology not only improved the health and wealth of the nation's citizens, they suggested that these twin forces could tackle any challenge, overcome any problem, and that improvements in the human condition were not just possible but almost inevitable. Certainly there were grave problems; the threat of communism and nuclear annihilation, along with the polio epidemic, remained as huge worries to many. But progress was the watchword, and most Americans believed that, with national unity and ingenuity, almost any threat could be neutralized.

The period during and especially after the Second World War saw a tremendous expansion of religion in America. Whether or not this was a national "revival" or "bubble" is still open for debate, but it is clear that almost all elements of religion grew dramatically, especially from 1945 to 1960. Partially, this was due to underlying economic and demographic factors, as the economic vitality triggered by and following World War II and the Baby Boom created a tremendous demand for religion. Americans moving to the new suburbs or migrating to new communities in the South and West of the country created a huge demand for new congregations, tens of thousands of which were established every year. But there was more to this religious expansion, which also drew from a nervous national religiosity based on the Cold War. The enemy was communism, which, because of its official atheism and political suppression of religion, was frequently referred to as "Godless communism." To be a good American then was to be religious—the two things were virtually synonymous—which led to increased rates of religious belief, identity, and participation that have rarely been matched, before or after this time period. Billboards erected at the edge of towns by local ministerial groups often urged Americans to "Attend the Church or Synagogue of Your Choice this Weekend," suggesting a noncreedal religious orthodoxy tinged with patriotism. "In God we Trust" was added to the currency and the phrase "Under God" was inserted into the Pledge of Allegiance.

Within American religion itself, broader prosperity was declared a "rising tide that floats all boats." The old mainline Protestant groups still maintained control over the American religious psyche, but increasingly their power was being challenged by rising groups such as Roman Catholicism, Reformed Judaism, and evangelical Protestantism. The new medium of television made national celebrities out of such figures as the Roman Catholic cardinal Fulton J. Sheen and evangelical revivalist Billy Graham. The election of a Roman Catholic, John F. Kennedy, to the presidency in 1960 was further indication of growing religious diversity. Since it was no longer possible to consider America as solely a Protestant or even Christian nation, many Americans sought to draw the religious tent wider by designating the United States as a "Judeo-Christian nation," which signaled the hope that, despite its diversity, America did have a common religious inheritance.

Beneath this religious conformity and growth were other trends. African Americans sought to appeal to this common religiosity as a basis for their push for civil rights, with only mixed success. Theologians wrestled with questions of meaning resulting from World War II and the Cold War, while new expressions of theology, such as existentialism and neo-orthodoxy moved into some areas of religion. Religious scholars began to consider the merits of more radical ways of thinking, such as higher biblical criticism, the "God is Dead" theology, and the implications of science and secularism. Such radical themes often had little direct impact on American religious life, except to be used by conservative religious critics as symbols of degeneration.

The Development of American Lutheranism, 1940–1965

As American Lutherans moved ever more firmly into the American social and religious mainstream in the twentieth century, their unique history came more and more to resemble that of the larger social and religious world around them. During this quarter-century, the larger schema of American religious developments had a profound impact on American Lutherans, most of whom were seeking to "catch up" to their American Protestant counterparts, whoever they might be. On the American religious scene, Lutherans were still considered a bit exotic, a bit regional, and exhibiting a mild but distinct ethnic Protestantism; but in the postwar period, these perceptions were fading. Although there were no Lutheran "stars" to match those of other groups, one Lutheran leader, Franklin Clark Fry, the president of the United Lutheran Church of America (ULCA), did make the cover of *Time* magazine in 1958 under the heading, "Mr. Lutheran." Lutherans were perceived as reliable Protestant partners in the larger religious project of American society and provided solid accomplishments in areas such as education, social services, postwar relief, missions, and ecumenism.

Lutherans grew numerically and financially during this period of time, from five million baptized members in 1940 to over nine million baptized in 1965.

Lutherans also increased as a percentage of the United States population, growing from about 3.8 percent of the population in 1940 to 4.6 percent in 1965, faster than the general rate of population growth. Those Lutheran institutions, such as colleges, seminaries, and social-service providers, that survived the Depression also grew during this time, providing a solid Lutheran infrastructure for their growth, and for their service to the larger communities beyond their own immediate spheres. Many Lutheran denominations joined newly formed ecumenical ventures, such as the Lutheran World Federation, the National Council of Churches, and the World Council of Churches, and participated in ongoing ecumenical discussions.

Within the American Lutheran world at this time, there was a widespread feeling that greater institutional unity was almost inevitable, although the exact contours of this unity were hotly debated. From the early 1940s to the early 1960s, there were intense rounds of merger negotiations and posturing, and though these activities led to the formation of two new consolidated Lutheran denominations rather than a single one, many contemporary observers were convinced that the final institutional unity of American Lutheranism was a matter of "when" rather than of "if." By 1963, the rounds of merger produced two new Lutheran denominations, the Lutheran Church in America (LCA), with 3.3 million baptized members, and the American Lutheran Church (ALC) with 2.5 million baptized members. Add the Lutheran Church–Missouri Synod (LCMS) with 2.9 million members, and the three denominations represented 95 percent of all American Lutherans.

Although questions of merger and structure dominated this period, American Lutherans were also at work in many other areas, nationally and internationally. Given better financial resources, American Lutherans went on a dramatic expansion of mission activities, not just the formation of thousands of new congregations in the United States, but also new and expanded mission activities in countries around the world. American Lutherans also donated millions of dollars to rebuild Lutheran religious life in Europe and Asia devastated by the effects of World War II, and resettled thousands of refugees in the United States. They began to grapple in a serious way with issues of national import, especially with the civil rights movement, the spread of communism, and the challenges and opportunities of the scientific and technological revolutions around them. Having "arrived," American Lutherans sought to make their voices heard.

American Lutherans and World War II

During the 1930s, many American Lutherans began to develop a negative response toward Adolf Hitler and the German Nazi party, thereby initiating a breakdown in traditional American Lutheran isolationism. This isolation eroded further with the Nazi invasion of Denmark and Norway in 1940, and it disappeared completely with the Japanese attack on Hawaii in 1941. Although during the late 1930s, several small Lutheran associations were formed to support pacifism and conscientious objectors, there was little or no Lutheran opposition when the time came to enter the war, which most American Lutheran denominations wholeheartedly supported. As the American government built up the armed forces in the years before 1941, the National Lutheran Council and the Missouri Synod each separately developed a pool of qualified military chaplains, who were ready to report for duty once the United States entered the war. German missions in Africa and Asia had already declined greatly even before the war due to Nazi currency restrictions, just as had happened during and after the First World War, and American Lutherans had to step in and take over these "orphaned" missions. After the German invasion of Norway and Denmark, and the Soviet invasion of Finland, there were even more orphaned missions to support.

All this, plus financial relief for war victims and the costs of chaplaincy, led American Lutheran leaders to initiate an emergency appeal for funds, which in its first year raised $240,000. In 1941, Lutherans also developed the Service Commission, which sought to coordinate and fund chaplaincy and ministry centers at military bases as well as relief to missions and war refugees. All of these activities were funded out of an ongoing financial appeal entitled Lutheran World Action, which over the next twenty-five years raised and disbursed over $80 million. Local Lutheran congregations were also encouraged to develop local programs to aid in the war efforts, while denominations developed their own larger responses. Young women and men from local Lutheran congregations enlisted in the armed forces, and soon the human costs of war became starkly aware to these communities. Homes flew blue-star flags to indicate that a member of the family was in the service; when those flags were replaced by gold-star flags, it indicated that there had been a military death in the family. Most Lutheran congregations had at least some families who had suffered this kind of loss.

As strange as it may seem, World War II was a time of financial prosperity for Lutheran congregations and denominations. Prewar unemployment vanished, and the desperate need for war workers meant that many women also found employment, greatly increasing their household revenue. For the time being, there were fewer traditional ministry initiatives on which Lutherans could spend their money. Congregations could not easily build new buildings due to wartime restrictions on materials, so they paid off their debts and stockpiled cash. Foreign-mission boards were cut off from missions in East Asia, and thus put funds into escrow for the future. On the other hand, Lutheran colleges continued to struggle financially, suffering from low enrollments due to the loss of young men to the service; some of these schools leased out parts of their facilities for military-training operations, such as the V-12 program. Seminaries, which a decade earlier had prolonged their programs, now accelerated their ministerial training to produce young pastors for local congregations and the military.

One of the great domestic effects of the war effort was the development of massive wartime industries, but these defense plants came at a great social cost; thousands of new workers flooded into communities that were ill-equipped to deal with them. At one such site, the Willow Run plant in Michigan, the National Lutheran Council (NLC) sent Sister Margaret Fry and Sister Margaret Schueder to develop social services to aid what was a real human mess. In her first report, Sister Fry told NLC officials: "Impression—a hodgepodge of all types of housing; and MUD everywhere, plus unsanitary conditions of sewage and garbage. Problems—need for housing, nursing (many expectant mothers, inoculation clinics, etc.), recreation facilities for children (the first three grades at Spencer School are running a double shift)."[1] Thousands of Lutherans moved to work at defense plants like these, spreading American Lutherans into areas of the South and West where there had not been a significant Lutheran presence previously. Some of these migrants chose to stay in these new areas and, after the end of the war, provided the nucleus for home-mission congregations.

Because of its nature as a "total war," World War II caused human suffering and destruction in a huge part of the world, affecting all areas of civilian life, devastating large portions of Europe and Asia, and creating millions of refugees or DPs ("Displaced Persons"). The eventual cessation of war did not end this human suffering, and the displaced and dispossessed became a major ongoing focus for American Lutherans. Their yearly financial appeal, Lutheran World Action, raised millions of dollars to address these problems. The NLC and the LCMS cooperated together in a new organization, Lutheran World Relief (LWR), which sent relief supplies to war-ravaged areas, shipping over a billion pounds of materials, worth $122 million, over about twenty years (1945–1965).

Important as these responses were, American Lutherans did more than just send money and material overseas; many of their leaders went abroad to direct and assist in the efforts to rebuild areas, especially in Europe. Ralph Long (NLC), P. O. Bersell (Augustana), Franklin C. Fry (ULCA), J. A. Aasgaard (Norwegian), and Lawrence Meyer (LCMS) all visited Europe shortly after the end of the war to survey conditions, to meet with European Lutheran leaders, and to plan for relief efforts. Other Lutheran leaders played a longer and more active role in the relief and rebuilding efforts, including Howard Hong, Stewart Herman, Sylvester Michelfelder, and Julius Bodensieck, as well as a number of others. They worked with many different organizations such as the United Nations, the International Refugee Organization, the Allied military powers, and European Lutheran leaders to help to alleviate the human suffering caused by the war.

The war had caused massive destruction and disruption in central Europe, especially Germany, where Lutheran churches were in physical and spiritual tatters after the war. American Lutherans provided materials and guidance to assist in the reconstruction of these churches, even though some American voices suggested that the Germans ought to be punished for the war and thus not assisted in reconstruction. American Lutheran leaders had to push a reluctant American government to be allowed to provide relief to Germany; the government eventually provided a pathway for such work called CRALOG (Council of Relief Agencies Licensed to Operate in Germany), of which Lutheran World Relief was a member.

The disruptions of the war were aggravated by the actions of the Soviet Union in Eastern Europe, where the Russian occupation of these countries was used as a vehicle to impose communism and atheism upon them. American Lutheran efforts to assist the rebuilding of European Lutheranism were very limited in communist-controlled territories, and millions of additional refugees were created by ethnic Germans and others fleeing or being expelled from Eastern Europe and eastern Germany ahead of the advancing Russian army. The Russian seizure of the Baltic countries (Estonia, Latvia, and Lithuania) added to this human flight, and many of these refugees were Lutherans. With American Lutheran assistance, Baltic Lutherans established national churches "in exile" in Scandinavia and North America, adding additional strains to the ethnic mix of Lutherans in the United States, and reinforcing Estonian and Latvian congregations already established by earlier immigrants.

The issue of refugees and displaced persons was a huge problem in the postwar reconstruction. Relief and governmental agencies had developed temporary camps in Europe to assist these refugees, but the ability of Western European countries to absorb them permanently was limited. Although many of them were eventually resettled in Europe, American Lutherans also assisted the resettlement of European refugees in North America and Australia; by 1952, seventy thousand Lutheran immigrants had been settled in the United States, with an additional twenty-two thousand in Canada and twenty thousand in Australia. Many of these refugees were sponsored by American Lutheran congregations, who provided housing and support for them until they could become self-sufficient. This huge logistical undertaking was coordinated by a large staff at the NLC under the direction of a remarkable Lutheran leader, Cordelia Cox.

The postwar situation among Lutheran missions around the world was equally unsettled, with the devastation in many countries and the continuing problem of supporting missions "orphaned" by the loss of support from European mission agencies. In 1948, American Lutherans formed the Commission on Younger Churches and Orphaned Missions (CYCOM), which spent millions of dollars towards these efforts, supporting as many as twenty-one different mission fields after the war, especially in Asia, where the devastations of war seriously affected many new Lutheran churches. Nor did the disruptions end in 1945, especially with the communist takeover in China in 1951 and the subsequent expulsion of Western missionaries. To deal with the problem of refugees and orphaned missions, CYCOM redirected missionaries and mission funding from China to meet the needs of other Asian populations, including refugees fleeing the communist takeover. China missionaries and resources were sent to Hong Kong and Taiwan, as well as to other Asian countries with sizable Chinese populations.

Home Mission and the Expansion of American Lutheranism

Everything was in place for an immense and unequaled expansion of American Lutheranism after 1945. The financial difficulties of the Depression and the war footing of the early 1940s were past, and there was a pent-up demand for religion just waiting to be satisfied. People were longing for a return to "normal," including buying houses in the new suburbs (often in new sections of the country), having children, and getting on with life. The question was, Would there be congregations available to serve them? And if so, who would plant these congregations, serve them, and finance them? The situation called for a massive outreach campaign, well-coordinated and financed, all on a scale not seen by American Lutherans before.

With the shift away from ethnic-specific home missions in the 1920s, many American Lutheran denominations had participated in a Lutheran Home Missions Council, founded in 1931, to coordinate efforts and reduce duplication; in 1942, these functions were absorbed by the NLC. After World War II, each of the major American Lutheran denominations geared up for the challenges and opportunities ahead by means of an organized home-mission strategy. The largest denominations, the ULCA, LCMS, American Lutheran Church, the Evangelical Lutheran Church,[2] and the Augustana Synod moved limited resources away from the maintenance of smaller existing congregations to the formation of new congregations. Among the eight member denominations of the NLC there was an unprecedented degree of coordination of these efforts, which seemed to blur the line between "internals" and "externals" that some had tried so hard to maintain. The tempo of new home-mission starts increased yearly, and by its peak in the late 1950s and early 1960s, American Lutherans were starting a new congregation every fifty-four hours, or over 160 new congregations a year.

A standard pattern was developed for the starting of a new congregation. Denominational staff would survey likely areas for expansion to ensure that conditions were ripe for a new congregation. A mission-developer pastor was sent to the area, who began to canvass the area for possible members, whether they were traditional Lutherans or totally new but receptive to Lutheranism. The mission board supplied funding and standardized materials such as hymnals, Sunday school lessons, and other publications for each new congregation, and would oversee the process by means of written reports and site visits. Evangelism and stewardship campaigns were organized, and the initial members of the new congregation would be enlisted to provide for its continued growth. Mission boards even supplied standard building designs, usually a minimal "first unit" onto which could be added future expansions. Careful and eager scrutiny was made of quantitative signs of growth; mission pastors even joked that they counted pregnant women as two members on their reports to the mission boards, such was the pressure for results.

Denominations developed national evangelism campaigns and strategies, the most successful of which was the Evangelical Lutheran Church's "Preaching-Reaching-Teaching" (PRT) program of the 1950s. These resulted in a strong growth in Lutheran congregations, from about 15,500 in 1940 to more than 17,300 in 1965. Lutheranism expanded as well into parts of the country where it had not previously been strong, especially in areas of the South and West. The number of Lutheran congregations in Florida grew from about forty in 1940 to over 240 by 1965, and in California from about 350 in 1940 to nearly 800 by 1965. The Wisconsin Synod spearheaded mission expansion into Arizona and the Southwest, while the Missouri Synod's director of home mission stated in 1956 that "Our church has had a proportionately larger growth in Home Missions than most other church bodies in America," though he also noted that even with this remarkable general increase in Christianity, the number of unchurched individuals continued to grow.[3]

American Lutherans and Relations with Other Christians

As American Lutherans began to make significant contributions to the nation and the world around them, they began to cooperate not just with other Lutheran bodies, but also with other Christian groups. This was the age of building organizations, and in short order American Lutherans cooperated with or led in the formation of three large ecumenical ventures: the National Council of Churches of Christ in the USA (1950), the World Council of Churches (1948), and the Lutheran World Federation (1947). Although the constituent members of the Synodical Conference (Missouri, Wisconsin, and others) did not participate in these groups, most other American Lutheran denominations did, although some of the more conservative members of the NLC hesitated on joining some of these organizations, especially the National Council of Churches of Christ (NCCC).

Before World War II, American and European Lutherans had met in three sessions of the Lutheran World Convention, but a fourth meeting, scheduled for Philadelphia in 1940, was cancelled. After the war, many concluded that a more permanent organization was needed, especially in light of the major challenges of the postwar reconstruction. American and Scandinavian Lutheran leaders planned an initial assembly of the new Lutheran World Federation (LWF) at Lund, Sweden, in 1947. The LWF headquarters was established in Geneva, Switzerland, with a permanent staff to continue the work of the organization between assemblies. American Lutheran leaders were prominently involved as members of the executive committee of LWF, and two American Lutherans served as its permanent executive secretary, Sylvester Michelfelder (1947–1951) and Carl Lund-Quist (1951–1960). The LWF struggled early on to overcome hard feelings involving the presence of the German Lutheran churches, but a second assembly at Hannover in 1952 went a long ways to resolving some of the lingering issues.

A second ecumenical organization, the World Council of Churches (WCC), was formed in Amsterdam in 1948, with its roots in prewar meetings of the Faith and Order conference and Life and Work conference in Great Britain, in 1937. Again, American Lutherans took a leading part in the movement to form this new organization, and especially pushed successfully for "confessional" rather than geographical representation in the organization. Five American Lutheran denominations joined immediately, the ULCA, Augustana, American Lutheran Church, and the two Danish-American denominations. Though the president of the Evangelical Lutheran Church, J. A. Aasgaard, pushed for his denomination to join, it withheld its agreement to do so until 1956. Eventually, other American Lutheran denominations joined, although not the Missouri and Wisconsin synods. For a number of years, ULCA president Franklin C. Fry was the chair of the WCC's central committee.

The third organization was the National Council of Churches of Christ in the USA (NCCC), formed in 1950. American Lutherans had not generally participated in its predecessor, the Federal Council of Churches. Only the General Synod had joined the FCC in 1908, but left that group as a result of the ULCA merger in 1918. When plans were circulated to develop the NCCC in 1950, many American Lutheran denominations were disinclined to join because of the presence of "liberal" mainline Protestant groups and because of doubts about its doctrinal ortho-doxy. Only two American Lutheran denominations joined the NCCC initially, the ULCA and the Augustana Synod. Eventually, through merger and decisions in the 1960s, many other Lutherans became involved in the work of the NCCC, although some American Lutheran denominations only became involved in NCCC activities through local and regional organizations.

The Road to American Lutheran Merger

During the 1940s and 1950s, the question was not whether American Lutheran denominations would merge, but how their merger process would work out. The rhetoric around merger was generally positive, if even at times a bit euphoric. One of the strongest proponents of merger was ULCA president Franklin Clark Fry, In a 1949 article entitled "Reaching Closer Relationships," Fry extolled the virtues of Lutheran union. Beginning with the premise that American Lutherans were already in "substantial agreement" with each other, Fry continued: "A unified Lutheran Church in America would honor and glorify its Savior with immensely increased effectiveness through a united testimony. The impact of the true Gospel upon Protestant life and thought in this pivotal western world would be strengthened mightily." Suggesting that each of the present groups could still maintain their dis-tinctive contribution to American Lutheranism within a unified Lutheran church, Fry concluded: "Keeping American Lutheranism frozen in its *present* divisions in these explosive, fermenting days for Christian faith cannot be in accordance with the divine will."[4] But not all American Lutherans agreed with Fry on at least one point, that is, his claim that American Lutherans were already in substantial agreement with one another. The Missouri Synod and other conservative American Lutheran denominations were still pushing for greater doctrinal unity (on their terms), and were deeply suspicious of the orthodoxy of the ULCA.

Even during World War II, with all the other demands on their time, American Lutheran leaders continued talks about greater unity and the path toward Lutheran merger. In 1941 and 1942, two "All-Lutheran Conferences" were held in Columbus, Ohio; various proposals were floated, including a federation of National Lutheran Council members, an enlargement of the American Lutheran Conference, and the calling of a "Free" conference to discuss merger. The situation stood roughly like this: the ULCA was open to a merger of all without preconditions, and the Missouri Synod insisted on complete doctrinal unity before merger. These two were the two largest American Lutheran denominations and stood as the "bookends" of the situ-ation. There were then roughly seven Midwestern denominations in between these two, with an aggregate membership roughly the same size as the ULCA and Missouri. Barring a miracle, it was generally believed there might be a merger between the middle group and either the ULCA or Missouri, but, realistically, there was not going to be at that time a merger that included *both* the ULCA and Missouri. The question of the day was, Which way would the centrist denominations move—toward Missouri or the ULCA?

This was assuming that the centrist denominations could agree among themselves, which often they could not. Five of the largest of these centrist denominations were together in the American Lutheran Conference (American Lutheran Church, Norwegian Lutheran Church in America, Augustana Synod, United Evangelical Lutheran Church, and the Lutheran Free Church). The main players here were the ALC, the NLCA, and Augustana, and their histories as well as some elements of ethnic rivalry came into play here. Despite their long-running feuds with the Missouri Synod, the ALC and NLCA still felt more comfortable with Missouri and questioned the orthodoxy of the ULCA. Meanwhile, Augustana had a long history as a part of the General Council, which had merged into the ULCA, and a rocky history with Missouri, resenting that synod's judgment of Augustana's orthodoxy, or alleged lack thereof.

In November 1942, the American Lutheran Conference met and, generally under the urging of Augustana leaders Ernest E. Ryden and Petrus O. Bersell, convinced the conference to invite all American Lutheran denominations to Lutheran merger negotiations without preconditions. Subsequently, however, the leaders of the ALC and NLCA undercut this offer, managing to insert doctrinal conditions and preconditions to the process that would effectively freeze the ULCA out of the negotiations. The irony is that, even with exclusion of the ULCA, there was neither any guarantee nor even a reasonable supposition that Missouri would join them. The next few years saw rounds of discussions and conferences that waltzed around conditions for merger, but they made little progress. In 1942, President Bersell of the Augustana Synod wrote to Norwegian leader Lars Boe, expressing a general hardening of attitudes: "The time has come for a federation that includes all but Missouri. The kindest thing we can do to Missouri is to ignore them until they come knocking at our door. And when that will happen they will find us strong and united and not . . . afraid of their bluster."[5] Leaders of the ALC and the NLCA were equally dismissive of the ULCA.

Finally in 1948–49, the merger negotiations started to move again, but quickly fell back into the old patterns of previous years. Augustana managed to secure a meeting of representatives from the eight members of the National Lutheran Council (the "Committee of 34") to discuss merger, but this, too, bogged down, and the process collapsed. The next approach was to consider a merger of the five member denominations of the American Lutheran Conference, which established the Joint Union Committee (JUC). The Augustana Synod was still hoping for a more inclusive merger process, and after decisions reached at its 1952 convention, its representatives literally walked out of the room where JUC negotiations were being held. The other four groups (ALC, ELC, UELC, and LFC) continued on with their joint negotiations, but the American Lutheran Conference itself collapsed in 1954.

While the four denominations continued their process toward merger, in 1955 the Augustana Synod and the ULCA issued an open invitation to all American Lutheran denominations to participate in merger negotiations. Missouri and the groups in the JUC both declined, but the invitation was accepted by two smaller groups, the Finnish Suomi Synod and the Danish American Evangelical Lutheran Church, and together the four formed the Joint Commission on Lutheran Unity (JCLU). Now, instead of one Lutheran merger process there were two—the JUC and the JCLU. From this point forward, the two parallel merger processes moved fairly quickly, given the complicated negotiations that each had to manage. Mergers, especially large ones, are inherently difficult to pull together, as differences in structure and ethos often differ widely among the denominations. The processes have to been perceived as "fair," a tough thing to do, especially given the disparity in size between the partners, especially in the JCLU.

The JUC finished its process first, and in 1960 formed the new American Lutheran Church (1960–1988), which consisted of the "old" ALC, the ELC, and the UELC. The Lutheran Free Church eventually joined the "new" ALC in 1963, but suffered the loss of a portion of its congregations, which formed the Association of Free Lutheran Congregations (AFLC). The JCLU finalized its merger in 1962, which joined together the ULCA, Augustana, Suomi, and the AELC into the new Lutheran Church in America (1962–1988). Thus, at the onset of the 1960s, there were now three major American Lutheran denominations, instead of the hoped-for single one.

American Lutherans and the Postwar Boom

American Lutheran educational institutions had lagged behind during the 1930s and 1940s because of reduced numbers of students, a prolonged situation attributable to the Depression and World War II. Everything changed rapidly and dramatically after 1945, however, with the beginning of an extended twenty-five-year boom in American higher education that strained the resources of colleges and universities around the country. The numbers of students enrolling in Lutheran institutions rose dramatically after 1945, with former soldiers swelling the student population. Most colleges had struggled to survive the past decades, and had certainly done little to maintain or expand their facilities. A new wrinkle was the sudden presence of older and often married students on campus; many institutions secured former military barracks or "Quonset huts" from the government as temporary housing for the influx of married students. Usually arranged on athletic fields or lawns, these temporary arrangements were given nicknames such as "the Fertile Crescent" or similar irreverent terms. A college education was becoming more broadly urged on young Lutherans, and the percentage of them that enrolled climbed steadily.

Suddenly, there was money. Returning soldiers brought with them federal scholarship aid in the form of the GI Bill, and the government also developed programs to assist with the building of dormitories and, because of Cold War pressures, scientific and technical facilities. A number of colleges received large and continuing grants from private educational foundations, which became a normal pattern. The Lutheran denominations also added more money to their colleges and universities, especially through special postwar appeals that focused especially on capital expansion. Although students and money were now abundant, qualified faculties were much harder to secure and, increasingly, bright young Lutheran students were urged to continue on in graduate education to build up the pool of qualified instructors. Sometimes, these graduate students were snapped up prematurely to supply the college's need, but most were able to complete their graduate degrees eventually. The percentage of Lutheran faculty with PhDs or other "terminal" degrees rose steadily during this period, and their exposure to American graduate education brought new ideas and worldviews to the colleges. There were several new colleges or expansions, including the founding of California Lutheran College in southern California (1959), and of Concordia College, Ann Arbor, Michigan (1963). Carthage College moved to a new campus in Kenosha, Wisconsin, and upgrading and consolidation proceeded at Concordia College in Selma, Alabama, in 1962, the only historically black Lutheran college.

Even with all these efforts, the majority of American Lutheran students did not attend Lutheran colleges, as their resources just were not adequate to do so. The majority of Lutheran students attended public colleges and universities; it was said, for example, that the largest "Lutheran college" in America was actually the University of Minnesota! Determined not to forget these students, American Lutherans developed an extensive postwar system of Lutheran campus ministries and other such outreach ventures. Much of this work was coordinated through the National Lutheran Council, with the Missouri Synod also undertaking extensive efforts in this area.

Seminary education went through a similar pattern. The postwar boom meant a huge strain on existing institutions, and the seminaries struggled with moving students through as quickly as possible to meet both student and denominational needs. The demand for new pastors was great, especially with the rapid home-mission expansion, and often the time toward granting degrees was abbreviated (and educational standards lowered) to produce new candidates for the ministry. In 1952, the ULCA opened a new seminary in Berkeley, California, and other seminary facilities were expanded. But many American Lutheran seminaries were still small and weak, and the Lutheran mergers of the 1960s produced a surplus of seminaries that would eventually be reduced by mergers and consolidation.

Lutheran social-service agencies traveled a similar path after World War II. There were large numbers of Lutheran hospitals, orphanages, homes for the elderly, and other such institutions, but they varied widely in quality and strength. The time when such facilities could be run on a prayer and a shoestring budget were rapidly passing, and these institutions were coming under pressure to professionalize and expand; if they could not do this, they had to merge or close. Government standards and oversight were becoming increasingly strict, especially for those institutions that took public funding, which was becoming increasingly both available and necessary. Increasingly, local and regional Lutheran councils were formed to coordinate Lutheran "welfare" efforts, and on the national level the NLC and the Missouri Synod were cooperating in areas where appropriate. Again, as with education, there was also a parallel stress on providing trained chaplains to work in non-Lutheran institutions and to provide professional training for clinical chaplains. With the postwar economic boom, Lutheran social-service ministries grew and expanded; it was estimated that by 1965 there were over five hundred agencies and institutions, with sixteen thousand employees, and cumulative annual budgets over $100 million. As a whole, Lutheran social services formed the second-largest private network in the country.

The numbers of Lutheran deaconesses peaked in 1938, and began to decline steadily after this, although, ironically enough, the range of activities and the professionalism of the deaconesses themselves expanded. It was becoming increasingly difficult to recruit young women into the movement, especially since there were now many more opportunities available to them in society and in the church. Several rounds of consolidations took place among the motherhouses, especially after the LCA merger in 1962, and reforms to the system attempted to make it more flexible and attractive. Deaconesses did continue to give devoted service to many Lutheran institutions and congregations.

There was also a corresponding expansion and reorientation of American Lutheran mission activities around the world. It has already been noted that

American Lutherans were forced to expand their range by taking on "orphaned" missions during and after World War II, and that the closing of China to Western missionaries in 1951 resulted in major shifts of focus and personnel. But these were only the beginnings of an immense shift in world-mission efforts after the war. Already in the 1930s, missiologists and other mission leaders were starting to consider major revisions to the far-flung American mission efforts oversea. The rapid collapse of the Western colonial system in Africa and Asia between 1945 and 1975 meant that the whole effort, including the relations among Christians in the West and in the global South would have to be reimagined. For American Lutherans, this meant expanded efforts to develop self-sustaining, indigenous, and independent Lutheran churches out of traditional mission fields. There were often multiple different European and American Lutheran mission efforts in a single country, and leaders struggled to combine these multiple efforts into larger, more sustainable, and indigenous Lutheran churches. Sometimes the legacy of denominational and theological differences, along with local and ethnic factors, did not make this entirely possible.

The tide of political independence in the former colonies meant the beginning of a new, and sometimes rocky, situation for Western Christian missionary work. Indigenous Lutheran leaders in the global South, along with many Western missionaries, pushed for autonomous control of local churches as quickly as possible. Many churches in Africa and Asia became independent during the 1950s and 1960s, though financial subsidies and other aid continued to flow from Western Lutheran denominations. Many newly independent churches became members of the Lutheran World Federation, slowly shifting the center of gravity of that organization southward. The role of American Lutheran personnel overseas shifted toward providing education and technical assistance and training leaders in these new churches. In 1954, one American Lutheran missiologist wrote: "But today an upsurge of national independence resents all forms of foreign paternalism. The missionary recognizes that the time is rapidly approaching when he is no longer needed . . . [and] adapts himself to the situation and becomes a counselor, advisor, or co-worker."[6] With the rush of anticolonial sentiment in newly independent countries, and even some suspicions that Western missionaries were covert operatives for the American Central Intelligence Agency, these missionaries had to tread cautiously.

American Lutheran mission work was therefore redirected to new areas and new countries. With the closing of mainland China, missionaries and funding were redirected to other areas of Asia, including Japan, Taiwan, Korea, Malaysia, and Borneo. Increasingly, after the war, Lutherans opened new mission work in Central and South America. There had been German and Danish immigrant Lutheran churches in these countries from the nineteenth century, but now American Lutherans were beginning to work with Spanish and Portuguese populations as well. At least four different groups began Spanish-language work in Mexico and along the United States border during the 1940s; the Missouri Synod began work in Uruguay (1942), Panama (1943), Venezuela (1951), and Chile (1954); and the World Mission Prayer League expanded into several different Latin American countries. In 1954, one reckoning placed the numbers of Lutheran mission personnel (European and American) at 2,735, working in forty-six countries, with a baptized membership of over 2.4 million people in the Lutheran churches in Africa, Asia, and Latin America.

American Lutherans in the Context of the 1950s and 1960s

During this quarter-century, all indications were that American Lutherans had fully assimilated into the mainstream of American social and economic life, and were solidly middle class. They generally ranked about in the middle in terms of income, social status, and education, usually right behind the Methodists and slightly ahead of the Roman Catholics. Data from right after World War II showed that 43 percent of Lutheran workers were classified as "manual urban workers," 26 percent farmers, 18 percent white-collar workers, and 13 percent businessmen or professionals; 20 percent were members of unions. Another survey from the late 1950s showed that American Lutherans were about 11 percent upper class, 25 percent middle class, 43 percent working class, and 21 percent lower class; about 5 percent of them had four-year college degrees. In 1962, the average yearly income for American Lutherans was $7,120 (as compared with a national average of $6,941), and by 1966 it had reached $10,375.[7] By most indications, American Lutherans were keeping up with, and at times exceeding, the national trends with their increases in income and educational level.

Americans quickly discovered after 1945 that one war had ended just as another one began—this time a "Cold War" that pitted the Western democracies against the communist powers, China and the Soviet Union. This was a long, drawn-out geopolitical struggle, lasting until 1991, that sometimes flared into open warfare, such as the Korean War (1950–1953) and the Vietnam War (1961–1973), with the apocalyptic specter of possible nuclear war always lurking in the background. American Lutherans had long been deeply suspicious of communism, and the post-1945 events in Eastern Europe and China, which deeply and negatively affected Lutheran populations in those areas, only confirmed and increased their opposition. Missouri Synod military chaplain and later seminary professor Martin Scharlemann wrote in the *Lutheran Witness* in 1951: "The Communist movement of today . . .

is basically a religion. In point of fact the present world-wide conflict is at heart a struggle between two absolutes: The forces of a man-god are in mortal combat with the follower of the God-Man. The party is in open conflict with the Church."[8] Official denominational pronouncements often decried communism during the 1950s and supported the efforts of American soldiers during the Korean War.

Although most Lutherans were strongly anticommunist during this period, this does not also mean that they were fully supportive of all of the actions of the U.S. government. Some Lutherans expressed their discomfort with the anticommunist frenzy in the early 1950s, with the activities of Senator Joseph McCarthy and the House Un-American Activities Committee, or decried the amount of money that was being devoted to military expenditures, or protested the peacetime conscription of soldiers. There was continued support in a number of corners for international efforts to reduce tensions and bring about peace, especially for arms-control agreements, international courts and policing, and the activities of the United Nations. One contributor to the *Lutheran Companion* in 1957 expressed his opinion that "The Christian conscience of America is deeply shocked over the possibility of an atomic conflict that may spell disaster for the whole human race," and urged all governments to turn their resources to peaceful activities.[9]

Small, scattered groups of American Lutherans continued to advocate for peace and pacifism, even though their activities during World War II were not widely honored; their efforts were generally limited to supporting conscientious objectors to the draft. In 1950, the head of the Lutheran Peace Fellowship, Paul Scherer, attempted to move his group from the limited aims of supporting conscientious objectors to a broader campaign for peace. He addressed his group: "Six years of war from 1939 to 1945 provided us with a world that promptly began to swap one totalitarian system for one even more demonic. The truth is that the problems of our Western civilization do not on the level of war yield themselves to even the faintest sign of any resolution."[10] But these groups remained small and scattered, and they did not have much of a public impact on American Lutherans until the late 1960s. The threat of communism as an atheistic tide rolling over Lutheran congregations remained, reinforced by the brutal Soviet invasion of Hungary in 1956, which created even more Lutheran refugees streaming to the West. Although it seems that American Lutherans were uncomfortable with the Cold War and militarism, they were perhaps even more threatened by communism.

The postwar era was also a time when the issues of race and civil rights for African Americans dominated the national scene. The equal rights promised in the post–Civil War amendments to the U.S. Constitution had long been submerged under popular and legal racial discrimination, but after World War II, African

Americans resumed their struggle for equality through the civil rights movement. Supreme Court decisions, such as the one that struck down the principles of segregation (*Brown v. Board of Education*, 1954) had opened the way for integration, but the long struggle for full inclusion had just begun.

By the middle of the twentieth century, the American Lutheran denominations had three areas of interaction with African American communities, each of which was subject to a pattern of initial and enthusiastic work only to be followed by years of neglect. The ULCA had African American congregations in the U.S. Virgin Islands and among Virgin Island immigrants on the mainland, especially in New York City. Because of work begun by the Joint Synod of Ohio, the ALC (1930–1960) had longstanding home missions in Alabama. The most successful of the three was the Synodical Conference outreach efforts in the South, with congregations stretching from North Carolina to Alabama and Louisiana. But all three areas suffered from intermittent interest from their sponsoring denominations, compounded by weak congregations and a lack of local commitment to training clerical and lay leaders. After years of neglect and dithering, the ALC decided in 1958 to transfer its remaining congregations in Alabama to the Synodical Conference. The Synodical Conference in 1947 decided to transfer responsibility for its African American congregations to the home-mission organizations of the regional districts of the Missouri Synod. The hope was to affiliate these African American congregations more closely into the local districts, but had the unintended effect of loosening bounds among these African American congregations. The ULCA and the National Lutheran Council also considered outreach with African Americans, with few substantial results.

The push for integration reconfigured many of these efforts, as the new strategy was to integrate African Americans into existing local Lutheran judicatories. The Missouri Synod began a process for doing exactly this from 1947 to 1961, by which time all African American pastors and congregations were integrated as full members of their local Missouri Synod districts. In 1956, Missouri adopted a policy that urged evangelical outreach "without discrimination," that "no mission shall be established with the expressed purpose of serving only one racial or ethnic group on a segregated basis" and urged that congregations in "changing areas" continue their ministry in that place, rather than relocating.[11] By the 1960s, most Lutheran denominations had a policy of integration and the full inclusion of African Americans, although carrying out these ambitious principles often stalled out on the local congregational level or were simply ignored. And though Lutheran leaders realized that segregated mission strategies would no longer work, dismantling these older structures often fatally reduced the cohesive bonds that tied African American

Lutheran congregations to one another, ties that provided support not readily available from the denominations themselves.

On the larger societal level, there were developments that appealed more broadly for full integration and inclusion on the national level. A Missouri Synod pastor who served African American Lutheran mission congregations in the North, Andrew Schultze, organized the Lutheran Human Relations Association of America (LHRAA) in 1953. The LHRAA eventually became a pan-Lutheran organization that lobbied American Lutherans and others for racial integration and acceptance. Schulze became a leading advocate for integration, but the subject was often a controversial one that played out occasionally in the pages of the denominational presses. When the *Lutheran Witness* ran a story cautiously urging integration in 1960, there was a raft of replies. Some of them were appreciative, some counseled patience, and a few dismissed the concept altogether. One angry correspondent wrote: "Any magazine as pro-integration as your Jan. 12 issue is unfit to be seen in any decent home. God separated the races. Keep it that way."[12] Few Lutherans or their congregations were as openly hostile to integration as this, but few Lutherans and their congregations went out of their way to make integration a local parish reality, either. Despite the urging of some denominational officials, many urban Lutheran congregations simply pulled up stakes and followed their members in "white flight" to the new suburbs, lessening the Lutheran presence in the inner cities. Integration, civil rights, and race continued to be difficult topics for American Lutherans.

New Developments in Theology and Worship

American Lutherans had always engaged in theological works and scholarship, most of which had traditionally been for "in-house" consumption; historically, much of it had been in languages other than English. Often, their theological orientation had been more toward Europe than the United States; these efforts generally engaged American Lutherans in intra-Lutheran discussions with European Lutheran scholars, and ignored the predominantly Reformed Protestant theology of the England and the United States. With their language transition in the twentieth century, American Lutherans began to produce significant works of theological scholarship in English and to engage with other Anglo-American Christians. This growing relationship also served as a conduit to introduce Lutheran theology and scholarship to many parts of the English-speaking world. After World War II, many bright and creative American Lutheran scholars went off to the leading graduate schools in America and Europe. Many of them returned to teach at Lutheran educational institutions or to run Lutheran denominations or agencies. Although the volume of their theological output was often limited during this period due to the intense demands placed on their energies for teaching and denominational leadership, many produced significant work. Other Lutheran scholars such as Jaroslav Pelikan, Martin Marty, Jerald Brauer, Sydney Ahlstrom, George Lindbeck, and Paul Holmer moved into prominent positions in leading American divinity schools.

Much of the theological work done in this period of time involved the dissemination of works on Luther and Lutheran theology into English, both for the use of American Lutherans themselves, and for use by seminarians, pastors, and scholars within the broader American denominational scene. The early twentieth-century "Luther Renaissance" in Europe created an upsurge in scholarship about Luther, which in the United States led to the publication of a fifty-five volume American edition of Luther's works in English, edited by Jaroslav Pelikan and Helmut Lehmann. The traumas of the Nazi movement and World War II caused postwar authors to reexamine the history and theology of Lutheranism itself. Some outside writers found a supposed causal link between Martin Luther's writings on the Jews and the Nazi movement, which American Lutheran scholars generally attempted to refute, or at least nuance. As an alternative to German Lutheran scholars, some of whom had been tainted by the war, American Lutherans began to translate and introduce the works of Scandinavian Lutheran theologians, including Gustav Aulén, Anders Nygren, and Gustaf Wingren, among others. Howard Hong spent his career translating the works of Søren Kierkegaard into English and introduced him to American audiences. The failure of German Lutherans to resist Hitler did, however, cause a searching reappraisal of Lutheran theology, especially in areas such as the relation of church and state, Christian social ethics, and topics such as the doctrine of the "two kingdoms." The theological works of German Lutheran resisters such as Dietrich Bonhoeffer and Martin Niemoeller were widely translated and studied as alternatives to traditional Lutheran positions.

After the war, other theological topics also came to the fore. American Lutheran debates resumed over the nature of biblical authority, including the term *inerrancy*, eliciting a number of books on the subject. Johan M. Reu forcefully defended the conservative position in his book *Luther and the Bible* (1944), while Joseph Sittler caused a stir with his searching reappraisal of the subject in his *Doctrine of the Word* (1948), which some conservative critics judged heretical. Merger activities caused a rush of scholarship in church history, led by Theodore Tappert, A. R. Wentz, Carl Meyer, E. Clifford Nelson, Conrad Bergendoff, and others. A major achievement was a new edition of the Lutheran *Book of Concord* in 1959. Lutherans paid close attention to other theological trends, such as the neo-orthodox theologies of Karl

Barth, Reinhold Niebuhr, and H. Richard Niebuhr, and the ecumenical implications of the new Roman Catholic theology coming out of the Second Vatican Council (1962–1965), which several American Lutheran scholars attended as observers. Lutheran denominational publishing houses began to produce significant numbers of both original and translated works of Lutheran theology and scholarship.

The period from 1940 to 1965 also saw significant developments in American Lutheran worship and hymnody. With the rapid transition to the use of English in the 1920s, all the American Lutheran denominations were forced to issue English-language hymnals and other worship materials quickly; the quality of these initial materials was often uneven. In their need to move quickly, many American Lutheran groups borrowed extensively from ULCA's *Common Service Book and Hymnal* (1918), and from the language of the Episcopal *Book of Common Prayer*. Hymnals were stocked with German and Scandinavian hymns translated into English, as well as favorite English and American hymns, especially the nineteenth-century gospel hymns. There was little in the way of homegrown American Lutheran hymns. European Lutheran hymns tended to predominate in the first parts of these hymnals, matching the rhythms of the church year, while the more subjective Anglo-American hymns crowded the areas of the hymnal dealing with devotional aspects of the Christian faith.

In 1941, the Missouri Synod and the Synodical Conference introduced a new English-language Lutheran hymnal, *The Lutheran Hymnal* (TLH) which served these denominations for over forty years. In 1945, the eight Lutheran denominations in the National Lutheran Council began to study and then produce a new joint English hymnal that they would all use. This process had some bumps along the way, as some Scandinavian denominations were wary of the new book becoming too "German" and too formally liturgical for their tastes, but eventually all the groups fell into line, and the *Service Book and Hymnal* (SBH) appeared in 1958. The use of a common hymnal to precede a merger process, such as the *Common Service* of 1888 was not new, and although this merger process ended eventually in two denominations rather than one, the congregations of both the ALC and LCA still overwhelmingly adopted the new "Red" hymnal (SBH). By the early 1960s, the great majority of American Lutherans used either *The Lutheran Hymnal* or the *Service Book and Hymnal*.

As has been seen, this was the age of standardization and consolidation, and this also was generally true about the ways in which American Lutherans worshiped during the postwar period. With the consolidation of hymnals and denominations came a degree of uniformity in worship that American Lutherans had never had before. To walk into a Lutheran congregation anywhere around the country, the worship experience was likely to be similar to what went on in one's home congregation. Lutheran denominations and publishing houses developed common worship materials that were dutifully employed by pastors and congregations around the country, especially in the new mission congregations. As Lutheranism expanded into new areas, especially in the South and West, Lutheran transplants to these areas could find a worship experience similar to that of their home congregations. The common pattern of worship was a modest version of formal liturgical worship, employing a chanted liturgy, the rhythms of the church year and lectionary, and traditional Lutheran ceremony. Holy Communion was most widely celebrated on the first Sunday of the month, although there were greater and lesser frequencies to this pattern.

The Reordering of American Lutheranism

Although excitement about the possibilities of Lutheran merger during the 1940s and 1950s sometimes bordered on the euphoric, the actual result in the early 1960s of two new denominations (ALC and LCA) and a third existing one (LCMS) was a bit deflating. Still, proponents were undaunted, believing that eventual Lutheran unification would happen. For the meantime, those in the two new Lutheran denominations had to get down to the difficult work of making the new churches actually work. This was not easy. Mergers and consolidations are actually very difficult to do well, and have considerable negative aspects rarely considered in the optimistic run-up to unification. Mergers disrupt the natural flow of organizations, and patterns of loyalty and affiliation that have been developed over decades are broken. The integration of different denominational and organizational cultures is daunting work. Mergers divert immense amounts of human time and energy away from the core mission of denominations, the direct proclamation of the gospel. And no matter how hard the participants try to order things, there are always "winners" and "losers" in any merger, with the inevitable hard feelings that can drain the life out of any denomination.[13] The period of the early 1960s, then, was a time when those in the ALC and LCA were focused on this type of institutional rearrangement.

Earlier mergers had not been quite so difficult to manage simply because there was much less denominational machinery to combine, and church institutions were more compactly located. When the ULCA was formed in 1918, no attempt was made to rearrange the basic synodical units of the new church immediately. The new ULCA simply brought all the existing regional synods into the new church, and only gradually were synodical consolidations attempted. In the 1960s, mergers formed completely new regional entities: districts in the ALC, and synods in the LCA. In each new church, there were four preexisting and separate publishing houses, pension programs, social ministry and mission boards, and auxiliaries for women, men, and youth ministry, all of which had to be consolidated into a single unit. It helped somewhat that these merging denominations had already been cooperating within the National Lutheran Council, but often the changes were wrenching.

The American Lutheran Church (1960–1988) perhaps had a smoother transition. Its four predecessor denominations were all based in the Midwest, and the two largest denominations, the old ALC and the ELC, were roughly the same size. Still, there were tensions, especially since most of the denominational machinery ended up in Minneapolis, home of the Norwegian-background ELC. Some in the two smaller denominations feared that they and their institutions would get lost in the big church. Especially reticent was the Lutheran Free Church, which delayed entering the new denomination until 1963, and then only by a fairly narrow congregational vote. There were some necessary consolidations, including the folding of Augsburg Seminary into Luther Seminary in St. Paul, Minnesota. Skirmishes about the ownership of educational institutions were eventually resolved.

The Lutheran Church in America (1962–1988) had a more difficult road concerning consolidation, especially because the institutional structures and cultures of the two larger groups, the ULCA and the Augustana Synod, were so different. Though the ULCA had developed a national bureaucracy, many of the institutions of the church, such as colleges, seminaries, and social-ministry organizations were owned by the regional synods rather than the national denomination; the situation was reversed in the Augustana Synod. The new LCA also faced the issue that it had inherited too many small, struggling seminaries. A study commission led by Augustana's Conrad Bergendoff urged several seminary consolidations; five midwestern seminaries were consolidated into a new seminary in Chicago, the Lutheran School of Theology at Chicago (LSTC), but the envisioned merger of the eastern Gettysburg and Philadelphia seminaries was scuttled by vested interests. On the other hand, the new LCA decided to mollify some constituencies by locating its national operations in three different cities (New York, Philadelphia, and Minneapolis), thereby winning some loyalty points, the location of "headquarters" being a point of pride.

Developments within the Missouri Synod

In 1947, the Missouri Synod celebrated its centennial with the usual festivities that rightly and customarily attend such occasions. Known officially since 1917 (when it dropped the word "German") as the Evangelical Lutheran Synod of Missouri, Ohio, and Other States, the denomination in 1947 streamlined its official title to

The Lutheran Church–Missouri Synod. This change of name signified other major changes in the Missouri Synod, which had gone through the same processes of language transition, acculturation, and social upheaval and transition that had affected other American Lutherans. After World War II, it had grown rapidly, doubling from 1.35 million members in 1940 to 2.8 million members in 1965, with a corresponding growth in missions and in educational and social-service institutions. It enjoyed the largest parochial school system of any Protestant group in the country. It was, and continues to be, the second largest Lutheran denomination in the United States.

All this growth was good, but it brought about internal tensions within Missouri that church leaders were constantly negotiating, in order to find some sort of balance. Never having merged with any other Lutheran denomination (Missouri did at times absorb smaller groups, such as the English District, the Slovaks, and the National Finns), the synod represented a continuity of theological and ecclesiastical traditions unmatched by any other American Lutheran group. Its traditional theology was codified by synodical theologian Franz A. O. Pieper (1852–1931) in his *Christliche Dogmatik* (later translated into English as *Christian Dogmatics*), and by the synodical statement on doctrine and unity, "A Brief Statement" of 1932. Underneath all of this were the ties of schooling and kinship that deeply knit together the clerical and lay leadership of the synod, which included several powerful clerical dynastic families.

But dramatic postwar growth in the Missouri Synod meant that more outsiders were coming into the synod both as clergy and laypersons; an estimate of new adult outsiders (baptized or confirmed) numbered 165,000 in the 1940s and 300,000 more in the 1950s.[14] Hundreds of new congregations were started in new suburban areas, while the rural and inner-city base of the synod dwindled. Although Missouri did not join the National Lutheran Council, it often worked together with, or in parallel to, the other Lutheran denominations in areas of chaplaincy, refugees and relief, education, social services, and many other endeavors. Missouri remained officially separate from the American Lutheran merger and ecumenical activities, but its representatives were often present at these functions to observe and to make the synod's opinions known.

One of the first definitive signs of increasing restlessness within the synod came in 1945, when a group of forty-four Missouri pastors and leaders issued a public "Statement" to the rest of the synod. Although they avoided any direct attack on the theology of the synod, even embracing the "inerrancy, certainty, and all-sufficiency" of the Scriptures, this group challenged Missouri to engage more gracefully the rest of American Lutheranism, especially around the issue of prayer with other Christians. The signers stated: "We therefore deplore the loveless attitude which is manifesting itself within the Synod. This unscriptural attitude has been expressed in suspicion of brethren, in impugning of motives, and in the condemnation of all who have expressed differing opinions concerning some of the problems confronting our Church today."[15] Although the signers were eventually persuaded to withdraw the statement, the appearance of this document and the controversy that it created highlighted the internal stresses within the synod and brought them to public notice.

In 1958, *Time* magazine quoted an unnamed member of the synod as saying, "the predictability of the Missouri Synod position had gone down considerably," and observed within the denomination "a growing restlessness with the literal attitude toward the Bible."[16] Certainly, there were growing tensions within Missouri, and a new generation of pastors, professors, and leaders attempted to push the synod toward more openness toward the world. Just as predictably, there were also strong countervailing forces within the synod that resisted these pressures, and saw the new stress on openness as being a call to compromise the synod's traditional stance against unionism. This latter group within Missouri won a significant victory in 1959 when a church convention at San Francisco approved a resolution reaffirming the synod's theological stance, as stated in "A Brief Statement" of 1932. At its next convention in 1962, the delegates forced a seminary professor to retract some of his statements about biblical authority. Synodical leaders, especially President John Behnken, tried to blunt the directness of this reaction, which led the 1962 convention to declare the 1959 resolution on the status of "A Brief Statement" as constitutionally invalid, but still expressed its support for the traditional theology of the synod.

Meanwhile, conservative critics of the Missouri Synod from within the Synodical Conference were worried about their perception that Missouri was drifting away from its traditional moorings. One of them, the small Evangelical Lutheran Synod (ELS), officially suspended its relations with the Missouri Synod in 1955, while the larger Wisconsin Evangelical Lutheran Synod (WELS) continued to protest developments through the 1950s, and in 1961 it, too, suspended fellowship with Missouri. In 1963, both WELS and the ELS withdrew from the Synodical Conference, which eventually brought about its formal demise. A rogue critic of Missouri, Herman Otten, kept up constant and often harsh criticism of "liberals" in the Missouri Synod through a self-published newspaper, the *Christian News*, the contents of which critics suggested were "neither Christian nor news."

In 1963, a moderate leader within Missouri, Oliver Harms, was elected as the new president of the synod. While his election was heralded as a movement of Missouri toward new engagement with other American Lutheran groups, it also stiffened resolve among conservative critics to oppose the current direction of the synod. To many contemporary observers, there were tensions building within Missouri, but it was unclear at the time how these seemingly irreconcilable differences would play out.

Conclusion

This twenty-five-year span represented both a period of major numerical growth within American Lutheranism, as well as major institutional realignments. These developments ushered in the modern period of American Lutheranism and delineated its basic structure going forward. There was an energy and an optimism to American Lutheranism during this period that is striking; though faced with large and difficult challenges, such as the reorientation of world Lutheranism, the rebuilding of Europe, and the transformation of American society, these Lutherans seemed quite confident of their ability to organize and to meet these challenges head-on. Moving into the 1960s and beyond, there was a sense of pride, growth, and momentum. This attitude would be sorely tested in the decades to come.

Notes

1. Sister Margaret Fry, "Report of first two weeks at Willow Run," March 14–21, 1943, as quoted in Sister Marilyn H. Stauffer, "Sister Margaret Fry at Willow Run," *Journal of the Lutheran Historical Conference* 1 (2011): 154–55.

2. The name of the Norwegian Lutheran Church in America was changed in 1946 to the Evangelical Lutheran Church (ELC).

3. H. A. Mayer, "Report of the Home Missions ---," Proceedings of the Convention of the LCMS, 1956, p. 369, quoted in E. Clifford Nelson, *Lutheranism in North America, 1914–1970* (Minneapolis: Augsburg, 1972), 136.

4. Franklin C. Fry, "Reaching Closer Relationships: The United Lutheran Church in America," *Lutheran Quarterly* 1, no. 2 (May 1949): 165–68.

5. "Letter, P. O. Bersell to Lars Boe," November 20, 1942, Lars Boe Presidential Papers, Archives of St. Olaf College, Northfield, Minnesota.

6. Andrew S. Burgess, ed., *Lutheran World Missions: Foreign Missions of the Lutheran Church in America* (Minneapolis: Augsburg, 1954), 18.

7. Economic data collected and summarized in Niel M. Johnson, "Lutherans in American Economic Life," in John E. Groh and Robert H. Smith, eds., *The Lutheran Church in North American Life* (St. Louis: Clayton Pub. House, 1979), 138–39.

8. Martin Scharlemann, "The Party or the Church?" *Lutheran Witness* 70, no. 5 (March 6, 1951): 73.

9. "Dim Disarmament Hopes," *Lutheran Companion* 103, no. 33 (August 14, 1957): 5.

10. Paul Scherer, "Remarks to the Lutheran Peace Fellowship," Syracuse, New York, 1950, quoted in Steven Schroeder, *A Community and a Perspective: Lutheran Peace Fellowship and the Edge of the Church, 1941–1991* (Lanham, MD: University Press of America, 1993), 51.

11. "Proceedings of the 1956 Convention of the Lutheran Church–Missouri Synod," St. Paul, Minnesota.

12. "Letter to the Editor," *Lutheran Witness* 79, no. 3 (February 9, 1960): 31.

13. There were a number of people in the old ALC (1930–1960) who could still be heard muttering about "losing out" in the 1960 merger, and similar conversations in Augustana about the 1962 merger.

14. Alan Graebner, *Uncertain Saints: The Laity in the Lutheran Church–Missouri Synod, 1900–1970* (Westport, CT: Greenwood, 1975), 160.

15. "A Statement of the 44," September 7, 1945, in Carl S. Meyer, ed., *Moving Frontiers: Readings in the History of the Lutheran Church–Missouri Synod* (St. Louis: Concordia, 1964), 422–24.

16. *Time*, April 7, 1958, cited in Leland Stevens, *A History of the Missouri Synod as Told by the "Lutheran Witness"* (Alamagordo, NM: n.p., 1997), 153.

Excursus 10

AMERICAN LUTHERAN AID TO REFUGEES

Although World War II in Europe ended in the spring of 1945, the people of that continent were living in perilous conditions. The war had been one the first modern examples of "total" warfare, which brought the destruction of combat to all sectors of society, not just the battlefield.

The lives and homes of many Europeans had been seriously disrupted, millions were without employment, housing, and food, and untold numbers of people had been displaced. Many Germans had abandoned cities destroyed by bombing and fighting, while countless Europeans (mostly from the East) had fled the advance of Russian troops and the Soviet takeover of the Baltic countries and Eastern Europe. The only major industrial power left, not directly subject to the destruction of war, was the United States, but it was unclear how this country would act.

Directly after World War I, the American people and their leaders had largely retreated from the world into a blanket of isolationism. But after World War II, Americans came to realize that if they wanted a peaceful world, they would have to assist the rebuilding of war-torn countries in Europe and Asia, and so they did.

During the war itself, many groups in the United States had already begun to plan for postwar relief and reconstruction; ready to take their place in this task were American Lutherans, especially in aid to their fellow Lutherans in Europe, as well as others. As early as 1940, American Lutheran groups began major annual fund drives to collect resources for these tasks, and in the decades to come they would raise almost $250 million. Almost as soon as the fighting ended in Europe, American Lutheran leaders headed that continent to assess the situation and to begin funneling aid to the people there. Organizationally, the National Lutheran Council (and in cooperation, the Lutheran Church–Missouri Synod) began to work with European Lutheran leaders, eventually constituting the Lutheran World Federation (LWF) in 1947; one of this group's first tasks was refugee assistance and resettlement (Service to Refugees).

The situation among the European Lutherans, especially in Germany, was grave, as the war had destroyed churches and other institutions, scattered pastors and church leaders, and the horrors of nazism and total warfare had scarred the people. Lutherans from the East had fled the expansion of Soviet communism and were refugees in Western Europe.

After first meeting the basic needs of people, American Lutheran relief personnel began to work with the Allied military government in Germany to plan for the rebuilding of the German Lutheran churches, and to assist in building churches-in-exile for Eastern European Lutherans. Individual Lutheran pastors and others began to work in camps directly with refugees (Displaced Persons, or DPs), helping them to begin to rebuild their spiritual lives and communities.

By the late 1940s, a major Lutheran organization in Europe was created to coordinate this work (LWF-SR), and an equally large organization in the United States to support and to fund it. In 1948, the U.S. government passed legislation to allow for up to 200,000 of these DPs to enter the United States, a figure that would later be expanded. This was the beginning of a refugee resettlement program, mainly to North America, that required both funding and organization to make it work.

In 1954, American Lutherans founded the Lutheran Refugee Service (now Lutheran Immigration and Refugee Services [LIRS]) to coordination this work. Lutheran congregations throughout the United States were called upon to help resettle the DPs in their communities and to support them in building new lives in North America.

Many congregations responded generously, and opened their arms to the refugees; by the 1960s it was estimated that American Lutherans had helped resettle 112,000 refugees in the United States, Canada, and Australia alone. As this task of resettling DPs from Europe wound down, it became clear that this service to refugees (and immigrants) would be a longstanding and permanent need. Wars and conflicts around the world continued to produce refugees; in the 1960s and 1970s, LIRS worked to resettle refugees from Asia, especially Southeast Asia, and more recently they have worked with refugees and immigrants from Africa.

American Lutherans took their place, and in many instances took the lead, in this work, and continue to support the work of assistance through LIRS, ministering to the continuing needs of a conflicted world and those people affected by it.

Chapter 11

TURMOIL, CHANGE, AND CONSOLIDATION, 1965–1988

A lthough there is a danger in describing a nation's history solely along generational lines, there is some modest justification in doing so in the case of the United States after 1945, because of the demonstrable social and demographic effects of the Baby Boom generation, those born between 1946 and 1964. This large group, seventy-eight million people, went through postwar America like the proverbial "pig in a python," affecting society in numerous ways. If the 1950s and early 1960s were largely the childhood of the Boomers, then the period after 1965 represented its adolescence and early adulthood, with all the changes and developments that might suggest. The youth culture of the 1960s and 1970s affected the United States in ways that are too numerous to detail here, except to suggest that it produced revolutions in social and political thought and attitudes that laid the foundations for the last fifty years of American history. It would be a mistake to overplay these changes, and there was quite a conservative reaction to them during the 1980s, but after the 1960s there was no realistic way to return to the world that had existed before. Change, and conflict about change, were dominant themes during this period, as the country sought to figure out the direction that it was going.

The United States grew by about 25 percent during this period of time, from a population of 194 million in 1965 to 244 million in 1988. Although it was not really noticed much at the time, a reform and liberalization of immigration policy in 1965 began a shift in American demographics that would only later become apparent, especially with the increased immigration to the United States of Hispanics and Asians. The internal population shifts from the North and East to the South and West continued unabated, as did the growth of the suburbs and demographic shifts within major urban areas. The early part of this time period was dominated by conflicts over American participation in the war in Vietnam (1961–1973), civil rights and race relations (including major urban riots), the "sexual revolution" and youth culture, and by the movement for women's rights. The 1970s saw further upheavals, including the Watergate political scandal, growing concern about the environment, and surging economic inflation and a severe recession. The conservative reaction of the 1980s, personified by the election of Ronald Reagan as president in 1980, brought continuing conflict over Cold War policies, military expenditures and weapons, and world issues such as policies toward Nicaragua and South Africa. The general optimism of the earlier period, including the general belief in progress and the benefits of technology, seemed to dim during this time period, and many Americans felt a sense of general malaise and unease.

American religion saw a commensurate shift of attitudes, a sharp sense of conflict both internal and external, and a parallel sense of drift and worry. During the early 1960s, some perceived America as quickly following the pattern of Western European nations, destined to become a modern, "secular" society. Although religion in America was strong due to the postwar revivals, some observers suggested that the dominance of secularism was inevitable, because an increasingly wealthy, educated, and "modern" society would no longer require belief in a divine being or religion. Some liberal theologians suggested that organized religion needed radical reform to survive. A *Time* magazine cover in 1966 asked, "Is God Dead?" and many observers thought the answer was "yes," seriously misreading not only the contemporary situation but also the long-term historical patterns, which showed a strong growth of organized religion in the nineteenth and twentieth centuries. There were, however, dramatic shifts in American religion during the 1960s, especially increasing polarization between religious liberal and conservatives, and conflict over the Vietnam War, race relations, and social morals. Young Americans, especially, experimented with sex, drugs, and rock and roll and explored new alternative religions, such as forms of Buddhism, Hinduism, new "authoritarian" cults such as Hare Krishna, the Unification Church, and the Children of God, and the elements of the "New Age" movement.

Almost no observers had predicted the conservative Christian revival of the 1970s and 1980s, when membership in evangelical and fundamentalist Christian congregations boomed just as mainline Protestantism began its long, dramatic, and painful decline in membership. Perhaps in reaction to contemporary social and political changes such as the legalization of abortion in 1973, conservative Christians came out of their self-imposed political isolation to organize and join groups such as the Christian Coalition and the Moral Majority, which helped elect Ronald Reagan as president. Suddenly, it seemed, conservative religious revivalists such as Jerry Falwell, Jimmy Bakker, and Jimmy Swaggart were all over the airwaves. Most surprising of all was the resurgence of Pentecostalism, which secularists believed had survived only in isolated pockets of Appalachia, and the dramatic growth of Mormonism. There were also other conservative religious revivals among traditional forms of American Judaism and Roman Catholicism.

Liberal to moderate forms of American religion, Protestant, Roman Catholic, and Jewish, saw their numbers stagnate or decline and their influence on American public life wane. Many of these mainline groups participated in the struggles for the rights of women and minorities, as well as against the Vietnam War, but they were curious to discover that their leadership in these areas did not bring them new members. Some of their rank-and-file members, often more conservative than their leaders, deserted the mainline denominations for more conservative groups.

American Lutheranism, 1965–1988

The dramatic membership and congregational growth experienced by American Lutherans during the quarter-century after 1945 plateaued after 1965. American Lutheran denominations had added thousands of new congregations and millions of new members, and hoped and even assumed that these conditions would continue. Membership figures in fact topped out in the late 1960s at nearly 9.2 million American Lutherans, who represented 4.6 percent of the total American population. Despite optimistic predictions and continuing efforts, the numbers of Lutherans in America declined slightly during this next twenty years, dropping to a total of 8.8 million Lutherans in 1988. In terms of total share of the religious "market," Lutherans then composed 3.6 percent of the total American population. As noted earlier, the three major denominations, the Lutheran Church in America (LCA), American Lutheran Church (ALC), and the Lutheran Church–Missouri Synod (LCMS) were roughly equal in size, representing about 95 percent of all American Lutherans. The Wisconsin Evangelical Lutheran Synod (WELS) was the largest of the smaller Lutheran denominations at about 300,000 members, and there were about fifteen other, much smaller groups.

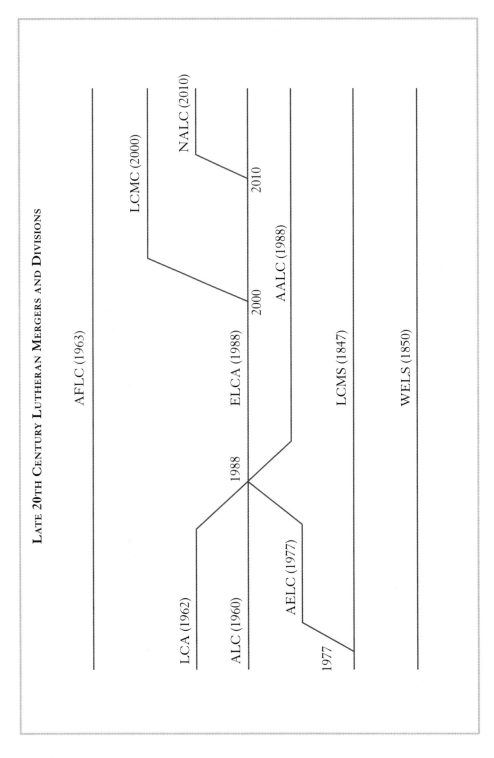

LATE 20TH CENTURY LUTHERAN MERGERS AND DIVISIONS

Three major studies, two in 1970 and one in 1980, attempted to survey American Lutherans on a wide variety of religious, social, and demographic factors, and these surveys taken together provide a fairly comprehensive view.[1] Not surprisingly, American Lutherans at the time were solidly middle-class Americans, more likely than average to be white (98 percent) and to live in the middle of the country. In the 1980 survey, 75 percent of Lutherans were born into Lutheran families, and another 15 percent became Lutherans by means of marriage, suggesting a solid degree of institutional loyalty. Most were of northern European background. A majority of Lutherans had at least some education beyond high school, and half of the Lutheran men had jobs considered "white collar," with a quarter in "blue-collar" jobs. Half of the Lutheran women worked outside of the home, while one-third listed their profession as "homemaker." The survey concluded that "Lutheran congregations appeal particularly to husband-and-wife couples, within the age of 35 to 65, together with their children still living at home," and wondered if Lutheran congregations were willing to reach out to those who were different from that norm.[2] Politically, more Lutherans identified as Republicans than Democrats, although here there were more differences between and within the three major denominations as well as between clergy and laypeople. The *Study of Generations* in 1970 identified differences in attitudes and "tensions" by age group, but did not see a "pervasive generation gap."[3]

Several interesting factors came through in these studies. First, the differences in attitudes and positions varied widely within each of the three major Lutheran denominations, which had apparently grown so large as to no longer have clusters of commonly held characteristics. The WELS respondents were, in general, fairly uniform in their responses, but the "big three" showed a wide variety of responses. Second, especially noticeable was a growing divide in religious and social attitudes between clergy and laity. While most laity still considered themselves "conservative" or "moderate," Lutheran clergy were much more likely to exhibit "liberal" attitudes or positions. And finally, laypeople were much less likely to understand or appreciate the distinctive ethos of Lutheranism, showing an alarming decline in catechesis and doctrinal preaching. In 1980, study author Carl Reuss concluded, "[These findings] suggest an erosion of laity understanding and acceptance of these Lutheran emphases. Implications are clear for confirmation instruction [and] for instruction of adults."[4] It is difficult to suggest trends from these findings, as these factors may always have been present in some form in American Lutheranism, but they were not good news for contemporary Lutheran leaders. However, they were very consistent with findings about other mainline American Protestants, of which American Lutherans had become a solid part.

There were also several other interesting pan-Lutheran developments in the late 1960s that bear brief examination. The first was the formation of a new inter-Lutheran entity for cooperation, the Lutheran Council in the USA, which included not only the LCA and ALC, but also the LCMS. There was also the unexpected rise of a pan-Lutheran movement for charismatic renewal and worship within these denominations.

The advocates of the National Lutheran Council (1918–1965) had long hoped to expand its reach to include Missouri and the other American Lutheran denominations not yet within it. But worries about unionism and the existence of the Synodical Conference did not allow the cooperation of Missouri or Wisconsin, though Missouri did coordinate its activities with the NLC at certain points. The coming mergers of the LCA and ALC in the early 1960s also suggested that perhaps the NLC would be less useful as an organization, now that it only consisted of two denominations. So in 1960 and 1961, planning started for creating a new organization to replace the NLC, leading in 1966 to the formation of the Lutheran Council in the USA (LCUSA). This new organization was carefully molded so that the LCMS could participate, stressing again only cooperation in external matters, and not implying fellowship in ministry, which the LCMS said was not yet doctrinally achieved. Certain cooperative functions that had become standard within the NLC, such as campus ministry and home missions, had to be carefully pruned back to meet objections. One LCMS writer urged caution in jumping to conclusions, positive or negative, about this affiliation: "Missouri reactions, almost inevitably, run the full spectrum from 'sellout' and 'compromise' to 'It's about time' and 'Long overdue!' . . . Both viewers with alarm and leapers before looking need especially to take a hard look at what the new council proposes to be and do."[5] The new LCUSA was launched in January 1966, and began to coordinate the activities of its member Lutheran denominations as best and as cautiously as it could.

The rise of Pentecostal or charismatic practices within American mainline Protestant denominations, particularly among the Episcopalians, Presbyterians, Lutherans, and even Roman Catholics, was quite an unexpected development. Pentecostal Christians were often derided as ignorant, backwoods, "holy-rollers," or were explained away in mechanistic or psychological terms. Few in the early 1960s would have paired them with middle-class mainline Protestants. But this is exactly what happened. Starting in the late 1950s, scattered American Lutheran pastors and congregations experienced the "gifts of the Spirit," including speaking in tongues. To say that denominational leaders were unprepared for this is an understatement, especially as the movement spread in the 1960s. But, to their credit, the various Lutheran denominations launched theological studies of the phenomenon that were actually balanced and nuanced and did not reject these developments out of hand.

The numbers of charismatic Lutheran pastors continued to grow, and one estimate was that in 1973 there were three hundred charismatic pastors in the LCMS and two hundred in the LCA.[6] Gatherings of charismatic Lutheran pastors occurred in the late 1960s and early 1970s, and in 1974 the Lutheran Charismatic Renewal Services and the National Leaders Conference were founded for encouragement and support. American Lutheran denominations issued cautious theological studies of the movement and of the theology of the Holy Spirit, including one by the ALC in 1964 and another by the LCMS in 1972. This latter document was supplemented by another LCMS study in 1977, this time with a somewhat more negative tone than the first one. Certainly, some charismatic Lutheran pastors sometimes came under suspicion and pressure, and the movement caused divisions in some congregations. The charismatic movement continued in major American Lutheran denominations as a subgroup within them, a sometimes uncomfortable experience for both parties.

American Lutherans and the Social Issues of the 1960s

The late 1960s were a time of immense social turmoil in the United States, and conflict at times turned into violence and open confrontation. The two issues that caused the most difficulty were conflicts concerning racial relations and the Vietnam War. It did seem during this period of time that the nation itself was deeply divided and in danger of spinning apart into hostile separate camps. College campuses and inner-city minority neighborhoods, especially, seethed with tension and anger, and in both settings violence was possible.

The push for greater rights for African Americans and the integration of social institutions had been an ongoing struggle in the United States since the 1950s. However, frustration with the glacial pace of progress and continuing economic inequalities meant that, by the late 1960s, radical groups such as the Black Panthers were gaining a following. Urban riots from 1965 to 1969, especially after the assassination of Martin Luther King Jr. in 1968, devastated African American communities and shocked the nation. African Americans pressed their concerns with increased vigor and rhetoric, leading to fears of a white backlash and open racial conflict.

American Lutheran denominations were concerned about improving relations and supported civil rights, but for the most part they moved cautiously. When Martin Luther King Jr. was invited to address an ALC Luther League gathering in 1961, there were strong internal pressures for the denomination to withdraw the invitation, though it did not do so. During the late 1960s, denominational leaders, especially in the LCA, expressed their support for racial equality and the elimination of poverty in a series of public pronouncements. Home-mission strategies were shifted to support inner-city congregations; congregations were encouraged not to pull out of the city and head for the suburbs, but to minister to the changing populations around them. There were a few notable successes in this endeavor, but many congregations moved anyway; most made rhetorical overtures toward welcoming minority members, but they probably took few practical steps to make such membership possible.

The LCMS had a significant number of African American congregations, especially in the South, but this ministry was not always well supported. African Americans in the LCMS formed a Black Clergy Caucus in 1968 to press for further support and encouragement of this ministry, and the denomination wrestled with expansion of African American membership outside of traditional congregations. By 1988, there were nearly 84,000 African American members in the LCMS, and eighty-eight pastors. In the ALC and LCA, organized efforts to increase African American membership during the 1970s and 1980s resulted in an African American membership of nearly 49,000, with 111 pastors by the late 1980s.[7] As has been the historical case with American Lutherans, there were often lofty goals and modest successes.

Conflict over the war in Vietnam touched nearly every Lutheran congregation. The American participation in this long-running war had begun in a limited way in the early 1960s, but starting in 1965 there was a massive escalation of military involvement, including the deployment of hundreds of thousands of troops. Unlike World War II or the Korean War, the public opposition to the war in Vietnam developed quickly, especially among young American men who were liable to be drafted into the military. The generational "gap" here can be overplayed, but it is true that older generations were proud of their military service during World War II and strongly anticommunist, and thus saw the Vietnam War in this light, whereas the younger generation were less likely to see any good purpose to the war. Initially, the American Lutheran denominations geared up (as they previously had) to supply chaplains and other forms of support to the troops. To conservative Lutheran supporters of the war, it was important to contain and defeat "atheistic" communism, and as citizens they wanted to believe their government and support its policies.

Opponents of the war demonstrated a number of different stances. Long on the periphery of American Lutheranism, advocates of total pacifism such as the Lutheran Peace Fellowship saw their message reach new audiences, and their numbers grew. A larger group of antiwar protestors were not necessarily pacifists, but opposed to this particular war as being unjust and unwinnable, and decried both the mission and methods of this war. Another element did not necessarily take a position on the war itself, but did support the rights of young men who were draft resisters or conscientious objectors not to go to war.

Lutheran periodicals during the period frequently printed articles and letters about the war. One supporter of the war wrote in 1970: "Communism is the great present-day enemy of the Church . . . you cannot compromise with evil, so [one] must oppose this world-wide movement strongly, even if it calls for the use of arms as in the case of Vietnam."[8] Opponents of the war dismissed the arguments about communism, and suggested that the war was brutally destructive, unnecessary, and was being waged unjustly against a people who were simply seeking self-determination. In this vein, one Lutheran writer suggested that "anyone who calls themselves a Christian should be greatly shocked by the wholesale slaughter in Vietnam."[9] The nature of this particular war, and of modern, technological warfare in general, caused many Lutherans to reexamine traditional just-war theory, and to wonder if such a position could be maintained any longer.

Cautiously at first, and then more boldly, American Lutheran denominations issued public pronouncements that raised questions about the war in Vietnam, and rethought Christian responses to war in general. One particular area of agreement was the issue of the rights of conscientious objectors; all three major Lutheran denominations issued statements supporting their legal status, and a Lutheran Selective Service Information office was established in New York at the LCUSA offices from 1971 to 1973, when the draft was suspended. Lutherans also generally supported an amnesty for draft evaders, which was issued in the late 1970s.

Changing Roles for Lutheran Women

Although these previous social conflicts did have longstanding effects, there was another development that perhaps had the greatest and most widespread impact on American society, namely the movement for equal rights for women, or in the language of the time, the Women's Liberation movement. Although American Lutherans did have a wide range of positions on these questions, from conservative to liberal, the growth in the numbers of women working outside the home was something that touched a great majority of families. Changes in how women's relations to men and to social and economic institutions were viewed would forever alter American society.

Although Lutheran women have always worked hard, and a number of them worked outside the home, this was not really the norm. During World War II, the shortage of labor allowed or even obligated women to work in defense industries and in positions usually reserved for men. But after the war, a longstanding notion returned to prevalence, namely, that ideally women would not work outside the home or have permanent careers. Certainly, there were women who defied these stereotypes, and some women found work teaching in Lutheran schools and colleges, or even working in Lutheran denominational offices. But by the early 1970s, changes in societal attitudes meant that women were beginning to work outside the home in record numbers. In the 1980 survey, 29 percent of Lutheran women worked full-time, and 22 percent part-time, while 37 percent self-identified as "homemakers."[10]

This shift, which only grew over time, had profound implications for local congregations, which had traditionally relied on unpaid women volunteers for much of their ministries, and for denominational women's auxiliaries, which during this period of time shifted from being independent organizations to an integral part of the denominational bureaucracy. Congregations began to find that they had to professionalize these formerly volunteer positions and to pay women to staff them. Lutheran parochial schools now had to consider pay equity for teachers and to forget the rationale that they could pay men more "because they had families to support." The numerical decline in the Lutheran deaconess communities, especially among younger members, came about in part because young women now had many more opportunities and fields available to them. Conservative Lutherans, both men and women, might decry the radical "women's libbers," but in practical terms these shifts affected every segment of the American Lutheran community.

The largest controversy, and perhaps one of the most important long-range developments, came with the decision of the ALC and LCA to ordain women as pastors in 1970, and the parallel refusal to do so by the LCMS. Lutheran churches in Europe and other mainline American denominations had previously decided to ordain women as pastors, and during the 1960s American Lutherans engaged this issue. Women already had roles within the Lutheran denominations that mimicked some of the duties of the ordained ministry, especially in campus ministry, but full participation in word-and-sacrament ministry was lacking. In 1966, the ALC asked LCUSA's Division for Theological Studies to do a background study on the question of women's ordination, while both the ALC and LCA started their own concurrent internal studies. The LCUSA report, issued in 1969, found that ". . . [in the] Biblical material and theological arguments we find the case both against and for the ordination of women inconclusive . . . sociological, psychological and ecumenical considerations do not settle the issue . . . [and] that variety in practice on this question is legitimate within common Lutheran confessions . . ."[11] Conservative critics of women's ordination suggested that the biblical account taken literally and authoritatively, as well as the "orders of creation," which held that differences between men and women were ordered by God, did not allow for the practice. They also suggested that ordaining women would cut off some American Lutheran denominations from others, as well as from other groups that did not ordain women—Catholics, Orthodox, or conservative Protestants.

In 1970, both the LCA and the ALC voted to change their constitutions to allow for the ordination of women. In the LCA, this came on clear majority voice vote, in the ALC by a 75 percent majority in the Church Council and, on a closer written ballot, 560 to 414 at its biennial convention. Women had been in theological study and church positions for a number of previous years, so the first ordinations were speedily held in 1970, with the distinctions going to Elizabeth Platz in the LCA and Barbara Andrews in the ALC. By 1988, there were over one thousand ordained women pastors in the two denominations, although their progress into the upper ranks of the clergy and into denominational leadership positions came slowly. In the LCMS, the internal conflict was much greater, with strong advocates on both sides, but the conservatives, led by new LCMS President J. A. O. Preus, blocked any consideration of the question. Indeed, the LCMS annual convention in 1971 issued an official statement expressing its "strong regret over The American Lutheran Church's action on the ordination of women to the pastoral office" and asked the ALC to reconsider its decision. The ALC, however, voted overwhelmingly in its 1972 convention to affirm its previous decision.[12] A sharp division was opened between American Lutheran denominations on this issue, with the ALC and LCA on one side and the LCMS on the other.

Conflict and Division within the Missouri Synod

The Lutheran differences over women's ordination were all the more unwelcome to many, as it had seemed through the middle of the 1960s that the three major Lutheran denominations were cautiously moving closer to one another. The formation of LCUSA in 1966 and Missouri's participation in it were seen by many as a positive development. But the most hopeful sign of the times was the official declaration of altar and pulpit fellowship between the LCMS and the ALC in 1969, a momentous decision especially for the LCMS, which in its history had rarely ever agreed to such an action. But these signs of closer relations between the three American Lutheran denominations were soon dashed by a strong conservative reaction within the LCMS, which led to strained inter-Lutheran relations and a painful schism within the Missouri Synod.

The fellowship agreement between the ALC and the LCMS essentially declared that the two groups were in doctrinal agreement with one another. This agreement had its roots in negotiations that began in the 1930s, and then returned in the late

1950s, before the actual formation of the ALC in 1960. As a part of the merger leading to the new ALC, the group adopted constitutional language declaring the Bible to be "inerrant" and "infallible," which the LCMS saw as a positive sign. Negotiations about fellowship continued on and off during the 1960s, and in 1967 they adopted a joint theological summary known as the "Joint Statement and Declaration," which permitted the LCMS leadership to bring fellowship to a vote. The vote came at the 1969 LCMS convention, when fellowship with the ALC was approved on a vote of 522 to 438, a momentous occasion in the synod's history. It was the same convention that allowed LCMS congregations to give women voice and vote in congregational government.

These votes were all the more surprising since at the time the LCMS was wracked by deep internal divisions between two opposing camps, the "moderates" and the "conservatives." Labels are tricky here, and trying to fit either group into a single category is difficult. The conservatives were essentially those who wished to maintain a traditional LCMS stance of strict doctrinal orthodoxy based on the seventeenth-century Lutheran Orthodox theologians, on the necessity of complete doctrinal agreement before fellowship, and on a deep suspicion of modernity. The moderates were those who, while still mostly conservative Lutherans, were much more willing to engage other Lutherans and the modern world, and who cautiously moved toward closer relations with the ALC and even LCA. During the term of President Oliver Harms (1962–1969), the moderates seemed to control the denominational machinery, as evidenced by the decision to join LCUSA and to pursue fellowship with the ALC, along with a new spirit of theological inquiry at Concordia Seminary in St. Louis.

But there were signs through the 1960s that LCMS conservatives were gathering power and seeking to challenge the moderates for control of the denomination. Later observers have seen this struggle as an early outbreak of the so-called culture wars of the late twentieth century. Conservatives rallied around the figure of J. A. O. Preus, and organized a campaign against Harms and the moderates. Preus himself was an outsider, a Norwegian from the "Little Norwegian" Synod (ELS), but had moved into Missouri to become the head of its "practical" seminary in Springfield, Illinois. Tensions came to a head at the synodical convention in 1969, when on the third ballot Preus defeated Harms for the presidency of the LCMS; ironically, this was the same convention that approved fellowship with the ALC, something Preus himself deeply opposed.

With his election in 1969, Preus set about to secure his hold on the administrative machinery of the synod and to ensure that conservatives dominated positions of authority. But moderates had their own power bases; in some of the district presidencies, and especially in the synod's flagship educational institution, Concordia Seminary in St. Louis. In May 1969, two months before the synod convention, John Tietjen was elected president of Concordia. A moderate like many others on the faculty, Tietjen proved to be Preus's chief opponent over the next five years. Preus soon moved against the St. Louis seminary, appointing a "fact-finding committee" to investigate the theological positions of the seminary professors; the key issue was the authority of Scripture, and especially whether professors held that the Bible was truly "inerrant" and infallible," and whether they actually taught from such a position. When this did not bring about the results he desired, Preus moved to gain closer authority over the seminary's board of control. After his reelection as president at the New Orleans convention in 1973, Preus and the board moved against Tietjen, who was removed as seminary president in January 1974.

Before the 1973 convention, moderates formed their own organization, Evangelical Lutherans in Mission (ELIM), to attempt to blunt the power of Preus and the conservatives. After Tietjen's removal, on February 19, 1974, forty-five (out of fifty) faculty and a large majority of Concordia seminarians walked out of the seminary campus, processed to nearby educational institutions, and constituted a new seminary, Christ Seminary in Exile, or Seminex. This was quite a blow to the LCMS, for Concordia Seminary, St. Louis, had long been a source of immense pride to the whole denominations, and its "exile" was a very strong statement indeed.

These developments also sent shock waves through the rest of American Lutheranism, although many outsiders just dismissed this as a case of "Missouri being Missouri," and either hoped or believed that this storm would pass, and that further Lutheran efforts toward cooperation and even merger would eventually get back on track. Writing in 1975 the conclusion to his standard history of American Lutheranism, ALC professor E. Clifford Nelson looked even beyond Lutheran unity to Lutheran ecumenical work as the next stage on the horizon, suggesting: "Lutheran unity, fifty years overdue, will come eventually because Missouri cannot forever escape the implications of its own confession."[13] Lutheran unity was, it seemed to him, inevitable, and an integral part of the Lutheran theological identity. But developments in Missouri continued to take an ominous turn, as the moderates were either further dispossessed from positions of authority in the synod or they left.

The immediate question in 1974 concerned the Seminex students, and how they might be called and ordained. Some moderate congregations were willing to have these graduates as their pastors, and some LCMS district presidents were willing to ordain them, and did so. At the heart of the matter was the traditional Missouri understanding of congregational autonomy within the synod, versus the power of the synod to control the clergy roster. At the 1975 LCMS convention, the conservative majority voted to condemn ELIM as schismatic, and agreed that district presidents who did not follow the procedures of the synod should be removed from office. During the spring of 1976, Preus removed four district presidents from office for refusing to follow synodical guidelines. Some moderates, who had hoped to remain in the LCMS, decided that it was time to leave the synod, and approximately 250 congregations (with a total of 108,000 members) and 550 pastors formed a new organization, the Association of Evangelical Lutheran Congregations (AELC).

The formation of the AELC in December 1976 was a watershed; LCMS moderates had to decide whether to stay in the synod or leave and join the new organization. Judging by some of the expectations of the time, far fewer moderates left the LCMS and joined the AELC than its founders had expected. John Tietjen recalled: "It had been expected that twelve hundred Missouri Synod congregations would join the new church, but only 250 did so. Even the English Synod . . . received only a little more than half the congregations that could have legitimately have been expected to leave the English District."[14] Leaving a denomination, even one you believe has wronged you, is a very difficult decision, and it seems that in the end many moderate members, congregations, and pastors could not make the break with Missouri. The new AELC had a number of daunting problems from the beginning, as the process of building a new denomination from scratch was difficult financially and organizationally. Seminex had to be supported, but what was to be its relation to the AELC, and to those in ELIM who remained in Missouri? Another issue was that the AELC was top-heavy with pastors, professors, and theologians, who had left Missouri in greater numbers than congregations, but, when combined with the Seminex graduates looking for call, there were far too many clergy in the AELC and far too few positions for them to fill. Quite a number of Missouri exiles had to move into either the ALC or LCA to find calls or teaching positions, a factor that had a long-range influence on these two denominations.

The main hope for the AELC was that it could engineer some sort of merger or cooperative arrangements with the LCA and ALC. The student numbers at Seminex declined over time, and eventually the resources of the seminary were dispersed to other Lutheran seminaries. By 1988, the AELC consisted of 267 congregations with 100,000 baptized members.

American Lutheranism during the 1970s

Unlike the 1960s, a decade that seemed to pulse with energy and excitement, though not always positively, the 1970s seemed rather sour and even dull at times. The way the Vietnam War ended, with an American withdrawal in 1973 and a communist victory in 1975, made the war seem all a big waste. The social challenges of the 1960s continued and deepened. The Watergate political scandal convulsed the nation and made many even more distrustful of government than they had been. The Cold War continued, oil-producing countries instigated the first energy crisis, financial inflation ate away at prosperity, and the ecological crisis came home in a big way. Even the two-hundredth anniversary of American independence in 1976 seemed more anticlimactic than celebratory. To many, the nation seemed to be drifting, unsure of how to proceed. Lutherans, too, seemed to feel this. For the three major American Lutheran denominations, the 1970s were dominated by two major pursuits: restructuring their activities and responding to the social crises around them.

The energy and excitement that characterized American Lutheranism in the early 1960s had dissipated by the 1970s, and by all signs the big three Lutheran denominations had plateaued, if they were not declining a bit. The rapid expansion of membership that characterized the period from 1945 to 1965 ran out of steam, and both membership and financial contributions were flat. The inflation of the 1970s sapped the assets of congregations, institutions, and denominations alike. For the ALC and LCA, the initial euphoria surrounding their mergers gave way to the realization that some, if not all, of the initial structuring of the new denominations would have to be rethought and reworked to meet contemporary realities. Mergers are very difficult to "digest," and the rebuilding of bonds of trust and loyalty in these Lutheran denominations took immense amounts of time and energy, as did dealing with those pockets of resentment and hard feelings that lingered among those who felt that they had "lost out" in the process. The church structures that resulted from the ALC and LCA mergers were in many ways overly complex, often due to political compromises and unrealistic expectations. Also, in the 1960s and 1970s, new groups were pushing for a seat at the table, and women and minorities wanted greater influence. A pervasive distrust of "the system" (left over from the revolts of the 1960s) colored the ways people looked at institutions.

Restructuring a denomination is not an easy thing to do, nor is it often a good omen. At best, the changes indicate a stall in momentum, but can also be a sign that an institution has lost its way. Already in the late 1960s, the ALC launched a process of restructuring called "Toward Greater Effectiveness in Mission," which was begun under President Kent Knutson (who died tragically in 1973) and was subsequently implemented under his successor, David Preus.[15] This restructuring seemed to be "digested" fairly well, and served the ALC for the remaining fifteen years of its life, under the leadership of President Preus. The LCA restructuring began in 1970, with the formation of a Commission on Function and Structure, which was to bring its report and recommendations to the 1972 convention in Dallas. This restructuring was more extensive than that of the ALC, and caused more political controversy. When some of the issues could not be decided they were deferred to the 1974 convention. The most contentious and far-reaching proposals revolved around dramatic changes in the nature and form of the LCA convention or, essentially, how the LCA governed itself on the national level. The proposal from The Committee for the Study of the Convention and Other Organizational Matters (TCFTS-OTCAOOM), was decisively defeated, and LCA governance on the national level remained as originally implemented.[16]

In the late 1970s, the LCMS faced the challenge of rebuilding a number of its own institutions after the Seminex walkout and the formation of the AELC. Hardest hit was the synod's flagship seminary, Concordia Seminary, St. Louis, which lost 90 percent of its faculty and 85 percent of its students. Although this was the most pressing instance, there were many other "holes" to be filled: new district presidents needed to be selected to replace those who had been dismissed; restive college faculties, such as at River Forest, Illinois, and Seward, Nebraska, had to be reined in; and denominational leaders who had left for the AELC had to be replaced. When changes in the Missouri educational system resulted in the closure of Concordia Senior College, Fort Wayne, Indiana, in 1977, the old "practical" seminary in Springfield, Illinois, was transferred to the Indiana campus.

One huge, perennial question that still haunted Missouri had to do with the authority of the synod itself, particularly as over and against the authority of the districts and congregations. Historically, these latter two had a fairly wide degree of latitude within the synod. This latitude was crucial to the bulk of Missouri moderates, most of whom had not left to join the AELC but remained in the synod. Many of them, no doubt, had hopes that this historical autonomy would allow them to continue in the synod relatively unscathed. Having gained power through the synod presidency, on the other hand, conservatives sought to use this new power to move against the moderates. The issue came to a boil in 1975 and 1976 when some local LCMS congregations voted to call Seminex graduates as pastors, and some district presidents allowed this. Responding to a 1975 convention resolution to discipline the presidents, one of them, Emil Jaech, responded that their stance: ". . . is neither new or unique in Missouri Synod history . . . the church [is] not an ecclesiastical government exercising coercive powers over its congregations but [is] the instrument of the Holy Spirit for carrying out the commission of our Lord to evangelize the people of the world . . ."[17] One letter to the *Lutheran Witness* spoke of the "right" of one congregation to call a Seminex graduate, and complained that in another case a "congregation was dissuaded from their call (what kind of theology goes into the revocation of a *divine* call?), [which] is more a tribute to the effectiveness of synodical headquarters than to the work of the Holy Spirit."[18] But the synod president also had powers, both direct and indirect, to discipline parts of the synod that seemed to him to be errant, and Preus often made use of these channels.

These kinds of tensions made any proposal to restructure the synod nationally, or to redefine the relationship between the national organization and the regional and local entities, problematic. Missouri went through a process of national restructuring during the late 1970s, with a task force that brought a recommendation to the synod's 1981 convention. The proposal was eventually passed by the convention, but not before considerable reworking on and off the convention floor.

As if internal issues were not enough, there were plenty of other things happening in the nation and the world to which American Lutherans felt compelled to respond. On the national scene, the struggle for rights for African Americans, Native Americans, and women continued. The Watergate political scandal and the larger public debate over the nature of American politics spilled over into the religious world, especially in a continuing distrust of institutions and structures. The dawning of ecological consciousness, questions surrounding the apartheid regime in South Africa, and the plight of refugees from Southeast Asia all concerned church people, some of whom increasingly began to believe that their church had to take not only positions, but direct action, on many, if not all, of these issues.

During the 1970s, these three denominations all established commissions, boards, or other organizations to address the concerns of women and minority populations, and to bring these concerns to the attention of the wider denomination. The LCA had a Consulting Committee on Minority Group Interests that made regular recommendations to LCA boards, divisions, and institutions, and an Association of Black Lutherans, which began meeting in 1978. Of course, all three of these denominations had women's organizations, which had generally been folded into the regular denominational structures, but the 1970s saw these new women's organizations taking a more forceful role in the affairs and direction of the denominations, a development that sometimes led to conflict. Having rejected the ordination of women, the LCMS nevertheless continued to wrestle with the issues of gender by means of a Task Force on Women created in 1974. The attempted passage of the Equal Rights Amendment (ERA) guaranteeing rights for women was as an issue to which many Lutherans reacted, positively and negatively, and which became an issue within the denominations. Lutheran supporters of the ERA saw passage as an issue of justice and morality, and believed the denominations had to take a stand on it. Some Lutherans, while not necessarily supporting or rejecting the ERA, suggested that taking a political stance on issues such as this was inappropriate for religious denominations. One writer to the ALC periodical *Lutheran Standard* wrote: "I am 100% opposed to mobilizing church bodies, either national or local to 'support' or 'oppose' this or any such issue. I believe it is the role of the church and its official organizations to get the gospel across . . . the church will pay a heavy price if it jumps on the bandwagon of politically oriented issues."[19] Yet other Lutherans concluded that the proposed amendment violated the biblically supported "orders of creation," gender differences mandated by divine creation.

Some sections of American Lutheranism felt differently, however, and held that merely taking a position on such issues was not sufficient; the denominations would have to take direct actions on its principles. The role of public-policy organizations, such as the LCA's Office of Governmental Affairs, grew more forceful. Advocates of particular positions endorsed the use of direct economic pressure for change, including boycott of states that had not passed the ERA, and the divestment of assets in companies doing business in South Africa, but these actions were often internally divisive and rarely worked. Beginning in the 1960s, the questions of the relation of church to society, and all the corollary issues, became both important and potentially alienating; in general, elements within the LCA tended toward a new position on the issue, the ALC was cautious, and the LCMS generally maintained its traditional distance on the question. The LCA and ALC issued numerous "social statements" beginning in the 1960s and 1970s, to provide guidance and resources for its members on controversial topics, and at times to help the denominations themselves to take a stand.

Native American concerns boiled over in 1973, when the American Indian Movement (AIM) took over the Sioux reservation at Wounded Knee, South Dakota, leading to a prolonged standoff with federal authorities. The ALC had a long history of support of AIM through its national staff person, Paul Boe, who was present and worked among the protesters at Wounded Knee during the conflict. Boe himself was arrested by federal authorities after the end of the standoff and charged with aiding and abetting the situation, but eventually the charges were dropped. A less controversial situation involved Lutheran resettlement of refugees from Southeast Asia—Vietnamese, Hmong, Laotians, and Cambodians who fled after the communist takeover. Just as after World War II, Lutheran Refugee Services facilitated the resettlement of thousands of these refugees in the United States, again working through local Lutheran congregations.

Changes in Mission and Direction

The 1970s and 1980s saw important changes in the ways in which American Lutherans structured and conceived of their mission to others, both in the United States and around the world. Traditional home- and foreign-mission work, at which

American Lutherans had become quite proficient, changed with the world around them, and they struggled to meet new challenges.

The home-mission outreach that had been so frenetic and successful in the two decades after World War II was based on a strategy of beginning new missions inexpensively, and then weaning them off of mission support quickly, freeing up funds for more mission starts. Inexpensive land in the new booming suburbs, inexpensive construction loan rates, standardized building and organizational plans, and a supply of young, inexpensive pastors powered the formation of hundreds of new congregations. But by the late 1960s and early 1970s, this system began to break down. The Baby Boom tailed off dramatically after 1964, and there were fewer young families to which to appeal. The suburban boom also declined, and everything became more expensive, including land, building costs, loan rates, and the costs to staff the new congregations. Furthermore, with concerns about increasing ethnic diversity, more home-mission funds were now intentionally channeled into starting and supporting new ethnic, urban congregations. These congregations were generally more expensive to start, and often required a prolonged commitment of funds. Coupling all these factors with the flat or even declining benevolence revenue (in real dollars) to the national denominations meant that progress was slowed. Sometimes, the denominations made special appeals for additional funding, such as the ALC's "50 More in 84," which was geared for new mission starts, but still the overall trend was downward.

Mission work outside of the United States continued, but the relationship between the American mission staff and the newly independent churches in the global South was changing and adapting. American mission staff had anticipated, and even longed for, this development, but it still was an uneasy and sometimes awkward transition. Churches in the newly independent countries in Africa and Asia could be sensitive to the appearance of being dependent on Western agencies, and sometime resented well-meaning advice or assistance. These new churches were becoming a force within the Lutheran World Federation and were eager to take their rightful place within this body. Sometimes, the evolution of local conditions meant the breaking of old Lutheran patterns, such as the relations between Lutheran church bodies in India, or with the confessional status of the Batak Church in Indonesia. Patterns of Lutheranism that had been important in the West were not always as crucial in the global South. One missiologist observed in 1969 that there was a "problematic" relationship between confessional identity and ecumenical relationships within Lutheranism, and that these "younger" Lutheran churches faced such problems as: ". . . the concept of confessional obligation, views on ministry and church leadership (including episcopacy), methods of overcoming confessional differences through transconfessional church unions including Lutherans . . ."[20]

Lutheran leaders in America would have to adjust to these new realities, as would mission workers on the ground.

Another shift came with the increasing dedication of world-mission funding to support development projects in the global South. Because of poverty and an exploding population, the assistance of Western denominations, especially mainline Protestants and Roman Catholics, was beginning to be shifted toward long-term projects to alleviate poverty, eradicate disease, and allow for greater self-sufficiency. These projects were especially important in those countries where overt Christian evangelism was prohibited, although some critics worried that without the explicit proclamation of the Christian gospel attached to them such work merely transformed the churches into well-meaning social-service agencies.

Women's and Youth Organizations, Education, and Worship

In the first half of the twentieth century, lay American Lutherans had built themselves impressive organizations for women and youth, organizations parallel to and usually supportive of the ministries of the denomination itself. These organizations, such as the various women's missionary societies, the Luther League, and the Walther League were generally independently run and financed, and in the case of the women's societies, made a substantial financial contribution to the mission work of the denomination. Changes in the second half of the twentieth century occasioned major shifts in these organizations.

The various women's organizations were strong going into the 1960s. Those in the merging denominations came together at the time of merger to create new, united women's organizations: the LCA's Lutheran Church Women (LCW) and the ALC's American Lutheran Church Women (ALCW). These new organizations were tied into the new denominations as auxiliaries, but they also became related to other denominational branches, such as for missions and for the status of women. The Lutheran Women's Missionary League (LWML) had become an official auxiliary of the Missouri Synod in 1942 and increasingly worked in concert with it.

The social upheavals and transitions of the 1960s and 1970s had a profound effect on these women's organizations, especially in terms of their membership. With the trend toward women working outside the home, fewer younger women joined these organizations or assumed active roles in them. The LCW, for example, achieved its highest membership in the mid-1960s, and by 1977 its membership had declined 27 percent, while revenues fell 21 percent by 1971. These organizations still contributed large amounts of money yearly to the missions and other projects, but they were gradually losing the power they once had. Some wondered aloud whether the time for such organizations had passed. These organizations had been a way for women to have influence in the church and the world at a time when women had few other opportunities, but now, with new paths open to them, perhaps the need for separate organizations was past. Leaders in these organizations were challenged to articulate a continuing mission for them in the new world of women's rights. The LCW and ALCW, especially, took the lead in championing women's opportunities and issues in their denominations, but they also had to worry about getting too far out in front of their rank-and-file members, many of whom were socially conservative, even on women's issues.

The 1960s and 1970s saw the death of the independent Lutheran youth organizations, the Luther League and the Walther League. These organizations had, in their earlier history, stretched the term *youth* beyond what it might be considered today. The heart of these leagues was young adults in their late teens and twenties, who provided the administrative skill and financial resources to run them. But after World War II, when attendance at college away from home became more of a norm, this base of young adults shrank rapidly, both in local congregations and within the youth organizations. It was becoming increasingly difficult to maintain these groups as autonomous entities, especially during the turmoil of the 1960s, when suspicion of such organizations was widespread among the youth themselves. As one participant from this time later observed:

> The mergers of ALC 1960 and LCA 1962 and their subsequent re-structuring had a devastating impact on teen-age work in the church bodies. . . . For reasons I never understood mainline Protestant churches began dropping their youth programs. Lutheran restructuring committees caught the fever and eliminated youth offices and programs, ostensibly as cost saving devices. In retrospect I see the drastic cutting of youth work as the beginnings of what came to full flower . . . 25–35 years later.[21]

The Luther League in the LCA was disbanded in 1968, and its assets and responsibilities were transferred to a new Commission on Youth Ministry. The Luther League in the ALC lasted longer, but it, too, was eventually closed.

The Walther League in the LCMS was, in terms of autonomy and of financial assets, the strongest of the three, but it, too, declined during the late 1960s. In its case, the leadership of the league moved toward dealing with the evolving needs of its members and championing their causes, but this led it into direct confrontation with synodical conservatives. A heated controversy over speakers invited to the league's convention in 1965 led to a long and pointed debate at the synod's convention that same year; while the league escaped official sanction, the issue did not go away. Some conservative local pastors reportedly refused to cooperate with the league or even to disseminate their materials. Plans to restructure the league and the other youth activities in the synod went forward, but the Walther League went into an organizational tailspin. Contributions to the league plummeted from $150,000 in 1965 to $2,000 in 1970, and by 1974 the league was essentially defunct.[22] Some elements of all three leagues remained on the local or regional level, but as national entities, their time was past.

In all three denominations, programing for ministry with youth became the responsibility of national staffers, directed by boards or commissions dedicated to this task. The main sphere of their activities was with high-school-age youth, and increasingly with middle-school youth. What did continue to work well were the large national youth gatherings, at which tens of thousands of Lutheran youth from around the country gathered for three-to-five days of music and worship, speakers and activities. Another popular activity during this time were the "hunger hikes," for which youth would receive pledges for every mile walked and contribute the money to world-hunger organizations.

As with the rest of Lutheranism, educational institutions changed dramatically over these decades. The boom in higher education after World War II meant a general expansion of Lutheran higher education, but also increased competition from publicly funded institutions. After 1970 or so, the decline in student numbers, the stagnation of denominational support, and difficult economic conditions caused major problems for Lutheran institutions. No colleges closed as a result, but there was still major concern for their futures. The denominations attempted to help with direct aid and with periodic special campaigns for capital improvements, but, increasingly, these Lutheran educational institutions were dependent on assistance from governmental sources and private foundations. During the 1960s, two colleges, Hardwick College in New York and Waterloo Lutheran University in Ontario, formally disassociated from their Lutheran denominations in order to receive greater public funding. As the Lutheran institutions attracted an increasingly diverse student population, they became less Lutheran in composition; Lutheran students declined from 66 percent in 1960 to 49 percent in 1970, with an proportional decline in Lutheran faculty.

Changes within the Missouri educational system during this time period were significant. The system had been built on the idea of a system of two-year teacher's colleges; a senior college in Fort Wayne, Indiana, primarily for preseminarians; and two seminaries. But there was great pressure from the two-year schools to upgrade their status to four-year institutions, and to be able to offer a wider curriculum;

in effect, making them four-year liberal-arts institutions. This trend doomed the senior college, which was closed in 1977. Missouri also opened new institutions in Ann Arbor, Michigan (1963), and in Irvine, California (1975), and all but two of its institutions became four-year institutions. Sometimes, attempts to transform an educational system did not work. The independent Lutheran Bible Institute in Minneapolis, Minnesota, attempted to become a degree-granting liberal-arts college in the 1960s, Golden Valley Lutheran College, but it did not have the financial base to achieve this goal and this institution was forced to close in 1985.

During the 1960s and 1970s, Lutherans paid renewed attention to their corporate worship life, but as with many other things in this period of time, these developments were not without their share of controversy. Although the recent past had seen uniformity in practice and usage through promotion of a common hymnal and worship practices, now others were experimenting with new forms and modes of worship. While some worship officials, influenced by the Liturgical Renewal movement within Roman Catholicism and other denominations, were seeking to move in direction of liturgical ecumenism, others were experimenting with evangelical worship and contemporary music and pushing the boundaries. Jazz services, folk-song masses, and contemporary language and rituals were being introduced at the congregational level and in youth meetings.

The denominations themselves attempted to make sense of all this and, after a time of study, introduced revised worship practices and new worship materials. The three denominations launched a joint study of confirmation and its practices, whose 1970 report made a number of key suggestions, the most important being a severing of first communion from the rite of confirmation, so that confirmation would not be seen as a form of adult "decision" or conversion. First communion was suggested for those children who had reached the fifth grade. This report was adopted by the ALC and LCA, but the LCMS simply suggested to its congregations that they reexamine their practices, without a synodical recommendation. Coming off this study, as well as a previous study of communion practices, the LCA also faced a minor controversy coming from proponents of infant communion, but the official prohibition of this practice remained in place.

Another joint project among the three denominations was a proposal to develop a new, joint hymnal, a proposal which, interestingly, originated with the LCMS at its 1965 convention at Detroit. A joint Inter-Lutheran Commission on Worship (ILCW) was formed in November 1966, with a very ambitious agenda not only to create this new hymnal for all American Lutherans, but also to experiment with and test out new liturgical language and services, as well as contemporary music and hymns. The tasks before them were large and, as is usual in the area of worship and music, the range of opinions on just what constituted "good" worship was wide. Some pushed for more formal and liturgical ("higher") worship and hymns, while others championed the new, contemporary, and "relevant" forms. In the early 1970s, the ILCW published a series of paperback contemporary worship materials for trial use within congregations, and attempted to incorporate the feedback from these materials into the larger hymnal project. The ILCW also incorporated ecumenical elements, such as a common lectionary and uniform English translations of liturgical texts, and began to implement gender-neutral, "inclusive" language for some of its elements.

The process of producing the new common hymnal proceeded slowly through the 1970s, but eventually the new "green" hymnal, the *Lutheran Book of Worship* (LBW) began to take shape. Controversies about the project continued, such as the inclusion of eucharistic prayers within the communion service, which some strongly opposed, while Scandinavian Americans felt that their hymn tradition was slighted in the new hymn section. But, finally, the proposed hymnal came into form and was eventually adopted by the ALC and LCA. In Missouri, the hymnal came under attack from certain quarters, and the 1977 convention established a special "blue-ribbon committee" to examine the proposed new hymnal. In May 1978, this committee proposed a list of twelve pages full of modifications to the proposed hymnal, but the ILCW replied that the project was too far advanced to admit such substantial changes. So, when the new LBW was published later that year, the LCMS did not participate in the production. This dashed the hopes of a common hymnal for all American Lutherans, and left some in the LCA and ALC fuming to the effect that the LCMS had "stuck" the rest of them with a bunch of unsingable sixteenth-century German hymns and then pulled out of the project. The LCMS moved forward with its own "blue" hymnal, *Lutheran Worship*, utilizing many of the common elements of the LBW, which was published in 1982. The two hymnals were visible symbols that closer worship and cooperation were being pushed further away from realization.

American Lutherans in the 1980s

The election of a conservative Republican, Ronald Reagan, as president in 1980, with the assistance of the so-called Religious Right, heralded a new and sometimes contentious decade. Reagan pushed to modernize and expand the American military; his more confrontational approach toward the Soviet Union led to its collapse in 1991 and the end of the Cold War. After the economic woes of the 1970s, the American economy boomed and ushered in a decade of economic advance, at least for some, sometimes disparaged as the "decade of greed." American foreign policy took a hard line against Soviet intervention in Afghanistan and against Latin American socialist governments and movements, such as the Sandinista revolutionaries in Nicaragua. Although there was a backlash against some of the social revolutions of the 1960s and 1970s in the United States, many of its changes remained in place, continuing to cause social conflict.

Although most American Lutherans continued to be in the moderate-to-conservative range, with a solid majority of them voting for President Reagan, there was also a growing liberal element, especially among the clergy in the ALC and LCA, which attempted to push for reforms and for "progressive" positions. Alarmed by the military positions of the Reagan administration, groups such as the Lutheran Peace Fellowship and others championed moves toward disarmament and the reduction or elimination of nuclear weaponry. While conservatives sought to reduce taxes and federal spending, more liberal elements sought to increase federal spending to alleviate poverty and to increase opportunities for the disadvantaged. In order to oppose South African apartheid, some in the Lutheran denominations began to push for church boards and organizations to divest their funds from corporations doing business in that country. Church pension agencies resisted this, citing their fiduciary responsibilities to individual plan participants. District and synod conventions saw a rise in resolutions aimed at a wide variety of social causes; during this time, the LCA issued social statements on such topics as on human rights, economic justice, peace and politics, and death and dying.

Several controversial headline-making groups and topics roiled American Lutheranism during the 1980s. To fight the effects of economic change and disadvantage, a group of pastors around Pittsburgh, led by Lutherans Daniel Solberg and Douglas Roth, formed the Denominational Ministry Strategy in the early 1980s. Their confrontational and militant actions resulted in alienation from their congregations and synod, their removal from the synod clergy roster, and stretches of time in jail. They bitterly blamed LCA officials for not supporting them and attempted to disrupt national LCA conventions. Opponents of the American policy against the Sandinistas in Nicaragua also protested against the government, and in solidarity ran informational study trips to that Central American nation. Not all Lutheran advocacy groups were liberal; the interdenominational Lutherans for Life was formed in 1979 and developed educational and strategic proposals to overturn the liberalization of American abortion policies. Although conservatives were wary of mixing church and state, some began to copy the organization and activities of the liberals against public policies they opposed.

There were also important developments during this decade concerning the relation of American Lutherans to other Lutherans and other Christians around the world. One of the nearest of these involved Lutherans in Canada. All three of the major American Lutheran denominations had congregations in Canada, but starting in the 1960s, Lutherans on both sides of the border concluded that an independent Canadian Lutheran denomination would be a good thing. The ALC congregations in Canada formed their own Evangelical Lutheran Church of Canada (ELCC) in 1967, and during the 1970s they were joined in merger talks with the Canadian congregations of the LCA and LCMS. The events in Missouri affected these talks, too, and eventually the ELCC and the LCA Canada Section merged to form the new Evangelical Lutheran Church in Canada (ELCIC) in 1985. The LCMS congregations formed their own independent denomination, the Lutheran Church–Canada (LCC) in 1987.

Lutheran relations in the United States took on a bipolar configuration, with the ALC, LCA, and AELC on one side of the equation, and the LCMS and WELS on the other, which led to the general feeling that the two groups were moving away from each other. The hopes that LCUSA would become a vehicle for Lutheran unity were not realized; rather, the LCMS began to pull back from a number of its joint commitments within LCUSA, such as the common hymnal, and increasingly went its own direction. While the other major groups participated in the Lutheran World Federation, in 1993 Missouri spearheaded the development of a parallel institution, the International Lutheran Council, to bind together conservative confessional Lutheran churches around the world.

The ALC and LCA joined in ecumenical dialogues and relationships beginning in the 1960s. Ecumenism was in the air; the Roman Catholic Church was changing rapidly after Vatican II (1962–1965); and mainline Protestants were working together in the National Council of Churches and the Consultation on Church Union, as well as in many bilateral discussions. The most important of these for American Lutherans were the joint dialogues between themselves and the Roman Catholic Church, the Protestant Episcopal Church, and the Reformed churches. These national discussions in the United States paralleled international discussions between the Lutheran World Federation and the various Christian communions.

In the United States, Lutheran–Roman Catholic dialogues were the oldest, beginning in 1965; they continued through eleven different rounds by 2005. Each round of these discussions was centered around a particular topic, such as the Lord's Supper, the papacy, authority and infallibility, and the thorniest of all, the doctrine of justification by faith, which resulted in a joint statement in 1985. Although these dialogues have not completely overcome the divisions between the two groups, they have led to greater understanding and appreciation. Lutheran–Episcopal dialogues (1969–1991) focused on similarly divisive issues, and resulted in an interim agreement and guidelines on sharing the Lord's Supper in 1982. Since the 1960s, the Lutheran–Reformed discussions have focused on similarly divisive issues, especially the nature of the Lord's Supper. By 1983, these talks resulted in a common statement, *Invitation to Action*, which called on the churches to recognize each other's ministry and sacraments. The ALC and the AELC were ready to move on these recommendations in 1986, while the LCA was slower to do so.

There was a great deal of internal politicking involved in these ecumenical dialogues. There were exceptions, but in general elements of the ALC wanted greater fellowship with the Reformed, while some elements within the LCA favored movement toward the Episcopalians and the Roman Catholics; much of this had to do with inter-Lutheran debates and conflicts. Both the ALC and LCA had begun to refer to their denominational leaders as "bishops" in the late 1970s, but without really clarifying whether there was a particular theological or ecclesiastical ideology behind this move, something that would come back to haunt them later. In this sense, then, these ecumenical dialogues were also about a search for allies to support each group's own internal Lutheran positions as over and against other American Lutherans.

Toward the Formation of the Evangelical Lutheran Church in America, 1988

With the LCMS moving away from the other American Lutheran denominations in the late 1970s, the dream of a pan-Lutheran merger involving all groups died, at least for the present. The formal impetus for a new Lutheran merger without Missouri came initially through the AELC, which realistically needed some kind of a merger to survive. The ALC and LCA, which had moved generally in concert since the 1960s, were both ready for such a step. An additional impetus for merger came from outside, from the LCMS, which in its 1981 convention finally suspended pulpit and altar fellowship with the ALC over the ordination of women and Missouri's worries about "liberalism" in the ALC. It seemed clear in the early 1980s that the path was clear for the ALC, LCA, and AELC to merge.

That path, however, proved to be a complicated one, and many issues had to be resolved before that goal could materialize. There was a fair amount of support for closer relations, but less for actually merging the three institutions together. Organizationally and culturally, there were some very significant differences between them. In the ALC especially, there were reservations about institutional unity with the LCA: ALC President David Preus later recalled that he had "argued for a 'unity in reconciled diversity' which assumed that the church at its best and most obedient did not have to be institutionally uniform."[23] There were any numbers of different types of relations suggested at this time, from closer working arrangements to a federative structure to full and complete integrative merger. Even in the ALC, the tide seemed to be moving toward some kind of merger, and so the three church conventions in 1982 voted to merge, creating the Commission for a New Lutheran Church (CNLC) to make this happen.

The CNLC was a new kind of path to Lutheran merger. Determined to avoid the tightly engineered mergers directed by denominational officials, the CNLC was set up to be representative of women, laypeople, and minority Lutherans, with a strict formula so that the seventy-member commission was "balanced." The CNLC itself often was an unwieldy organization, so it was proposed that a smaller planning committee could do some of the work between main sessions, but the full commission was wary of giving over too much power to this group. The CNLC had some very difficult conflicts to overcome, as the three different merging churches had very different structures as well as significant differences in ethos. Controversies about key structural issues included the relation of the congregation to the regional and national expressions of the church; how educational and social-service agencies should relate to the denomination; the question of "quotas" for equal representation; the merging of pension plans, rosters, and auxiliary organizations; the nature of ordained and other forms of rostered leadership; participation in various ecumenical organizations; and even where the national denominational headquarters would be located. All these, and many more, still needed to be addressed, and the deadline was tight. The basic outlines of the plan were scheduled to be voted on by the denominational conventions in 1986, so that the new denomination could come into existence by January 1988.

There was a real sense of a generational shift during the CNLC process. The leaders of the existing denominations had much less say in the process than in previous mergers, and there were times when their advice and cautions were ignored. The emphasis was on the word *new*. It was repeatedly said that this would be a *new* Lutheran church, and not simply a merger of the old. But the tight timeframe toward the new church, and the sometimes unwieldy decision-making structure of the CNLC, meant that some important issues could not be solved within the time allotted, and were left unresolved for the new denomination to decide. By 1986, enough of the plan was in place so that all three of the denominations could vote on it, and they all approved the new church at their respective conventions in 1986, although the ALC had to hold a congregational referendum before it was official. Ultimately, this referendum was successful and the ALC approved the merger. A ten-member transition team was selected to implement the decisions of the CNLC, and the Constituting Convention of the new denomination, the Evangelical Lutheran Church in America (ELCA), was held in Columbus, Ohio, in 1987. As presiding bishop, the new denomination elected Herbert Chilstrom, the bishop of the Minnesota Synod of the LCA, over ALC presiding bishop David Preus.

The new ELCA was launched. But where would it go? And where, too, was Missouri headed? In what direction or directions were American Lutherans going? There were more questions than answers.

Notes

1. The three surveys are summarized in Lawrence L. Kersten, *The Lutheran Ethic: The Impact of Religion on Laymen and Clergy* (Detroit: Wayne State University Press, 1970); Merton Strommen, et al., eds., *A Study of Generations* (Minneapolis: Augsburg, 1972); and Carl F. Reuss, *Profiles of Lutherans in the USA* (Minneapolis: Augsburg, 1982).

2. Reuss, *Profiles of Lutherans*, 91–101.

3. Strommen, *Study of Generations*, 258.

4. Reuss, *Profiles of Lutherans*, 34.

5. "In Perspective: Lutheran Cooperation," *Lutheran Witness*, 83, no. 25 (December 8, 1964): 3–4.

6. *Christianity Today*, August 31, 1973, cited in Carter Lindberg, *The Third Reformation? Charismatic Movements and the Lutheran Tradition* (Macon, GA: Mercer University Press, 1983), 193.

7. Jeff Johnson, *Black Christians: The Untold Lutheran Story* (St. Louis: Concordia, 1991), 198–220.

8. Ralph Michaels, "A Case for Political Conservatism," *Lutheran Forum* 4, no. 10 (November 1970): 12, cited in David Settje, "Lutheran Responses to the Vietnam War, 1964–75," in *Lutherans in America—A Twentieth-Century Retrospective (20th Meeting, 2000): Essays and Reports of the Lutheran Historical Conference* 19 (2005): 23–24.

9. J. Louise Owens, "Vietnam Opinions," *The Lutheran* 5, no. 21 (October 11, 1967): 49, in Settje, "Lutheran Responses," 44.

10. Reuss, *Profiles of Lutherans*, 98.

11. Department of Theological Study, LCUSA, "A Statement of Findings Related to the Requested Study on the Subject of the Ordination of Women," March 7–8, 1969, in Raymond Tiemeyer, ed., *The Ordination of Women* (Minneapolis: Augsburg, 1970), 52.

12. *Proceedings of the Annual Convention of the Lutheran Church–Missouri Synod, 1971*, 136. See Mary Todd, *Authority Vested: A Story of Identity and Change in the Lutheran Church–Missouri Synod* (Grand Rapids: Eerdmans, 2000), 221.

13. E. Clifford Nelson, ed., *The Lutherans in North America* (Philadelphia: Fortress Press, 1975), 539.

14. John Tietjen, *Memoirs in Exile: Confessional Hope and Institutional Conflict* (Minneapolis: Fortress Press, 1990), 269.

15. The president of the ALC, David Preus, and the president of the LCMS, J. A. O. (Jack) Preus were related, and knew each other well. This made the strained ALC–LCMS relations over fellowship in the 1970s all the more interesting. See David W. Preus, *Pastor and President: Reflections of a Lutheran Churchman* (Minneapolis: Lutheran University Press, 2011), 72–81.

16. Lutherans, it seems, are fond of acronyms, but so far as this author knows, TCFTSOT-CAOOM is the longest and most complicated one in American Lutheran history.

17. "Statement by Rev. Emil Jaech," in *Proceedings of the Annual Convention of the Lutheran Church–Missouri Synod, 1975*," 77, cited in August R. Sueflow, ed., *Heritage in Motion: Readings in the History of the Lutheran Church–Missouri Synod* (St. Louis: Concordia, 1998), 187.

18. "Letter of Donald Hinchey," *Lutheran Witness* 94, no. 16 (October 5, 1975): 21.

19. Betty Ulrich, "A sledge to pound tacks," *Lutheran Standard* 13, no. 10 (May 1973): 9, quoted in Elisabeth Annice Unruh, "Equality Denied: Lutheran Responses to the Equal Rights Amendment," *Journal of the Lutheran Historical Conference* 1 (2011): 225.

20. James A. Sherer, *Mission and Unity in Lutheranism: A Study in Confession and Ecumenicity* (Philadelphia: Fortress Press, 1969), 3.

21. Private email correspondence with former ALC President David Preus, March 29, 2014.

22. Jon Pahl, *The Hopes and Dreams of All: The International Walther League and Lutheran Youth in American Culture, 1893–1993* (Chicago: Wheat Ridge Ministries, 1993), 277.

23. Preus, *Pastor and President*, 88.

Excursus 11

LUTHERAN COOPERATION

By the beginning of the twentieth century, American Lutheranism had grown to be the third largest Protestant family in the United States, after the Baptists and Methodists. Fueled by the arrival of millions of Lutheran immigrants from Europe, there were more than two dozen different Lutheran denominations divided by language and theology. Most wanted to become American and take their rightful place in the American religious scene, but their divisions made them less ineffective on the national level.

During the First World War, these Lutherans sought to demonstrate their patriotism and to support their troops, but this required a degree of mutual coordination between the various Lutheran groups that had previously not existed. In 1917, they formed the National Lutheran Commission for Soldiers and Sailors Welfare to raise funds and employ chaplains for the military camps. As that war was winding down in 1918, eight Lutheran denominations formed a more permanent organization, the National Lutheran Council (NLC), to explore more ways in which American Lutheran groups could cooperate and do their work more efficiently. One of the largest Lutheran denominations, the Missouri Synod, did not formally join the NLC, but did coordinate some of its efforts with the new group.

There were many things for the NLC to do, things better accomplished in a coordinated fashion rather than separately. Two initial concerns were the support for and reconstruction of war-ravaged Lutheran churches, and support for Lutheran missions in Africa and Asia. It also coordinated many things domestically, including Lutheran efforts in education, social services, and home-mission expansion, as well as services such as planning and publicity. The NLC became a clearinghouse and coordinating center for the great expansion of this work that American Lutherans carried out in the first part of the twentieth century.

During the Second World War (1941–1945), the NLC again mobilized American Lutherans for action, to support the troops, coordinate chaplains, provide assistance at home for the workers in the new defense industries, and other similar tasks. During and after this war, it helped sponsor a major fund drive, Lutheran World Action, which raised millions of dollars for war relief. Together with the Missouri Synod, the NLC cooperated in a new group, Lutheran World Relief, which shipped over a billion pounds of relief supplies to troubled areas around the world in the twenty years after 1945. The NLC also coordinated the assistance for European Lutheran churches, and resettled war refugees in the United States and Canada.

During and after World War II, the NLC also broadened its work in North America. Important areas of this service included campus ministry, Lutheran higher education, social-welfare services, aid to migrants and refugees, and planning and coordination for the massive postwar founding of new Lutheran congregations, especially in the new suburbs, and in the growing areas of the South and West. One particular area was the expansion of Lutheran media presence through radio, television, and even motion pictures.

As American Lutherans continued to work together, many thought that this successful cooperation demonstrated the viability of the merger of American Lutheran denominations, and throughout the 1940s and 1950s, merger negotiations gained ground. At this time, it proved impossible to get all eight Lutheran groups into a single merger, so in 1960 four groups formed the American Lutheran Church (ALC), and in 1962 four others formed the Lutheran Church in America (LCA). These mergers were made possible in part by the relationships and cooperative efforts that had been accomplished through the years by the NLC.

In the early 1960s, the ALC, LCA, and Missouri Synod forged even closer working relationships in many of these minstry areas, and by 1966 they had decided to form a new cooperative body, the Lutheran Council in the USA (LCUSA), which took over and expanded many of the functions of the NLC. LCUSA embodied an unprecedented level of cooperation between Lutherans in America, representing over 95 percent of all American Lutherans. LCUSA also continued and expanded the traditional efforts of the NLC in areas of social service, education and campus ministry, assistance to refugees and immigrants, and many other activities. LCUSA became an important agency for planning and research, for historical and archival preservation, and as the public face of American Lutheranism.

As the ALC and LCA moved toward merger into the Evangelical Lutheran Church in America (ELCA) in 1988, the continuing need for LCUSA was diminished. The new ELCA and the Lutheran Church–Missouri Synod decided that many of LCUSA's functions could now be handled on a bilateral basis between the two denominations, or spun off into other groups, so LCUSA came to an end. But these two groups, NLC and LCUSA, played an important role in the larger development of twentieth-century American Lutheranism, and in its ministries to the nation and the world.

Chapter 12

Uncertain Present, Uneasy Future, 1988–2013

H istorians are rightly uneasy when faced with the prospect of describing recent or contemporary events and then analyzing them. There are far too many examples of such descriptions and analyses turning out not only to be wrong, but in some cases spectacularly wrong. Those who do historical analysis customarily wait for an extended period of time before pronouncing judgments on the past, hoping that time will clear away the "fog" of present perceptions, or at least that the principal actors will have died so that no one can contest the analysis. But it is perhaps at least valuable to set out a record of recent historical events that seem, at the time of writing, to be important, and to make a cautious initial attempt at describing them and suggesting major trends. This work will follow Martin Luther's advice to "sin boldly," so that perhaps future readers and historians will themselves have the chance to consider the recent history of American Lutheranism and, where necessary, to correct this work's mistakes.

The last quarter-century of American history, 1988 to 2013, is difficult to encapsulate in a few ideas or phrases. Certainly, the United States continued to grow in terms of population, from 244 million people in 1988 to 315 million by 2012. This period of time has seen economic growth, even booms, followed by deep recessions, caused in part by collapses in the stock market, in 2000–2001, and the housing market, in 2007–2009. The full effects of the immigration reforms of 1965 and 1986 have begun to be noticed, with legal immigration at about seven to eight million persons in each of the decades of the 1980s and 1990s, with an additional untold number of illegal immigrants. The technological or digital revolution has transformed American society in ways that have yet to be calculated, but it is clear that the prevalence of personal computers, tablets, smartphones, and other mobile devices, along with the World-Wide Web and Internet, have had a tremendous effect on everyday life. American society has grown more diverse in many ways, including racially, with Hispanic Americans becoming the largest minority group in the country. Since the terrorist attacks of September 11, 2001, the United States has been deeply involved in a "war against terrorism," including extended wars in Iraq and Afghanistan. Social and cultural trends are difficult to quantify from this vantage point, but it is clear that they have changed in important ways since 1988.

The situation of religion in America has also grown and developed since 1988. Trends from the recent past have continued, with the mainline Protestant denominations continuing to lose members and influence, while evangelical groups have grown or at least held their own, buoyed by the explosive growth of large, non-denominational "megachurches," that is, those congregations with over two thousand worshipers each Sunday. The major Protestant consolidations of midcentury are complete, but they occurred just as there was a major cultural shift away from "big" entities and a flattening of hierarchical structures. Quite surprisingly to some, the immigration boom has had the effect of strengthening Christianity in America. Two-thirds of all immigrants were already Christians when they entered the United States, while a number of others converted once in the United States. These new arrivals have meant numerical stability for Roman Catholicism and growth for evangelical groups, such as the Assemblies of God. Only 15 percent of immigrants are Hindus, Muslims, or Buddhists, but their arrival has meant a noticeable proliferation of temples and mosques, especially in metropolitan areas. Overall, the numbers for membership in organized religion (two-thirds of Americans) and those believing in some sort of God (about 90 percent) have remained steady, but internal fluctuations have caused some observers to see religious decline. Recent surveys showing a rise in the number of Americans claiming "no religion," also known as the "Nones," have attracted some attention, but the overall trends are far from clear. There are also significant regional variations in all these patterns.

American Lutherans shared in many of these larger trends, although they have tended to lag behind other Protestant groups in the date that these trends appear in their midst. The whole push for merger and consolidation that characterized the twentieth century for Lutherans essentially came to an end in 1988 with the formation of the ELCA; a further consolidation to bring together the ELCA and LCMS is highly unlikely—in fact, the two groups are cooperating in increasingly fewer areas. The numerical decline of American Lutheranism, which started modestly in the 1970s, has become more pronounced, and is a dangerous trend that Lutheran denominations and most congregations seem unable to address. From about 8.5 million baptized Lutherans in America in 1988, the latest figures show a total of 7.5 million baptized in 2010, lessening the Lutheran share of the religion "market" from 3.5 percent in 1988 to 2.4 percent in 2010. In contrast, the number of Lutherans in Africa has grown dramatically (18.7 million in 2009), so that there are now more than twice as many Lutherans in Africa than in the United States. On the financial side, giving to local Lutheran congregations is generally steady, though benevolent giving to the denominations and related causes is down substantially.

The beginnings of the ELCA in 1988 were rocky, and the denomination itself has continued to suffer one major controversy after another (many self-inflicted), including over the doctrine of the ministry, over ecumenical relations, and especially over positions on human sexuality. The ELCA has had to go through several painful rounds of reorganization and budget cutting on the national and synodical levels. Benevolent giving to the national ELCA, which was around $65 million in the 1990s, and up as high as $70 million by 2000, had dropped to $50 million by 2012, which in real dollars means a decline in giving of 60 percent.[1] Membership in the ELCA has declined from 5.2 million members at its beginning in 1988 to 3.95 million members in 2012.[2] During the decade of the 2000s, disaffected ELCA congregations who opposed ELCA positions on ecumenism and on human sexuality began to leave the denomination in large numbers. These actions led to a sort of "slow-motion" schism through the decade, resulting in the largest Lutheran schism since the General Council was formed in 1867, and one of the largest Protestant schisms in America since that time. Those who left formed two new American Lutheran denominations, the Lutheran Congregations for Mission in Christ (LCMC) in 2001, and the North American Lutheran Church (NALC) in 2010, with a combined membership of 450,000 in over one thousand congregations. The LCMS has not suffered such dramatic losses as the ELCA, but still has declined from 2.7 million members in 1988 to 2.3 million members in 2010, and its benevolent giving has been flat, which also means a significant decline in real dollars. It has continued to battle internally, however, with certain groups charging that other Missourians are not yet conservative enough, and ready to pounce on any sign of possible "unionism."

Much of this Lutheran malaise mirrors dramatic ways in which Americans relate to religious denominations in general. The former patterns of institutional uniformity and loyalty declined dramatically in the final decades of the twentieth century, and most Americans now rank many other factors much higher than denominational label when choosing a congregation. Lutheran congregations themselves have become much more diverse; if one were to select and attend a random dozen Lutheran congregations in any major metropolitan area, one would find an amazing array of different worship experiences and congregational patterns. Many congregations have, in effect, positioned themselves in "niche markets," emphasizing distinctive types of worship and activities to attract a certain variety of potential members.

The Consolidation of the ELCA

The ELCA began in January 1988 with high hopes and great expectations. It also began with completely unrealistic budget and revenue projections, with a complex, some said bloated, administrative structure, and with nagging and potentially divisive internal issues bequeathed to it by the CNLC, which could not figure how to resolve them. All these difficulties were in the context of larger societal challenges; one observer suggested the ELCA launch was troubled by "Loss of confidence in large institutions, high degrees of individualism, gay/lesbian issues, high visibility and forthright demands by women and minorities, the appeal of fundamentalism to a harried populace—all mitigated against a smooth start."[3] The ELCA also started out without most of the experienced national leaders and staff members of the three predecessor denominations. The decision to locate the ELCA national headquarters in Chicago meant that officials and staff from Minneapolis, Philadelphia, and New York were less likely to make the move. Many other staffers complained that they were not even given the chance to move; whatever the case, the ELCA lost a generation of seasoned leaders and staff, perhaps another factor in the rocky transition.

The structural issues were perhaps the biggest initial problem. The CNLC recognized that the three predecessor church bodies would need a significant amount of money to conclude their operations, as well as to fund the start of the new ELCA, and budgeted $112 million to cover the costs. That was not enough to keep the ELCA from falling $15.8 million in the "red" in 1988; and sizable deficits in the two subsequent years drained a $21.6 million reserve fund from the previous denominations. Presiding Bishop Herbert Chilstrom was forced to initiate substantial budgetary reductions that trimmed budgets from $87 million in 1989 to $70 million in 1995, with corresponding reductions in staff and in mission support. There are a number of factors that might account for the loss of revenue, but perhaps the most important aspect was the structure of the ELCA itself. In order to satisfy critics who worried about the new denomination being too centralized and "remote," the

CNLC approved a costly, multilayered structure that was built on sixty-five smaller synods and nine larger regional units, all under the national structure. There is some evidence that while congregational giving to the synods rose annually, much of the increase was absorbed on that middle level and never reached the national office. One calculation in 1991 was that the new ELCA was receiving $25 to $35 million less income than the three predecessor bodies might have expected.[4] This might have been anticipated, as similar problems dogged the history of the LCA and ALC through the first decade of their existence.

It is always difficult to ascertain the specific reasons why giving to a denomination declines; actually, there may be many reasons. Some people choose to direct their benevolence dollars to local projects; they could be dissatisfied with national priorities; or they could simply be concerned with local, congregational budget issues. And certainly, the ELCA was not alone in its troubles; there were similar problems in other mainline Protestant denominations, although not to the level as in the ELCA. The loss of funding for staff and programs was a troubling and discouraging development for the new church, launched with such fanfare and expectations. One observer put part of the blame on the CNLC itself, in its quest to create a dramatically "new" denomination: "Lutherans are basically conservative, both politically and theologically, yet the new church was focused much on 'newness.'"[5] Perhaps impatient with the rate of change, elements in the CNLC and the new ELCA attempted to "jump-start" the pace of change, bypassing the old structures and ways of doing things. One of the most important, and controversial, elements of this newness was the insistence on binding quotas for equal representation on all levels, synodical and national. There was a mandated balance of men and women, lay and clergy, and minorities (racial and linguistic) on all levels of the church. While this was perhaps an admirable goal, it created large amounts of hard feelings and, ironically, often siphoned minority and female leadership away from local congregations.

Other issues, left over from the CNLC and from predecessor denominations, also troubled the new ELCA. One of the thorniest issues in the merger was the question of the nature of the ministry, especially different forms of ordained and nonordained rostered leadership. To be fair, this had been a perennial issue in American Lutheranism. Each denomination had its own special categories: the rostered teachers of the AELC, the deaconesses in the LCA, and lay rostered personnel in the ALC. Unable to reconcile these and other theological issues about the nature of the ministry, the CNLC decided to limit rostering to ordained individuals for a period of six years, until the ELCA could complete a major study of the ministry to resolve these issues.

Another difficult and very public issue was that of sexuality, especially the ordination of noncelibate gay and lesbian pastors, which was sparked by a case of three such candidates for ordination from San Francisco. In 1988, three male certified pastoral candidates from Pacific Lutheran Theological Seminary announced publicly that they were gay and were subsequently denied calls. In 1990, two local California congregations called two lesbian women in a committed relationship and a noncelibate gay male, and ordained them independently of the local synod and of ELCA policy. The candidates refused to promise to adhere ELCA regulations requiring celibacy for nonmarried pastors, and these independent (or irregular) ordinations led to the suspension of these congregations from the ELCA. The uproar was intense, both from supporters and opponents of these actions, and the ELCA was convulsed by controversy over the issue of homosexuality. Although personally sympathetic to the cause of the ordination of gays and lesbians, Bishop Chilstrom did enforce the standing rules and the actions against the California congregations, but this issue did not die away.

Issues in the Missouri Synod

The difficulty in tracking the recent issues in the LCMS is the question of nomenclature, or, what to call the various factions and groups. To use the terms *moderate* or *conservative* is problematic at best, because these terms are loaded with meanings, many of them pejorative. A further complication is that there is no scale by which to judge them: "moderate" in regards to what? Or in relation to whom? To use the term *moderate*, for example, to denote those who left the LCMS in the 1970s is a problem. As their subsequent history unfolded, some of the AELC moderates actually turned out to be rather conservative in the ELCA, while many others eventually became quite liberal; these AELC theologians and pastors came to have an influence in the new denomination beyond what their numbers might have indicated. As has been seen, there were many more "moderates" who remained in the LCMS and continued to support its theological positions. The terms *moderate* and *conservative* in the LCMS, then, seem to be situated on a scale of relative conservativeness, or moderate in the degree to which one is open to the outside world. Some on the more conservative side of the LCMS tend to scour the moves and the motives of those who are judged less conservative, searching for the tiniest hint of impending nonorthodoxy. The levels of internal distrust and suspicion seemed to be intense at times.

After twelve years as LCMS president, J. A. O. Preus stepped down from his position in 1981. His last years in office were marked by struggle and conflict with elements of the very conservative movement that had elected him in the first place, and it made the internal development of the synod very difficult and complicated in the 1980s and 1990s. One historian of the LCMS summarized: "With moderates defeated and exiled, conservatives had the synod in their hands, but they still needed heretics to hunt and a church to purify. . . . For twenty years following the church consumed itself with charges and counter charges, sometimes about liberals but often conservative-against-conservative."[6] There is a sense that this last statement might be overstated; certainly, the LCMS continued to do good ministry in many areas, but it does explain an air of great political caution and reticence that has existed in the LCMS since the 1970s.

In 1981, Ralph Bohlmann, one of the "Faithful Five" Concordia faculty who remained in St. Louis after the Seminex walkout, was elected president of the LCMS. Through his term, he was attacked increasingly as a moderate, and was drawn into an ongoing battle with Robert Preus, brother of J. A. O. Preus, and president of Concordia Theological Seminary, Fort Wayne, Indiana. At the 1989 LCMS convention, Bohlmann was narrowly defeated for reelection by a more conservative candidate, Alvin Barry, one of the LCMS district presidents. The Barry presidency was marked both by a more conservative tone and by increased intraconservative rivalries, often over issues of ministry and leadership. Tensions were also stoked by an abortive proposal in 1998 by a blue-ribbon committee to restructure the synod, which critics from a number of sides interpreted as an attempt to locate more power in the president's office.

Barry died in 2001, just before the LCMS convention, leading to the election of someone considered more moderate, Gerald Kieschnick. He immediately found himself in trouble for authorizing Atlantic District president David Benke to participate in a prayer event at Yankee Stadium to commemorate the terrorist attacks of September 11, 2001. Several pastors filed charges against both Kieschnick and Benke, and although both were eventually acquitted, the rancor over the issue remained. In 2010, Matthew Harrison was elected as the new LCMS president.

Denominational Culture and Factionalism

Shifting contemporary social and religious patterns have deeply affected the organization of the large Protestant denominations, especially in the ways that they relate internally and externally. The modern, centralized, and bureaucratized mainline Protestant denomination is largely the product of the middle decades of the twentieth century; it parallels the development of the modern business corporation. Centralized planning and economies of scale were intended to introduce efficiency into organizational operations, and the size of the new entities was designed for them to be able to dominate the marketplace, whether that market was commercial or, in this case, religious. The American Protestant urge for merger—some might say it was a mania—was at least partially concerned with developing larger entities in order to fulfill their mission more efficiently, reduce "needless duplication and rivalry," and to be able to have a strong and united voice with which to influence American public opinion. There was also, in part, a hegemonic element to all this. The development of the big mainline Protestant denominations was partially in response to the breakaway groups of evangelicals and fundamentalists that left during the 1930s and 1940s; "bigness" was also a way to freeze them out of competition and public life.

American Lutherans came late to this movement toward the large, centralized denomination; the formation of the ELCA in 1988 was perhaps the last major Protestant denominational merger; certainly it was the last one of the twentieth century. This development also suggests some of the reasons for anxiety within the Missouri Synod during the twentieth century, with one portion of the synod perhaps worried that they were "missing out" on the merger process and another portion worried that the LCMS would lose influence to the larger ELCA. However it may have played out, Lutherans came to the movement of the large Protestant denominations at just about the time that this movement was collapsing, beginning in the late 1960s. In the last third of the twentieth century, American businesses realized that the large, centralized corporate model was not working; largeness reduced innovation, insulated officials and staff from customer feedback, dampened the ability to respond nimbly to changing conditions, and cost too much. So, late in the twentieth century, corporations started to change by spinning off divisions, reducing and decentralizing bureaucracies, and refocusing their activities for a better sense of their core mission. American Protestant denominations, including the ELCA and LCMS, have been much slower to recognize these trends and react to them, although reductions in national benevolence giving are forcing these changes upon them.

Another factor about the size of the two large American Lutheran denominations, as they presently exist, is the shift of the primary location of competition and contention from being external to being internal. When there were twelve or fifteen good-sized American Lutheran denominations, as was the case around 1900, these individual denominations had a relatively greater degree of internal theological and cultural coherence (note the word *relatively*), and much of the competitive focus was directed at other, outside groups; that is, other American Lutheran denominations. Each denomination had its own specific identity, and one could join or transfer to the group that most closely matched one's own position or principles. With growth (LCMS) and merger (ELCA), the loci for competition and contention shifted inwards;

now, disputed questions were being fought out within the denomination and against other parties within one's own group. Merger actually encouraged this type of contention, since various groups thought and feared that their particular positions would be lost in the new entity because of the dominance of others in the new denomination.

What this has meant is the rise of internal factionalism (whether organized or not) within the recent history of the LCMS and ELCA. These multimillion-member denominations are probably just too large to have a single, coherent identity but, rather, are marked by the shifting competition and alliances of internal groups, all seeking to make sure their voices are heard and their concerns are addressed. The late twentieth-century American cultural loss of faith in large entities (business, government, or religious) has probably exacerbated this trend; the practice of being loyal to, and taking your identity from, participation in an organized group has seriously declined. Full commitment to the organization is difficult when one held serious differences with the organization as a whole.

The internal development of both the ELCA and LCMS has been greatly affected by these trends, and to understand their recent history, one must understand the nature of the factions involved. First, the ELCA, and then the LCMS. The ELCA itself is a broad coalition of diverse religious and social views, and the range of ideological positions runs the gamut from conservative to liberal (recognizing the limitations of these terms). It is sometimes tempting to trace this diversity back to the positions within predecessor denominations, and say, for example, that the ALC was more conservative and the LCA more liberal, but such judgments are too sweeping to mean much. For example, Mark Hanson, presiding bishop of the ELCA from 2001 to 2013, was considered liberal, but his roots are in the low-church, Haugean movement in the ALC.

One group within the ELCA is a broad range of congregationally oriented, culturally conservative, low-church pastors and members, mainly but not exclusively in the upper Midwest. They are not generally organized into particular groups, but their voice can be heard in a number of synods and organizations. One might refer to them as "denominational" Lutherans, who are loyal to their Lutheran heritage(s) and yet see nothing wrong with being identified as Protestants. Charismatic Lutherans would be a subgroup within this section. Another group would be the self-identified "Evangelical Catholics," who are marked by a high view of the ministerial office and historical liturgical forms of worship. Many of them see Lutheranism not so much as a permanent denomination, but as a "movement" within the church universal, with the ecumenical goal of uniting the whole Christian movement. This movement itself has different wings; some Evangelical Catholics are quite liberal socially, while others are conservative. Some in this movement, especially the more conservative, have expressed their displeasure with contemporary American Lutheranism by "swimming the Tiber," that is, going over to the Roman Catholic Church. Another group within the ELCA is the Lutheran Left; traditionally, members of this group have been outsiders, urging more liberal religious and social positions on the churches; their numbers were greatly augmented during the 1960s and 1970s. The interesting thing here is how, through the CNLC merger process, and especially by means of the quota system, this group moved from "outside" to "inside" the ELCA, dominating the synodical and national organizations of the denomination. Finally, there are what might be called the "pragmatic institutional loyalists," those within the ELCA for whom the denomination itself provides a primary identity; these individuals are often those working to build coalitions and compromises among these various factions to enable the denomination to keep operating. Much of the history of the ELCA itself can be explained through the interaction of these four distinct groups and the shifting alliances between them.

Within the LCMS, there are similar groups, though their complexion and nature differ within this denomination. On the conservative side, there is a group which is similar to the ELCA's Evangelical Catholics, devoted to a (very) high view of ministerial authority and to formal liturgical practices, although socially they are very traditional. Unlike their ELCA counterparts, however, this group is also greatly devoted to a strict Lutheran confessionalism, especially to seventeenth-century Lutheran Orthodox theology. There are other movements of strict confessionalism in the LCMS that are less concerned with ministerial office and formal liturgy, but share the concerns about keeping Missouri theologically "pure," and which tend to be rather active in attacking any signs they see of incipient "liberalism" within the synod. A number of these strict conservative groups are politically quite well organized and savvy, producing "slates" of conservative candidates for synodical office and aggressively organizing to elect them. Among the moderate conservatives in Missouri a number of organized groups, such as Daystar and Jesus First, have organized to counter the influence of the strict conservatives. Many of these groups represent the old-line LCMS, especially concern for congregational autonomy within the synod itself. Part of this moderate conservative wing also consists of those pastors and congregations who have adopted elements of the church-growth movement, which focuses on evangelism, contemporary worship, and other elements to reach out to the "unchurched." Of course, like the ELCA, the LCMS has its own group of pragmatic denominational loyalists, seeking to control power and broker compromises within the denomination.

This may seem like a rather long and theoretical discussion of contemporary Protestant denominationalism and the place of American Lutheranism within it, and perhaps it is. But understanding these dynamics is crucial to a better knowledge of contemporary American Lutheranism, not only what they fight about, but *how* they go about fighting. Many lay Lutherans, pastors, and congregations continue on with the faithful ministry that they carry out in their local communities, doing the day-to-day work of the church. They try to stay out of the way of divisive issues and church politics, but often these questions intrude into their local ministries, as conflicts that are national in scope can become local, too. In this media-saturated age, it is almost impossible to escape the local implications of national politics, secular or religious.

Recent Developments in the ELCA and LCMS

As has been alluded to previously, the CNLC decided to move the merger process along by deferring certain intractable problems for a later date, suggesting that the new ELCA set up a process to deal with them. Chief among these were questions of ministry, ecumenism, and sexuality; the ELCA was left in its formative years to handle these "hot" issues, just at the time that it was also dealing with serious financial and organizational problems.

The question of ministry was the most structurally important of these three issues. Throughout its history, American Lutherans had argued about the doctrinal and practical issues surrounding the ministry. Was the ministry a divine call to the pastor, or was it the delegation of the powers implicit in the priesthood of all believers to a selected leader? What happens to a pastor without a call, or designated for some special ministry, such as teaching and administration? Is the ordained ministry limited to those called to preach the word and administer the sacraments? What about those called to service, such as rostered teachers and deaconesses? Each of the three predecessor denominations had different groups of rostered lay leaders, and it was unclear how the new church would deal with them.

The traditional Lutheran understanding was that there was a single ordained ministry of word and sacrament. However, this does not always account for bishops and rostered laypeople. Some Lutherans of a more high-church, Evangelical Catholic leaning thought that this study would be a good opportunity to bring into American Lutheranism the Roman Catholic and Episcopalian idea of a three-tiered structure of ministry, of separately ordained bishops, pastors or priests, and deacons. This might solve some problems, perhaps, but, argued the critics, it would import an alien understanding of the ministry into American Lutheranism. The Task Force for the Study of the Ministry (1989–1993) brought forth a series of recommendations to the ELCA in 1993, which argued for a separate category of ordained "diaconal ministers," which was not adopted; instead, the diaconal ministers were "certified and approved" for their own separate roster. The term *bishop* was retained, but without an additional "ordination"; rather, the term used was "installation." The issues involved were complex, and sometimes indistinct or ambiguous terminology was employed, solving the present problem but allowing for more conflict in the future. The questions would surface again in regard to ecumenical relations with the Protestant Episcopal Church in the late 1990s.

The Study on Ecumenism was a largely theoretical affair, trying to straighten out the various ecumenical arrangements of the various bilateral dialogues, and establishing a policy for ecumenical work in the ELCA. Internal tensions revolved around the unwritten implications of the statement itself, whether the document would incline the ELCA more toward the Roman Catholic and Episcopal churches, or toward other Protestant churches, such as the Reformed and Methodist. The statement, adopted in 1991, called for the ELCA to move toward "full communion," including interchange of ministries, whenever possible, a goal that would also come back to haunt the ELCA in the late 1990s.

While many lay Lutherans do not have strong opinions on polity issues such as ministry and ecumenism, thinking of these as things for pastors to argue about, there were very few Lutherans without some sort of opinion about the topic of sexuality— often very strongly held opinions. The irregular ordinations in California at the beginning of the ELCA were signs that advocates for the ordination of non-celibate gay and lesbian persons would attempt to make a strong push on this issue in the new church. A study commission to produce a new document and position paper on these issues was formed, with the intent of producing a document for the ELCA Churchwide Assembly in 1995. Most of the work on the commission was uncontroversial, but the issue of homosexuality was incendiary and volatile. The work of the commission was doomed when, in October 1993, an advance draft of its report, including language accepting of the ordination of gays and lesbians in monogamous relationships, was prematurely published in the St. Louis *Post-Dispatch*. A firestorm of criticism hit the media and the national offices, and many pastors and bishops felt blindsided. Although some wanted to continue the study process to its end, eventually it was decided to shelve the whole issue indefinitely. In this case, indefinitely meant about ten years.

For the LCMS, the initial adjustment in 1988 was to determine its relationship with the ELCA and, more importantly, to affirm its own separate identity in American Lutheranism apart from the now twice-larger new denomination. With all the hoopla going on about the new ELCA, the leaders of the LCMS had to remind the world that they continued to exist, that the ELCA did not speak for all American

Lutherans, and that they would stick to their guns and not rush into any form of fellowship without full doctrinal agreement. Samuel Nafzger, LCMS executive secretary for its powerful Commission on Theology and Church Relations, said at the time that this attention was "a wonderful opportunity at just this point in history to be what we are—a positive, forward-looking, Christ-centered, confessional Lutheran church—eager to share the Good News of the Gospel of Jesus Christ."[7] Although this was probably true, the LCMS had its share of conflicts and controversies after 1988, often having to do with lingering suspicions and internal politics that caused a great deal of continuing trauma.

One of the first controversies came in 1989, when the board of Concordia Theological Seminary, Fort Wayne, Indiana, voted to "honorably retire" its then-president, Robert Preus. Preus and many of his conservative allies were convinced that LCMS president Ralph Bohlmann was behind the action, an assertion that he denied. The case wound its way through the secular courts and through layers of the LCMS bureaucracy, until 1992, when the process came to a standstill. A compromise was brokered that allowed Preus to return for a temporary and limited appointment, but the controversy perhaps led to Bohlmann's defeat for reelection as synod president at the synod convention later that year. The editor of the *Lutheran Witness*, David Strand, suggested of Bohlmann: "His critics had long accused him . . . of [being] too soft on allegedly errant pastors and professors . . . that his opinions on the service of women in the church were questionable . . . and that his administration had sought to centralize authority."[8] Bohlmann had personally appointed a Presidential Commission on Women in the early 1980s, and the work of this group continued to worry synodical conservatives, even though it never did suggest that women be ordained as pastors; that "would not happened in God's lifetime," as one observer suggested. Even though the next president, Alvin Barry, kept the commission itself in operation, the whole "women's question" became bogged down in theological turf wars within the synod.

With the death of Barry in 2001, and the election of Gerald Kieschnick as synodical president, synod moderates were cheered, while conservatives fretted. The events surrounding district president David Benke and the 9/11 prayer service, mentioned above, exposed the LCMS to public disapproval, with many outsiders and more than a few insiders unable to believe that in a time of such extraordinary crisis, such rules could not be relaxed, even temporarily for the sake of public witness. The entire process of charges and proceedings against Kieschnick and Benke also exposed the LCMS to more criticism. But the issue had not been resolved, and surfaced all over again in 2012 because of a shooting rampage at a school in Newtown, Connecticut. A local LCMS pastor again participated in a community event, critics howled, and new LCMS President Matthew Harrison was caught in the crossfire between critics and supporters.

New Developments in American Lutheranism

Since the 1980s, there have been two interesting developments in American religion generally that have affected American Lutheranism as well: the rise of the Protestant "megachurches" and the parallel growth of new ethnic congregations, constituted by outreach to American minorities as well as to new immigrants from the global South. While these trends have mainly been located among the American evangelical denominations, their influence has spread within both the ELCA and LCMS. In the case of the megachurches, this rise has been occasioned mainly by entrepreneurial pastors working more or less independently, but the rise of ethnic ministries has been encouraged and funded to a large extent by the denominations themselves, seeking to diversify their membership racially.

Strictly speaking, a megachurch is by definition a congregation that averages over two thousand people in worship on a weekend; by the early 2000s, the ELCA had seven of these congregations, while the LCMS had four.[9] If the parameters are expanded to include congregations with between one and two thousand worshipers weekly, there would be thirty-six additional ELCA and thirty-four additional LCMS congregations considered as megachurches, for a total of eighty-one. This is all the more impressive when one considers that perhaps as many as half of all Lutheran congregations in the United States have fewer than one hundred worshipers.

There have always been a few very large Lutheran congregations, and some of these megachurches go back to the turn of the twentieth century; the largest Lutheran congregation, Mt. Olivet (ELCA) in Minneapolis, averaging six thousand worshipers a weekend, was founded in 1920. But the majority of these Lutheran megachurches were founded after 1970, and most of them achieved their size in the 1980s and 1990s. Many of these megachurches grew much more rapidly than the average Lutheran congregations; the ELCA megachurches collectively grew 37 percent in the period from 1993 to 2000, when most Lutheran congregations declined. Most of the Lutheran megachurches were founded and developed by a dynamic, visionary lead pastor, who built the church up to its present size; most are suburban or exurban in location, mainly in the Midwest, although a significant number of them are found in the Southwest—Arizona, Nevada, and California.

A common characteristic of these megachurches is that many of them follow the traits and philosophy of the church-growth movement: they worship in a casual, contemporary style; pay close attention to inviting and retaining religious "seekers"; provide numerous small-group affiliation activities for members; and challenge their members to be involved by donating significant time and money to the congregation. They often take on the dominant traits of the evangelical megachurches around them, with their leaders frequently moving in the same or similar circles. In the ELCA, these megachurches are, fairly consistently, more theologically and socially conservative than the denomination itself; in the LCMS, most of these megachurches tend toward the moderate side of church politics.

It is difficult to assess the impact of these Lutheran megachurches on the wider American Lutheran scene. For one thing, they are a relatively new phenomenon, and it remains to be seen how they track into the future. But as well, many of these congregations are not always deeply integrated in the common life of the denominations to which they belong. Some Lutheran megachurches have their own ministry missions that they support directly, and some even train many of their own staff internally. As shall be seen later, a number of the ELCA megachurches became involved in the internal disputes within the denomination over ministry and sexuality, and some of the largest ELCA megachurches have left the denomination over these issues. The LCMS megachurches seemingly have avoided becoming too involved in internal LCMS scuffles, focusing their energy in other directions. To some extent, these megachurches are functionally independent of the Lutheran denominations; the ELCA and LCMS need the megachurches more than the megachurches need them.

With the rise of immigration since the 1965 and 1986 reforms, large numbers of people have settled in the United States, primarily from Latin America, but also from Asia, and a smaller but increasing number from Africa. As has been noted, about two-thirds of these immigrants are Christian already when they come to the United States, and a significant additional number convert to Christianity after they arrive, often those from Asia who have no religious background. In the case of Lutherans, there were already significant younger Lutheran churches in Asia and Africa, and growing Lutheran churches in Latin America. Given the numerical growth of immigration, and the increased pressure within the Lutheran denominations to diversify their membership racially and ethnically, these new immigrants, together with existing minority populations, were seen as prime targets. The major Lutheran denominations have expended a growing portion of their funding for home missions in developing and supporting minority congregations, usually with mixed success. At the founding of the ELCA, its stated goal was to reach a total membership of which 10 percent would be "persons of color or whose primary language is not English," while the LCMS had similar goals of doubling its African American population, and creating one thousand new cross-cultural ministries. These were laudable goals, but ones of which the denominations fell short. Nevertheless, as of 2000, the ELCA listed congregations worshiping in thirty-three different languages, while the LCMS reported twelve different, non-European languages.

African American Lutherans numbered more than 100,000 by 2000, and there were over 220 ordained African American pastors. These numbers actually saw their greatest increase in the 1960s and 1970s, and have remained roughly steady since then. Both denominations have created specific organizations for African Americans within their structures, but these and other efforts have too often been sporadic, with bursts of energy and enthusiasm followed by periods of inaction. The decline of national denominational budgets since the 1990s has meant that funding for minority congregations has also declined.

Although American Lutherans have been doing mission work in Latin America since the beginning of the twentieth century, the only sizable element of this ministry within the denominations is the ELCA Spanish-speaking congregations in Puerto Rico. There are several Lutheran denominations in Mexico, but the bulk of Hispanics in Lutheran congregations have come through their joining Lutheran congregations after coming to the United States, and not from the immigration of those who were already Lutheran. In the year 2000, the ELCA listed about 39,000 Hispanic members, with about 180 congregations reporting at least one service offered in Spanish. This was a 45 percent increase since 1988. The LCMS has about 120 Hispanic congregations, and reports almost one hundred "Hispanic workers." Both churches have separate organizations for the encouragement of Hispanic ministries and publish worship and educational materials in Spanish.

Asian immigration has increased rapidly since 1965, and both denominations show Asian-ethnic congregations: sixty-three congregations in eleven different languages in the ELCA, and seven different worship languages in the LCMS. Most of these Asian American Lutherans are East Asian (Chinese, Japanese, and Korean), many of them from already-established Lutheran churches in Asia. The LCMS has been particularly strong in its Korean congregations. Lutheranism has also made some inroads into the Southeast Asian refugee populations (Hmong, Vietnamese, Laotian), especially in Minnesota. There is a small number of South Asian (India and Pakistan) and Arab Lutheran congregations as well.

Some of the fastest-growing Lutheran churches are in Africa, especially East Africa, and, with the small but rising numbers of African immigrants, American Lutheranism is seeing increasing numbers of African congregations, especially Ethiopian, Sudanese, Liberian, Ghanaian, and Nigerian. These congregations usually consist of Lutheran immigrants or refugees from Africa who have strong ties back to the Lutheran churches in their home countries.

Often these minority and new immigrant ministries are built on the personal efforts of a few key leaders, who then are responsible for recruiting and developing other pastors and congregations to affiliate with the Lutheran denominations. One major problem, especially for the ELCA, is that many of these minority and immigrant pastors and congregations are quite socially and theologically conservative, and because of recent decisions to which they are opposed, especially related to sexuality, a sizable number of them have withdrawn from the ELCA or have seen members defect from their congregations over these controversies.

One other important new development, at least in the ELCA, was the rise in the numbers of women ordained into the pastoral ministry and their corresponding rise into positions of prominence in that denomination. In 1991 there were a total of 1,400 women who were ordained pastors in the ELCA, or about eight percent of the total number of pastors. By the beginning of 2013, that number had grown to 3,849 women ordained pastors; this was twenty-three percent of the total number of pastors, and thirty-two percent of all active pastors (that is, not retired or unable to work). This number also included 212 ordained women who were members of racial or linguistic minority groups.[10] Although it appears that women pastors have not completely broken through the "glass ceiling" and into leadership in the larger ELCA congregations, they have increasingly been moving into synodical leadership as bishops. The first woman elected as an ELCA bishop was Pastor April Larson, who became the bishop of the LaCrosse Area Synod (Wisconsin) in 1992; by the summer of 2014 there were approximately ten female ELCA bishops. The most visible sign of women's leadership in the ELCA came in the summer of 2013, with the election of Bishop Elizabeth Eaton as the Presiding Bishop of the ELCA. Increasing numbers of women, lay and ordained, are assuming other leadership roles on the synodical and national levels, such as in elective offices and on synodical and national staffs.

Worship, Education, and Social Ministry

Of all the ways that American Lutheran congregations proclaim the gospel of Jesus Christ to the world, the most easily apparent and accessible to most people is their public worship. People judge a congregation by its music, its liturgy, and its preaching. Since these are so important, they are also often some of the most contentious items within Lutheranism, as people debate the various forms and functions of worship. Particularly sharp have been the "worship wars" of the last thirty-five years, pitting proponents of traditional forms of liturgical worship against those who champion new, "contemporary" forms of worship, with guitars, drums, and synthesizers.

This divide is not a simple one; there are different forms of both traditional and contemporary worship, and different models and theologies of worship on all sides.

Fifty years ago, the stress was on liturgical uniformity; the hope was that every Lutheran church would worship roughly in the same way, using a common set of worship materials. The denominational hymnal was seen as the unifying force that tied all these former immigrant churches together now as "American" Lutherans, and tied together Lutherans from Alaska to Florida. It has already been noted that hymnals themselves, both the *Service Book and Hymnal* of the 1950s and the *Lutheran Book of Worship* in the 1970s, were intended to pave the way for merger, on the assumption that commonality in worship would hopefully lead to living together in common denominational structures. But the events of the late 1960s and following have driven a diversification in worship styles and materials that seems only to be increasing.

The arguments of the "worship wars" seem reminiscent of the debates over the transition to the use of the English language among the ethnic denominations ninety years ago. On one side, advocates of traditional liturgical worship (organ music, traditional hymns) argue that these forms hold worshipers in the great traditions of Christianity, and are richly and deeply expressive of the core elements of Christian theology. They find contemporary worship to be shallow, trendy, and impermanent; nothing becomes as dated as the "relevance" of former years. On the other side, advocates for contemporary worship suggest that the use of new musical forms (guitars, drums, etc.) and new informal language and style speaks directly to the needs and concerns of present generations, especially youth, who otherwise would be turned off by organized religion. Contemporary advocates find traditional worship to be outmoded, overly complex, and off-putting to modern people—essentially an "in-group" behavior that fewer and fewer people understand or appreciate. These conflicts are often expressed within congregations themselves, leaving pastors and congregational leaders in a difficult position. Often a solution is to have separate services for each style on Sunday mornings, but this solution is not without its own difficulties.

From the 1990s forward, technology has dramatically shifted the worship of most Lutherans away from traditional hymnals, and introduced a diversity of worship materials and music into Lutheran worship. Computers allow congregations to arrange and edit worship materials and hymns in any way that suits them, which they then either print themselves or display on various types of screens in the sanctuary. The ubiquity of the Internet and music-licensing agreements allow congregations easily to access a much wider range of materials than ever before. Congregations now define themselves by their unique forms of worship, pointing to a particular "audience" for their worship style. There is one traditional-worship

Lutheran congregation in the Minneapolis-St. Paul area, for example, that advertises itself as the "Alternative to Alternative Worship." Especially in major metropolitan areas, one can find a wide array of different Lutheran worship styles, and one can affiliate with the style that "fits" best. Worship style, then, has become a marketing tool to attract individuals to one or another congregation.

Since bound and printed hymnals have a definite shelf life, probably twenty to thirty years, they either need to be reprinted, or have new ones replace them, so during the 1990s and 2000s each denomination developed its own new hymnal. The Wisconsin Evangelical Lutheran Synod (WELS) was the first to adopt a new hymnal, *Christian Worship*, in 1993, followed by *Evangelical Lutheran Worship* (ELCA) and the *Lutheran Service Book* (LCMS), both in 2006. There has been a great recent proliferation of American Lutheran hymnwriters and composers, with Herb Brokering, Marty Haugen, John Ylvisaker, and David and Susan Cherwin working in more contemporary styles, and Martin Franzmann and Jaroslav Vatja working more traditionally. These hymnals have also introduced American Lutherans to new hymns from Latin America, Africa, and Asia, as well as traditional and contemporary American hymns from other denominations. Some hymnwriters, such as Gracia Grindal, have been working to reintroduce neglected traditional Lutheran hymns from the Scandinavian traditions, as well as contemporary Scandinavian hymns and liturgies.

Lutheran educational institutions, especially colleges, universities, and seminaries, are also dealing with major changes in the last twenty-five years, including reduced funding from the denominations, greater diversity in students and faculty, and a corresponding and perennial process for reimagining and rethinking their Lutheran identity—and in some cases, whether such an identity continues to be useful or beneficial to that institution's own self-understanding and mission. Financially, all of these institutions have been stressed by the demands and the economic conditions of the past decades; to be competitive, many have felt it necessary to expand their student and revenue bases, to implement more specialized programs and expansive campus amenities, and to maximize all sources of income. Fundraising seemingly has become nearly a full-time job for most college and university presidents. Many of the elite Lutheran schools have survived and even thrived during this time, but some of the weaker schools have struggled to keep their doors open. A few of them have been lost to Lutheranism, including Waldorf College, Forest City, Iowa, which was sold to a for-profit school, and Dana College, Blair, Nebraska, which closed in 2010.

The ten LCMS colleges and universities have been organized together in the Concordia University system, formed in 1992, for the purposes of tying the institutions more closely to each other and to the synod, and to develop new programs and cooperation between them. It is also sometimes a source of contention, especially for those who fear that the system is a cover for tighter synodical control, especially over the content of teaching. The ten schools themselves range in size and financial health, and several of the schools are in perennial financial difficulty.

Lutheran seminaries are likewise stressed by financial issues and by theological controversies, but they themselves are much more tightly affected by the relative financial and theological health of the denominations they serve. Lacking a real opportunity to diversify, dependent on denominational support that is simultaneously decreasing, and unable to shift too much of the financial burden onto students whose educational debt-load is increasing, seminaries are faced with deep-seated, intractable issues. As the denominations and congregations they serve continue to contract, there is less need for full-time pastors and fewer congregations able to afford such ministries. This decline also put stress on the ELCA seminaries, with fewer pastoral candidates entering their programs. The need for new ethnic pastors, and those fluent in languages other than English, is rising, but these pastoral candidates do not always have the traditional educational background usually assumed by seminaries.

Starting in the 1970s and 1980s, the complexion of the seminary student population has been shifting. There was a large movement toward second-career, and thus older, seminarians through the 1980s and 1990s, although there has been a rebalancing of this trend in the last decade, with increasing numbers of younger students. In the ELCA seminaries, the large enrollment of women seminarians has shifted the complexion of these institutions. New pedagogical approaches and technologies have shifted the paradigms of seminary attendance and formation; distance learning and online classes, combined with short-term intensive classes, have allowed some students to remain in their local faith communities, where they minister while receiving further education for ministry. Both denominations have programs, such as the TEEM program in the ELCA, which offer alternate paths to ordination for students and minority congregational leaders who might not have the educational background to enter a traditional seminary program. Given their severe financial issues, several freestanding ELCA seminaries have recently sought affiliation with Lutheran colleges or universities. It is still an open question whether both the ELCA and LCMS have too many seminaries, and whether consolidation or closure loom on the horizon. Theological education is changing rapidly, and the Lutheran seminaries are attempting to keep up with the changes.

Many of the issues of identity, organization, and finance that affect the Lutheran educational institutions also are a part of the Lutheran network of social-service ministries and institutions. For a number of years, many of these institutions had been tied together regionally in networks of organizations called Lutheran Social Services (LSS) of whatever territory these are located; historically, the ELCA and LCMS had cooperated in these organizations. In 1997, a national organization, Lutheran Services in America, was formed, bringing together over three hundred different institutions into a single network, the largest such private network on the basis of revenue in the United States. These institutions together interact with some six million people every year, have an annual income over $18 billion, and employ nearly 250,000 workers. This is an impressive achievement of Lutherans in America, and a great legacy for all those who founded such institutions in the past, usually out of faith and hard work, and not much money.

Of course, as with every other segment of American Lutheranism, these social-ministry providers face contemporary issues. Although many of these institutions receive some funding from congregations, synods, and denominations, the bulk of their income comes through fees, insurance, private foundations, and, above all, from federal and state programs. Indeed, these institutions have, in general, become heavily dependent on governmental funding. But government aid and assistance is often a two-edged sword, as the government agencies demand standards and accountability from the Lutheran institutions. Generally, these standards are good and ensure professional care, but at times government demands, especially in areas involving ethical and social issues, can come into tension with the institution's own standards and beliefs, such as in the case of abortion. Lutheran social-ministry institutions have also struggled with the question of Lutheran identity, and its nature and utility, and there are inter-Lutheran disputes that also complicate matters. Finally, there is increasing consolidation in this area, leading to larger and larger institutions and systems.

Ecumenism and Controversy

With the formation of the ELCA in 1988, the century-long process of Lutheran fellowship and merger negotiations has come to an end, at least for the foreseeable future. In truth, the ELCA and LCMS have moved further apart, and cooperation between the two has diminished. With the formation of the ELCA, the need for the Lutheran Council in the USA also came to an end, as there were then only two church bodies left in it, and it was felt that whatever cooperation or coordination was necessary could be handled directly on a bilateral basis. But while merger and formal inter-Lutheran cooperation have faded, the activity seems to have shifted toward ecumenical ventures on a national and worldwide basis, especially in the

ELCA. The "urge to merge" seemingly has popped up again, but now in the form of ecumenical activities. American Lutherans have been very busy with dialogues, negotiations, and activities with other religious groups since the 1980s.

One of the longest-running dialogues has been between Lutherans and Roman Catholics, which have been underway nationally and internationally since the early 1960s. The early dialogues were focused on easier matters, but starting in the 1990s the international dialogue between the LWF and the Roman Catholic Church began to focus on one of the toughest theological issues between them, the doctrine of justification. Differences between Lutherans and Roman Catholics over this issue were at the heart of the sixteenth-century divisions, and both the Catholic and Lutheran doctrinal documents of that period contained harsh condemnations of the others' formulation of this doctrine. In what some have hailed as a "breakthrough," the LWF and the Roman Catholic Pontifical Council for the Promotion of Christian Unity came to a joint agreement in 1997, the "Joint Declaration on the Doctrine of Justification" (JDDJ), which was signed October 31, 1999, at Augsburg, Germany. This agreement claims to have reached a "common understanding of justification," and suggests that the mutual condemnations of the sixteenth century no longer apply. The exact status of this document is, however, unclear; it tends to trade on certain linguistic and theological ambiguities and there is also uncertainty about its official status within the two groups. The Commission on Theology and Church Relations in the LCMS welcomed certain clarifications in the dialogue, but observed: "Although change has taken place in the Roman Catholic church since Vatican II, JDDJ shows how very little headway has been made toward a genuine resolution of the differences between Lutherans and Roman Catholics on justification. This statement is not a 'breakthrough.'"[11] Changes in the Roman Catholic Church and ambiguous statements by some of its officials since 1997 have also called some of the elements of JDDJ into question.

Lutherans have also attempted to overcome other divisions that came out of the sixteenth-century Reformation. Ever since the Jewish Holocaust during World War II, Lutherans have been attempting to deal with the issue of antisemitism, and particularly the harsh writings against the Jews that Martin Luther produced later in his life, disappointed that the Jews of his day were rejecting the new Evangelical gospel. A series of ongoing discussions have taken place between Lutherans and Jews in America, leading to a number of actions formally repudiating Luther's harsh statements. Already in 1983, the LCMS formally disapproved of Martin Luther's "hostile attitude" toward the Jews, and in 1994 the ELCA Church Council voted to repudiate Luther's writings on the Jews. Also, through a series of talks and negotiations between the LWF and World Mennonite organizations, the LWF in 2010 was moved to "ask for forgiveness" from the Mennonites for the part that Lutherans had played historically in the persecution of Mennonite and other Anabaptist groups. In 2012, ELCA and American Mennonite officials formally recognized this action at an American Mennonite convention.

Although the LCMS has had participants in a number of these various dialogues, it is not a member of the LWF and has not formally participated in these agreements. The LCMS did play a leading role, however, in the formation of an organization parallel to that of the LWF, the International Lutheran Council, formed during a meeting in Guatemala in 1993. This organization is a grouping of more strictly confessional Lutheran churches around the world; the LCMS, the Evangelical Lutheran Church in Brazil, and the Lutheran Church–Canada are the largest of the member churches.

Following up on its 1991 Declaration of Ecumenism, and working off its stated goal of moving toward full communion wherever possible, the ELCA has moved toward ecumenical agreements with several American denominational groups. Full communion, here, means the full ability to interchange ministers between the two groups, and the ability to receive communion from each other as well. There have been in the ELCA three such agreements since 1991, with the Reformed, with the Methodists, and with the Episcopalians. In dialogue with the Reformed denominations, the Reformed Church of America, the United Church of Christ (UCC), and the Presbyterian Church (USA), the key issue revolved around historical and theological differences over the Lord's Supper. On the Lutheran side, there has also been concern about the noncreedal status of the UCC, and the fact that some UCC congregations hold dual status in the Unitarian Universalist Association. In 1997, the ELCA and the Reformed denominations reached the "Formula of Agreement," which was passed by the various groups, initiating full communion between them. Similarly, the ELCA–United Methodist talks produced a full communion agreement in 2009, and these two denominations are now also joined ecumenically. But the third ecumenical agreement, between the ELCA and the Episcopal Church, had a much more difficult path.

There had already been tensions during the 1980s within and among the predecessor bodies that created the ELCA, especially but not exclusively among conservatives in the ALC, who were upset about the direction of the CNLC, the loss of the term *inerrant* in its theological documents, quotas, and alleged centralization of power. At the time of the formation of the ELCA in 1988, about one hundred ALC congregations decided not to enter the ELCA; some of these joined smaller existing Lutheran groups, such as the Association of Free Lutheran Congregations, or formed their own new group, the Association of American Lutheran Churches

(AALC), in 1988. The AALC began to move toward greater relations with the LCMS during the 2000s, at which time some of its charismatic congregations left the AALC. Charismatic Lutherans, led by a Lutheran megachurch, North Heights Lutheran Church in Arden Hills, Minnesota, formed their own organization in 2002, the Alliance of Renewal Congregations.

The politics of ecumenism had long been a part of the formation of the ELCA. Although not strictly an ALC–LCA division as some have framed it, there was a sense that many low-church Lutherans in the ALC were more comfortable with the Reformed denominations, while high-church and Evangelical Catholics wished closer relations with the Episcopal denomination. Partially, this was also a search for outside allies to support their own internal preferences for the new ELCA. Since the question of the nature of the ministry was left by the CNLC for the new ELCA to resolve, these ecumenical questions became enmeshed with internal ELCA politics. The high-church, Evangelical Catholic party was deeply disappointed in the results of the Study of the Ministry, especially its failure to adopt the threefold ordained ministry, and to have "real" bishops in the new church.

As the Lutheran–Episcopal dialogues moved through the 1990s, they ran into difficulties over the question of how to achieve full communion and full inter-change of ministries between the two churches. The problem was that the Episco-pal Church, by its own self-definition, must have the threefold orders of ministry (deacon, priest, bishop), and these orders must be ordained by a bishop who is in the historic episcopate, the succession of bishops down through the ages. To achieve full interchange of ministries, there would have to be some significant readjustments of the ELCA's own system of ministries, the kind of changes that the ELCA had previously rejected in the Study of the Ministry. The Lutheran–Episcopal dialogue team decided in 1991 to put forward a plan for full communion between the two denominations, the "Concordat of Agreement," which called for the ELCA to adopt the historic episcopate and the threefold ordering of ministry to reach full com-munion. There was significant dissent on the Lutheran side of the team, however, which voted for the deal by a margin of five to three; the three in opposition issued a blistering dissent against the proposed Concordat. At the 1997 ELCA Church-wide Assembly, the Concordat ran into trouble and failed by six votes to pass by the needed two-thirds majority. Proponents vowed to make changes to the document and bring it back to the Assembly in 1999. A joint drafting team came up with a revised proposal, entitled "Called to Common Mission" (CCM), which still called for bishops in the historic episcopate, but backed off from other changes, including the threefold ministry. Again, the Lutheran side of the drafting team was split, this time two in favor and one against. There was considerable discussion within the

ELCA over this new agreement, and the Lutheran media was full of discussions for and against the revised proposal.

Although there was considerable opposition to this proposal, especially among the low-church conservatives in the ELCA, organized opposition did not gel until about late 1996, this time through a computer list-serve. This new technology linked opponents from around the country, who finally met in February 1999, at a Lutheran megachurch in Mahtomedi, Minnesota, to plan strategy and to form a new group, the Word Alone Network (WAN). The central matter of contention was a confessional one, linked to article seven of the Augsburg Confession, which states: "For the true unity of the Church it is enough [*satis est*] to agree concerning the teaching of the Gospel and the administration of the sacraments. It is not necessary that human traditions or rites and ceremonies, instituted by men, should be alike everywhere."[12] Proponents of CCM suggested that as long as there was agreement on the gospel and on the sacraments the ELCA was free to agree to whatever additional structures it wished to adopt. Opponents of CCM said that, in effect, the Episcopal demand for the ELCA to adopt the historic episcopate as a precondition for full communion was a violation of the *satis est*, something additional to gospel and sacraments demanded for unity. A heated and prolonged discussion over the issue took place at the 1999 ELCA Churchwide Assembly in Denver, but CCM was passed by twenty-seven votes over the two-thirds threshold. After several years of intense controversy and activity, the proponents had managed to shift just thirty-three votes, barely enough to approve the proposal. A coalition of theological liberals, who liked the social and political stances of the Episcopalians, and the Evangelical Catholics, who longed to institute the historic episcopate in the ELCA, carried the day, convincing the majority of convention attendees, many of whom liked the idea of closer relations with the Episcopalians.

The Word Alone Network continued on after its defeat in Denver, becoming the voice for the opposition within the ELCA. But there were those pastors and congregations for whom the passage of CCM was the last straw, and they began to make plans to leave the ELCA. Word Alone helped create, in 2001, a new American Lutheran denomination, the Lutheran Congregations in Mission for Christ (LCMC), which was intended more as an association of congregations than a traditionally oriented Lutheran synod. The nature of the LCMC is rather varied; it consists of at least thirty-two former ELCA megachurches, and many smaller, mainly rural, conservative congregations. By 2012, the LCMC consisted of over 770 congregations in the United States, with over 350,000 members, making it the fourth largest Lutheran denomination in America. The Word Alone Network continued on for another few years as the vehicle for "loyal dissent" within the ELCA, but it eventually disbanded.

The traumas of the first ECLA sexuality study did not deter those within the ELCA who sought to move the denomination further toward the ordination of gays and lesbians in monagomous relationships, so a second sexuality study was commissioned. Since the mid-1970s an interest group, Lutherans Concerned/North America, had advocated for such official Lutheran recognition, and by the 2000s they had over 375 "Reconciled in Christ" congregations that openly welcomed gay and lesbian persons. The second sexuality study brought forth another major round of controversy and contention over its proposal to allow congregations to call gay and lesbian pastors in "committed, monogamous relationships." Another group, Lutheran CORE (Coalition for Reform), was organized to attempt to defeat the measure. At the 2009 ELCA convention, the proposal was again passed by a similarly close vote; just barely over the two-thirds majority required.

The 2009 assembly vote on sexuality was the impetus for the formation of another new Lutheran denomination, the North American Lutheran Church (NALC), in 2010. Lutheran CORE remained as the voice of the opposition within the ELCA, while the NALC was the group for those who wished to leave. NALC is a more traditional synodical organization than is LCMC, but the two share the intent to be centrist Lutheran denominations, between the ELCA and the LCMS. Since its formation in 2010, the NALC has grown to over 100,000 members and three hundred congregations. In 2010 and 2011, the ELCA lost on average about 250,000 members and over 350 congregations a year, though by 2013 the rate of loss had slowed somewhat (see footnote 2 for further details).

The schism that has produced the LCMC and the NALC has become the largest Lutheran schism since the 1860s, dwarfing the walkout of Missouri moderates that formed the AELC in 1976, and perhaps the largest American Protestant schism since the nineteenth century. Combined figures for the LCMC and NALC represent almost 450,000 members and over one thousand congregations. The ELCA has suffered a 20 percent loss in membership, from about 5.1 million members in 2001 to 4 million in 2011, and the loss of over 1,200 congregations. This is a different kind of schism, a "slow-motion" schism that has evolved over the course of a decade, rather than the sharp and quick defections that have been seen in the past. Perhaps this is due to the fact that in the twenty-first century it is much harder, legally and constitutionally, for congregations to leave already-established denominations. The combined membership figures of the NALC and LCMC also only account for about half the ELCA's losses; where the other half-million ELCA members have gone is unclear. And these losses are not the only problem for the ELCA; there were many other members, pastors, and congregations who decided that leaving the denomination was just too difficult, and have "dropped out" within the ELCA itself. These internal disaffected members could hardly be relied upon to support the ELCA fully. While some have suggested that conservative losses might be offset by gains of liberal membership, this has not yet been seen; in fact, from 2003 to 2010 the average rate of congregational decline for the liberal "Reconciled in Christ" congregations has been twelve percent, compared to the average of eight percent for all other ELCA congregations.[13] By these indicators, and by the sharp financial losses, it might be concluded that the ELCA has suffered a significant loss of strength over the issues of ministry and sexuality since 1999.

Conclusion

If there is anything that historians fear more than contemporary history, it would be attempting to draw any kind of conclusion from a historical record that brings the analysis down to the present day. Stopping the historical analysis at any arbitrary point, in this case the year 2013, is somewhat like leaving a movie in the middle and then trying to make an educated guess about the ending. Where Lutherans in America are headed is difficult to say; one can draw conclusions from the present trajectories, but who knows what kind of forces will modify or shift those trajectories in the future. Yet, it would be completely inadequate to just drop the narrative at an arbitrary point and not attempt to set forth a sense of how things look from this time and place, knowing, however, that such an attempt would be provisional.

The last quarter-century of American Lutheranism has seen the culmination of several trends and the beginning of others. Certainly, by the beginning of the twenty-first century, Lutherans faced the end of one of the grand narratives of their history in America, the 175-year-long concern with its institutional arrangements. To merge or not to merge, that was the question. Well, for the foreseeable future, this question is moot; the ELCA is the end of that process, while the LCMS and WELS have maintained their independent stances. The LCMC and NALC are just too new to really know how their attempted centrist positions will hold, and the other smaller groups are only a footnote to the narrative. So, given the end of one grand narrative, what other narratives will replace it, if any?

On the other hand, Lutherans, whatever their theology and their polity, face the twenty-first century with questions that are really common to all religious groups in America. The last forty or fifty years have seen a seismic shift in the location of religious groups in American culture, in the ways that Americans relate to their denominations, and in what they want out of organized religion in the first place. This is a time when institutions have been "flattened" and deemphasized, and in which "brand loyalty" and conformity are dead; now religious seekers will no longer buy religion by its label, but will instead seek to probe much more deeply into the organization to see its value and worth.

Certainly, this prospect is terrifying to many religious leaders, lay and clergy alike, because so much of what they themselves hold dear is being called into question. Those who lead denominations do so because they have a history with them and a stake in their success. Religious leaders are often deeply committed to their institutions and it is hard for them to understand those who are not similarly committed, either to one specific denomination or to any denomination at all. Yet, this situation is really not new at all; this problem, caused by the distinctly American way of viewing and ordering religious life, is as old as the country itself. Religious seekers might say, "Your religious group is all well and good, but what do you have to offer me that makes my investment of time and energy worthwhile?" What, then, is the Lutheran answer to this perennial question?

Certainly, it seems clear at this point that though the national institutional variation of American Lutheranism has been greatly condensed, and that the varieties of Lutheranism on the local, congregational level are as diverse or more diverse than ever before. If the questions of Lutheranism's future in the United States are to be determined, it will be through the leadership of those who work on this diverse, local level. In these local places, Lutherans attempt to shape their message in such a way that the distinct power of the Lutheran understanding of the gospel is presented in all of its power and relevance. Lutheran leaders on the regional and national level would be well served to learn from and support such ministries, for if there is a future for Lutheranism in America, it will come through those channels and be built off of these insights.

Notes

1. According to the U.S. Bureau of Labor Statistics, the Consumer Price Index has roughly doubled from 1988 to 2012, meaning that the $65 million level in 1988 would be the equivalent of about $130 million in 2012; the actual figure of $50 million is thus about 40 percent of that total in real, inflation-adjusted numbers.

2. The membership declines have accelerated during the history of the ELCA. From 1988 to 1999, the yearly losses were modest, approximately 12,500 members per year. From 2000 to 2009 the yearly losses grew to an average of 63,000 members per year. After the 2009 vote to allow gay and lesbian pastors in monogamous relationships, the losses rose to 270,000 members in 2010 and 212,000 members in 2011. This loss was reduced to 108,000 members in 2012. But the trend lines for ELCA membership remain difficult. The figures are difficult to fully and completely interpret, and often lag behind for years; congregations may "carry" long-departed members on their membership rolls for many years, until the books are adjusted. One can conclude that the surge in ELCA membership losses in 2010 and 2011 may be attributed primarily to the loss of members dissatisfied with the 2009 vote.

3. Edgar R. Trexler, *Anatomy of a Merger: People, Dynamics, and Decisions That Shaped the ELCA* (Minneapolis: Augsburg Fortress, 1991), 247.

4. Ibid., 253.

5. Ibid., 258.

6. James C. Burkee, *Power, Politics, and the Missouri Synod: A Conflict That Changed American Christianity* (Minneapolis: Fortress Press, 2011), 179.

7. "Reflections on the New Lutheran Church," *Lutheran Witness* 105, no. 3 (March 1986): 20–21.

8. "Special Report: Eight Days in Pittsburgh," *Lutheran Witness* 110, no. 8 (August 1992): 2.

9. Beyond the official ELCA and LCMS records, further data and analysis of these Lutheran megachurches can be found in two sources: the "Faith Communities Today" (FACT) study of megachurches (Hartford Seminary, 2001); and in Scott Thumma and Jim Petersen, "Goliaths in our Midst: Megachurches in the ELCA," in Richard Cimino, ed., *Lutherans Today: American Lutheran Identity in the Twenty-First Century* (Grand Rapids: Eerdmans, 2003), 102–124.

10. "Fact Sheet about Ordained Women," Office of Research and Evaluation, ELCA, February 2013. Accessed at elca.org/ELCA%20Resource%20Repository/Fact_Sheet_About_Ordained_Women.pdf

11. "The Joint Declaration on the Doctrine of Justification in Confessional Lutheran Perspective," Commission on Theology and Church Relations, Lutheran Church–Missouri Synod, 1997.

12. Article 7, "The Augsburg Confession (Latin version)," in Theodore Tappert, trans. and ed., *The Book of Concord: The Confessions of the Evangelical Lutheran Church* (Philadelphia: Muhlenberg Press, 1959), 32.

13. Membership statistics are notoriously difficult to assess, and so there might be many different reasons for the decline of these congregations. Yet these numbers do show, at least in part, that these "Reconciled in Christ" congregations are not immune from the general membership decline, and may be suffering these trends at a rate greater than that of ELCA congregations as a whole.

Excursus 12

HISPANIC LUTHERANISM

It all started with a Swedish American theological student from Rock Island, Illinois, who in 1898 decided that the people of Puerto Rico needed to hear the Lutheran proclamation of the gospel. Never mind that he himself had only been in America for nine years, that he was not ordained, and had no official or financial backing—no, he was going to Puerto Rico. And one other thing: he didn't know a word of Spanish. But Gustav Swensson traveled to Puerto Rico, learned the language quickly, and began to preach in San Juan in 1899, the beginnings of Spanish- and Portuguese-speaking Lutheranism that now counts over one million Lutherans in Latin America, and tens of thousands of Hispanic Lutherans in the United States.

There had been Lutherans in Latin America for centuries—not in Spanish or Portuguese territories, but in the Virgin Islands and Guyana. In the nineteenth century, European Lutherans began to immigrate to South America, especially Brazil, Argentina, and Chile, and founded Lutheran congregations there. But they founded immigrant congregations in their immigrant languages, especially in German. Although they lived in countries that spoke Spanish or Portuguese, they did not initially consider an outreach to their neighbors who used those languages. Mission work, it seems, was proper to Africa and Asia, but not to the Latin America.

All this changed in the twentieth century. Swensson's initial efforts in Puerto Rico were taken over by one American Lutheran group, while another started a mission in Argentina in 1908, and a third began in Columbia and Bolivia in the 1930s. But in the 1940s and 1950s, American Lutherans began serious efforts to reach out to Latin American populations in over eighteen countries in the region. And the descendants of European Lutherans in Latin America began to make the transition to the use of Spanish or Portuguese within their communities, and to reach out themselves to the local populations. After World War II, there was a serious growth of Lutheranism and Lutheran churches in Latin America, which soon became autonomous and independent of their mission sponsors.

Spanish-speaking Lutheranism in Mexico and the United States actually began north of the border, and was taken back into Mexico by Hispanic converts and American Lutheran missionaries. As early as 1916, a few pastors from the Texas Synod began work among Mexican Americans in the Rio Grande valley, which eventually grew into a full-fledged home mission project. The Texas District of the Missouri Synod also began outreach to Mexican Americans in the same state in 1926, and their official records in 1932 list Spanish (Mexican) mission work in Chicago and Los Angeles as well. Both of these were considered "home" missions (rather than foreign missions), and both included the formation of Spanish-speaking congregations, as well as Lutheran periodicals, theological books, and worship materials translated into Spanish. The Missouri Synod even established a Spanish-language edition of its popular radio ministry, *The Lutheran Hour*.

It was from these bases in the southern United States that American Lutherans eventually took Lutheranism south of the border into Mexico. Building on earlier efforts among German immigrants to Mexico, the Missouri Synod began mission work in Mexico in 1940, and eventually formed the Lutheran Synod of Mexico. In 1936, Myrtle Nordin, of Lake Lillian, Minnesota (who had studied Spanish as an independent missionary in Columbia), gathered a group to form the Latin American Lutheran Mission (LALM), which began outreach with Spanish-speaking populations in south Texas and northern Mexico, forming congregations in Mexico that would eventually form the Evangelical Lutheran Church of Mexico. Beginning in 1945, the World Mission Prayer League began their own mission work in Mexico, leading to the formation of the Lutheran Apostolic Alliance of Mexico (1977). Finally, the American Lutheran Church began work in Mexico in 1947, building off the earlier work in south Texas, which led to the formation of the Mexican Lutheran Church (1957). There are currently about ten thousand Lutherans in Mexico itself.

Although a few Hispanic Lutherans in the United States came by way of immigration (notably Puerto Rican Lutherans to New York), most of the Spanish-speaking Lutherans in America converted to Lutheranism while in this country. Outreach to Hispanic Americans had begun early in the twentieth century in Texas (as we have seen), but this work really took off after 1960 or so, with specific and targeted home-missions work. By 2000, the Evangelical Lutheran Church in America listed 180 congregations that used Spanish in worship (including those in Puerto Rico), with a total Hispanic membership of over 39,000 people. The Lutheran Church–Missouri Synod listed 120 Hispanic congregations, with ninety-six "Hispanic workers" on its rolls. Both denominations have special associations or conferences for Hispanic work. With the Hispanic population in the United States growing rapidly, this portion of the population will continue to be an important sector for Lutherans in America.

Epilogue

HOPE

T he beginning of the final chapter of this history mentioned the dangers of writing contemporary history, dangers that were noted but did not finally deter this attempt to bring the history of Lutherans in America up to the date of this work's publication. Certainly, the last two chapters of this history must be seen as provisional attempts, and certainly (and devoutly to be wished), future historians will revisit the narratives and conclusions of these chapters and revise them in light of further historical developments and understandings. But having braved the inherent limitations of writing contemporary history, one is emboldened to even further dangers, namely some brief thoughts about the immediate future for Lutherans in America.

In the process of writing this history, this manuscript was sent out to a number of American Lutheran historians and leaders around the country for their comments and suggestion, and a number of them were kind enough to return very helpful responses. Definitely, the most pointed comments were received about the final two chapters, which cover the most recent fifty years of American Lutheran history; these reactions were quite divided. Some of these respondents commented that, in their opinion, the tone of the final chapters was too pessimistic, with too much stress on the decline and difficulties experienced in the last few decades. These commentators suggested that perhaps there were more areas of optimism than the narrative allowed. On the other hand, an equal number of respondents thought that these final chapters were not actually tough enough, and that in places the narrative actually understated the magnitude of the problems facing American Lutherans. Taking these divergent readings into account, the last two chapters were reworked and readjusted in places, but, in all honesty, the general thrust of the chapters was not materially altered. Time is the only thing which will shed further light on this period of time, and the provisional nature of the chapters will be revised.

This whole experience, however, does raise the question of the health of American Lutheranism, and prospects for its future. Certainly, the Lutheran traditions in America face a number of strong challenges to their continued vitality, and these challenges are applied equally across the board, from one Lutheran denomination to another, and from national to regional to local levels. These challenges are recorded in the last two chapters and do not need to be restated. But the history of Lutherans in America shows that there have often been such periods of difficulty and challenge in the past, and that Lutherans have found ways to meet and adapt to these new conditions. Not to say that any of this was automatic, in some form of historical progression or Hegelian dialectic; rather, it is to say that in the past Lutherans have found ways to address their difficulties.

This history also records that Lutherans have often reached back into their history and found creative ways to reappropriate their theological and spiritual traditions to meet the needs of the future. When this is done well, it is not some wooden attempt to repristinate some "golden age" of the past, as if there ever was such a golden age or such a repristination were possible. Rather, the best ways of using the insights of the past were those that delved deeply into the past to discover the creating and motivating elements of historical events that energized whatever transformative actions were developed to meet the challenges head-on. History should not be a room from which to retreat from the present, but a creative resource to meet the present and future squarely.

There are two contemporary problems that must be addressed before such a creative retrieval is possible. The first is the general American tendency to believe that history has little value or worth—it is just the record of a past to be overcome. America was built on the almost divine belief in progress, that as a nation and as a society we are always progressing and getting better. This is a secular theology, which states that the telos or salvivic goal can be realized in time and space, especially in America—this is quite literally a secular version of realized eschatology, or the building of God's millennial kingdom right here in the United States. A healthy Lutheran skepticism, along with a solid understanding of the distinction between law and gospel, church and state, ought to be more than enough to demolish these pretensions. But this leads us directly to the second problem: most Lutherans do not really know or understand their theological tradition very well, and would not be able to apply its critiques to the secular and religious theologies that dominate American society. This problem, the ignorance of the essence Lutheran theology and insights, seems to be across the board. Lutheran laypeople have not been well catechized and have not been continually exposed to these insights as adults. Many Lutheran pastors seem to be not much better prepared, with a limited understanding of Lutheran history and theology. It is not possible to critique society without a clear position from which to do this.

Nevertheless, Lutherans in America have rich traditions from which to draw, and there are many places where the Lutheran understanding of the gospel is being lived out. Certainly, on the local level, there are very strong and renewing Lutheran congregations in which the gospel is daily proclaimed and lived out. These congregations have always been the backbone of American Lutheranism, and their maintenance and expansion are causes for great hope for the future. The example of these congregations should be celebrated and lifted up as examples for others who need the same sort of inspiration. Certainly, regional and national Lutheran structures have come under deep challenges in the past decades and are struggling to find their purpose and impact. It would seem that the way forward for these elements of American Lutheranism would be to refocus and recommit to the service of local congregations as the core of their purpose. They should be in the business of recognizing and celebrating the best of these local Lutheran congregations, and assisting struggling congregations to find their way to a better future. Perhaps Lutheranism might need a great deal of flexibility and reimagination to allow this to happen, but the effort might well be worth the price. This is not a call for a Lutheran congregationalism (necessarily) but, rather, a suggestion that the revitalization of our tradition will be most effective if rooted in such local communities of faith.

Certainly, Lutherans will continue to be an important and creative element within American Christianity, although the ways they have an impact might well change and develop over time. The Lutheran understanding of the gospel of Jesus Christ, and its impact on the lives of believers, is a strong and timeless message of faith and trust in God. Hopefully, American Lutherans will be revitalized by this message, to continue to be worthy of their calling. For American Lutherans, and for all American Christians, this tradition must continue to bring its voice to the needs of the world of which it is a part.

ABBREVIATIONS AND ACRONYMS

AALC (1987–)   American Association of Lutheran Churches

AALC (1987–)	American Association of Lutheran Churches
AELC (1872–1962)	American Evangelical Lutheran Church (name change 1953; formerly Danish Evangelical Lutheran Church in America)
AELC (1976–1987)	Association of Evangelical Lutheran Congregations
AFLC (1962–)	Association of Free Lutheran Congregations
ALC (1930–1960)	American Lutheran Church
ALC (1960–1988)	American Lutheran Church
ALConf (1930–1954)	American Lutheran Conference (cooperative body)
ALCW (1960–1988)	American Lutheran Church Women
Augustana (1860–1962)	Augustana Evangelical Lutheran Church (name change 1948; formerly Augustana Synod)
Buffalo (1845–1930)	Buffalo Synod
CCM (1999)	Called to Common Mission (ecumenical agreement)
CLB (1900–)	Church of the Lutheran Brethren of America
CNLC (1982–1987)	Commission for a New Lutheran Church (merger committee)
CSB (1917)	*Common Service Book* (hymnal)
CYCOM (1948–1955)	Commission on Younger Churches and Orphaned Missions
ELC (1917–1960)	Evangelical Lutheran Church (name change 1946; formerly Norwegian Lutheran Church in America

ELCA (1988–)	Evangelical Lutheran Church in America
ELCC (1960–1985)	Evangelical Lutheran Church of Canada
ELCIC (1985–)	Evangelical Lutheran Church in Canada
ELIM (1973–1988)	Evangelical Lutherans in Mission
ELS (1917–)	Evangelical Lutheran Synod
ELW (2006)	*Evangelical Lutheran Worship* (hymnal)
GC (1872–1918)	General Council
GS (1820–1918)	General Synod
GSS (1863–1886)	General Synod, South (name change 1865; formerly General Synod in the Confederate States)
ILC (1993–)	International Lutheran Council (cooperative body)
ILCW (1966–1978)	Inter-Lutheran Commission on Worship (hymnal committee)
Iowa (1854–1930)	Iowa Synod
JCLU (1955–1962)	Joint Committee on Lutheran Union (merger committee)
JUC (1952–1960)	Joint Union Committee (merger committee)
LBA (f. 1918)	Lutheran Brotherhoods of America
LBW (1978)	*Lutheran Book of Worship* (hymnal)
LCMC (2001–)	Lutheran Congregations in Mission for Christ
LCMS (1847–)	Lutheran Church–Missouri Synod (name change 1947)
LCUSA (1966–1988)	Lutheran Council in the USA (cooperative body)
LCW (1962–1988)	Lutheran Church Women
LFC (1897–1963)	Lutheran Free Church
LHRAA (1953–2013)	Lutheran Human Relations Association of America
LIRS (1939–)	Lutheran Immigration and Refugee Services (name change 1967)
LLL (1917–1992)	Lutheran Laymen's League (continued by Lutheran Hour Ministries)
LSA (1997–)	Lutheran Services in American
LSS	Lutheran Social Services
LW (1982)	*Lutheran Worship* (hymnal)
LWA (Post WWII)	Lutheran World Action (relief appeal)
LWC (1923–1935)	Lutheran World Conventions (cooperative body)
LWF (1947–)	Lutheran World Federation (cooperative body)
LWR (1945–)	Lutheran World Relief
NALC (2010–)	North American Lutheran Church
NCCC (1950–)	National Council of Churches of Christ (ecumenical agency)

NLC (1918–1966)	National Lutherans Council (cooperative body)
NLCA (1917–1948)	Norwegian Lutheran Church in America (continued by the ELC)
NLCSSW (1917–1918)	National Lutheran Commission for Soldiers and Sailors Welfare
Ohio (1820–1930)	Joint Synod of Ohio
SBH (1958)	*Service Book and Hymnal* (hymnal)
SC (1872–1962)	Synodical Conference (cooperative body)
Suomi (1890–1962)	Suomi Synod
UELC (1896–1960)	United Evangelical Lutheran Church (name change 1946; continued as United Danish Evangelical Lutheran Church)
ULCA (1918–1962)	United Lutheran Church in America
UNLC (1890–1917)	United Norwegian Lutheran Church
USS (1886–1918)	United Synod South
WAN (2000–)	Word Alone Network
WCC (1948–)	World Council of Churches (ecumenical agency)
WELS (1892–)	Wisconsin Evangelical Lutheran Synod (name change 1959; formerly the Evangelical Lutheran Synod of Wisconsin)
WMPL (1937–)	World Mission Prayer League (name change 1945)

Selected Annotated Bibliography

E very academic history must deal the issue of issue of notation and citation. A work must have enough citations to be able to direct the reader to further areas of research and study, but not so many notes as to overwhelm the reader, or distract the reader's attention from the central narrative. In some scholarly books, there is a rich sidebar of historical discussion within the notes themselves, but this, too, can be distracting. This book deals with these issues in two ways. First, the discussions that perhaps could have been in the notes have been moved into the body of the main work, wherever possible; the notes themselves are primarily for reference. Second, this work has minimized the notes themselves, relying instead on this bibliographical essay to flesh out for the reader the multitude of additional resources for the history of Lutherans in North America, resources to which they might wish to turn for further information and reading. The hope is that this arrangement will be the most useful and efficient means of communication with the reader.

Historical Guides, Reference Works, and Bibliographies

DeBerg, Betty. *Women and Women's Issues in North American Lutheranism*. Chicago: Commission for Women of the ELCA, 1992.

McArver, Susan Wilds. "Lutherans," in Philip Goff, ed., *Blackwell Companion to American Religion*, 614–35. Malden, MA: Wiley Blackwell, 2010.

> *A detailed and very helpful historiographical essay on the writing of American Lutheran history, with an extended bibliography of sources at its end. Extremely useful, especially because it is relatively current.*

Voigt, Louis Charles. "The Development of Official Titles Used By Lutheran Church Bodies in North America, 1748–1966." Unpub. MA thesis. University of Chicago, 1967.

Wiederaenders, Robert C. *A Bibliography of American Lutheranism, 1624–1850*. N.p.: 1956.

————, ed., *Historical Guide to Lutheran Church Bodies of North America*. 2d ed. Lutheran Historical Conference Publication 1. St. Louis: Lutheran Historical Conference, 1998.

> *This reference work is indispensable as a guide to American Lutheran history, giving the historical outlines of its institutional formation. Includes bibliography, maps, charts, and texts. A first edition of this work by the same editor is entitled* The Synods of American Lutheranism.

Encyclopedias and Reference Works

Bodensieck, Julius, ed. *The Encyclopedia of the Lutheran Church*. 3 vols. Minneapolis: Augsburg, 1965.

> *A standard resource, especially good for the breadth of its coverage.*

Gassmann, Günther. *Historical Dictionary of Lutheranism*. 2d ed. Lanham, MD: Scarecrow, 2011.

> *Has some useful entries, but is limited and in places inaccurate.*

Lueker, Erwin L. *Lutheran Cyclopedia*. St. Louis: Concordia, 1975.

> *A very useful single volume reference. Entries are not lengthy but can be very helpful for basic details. Also online as the "Christian Cyclopedia":* http://cyclopedia.lcms.org/.

Wengert, Timothy, ed. *The Dictionary of Luther and the Lutheran Tradition*. Grand Rapids: Baker Academic, 2016.

> *A forthcoming reference book which will be useful and current.*

Almanacs and Directories

These kinds of works, which have been issued in various forms from the middle of the nineteenth century, can be very useful for locating congregations and individuals, as well as other important information. Two notable versions of this genre are:

Kieffer, G. L., et al., eds. *The Lutheran World Almanac*. New York: National Lutheran Council. Vol. 1 (1920) through vol. 8 (1937).

Knubel, Helen M. *Lutheran Church Directory for the United States and Canada*. New York: National Lutheran Council (later by the Lutheran Council in the USA).

Journals and Periodicals

Concordia Historical Institute Quarterly.

Journal of the Lutheran Historical Conference. Since 2011; replaces: *Essays and Reports of the Lutheran Historical Conference*. Biennial, 22 vols., 1966–2006.

Lutheran Quarterly. New series since 1987; previous series 1948–1976. Older series are also
valuable.
Wisconsin Lutheran Quarterly.

Sourcebooks and Readers

Meyer, Carl S., ed., *Moving Frontiers: Readings in the History of the Lutheran Church–Missouri
Synod.* St. Louis: Concordia, 1964.
Suelflow, August, ed., *Heritage in Motion.* St. Louis: Concordia, 1988.
Two volumes covering the history of the Lutheran Church–Missouri Synod.
Wolf, Richard C., ed. *Documents of Lutheran Unity in America.* Philadelphia: Fortress Press,
1966.
Best anthology of official documents and other materials.

Biographies

There is no good standard collection of Lutheran biographies available. There are many
places to go for American Lutheran biographies, however, especially synodical histories,
alumni volumes (especially for the Luther seminaries), and other regional and localized historical works. The encyclopedias and references books listed above are also generally good
in this area.

Jensson [sometimes Roseland], J. C. *American Lutheran Biographies.* Milwaukee: N.p., 1890.
Helpful for Lutheran pastors from the eighteenth and nineteenth centuries.
Nothstein, Ira O. *Lutheran Makers of America: Brief Sketches of Sixty-Eight Notable Early
Lutherans.* Philadelphia: United Lutheran Publication House, 1930.
Helpful for colonial Lutheranism, both lay and clergy.

General Histories

Groh, John E., and Robert H. Smith, eds. *The Lutheran Church in North American Life.* St.
Louis: Clayton Pub. House, 1979.
Another interesting topical history, concentrating on Lutherans and American culture.
Jacobs, Henry Eyster. *A History of the Evangelical Lutheran Church in the United States.* New
York: Charles Scribner's Sons, 1893.
*This and Neve/Allbeck (below) are two older histories, but each has interesting and
important materials.*
Lagerquist, L. DeAne. *The Lutherans.* Denominations in America 9. Westport, CT: Green-
wood, 1999.
*An excellent interpretative history, though not as detailed as Nelson or Wentz (below).
Hardcover edition has a fine biography section in the back.*

Nelson, E. Clifford ed. *The Lutherans in North America*. Philadelphia: Fortress Press, 1975.
The standard history on the subject, especially good on the institutional history.

Neve, J. L., and Willard Allbeck, *History of the Lutheran Church in America*. 3d ed, Burlington, IA: Lutheran Literacy Board, 1934.

Wentz, Abdel Ross, *A Basic History of Lutheranism in America*. Rev. ed. Philadelphia: Fortress Press, 1964.
Prior to Nelson, this was the standard history, and is still very useful.

Specialized Histories

Bergendoff, Conrad. *The Doctrine of the Church in American Lutheranism*. Philadelphia: Muhlenberg, 1956.

Solberg, Richard W. *Lutheran Higher Education in North America*. Minneapolis: Augsburg, 1985.

Tietjen, John H. *Which Way to Lutheran Unity?* St. Louis: Clayton, 1966.

Colonial Lutheranism

Qualben, Lars P. *The Lutheran Church in Colonial America*. New York: Thomas Nelson, 1940.
Some good information, but must be used carefully; some parts are inaccurate.

New York

Clark, Delber Wallace. *The World of Justus Falckner*. Philadelphia: Muhlenberg, 1946.

Hart, Simon, and Harry Kreider, trans. *The Lutheran Church in New York and New Jersey, 1772–1760*. N.p.: United Lutheran Synod of New York and New England, 1962.

Van Laer, Arnold J. H. trans. *The Lutheran Church in New York, 1649–1772*. New York: New York Public Library, 1946.

Williams, Kim-Eric. *The Journey of Justus Falckner*. Delhi, NY: ALPB Books, 2003.

New Sweden

Craig, Peter Stebbins, and Kim-Eric Williams, eds. *Colonial Records of the Swedish Churches in Pennsylvania*. 4 vols. (so far). Philadelphia: Swedish Colonial Society, 2006– .

Johnson, Amandus. *The Swedish Settlements on the Delaware, 1638–1664*. 2 vols. New York: D. Appleton and Co., 1911.

Lindmark, Daniel. *Ecclesia Plantanda: Swedishness in Colonial America*. Skrifter Från forskningsprogrammet 52. Umeå, Sweden: n.p., 2005.

German Immigration

Documentary History of the Evangelical Lutheran Ministerium of Pennsylvania, 1748–1821. Philadelphia: General Council, 1898.

Grabbe, Hans-Jürgen, ed., *Halle Pietism: Colonial North America, and the Young United States.* USA-Studien, Band 15. Stuttgart: Franz Steiner Verlag, 2008.

Rigforgiato, Leonard R. *Missionary of Moderation: Henry Melchior Muhlenberg and the Lutheran Church in English America.* Lewisburg, PA: Bucknell University Press, 1980.

Roeber, A. G. *Palatines, Liberty, and Property: German Lutherans in Colonial British America.* Baltimore: Johns Hopkins University Press, 1993.

Schmauk, Theodore E. ed. *The Lutheran Church in Pennsylvania, 1638–1820.* Philadelphia: General Council Publication House, 1903.

Splitter, Wolfgang. *Pastors, People, Politics: German Lutherans in Pennsylvania, 1740–1790.* Trier: Wissenschaftlicher, 1998.

Tappert, Theodore, and John Doberstein, trans. *The Journals of Henry Melchior Muhlenberg.* 3 vols. Philadelphia: Muhlenberg, 1942.

Wallace, Paul A. W. *The Muhlenbergs of Pennsylvania.* Philadelphia: University of Pennsylvania Press, 1950.

Georgia

Kleckley, Russell, trans., *The Letters of Johann Martin Boltzius, Lutheran Pastor in Ebenezer, Georgia.* 2 vols. Lewiston, NY: Edwin Mellen, 2009.

Jones, George Fenwick, et al., trans. *Detailed Reports on the Salzberger Emigrants Who Settled in America.* 18 vols. (so far). Athens: University of Georgia Press, 1968– .

Nineteenth Century

Eastern Lutheranism

Allbeck, Willard D. *A Century of Lutherans in Ohio.* Yellow Springs, OH: Antioch, 1966.

Kreider, Harry J. *History of the United Lutheran Synod of New York and New Jersey.* Philadelphia: Muhlenberg, 1954.

Kurtz, Michael J. *John Gottlieb Morris: Man of God and Man of Science.* Baltimore: Maryland Historical Society, 1997.

Wentz, Abdel Ross. *Pioneer in Christian Unity: Samuel Simon Schmucker.* Philadelphia: Fortress Press, 1967.

———. *A History of the Evangelical Lutheran Synods of Maryland, 1820–1920.* Harrisburg, PA: Evangelical Press, 1920.
  See also the histories of the other various synods.

"American" Lutheranism and Confessionalism

Conser, Walter H., Jr. *Church and Confession: Conservative Theologians in Germany, England, and America, 1815–1866*. Macon, GA: Mercer University Press, 1984.

Ferm, Vergilius. *The Crisis in American Lutheran Theology*. New York: The Century Co., 1927.

David A. Gustafson, *Lutherans in Crisis: The Question of Identity in the American Republic*. Minneapolis: Fortress Press, 1993.

Kuenning, Paul P. *The Rise and Fall of American Lutheran Pietism: The Rejection of an Activist Heritage*. Macon, GA: Mercer University Press, 1988.

Repp, Arthur C., Sr. *Luther's Catechism Comes to America*. Metuchen, NJ: Scarecrow, 1982.

Tappert, Theodore G., ed. *Lutheran Confessional Theology in America, 1840–1880*. New York: Oxford University Press, 1972.

> *Note that books on the "American Lutheranism" controversy can lean toward one side or the other, and should generally be read critically.*

Southern Lutheranism

Anderson, Hugh G. *Lutheranism in the Southeastern States, 1860–1886*. The Hague: Mouton, 1969.

Bost, Raymond M. *History of the Lutheran Church in South Carolina*. Columbia, SC: R. L. Bryan Co., 1971.

———, and Jeff L. Norris. *All One Body: The Story of the North Carolina Lutheran Synod, 1803–1993*. Salisbury, NC: North Carolina Synod ELCA, 1994.

Eisenberg, William E. *The Lutheran Church in Virginia, 1717–1962*. Roanoke: Virginia Synod, LCA, 1967.

General Council and Later Eastern Lutheranism

Evjen, John O. *The Life of J. H. W. Stuckenberg*. Minneapolis: Lutheran Free Church Press, 1938.

Gerberding, G. H. *The Life and Letters of W. A. Passavant*. Greenville, PA: The Young Lutheran Co., 1906.

Ochsenford, S. E. *Documentary History of the General Council of the Evangelical Lutheran Church in North America*. Philadelphia: General Council Publication House, 1912.

Scholz, Robert F. *Press Toward the Mark: History of the United Lutheran Synod of New York and New England, 1830–1930*. Metuchen, NJ: Scarecrow, 1995.

Conservative Midwestern Germans

Baepler, Walter A. *A Century of Grace: The Missouri Synod, 1847–1947*. St. Louis: Concordia, 1947.

Forester, Walter O. *Zion on the Mississippi: The Settlement of the Saxon Lutherans in Missouri, 1839–1841.* St. Louis: Concordia, 1953.

Hoek, Albert Llewellyn. *The Pilgrim Colony: The History of the St. Sebald Congregation, the Two Wartburgs, and the Synods of Iowa and Missouri.* Minneapolis: Lutheran University Press, 2004.

Mauelshagen, Carl. *American Lutheranism Surrenders to Forces of Conservatism.* Athens: University of Georgia, 1936.

> *Some good information, but with a definite slant.*

Meuser, Fred W. *The Formation of the American Lutheran Church.* Columbus: Wartburg Press, 1958.

> *On the Iowa, Ohio, and Buffalo Synods.*

Ottersberg, Gerhard. "The Evangelical Lutheran Synod of Iowa and Other States, 1854–1904," Unpub. PhD diss. University of Nebraska, 1949.

Sheatsley, C. V. *History of the Evangelical Lutheran Joint Synod of Ohio and Other States from the Earliest Beginnings to 1919.* Columbus: Lutheran Book Concern, 1919.

Spitz, Lewis W., Sr. *The Life of Dr. C. F. W. Walther.* St. Louis: Concordia, 1961.

Suelflow, August Robert. *Servant of the Word: The Life and Ministry of C. F. W. Walther.* St. Louis: Concordia, 2000.

Ziehe, H. C. *Centennial Story of the Lutheran Church in Texas, 1851–1951.* 2 vols. Seguin, TX: South Texas Printing Co., 1951.

Norwegian Lutherans

Aaberg, Theodore A. *A City on a Hill: A History of the Evangelical Lutheran Synod.* Mankato, MN: Evangelical Lutheran Synod, 1968.

Fevold, Eugene L. *The Lutheran Free Church: A Fellowship of American Lutheran Congregations, 1897–1963.* Minneapolis: Augsburg, 1969.

Gjerde, S. S., and P. Ljostveit, eds. *The Hauge Movement in America.* Minneapolis: Hauge Inner Mission Federation, 1941.

Levang, Joseph H. *The Church of the Lutheran Brethren, 1900–1975.* Fergus Falls, MN: Lutheran Brethren Pub. Co., 1980.

Nelson, E. Clifford, and Eugene L. Fevold. *The Lutheran Church Among Norwegian-Americans.* 2 vols. Minneapolis: Augsburg, 1960.

Nichol, Todd, ed. *Crossings: Norwegian-American Lutheranism as a Transatlantic Tradition.* Northfield, MN: Norwegian-American Historical Association, 2003.

Rohne, J. Magnus. *Norwegian American Lutheranism up to 1872.* New York: MacMillan, 1926.

Swedish Lutherans

Arden, G. Everett. *Augustana Heritage: History of the Augustana Lutheran Church.* Rock Island, IL: Augustana Press, 1963.

Erling, Maria, and Mark Granquist. *The Augustana Story: Shaping Lutheran Identity in North America*. Minneapolis: Augsburg Fortress, 2008.

Olson, Oscar. *The Augustana Lutheran Church: Pioneer Period, 1846–1860*. Rock Island, IL: Augustana Book Concern, 1950.

Söderström, Hugo. *Confession and Cooperation: The Policy of the Augustana Synod in Confessional Matters . . .* Lund: C. W. K. Gleerup Bokförlag, 1973.

Danish Lutherans

Hansen, Thorvald. *Church Divided: Lutheranism among the Danish Immigrants*. Des Moines: Grand View College, 1992.

Jensen, John M. *The United Evangelical Lutheran Church*. Minneapolis: Augsburg, 1964.

Kjølhede, Peder, et al. *Danes in America: Danish-American Lutheranism from 1860–1908*. Blair, NE: Lur Publications, 2001.

Mortensen, Enok. *The Danish Lutheran Church in America*. Philadelphia: Board of Publications LCA, 1967.

Finnish and Slovak Lutherans

Alexander, June Granatir. *The Immigrant Church and Community: Pittsburgh's Slovak Catholics and Lutherans, 1880–1915*. Pittsburgh: University of Pittsburgh Press, 1987.

Bódy, Ján, ed. *History of the Slovak Zion Synod LCA*. N.p.: n.p., 1970.

Foltz, Aila, and Miriam Yliniemi, eds. *A Godly Heritage: Historical View of the Laestadian Revival and Development of the Apostolic Lutheran Church in America*. N.p.: n.p., 2005.

Heikkinen, Jacob. *The Story of the Suomi Synod: Finnish Evangelical Lutheran Church of America, 1890–1962*. New York Mills, MN: Parta Pub., 1985.

Jalkanen, Ralph J., ed. *The Faith of the Finn: Historical Perspectives on the Finnish Lutheran Church in America*. East Lansing: Michigan State University Press, 1972.

Kortekangas, Paavo, and Antti Lepisto, eds. *The Faith of the Finns on a New Continent*. N.p.: N.p., 2000.

Twentieth Century

Bachmann, E. Theodore, with Mercia Brenne Bachmann. *The United Lutheran Church in America, 1918–1962*. Ed. Paul Rorem. Minneapolis: Fortress Press, 1997.

Devol, Edmund. *Sword of the Spirit: A Biography of Samuel Trexler*. New York: Dodd, Meade, & Co., 1956.

Fischer, Robert H., ed. *Franklin Clark Fry: A Palette for a Portrait*. Springfield, OH: Lutheran Quarterly, 1972.

Nelson, E. Clifford. *Lutheranism in North America, 1914–1970*. Minneapolis: Augsburg, 1972.

Nichol, Todd W. "The American Lutheran Church: An Historical Study of Its Confession of Faith according to Its Constituting Documents." Unpub. PhD diss. Graduate Theological Union, 1988.

Pannkoke, O. H. *A Great Church Finds Itself: The Lutheran Church between the Wars.* Quitman, GA: n.p., 1966.

An eccentric history, but with some interesting information.

Schuetze, Armin W. *The Synodical Conference: Ecumenical Endeavor.* Milwaukee: Northwestern Pub. House, 2000.

Spaude, Paul. *The Lutheran Church under American Influence.* Burlington, IA: Lutheran Literacy Board, 1943.

Wentz, Frederick K. *Lutherans in Concert: The Story of the National Lutheran Council, 1918–1966.* Minneapolis: Augsburg, 1968.

The ELCA and Its Constituent Denominations

Gilbert, W. Kent. *Commitment to Unity: A History of the Lutheran Church in America.* Philadelphia: Fortress Press, 1988.

Knutson, Johannes. *The Formation of the Lutheran Church in America.* Philadelphia: Fortress Press, 1978.

Lutz, Charles P., ed. *Church Roots: Stories of the Nine Immigrant Groups That Became the American Lutheran Church.* Minneapolis: Augsburg, 1985.

Nichol, Todd W. *All These Lutherans: Three Paths toward a New Lutheran Church.* Minneapolis: Augsburg, 1986.

Rogness, Alvin N. *The Story of the American Lutheran Church.* Minneapolis: Augsburg, 1980.

Trexler, Edgar R. *Anatomy of a Merger: People, Dynamics, and Decisions That Shaped the ELCA.* Minneapolis: Augsburg, 1991.

Missouri, Wisconsin, and the AELC

Adams, James E. *Preus of Missouri and the Great Lutheran Civil War.* New York: Harper & Row, 1977.

Braun, Mark E. *The Tale of Two Synods: Events That Led to the Split between Wisconsin and Missouri.* Milwaukee: Northwestern Pub. House, 2003.

Burkee, James C. *Power, Politics, and the Missouri Synod: A Conflict That Changed American Christianity.* Minneapolis: Fortress Press, 2011.

Danker, Frederick D. *No Room in the Brotherhood: The Preus-Otten Purge of Missouri.* St. Louis: Clayton Pub. House, 1977.

Marquart, Kurt E. *Anatomy of an Explosion: Missouri in Lutheran Perspective.* Fort Wayne, IN: Concordia Theological Seminary Press, 1977.

Rudnick, Milton L. *Fundamentalism and the Missouri Synod.* St. Louis: Concordia, 1966.

Tietjen, John H. *Memoirs in Exile: Confessional Hope and Institutional Conflict.* Minneapolis: Fortress Press, 1990.

Todd, Mary. *Authority Vested: A Story of Identity and Change in the Lutheran Church–Missouri Synod.* Grand Rapids: Eerdmans, 2000.

Zimmerman, Paul. *A Seminary in Crisis.* St. Louis: Concordia, 2007.

Recent American Lutheranism

Cimino, Richard, ed. *Lutherans Today: American Lutheran Identity in the Twenty-First Century.* Grand Rapids: Eerdmans, 2003.

LCMC: The First Ten Years. N.p: Lutheran Congregations in Mission for Christ, 2010.

Lindberg, Carter. *The Third Reformation: Charismatic Movements and the Lutheran Tradition.* Macon, GA: Mercer University Press, 1983.

Settje, David. *Lutherans and the Longest War: Adrift on a Sea of Doubt about the Cold and Vietnam Wars, 1964–1975.* Lanham, MD: Lexington Books, 2007.

Ecumenical Relations and Social Policy

Flesner, Dorris. *American Lutherans Help Shape the World Council: The Role of the Lutheran Churches of America in the Formation of the World Council of Churches.* Dubuque, IA: Lutheran Historical Conference, 1981.

Galchutt, Kathryn M. *The Career of Andrew Schulze: Lutherans and Race Relations in the Civil Rights Movement, 1924–1968.* Macon, GA: Mercer University Press, 2005.

Klein, Christa. *Politics and Policy: The Genesis and Theology of Social Statements in the Lutheran Church in America.* Minneapolis: Fortress Press, 1989.

Marty, Myron A. *Lutherans and Roman Catholicism: The Changing Conflict, 1917–1963.* Notre Dame, IN: University of Notre Dame Press, 1968.

Nelson, E. Clifford. *The Rise of World Lutheranism: An American Perspective.* Philadelphia: Fortress Press, 1982.

Schroeder, Steven. *A Community and a Perspective: Lutheran Peace Fellowship and the Edge of the Church, 1941–1991.* Lanham, MD: University Press of America, 1993.

Social Ministry and Relief Work

Bachman, John W. *Together in Hope: 50 Years of Lutheran World Relief.* New York: Lutheran World Relief, 1995.

Lueking, F. Dean. *A Century of Caring, 1868–1968.* St. Louis: Board of Social Ministry, LCMS, 1968.

McCurley, Foster R., ed. *Social Ministry in the Lutheran Tradition.* Minneapolis: Fortress Press, 2008.

Solberg, Richard W. *Open Doors: The Story of Lutherans Resettling Refugees.* Concordia, 1992.

———. *As Between Brothers: The Story of Lutheran Response to World Need.* Minneapolis: Augsburg, 1957.

Women

Bengtson, Gloria, ed. *Lutheran Women in Ordained Ministry, 1970–1995.* Minneapolis: Augsburg, 1995.

Coburn, Carol K. *Life At Four Corners: Religion, Gender, and Education in a German-American Community, 1868–1945.* Lawrence: University Press of Kansas, 1992.

Grindal, Gracia, and Marvin Slind, eds., *Linka's Diary: A Norwegian Immigrant Story in Words and Sketches.* Minneapolis: Lutheran University Press, 2008.

Lagerquist, L. DeAne. *From Our Mother's Arms: A History of Women in the American Lutheran Church.* Minneapolis: Augsburg, 1987.

Meyer, Ruth F. *Women on a Mission: The Role of Women in the Church from Bible Times up to and Including a History of the Lutheran Women's Missionary League During Its First Twenty-Five Years.* St. Louis: Concordia, 1967.

Nauman, Cheryl. *In the Footsteps of Phoebe: A Complete History of the Deaconess Movement in the Lutheran Church–Missouri Synod.* St. Louis: Concordia, 2007.

Reishus, Martha. *Hearts and Hands Uplifted: A History of the Womens' Missionary Federation of the Evangelical Lutheran Church.* Minneapolis: Augsburg, 1958.

These Fifty Years: 1892–1942. Chicago: Women's Missionary Society of the Augustana Synod, 1942.

Todd, Mary. *Authority Vested: A Story of Identity and Change in the Lutheran Church–Missouri Synod.* Grand Rapids: Eerdmans, 2000.

Weiser, Frederick S. *To Serve the Lord and His People, 1884–1984.* Gladwyne, PA: Deaconess Community of the LCA, 1984.

———. *Love's Response: A Story of Lutheran Deaconesses in America.* Philadelphia: Board of Publication of the ULCA, 1962.

African, Asian, and Hispanic-American Lutheranism

Beatty, Paul B. *A History of the Lutheran Church in Guyana.* Georgetown, Guyana: Daily Chronik, 1970.

Branch, Lonnie L. *Reflections of Light: The Odyssey of a Black American Lutheran Pastor During the Civil Rights Era.* Minneapolis: Kirk House Publishing, 2014.

Dickinson, Richard C. *Roses and Thorns: The Centennial Edition of Black Lutheran Mission and Ministry in the LCMS.* St. Louis: Concordia, 1977.

Galchutt, Kathryn M. *The Career of Andrew Schulze: Lutherans and Race Relations in the Civil Rights Movement, 1924–1968.* Macon, GA: Mercer University Press, 2005.

Johnson, Jeff G. *Black Christians: The Untold Lutheran Story*. St. Louis: Concordia, 1991.

Larsen, Jens. *The Virgin Islands Story: A History of the Lutheran Church in the Virgin Islands*. Minneapolis: Augsburg, 1968.

Rosales, Raymond S. *It's about Mission: Ventures and Views of a Pilgrim in Hispanic Ministry*. St. Louis: Concordia, 1998.

Yee, Edmond. *The Soaring Crane: Stories of Asian Lutherans in North America*. Minneapolis: Augsburg Fortress, 2002.

Laymen's Movements

Avery, William O. *Empowered Laity: The Story of the Lutheran Laity Movement*. Minneapolis: Fortress Press, 1997.

Graebner, Alan. *Uncertain Saints: The Laity in the Lutheran Church, Missouri Synod, 1900–1970*. Westport, CT: Greenwood, 1975.

Youth Movements

Bogh, Molly Schultz. *Disturbing the Peace of the Church: Lutheran Youth Ministry and Social Change in the 1960s*. Minneapolis: Kirk House, 2012.

Pahl, Jon. *The Hopes and Dreams of All: The International Walther League and Lutheran Youth in American Culture, 1893–1993*. Chicago: Wheat Ridge Ministries, 1993.

World Missions

Drach, George. *Our Church Abroad: The Foreign Missions of the Lutheran Church in America*. Minneapolis: Augsburg, 1926.

Lueking, F. Dean. *Mission in the Making: The Missionary Enterprise among Missouri Synod Lutherans, 1846–1963*. St. Louis: Concordia, 1964.

Swanson, S. Hjalmar. *Foundation for Tomorrow: A Century of Progress in Augustana World Missions*. Rock Island, IL: Augustana Book Concern, 1960.

Worship

Olson, Oliver K. *Reclaiming the Lutheran Liturgical Heritage*. Minneapolis: ReClaim Resources, 2007.

Reed, Luther. *The Lutheran Liturgy: A Study of the Common Liturgy of the Lutheran Church in America*. Philadelphia: Muhlenberg, 1947.

Stulken, Mary Kay. *Hymnal Companion to the Lutheran Book of Worship*. Philadelphia: Fortress Press, 1981.

Sundberg, Walter. *Worship as Repentance: Lutheran Liturgical Traditions and Catholic Consensus.* Grand Rapids: Eerdmans, 2012.

Truscott, Jeffrey A. *The Reform of Baptism and Confirmation in American Lutheranism.* Lanham, MD: Scarecrow, 2003.

Westermeyer, Paul. *Hymnal Companion to Evangelical Lutheran Worship.* Minneapolis: Augsburg Fortress, 2010.

Canadian Lutheranism

Cronmiller, Carl R. *A History of the Lutheran Church in Canada.* N.p.: Evangelical Lutheran Synod of Canada, 1961.

Eylands, Valdimar J. *Lutherans in Canada.* Winnipeg: Icelandic Evangelical Lutheran Synod, 1945.

Threinen, Norman J. *A Religious-Cultural Mosaic: A History of Lutherans in Canada.* Vulcan, AB: Today's Reformation Press, 2006.

———. *Fifty Years of Lutheran Convergence: The Canadian Case-Study.* Dubuque, IA: Lutheran Historical Conference, 1983.

Index

Apostolic Lutherans, *see Laestadians*
Apprentice training of pastors, 133, 151
Arnzius, Bernard, 43, 47, 51
Asia, 8, 19, 27, 31, 33, 41, 112, 199, 202-203, 213, 218, 232, 237, 240, 253, 261, 264-266, 268, 276-277, 289, 290, 292, 307-309, 321, 337-338, 341, 353, 373-374
Asian American Lutherans, 338
Association of American Lutheran Churches (AALC), 345
Association of Black Lutherans, 307
Association of Evangelical Lutheran Congregations (AELC), 234, 304, 359
Association of Free Lutheran Congregations (AFLC), 234, 273, 345, 359
Augsburg College, 206, 229, 230
Augsburg Confession (1530), 14-15, 17, 54, 73, 89, 132, 148, 149, 161, 163-165, 179, 180, 186, 223, 243-244, 347, 351n12
Augsburg Publishing House, 255
Augustana Seminary, 186, 251
Augustana Synod, 174, 185-187, 193, 195, 207, 211-213, 215, 219, 220, 224, 240-241, 248, 250-253, 256, 258n14, 268, 271-273, 284, 359, 370, 373

Bachman, John, 157, 175, 198n3, 372
Baltic Lutherans, 207, 240, 267
Barry, Alvin, 329, 335
Behnken, John, 286
Benke, David, 329, 335
Berg, Carolina Sandell, 28, 193
Bergendoff, Conrad, 281, 284, 366
Berkenmeyer, William C., 62-64, 74-76, 79, 84n10, 90, 92-93, 99, 102
Bilateral discussions, 248, 316, 334
Bjork, Erick, 47, 48, 51, 55, 67
Black Clergy caucus, 298
Bodensieck, Julius, 267, 364
Boe, Lars, 242, 258n9, 272, 287n5
Boe, Paul, 308
Bohlmann, Ralph, 329, 335
Boltzius, Gertraut Kroehr, 99, 100
Boltzius, Johann Martin, 70, 71, 81, 82, 83, 84n4, 84n12, 84n18, 96-97, 99-100, 102-103, 110n9, 367
Book of Concord, 14, 15, 19, 20, 54, 161, 223, 281, 351n12
Brandelle, G. A., 240, 251, 258n14
Braun, Caspar, 146

"Brief Statement," Missouri Synod (1932), 248, 285-286
Brown, G. H., 145
Buehler, J. M., 182
Buenger, Johan, 197
Buffalo Synod, 29, 146, 150, 152, 161-163, 174, 236, 246, 249, 359, 369
Bureaucratization, 257

California Lutheran College, 274
"Called to Common Mission" (CCM), 346-347, 359
Cameroon, 219, 240-241, 252-253
Campanius, Johan, 45, 46, 57n2, 103, (center section)
Capital University, 154
Carthage College, 154, 274
Catechism, Large, 12
Catechism, Small, 12, 14-15, 45, 54, 98, 103, 111, 127, 129, 131-132, 164 (center section)
Catechists, 75, 123, 133, 134, 151, 155, (center section)
Central Missionary Society, 155, 156, 166n8
Centralization, 179, 257, 257, 345
Chaplains, 41, 177, 226, 259-260, 265, 275, 277, 285, 298, 321
Charismatic Lutherans, 296–297, 319n6, 331, 346, 372
Cherokee mission, Oaks, Oklahoma, 195
Chicago Theses (1919), 243, 246, 248
Chilstrom, Herbert, 319, 326, 328
China Mission Society, 199, 219
China, 31, 33, (center section), 199, 200, 219, 231-232, 241, 252-254, 268, 276-277
Christ Seminary in Exile (Seminex), (center section), 303, 304, 306, 329
Christian News, 286
Christian Worship (WELS), 112, 341
Church Book (1868), 192
Church headquarters, 257
Church of the Lutheran Brethren, 206, 222, 252, 359, 369
Churchly Pietism, 77
Civil War, 145, 154-55, 157-158, 160-161, 168, 172-173, 175–178, 181, 185, 197, 201, 210, 216, 218, 220, 223, 278, 371
Classical Assembly, 64, 75
Cold War, 261, 262, 263, 274, 277, 278, 292, 305, 314
Collin, Nicholas, 102, 109, 110n14, 110n25

Hartwick Synod, 150, 158, 161, 173

Hartwick, John Christian, 74, 75, 90, 92-93

Hasselius, Samuel, 102

Hasselquist, Tuve Nilsson, 186

Hauge, Hans Nielsen (1771–1824), 27, 28, 184, 186

Hauge's Norwegian Evangelical Lutheran Synod, 174, 186, 206, 222

Hausihl, Bernard Michael, 108

Hedberg, Frederick Gabriel, 28, 208

Helmuth, J. H. C., 128, 134

Henkel, Anthony Jacob, 53, 61, 67

Henkel, Paul, 128, 130-131, 135, 136, 137n16, 138n20, 147

Herman, Stewart, 267

Hermannsburg Mission in India, 219

Hessian Soldiers, 108

Heyer, Father J. F. C., 145, 156, 166n8, 166n8, 218

Higher Biblical criticism, 245

Hispanic Lutheranism, 353–354

Holm, John Campanius, 103

Holston Synod, 178-179

Homes for physically and mentally handicapped, 172, 195, 197

Homes for the elderly, 195, 197, 235

Home missions, 145, 155–156, 183, 192, 194, 203, 209, 218, 220, 224, 235, 242, 250-251, 268-269, 279, 287n3, 296, 298, 309, 321, 337, 353-354

Home Missionary Society of the General Synod, 155

Home missionaries, 151, 155-156, 182, 182, 194

Hong, Howard, 267, 281

Hospitals, 2, 108, 172, 184, 195-196, 197, 203, 211-213, 226-227, 235

Human sexuality, 325, 328, 333, 334, 337, 339, 348, 349

Hymnals, Lutheran, 111–112, 131, 135, 136, 282, 313-314, 360

Icelandic Evangelical Lutheran Synod of America, 208-209

Illinois Synod, 180, 189

Immigration and language transition (1918–1940), 237–240

Immigration, 7, 18, 32, 49, 52-53, 62, 65, 67, 95-97, 126, 145, 150, 160-161, 165, 171-172, 183, 201, 202, 207, 209, 231-233, 235, 237-238, 249, 290, 292, 324, 337-338, 354, 360, 367

Indenture, 37, 50-51, 53, 67, 78, 97

Independent Horse Troop, 108

India, 30-31, 33-34, 72, 199, 213, 219, 240-241, 252, 309, 338

Inerrancy of the Bible, 244-247, 281, 285, 302-303, 345

Infallibility of the Bible, 82, 244, 245, 302, 303, 316

Inner Mission movement, 28, 30, 32, 188, 235

Integration, racial, 279-280, 283, 297, 337

Inter-Lutheran Commission on Worship (ILCW), 313, 360

Intermarriage, 65, 94, 126

International Lutheran Council, 316, 345, 360

Intersynodical (Chicago) Theses, (1925), 248

Invitation to Action, 317

Iowa Synod, 30, 146, 150, 152, 154, 161-163, 174, 180-181, 189-191, 193-195, 197, 198n13, 206, 212, 236, 241, 246, 247, 249, 360, 369

Irregular ordinations, 328, 334

Isolationism, 224, 231, 256, 261

Jacobs, Charles M., 243, 246, 258n10

Jaech, Emil, 306, 320n17

Jensen, Rasmus, 33–34, 41, 48

Jesus First, 332

Jewish mission efforts, 194

Joint Commission on Lutheran Unity, 273

Joint Declaration on the Doctrine of Justification (JDDJ), 344, 351n11

Joint Synod of Ohio, 137n9, 160-161, 163, 165n3, 189-191, 193, 219, 221, 279, 361, 369

Joint Synod of Wisconsin, 203, 207

Joint Union Committee (JUC), 273, 360

Jones, Jehu, 157

Kansas Synod, 182

Keffer, Adam, 139-140

Kieschnick, Gerald, 329, 335

King, Martin Luther, Jr., 297

Knoll, Michael Christian, 63-64, 83n1, 92

Knubel, Frederick, 243, 246, 258n10

Knutson, Kent, 305

Kocherthal, Beinigna Sybilla, 99

Kocherthal, Joshua, 52, 61, 99

Koehler, J. P., 236

Koontz, David J., 220

Walther, C. F. W., 29, 146, 152, 160-163, (center section), 175, 176, 189-190, 193, 198n5, 206, 207, 369
Wartburg College, 154
Wartburg Seminary, 152, 162
Wartburg Synod, 194
Washington Declaration (1920), 243
Washington Service, 1869, 192
Watergate, 292, 305, 307
Waterloo Lutheran University, 312
Wauwatosa Theology, 236
WCAL, St Olaf College Radio Station, 255
Weiser, Anna Maria, 73, 91, 99, 100
Weiser, Conrad, 73-75, 91, 99
Wends, 209
Wentz, Abdel Ross, 190, 281
Western Virginia, 69, 122, 175, 177
Whitefield, George, 82-83, 85, 129
Wisconsin Synod, 59, 174, 181, 189, 195, 203, 207, 234, 236, 269, 270, 286, 293, 339, 341, 361, 371
Wiseman, Daniel, 220, 221
Wittenberg College, 152, 165, 224
Wittenberg Synod, 150, 161, 175
Wittenberg Native American mission to the Winnebagos, 195
Wolf, Johan August, 63, 64, 74, 80, 90
Woman's Home and Foreign Mission Society, Augustana Synod, 211
Women ordination, 339
Women teachers, 212
Women voting and holding office in American Lutheran congregations, 209, 213, 302
Women, 1, 2, 22, 98-102, 154-155, 172, 183, 200, 202, 209, 210–214, 216-218, 223, 226, 227, 232, 253-254, 260, 265, 269, 275,

283-284, 292, 295, 299-302, 305, 307, 310-311, 317-318, 319n11, 326-328, 335, 339, 342, 351n10, 363, 373
Women's Foreign Mission Society of the General Synod, 211
Women's Missionary Federation, 211
Women's Missionary Society, 211, 310, 373
Women's organizations, 210, 211, 213, 226, 307, 310–311
Women's seminaries, 216
Word Alone Network (WAN), 347, 361
World Council of Churches, 264, 270, 361, 372
World Mission Prayer League, 253, 277, 354, 361
"Worship wars," 168, 339, 340
Worship, 11, 13, 16-17, 19, 34, 41, 43, 45, 48, 54, 60, 66, 72, 77, 78, 79–81, 83, 105, 111-112, 126-127, 129-130, 132, 135-137, 146-147, 149-150, 153, 158-159, 168, 192-193, 223, 225, 238-240, 260, 260n2, 280, 282-283, 296, 310, 312–314, 324, 326, 331-332, 336, 338-341, 354, 374–375
Wounded Knee, South Dakota, 308
Wrangel, Carl Magnus, 95, 104
Wyneken, Friedrich, 162

Youth, 199, 210, 213–215, 239
Youth organization, 213, 254, 310, 310, 311–312

Ziegenbalg, Bartholomaeus, 30
Ziegenhagen, Frederick, 72
Zinzendorf, Ludwig von, 23, 73, 76, 83, 89
Zion Society for Israel, 194